PRAISE FOR *PUBLIC PARTICIPATION FOR 21ST CENTURY DEMOCRACY*

"Around the world, citizens are demanding new forms of democracy, in which their engagement extends beyond the ballot box and tokenistic consultation. In a *tour de force* of the field, this book provides a practical, comprehensive, and insightful overview of how the field of public participation in the United States has been transformed over the last half century, and why it must continue to be re-invented for this century and beyond. This book will be a great resource for students, policy makers, practitioners, and others concerned about creating a more democratic, participatory, and sustainable society."

—**Professor John Gaventa**, Director of Research, Institute of Development Studies

"If you care about democracy and its future, please read this book! Nabatchi and Leighninger have produced a conceptually rich and immensely practical overview of public participation and how we the people, our elected officials, and leaders of all kinds can improve our lives together as free people in a democratic society."

—**John Bryson**, McKnight Presidential Professor of Planning and Public Affairs, Hubert H. Humphrey School of Public Affairs, University of Minnesota

' "Grand plans are made of small elements," say the authors of *Public Participation for the 21st Century*. In this tour-de-force, Nabatchi and Leighninger vividly capture the small elements of change stirring across the country in which citizens are asserting their central role in America's greatest adaptive experiment—democracy. The authors provide a framework that moves from the theoretical to the practical and back to help us make sense of the current chaos and experimentation that always accompanies deep systemic change. In this unflinching examination of how public policy could be better with more citizen participation, they inspire us to think grandly and also to roll up our sleeves to create the future we want."

—**Paula Ellis**, Civic Entrepreneur, Former Media Executive, Journalist, Community Builder, and Philanthropist.

"A thoughtful, comprehensive, and original work, this book reveals the state-of-the-art on public participation in the 21st century. This book offers one of those rare occasions on which you get the best of theory and practice in just one volume. It is a must-read for scholars, a go-to for practitioners, and a wake-up call for those who doubt citizens' capacity to make things work."

—**Tiago Peixoto**, Team Lead, Digital Engagement Unit at the World Bank

"Today, people worldwide are crying out to have more say in the public decisions that most impact their lives locally and nationally. Nabatchi and Leighninger have written an engaging, accessible, and comprehensive book that will enable thousands of students, practitioners and government officials to improve public participation to meet the challenges facing 21st century democracy."

—**Dr. Carolyn J. Lukensmeyer**, Executive Director of the National Institute for Civil Discourse

"Nabatchi and Leighninger authors deftly slice and dice conventional participatory processes and replace them with new ideas for quality public participation. Examples from real world policy areas, as well as 'participation scenarios and tactics,' drive home the everyday relevance of this book. Questions for discussion make this a natural for classroom use, but its reach is far broader: This book is a 'must read' for those around the world who hope to foster true democratic participation."

—**Rosemary O'Leary**, Edwin O. Stene Distinguished Professor, School of Public Affairs, University of Kansas

"Community engagement is essential to building public trust, which will increasingly be the working capital for local governments. Knowledge of emerging approaches for both high-tech and high-touch engagement are now essential for all elected and appointed officials. Public *Participation for 21st Century Democracy* is a practical guide for officials who understand these challenges and want to encourage citizen contributions to governance."

—**Robert O'Neill**, Executive Director, International City/County Management Association

"*Public Participation for 21st Century Democracy* is an extremely valuable resource for public participation practitioners, educators, and researchers. Far more than a 'how-to' manual, the authors demonstrate the necessity of recognizing and responding to the ever-changing social, political, organizational, and sector-specific dynamics that influence how, when, and why public participation efforts succeed or fail. Perhaps most importantly, the authors offer practical strategies and guidance to assist readers in strengthening the quality *and* impact of public participation initiatives."

—**Kyle Bozentko**, Executive Director, Jefferson Center

Public Participation

FOR

21ST CENTURY DEMOCRACY

Tina Nabatchi

Matt Leighninger

JB JOSSEY-BASS™

A Wiley Brand

**Library of Congress Cataloging-in-Publication Data has been applied for and is on file with the
Library of Congress.**

ISBN 9781118688403 (Hardback)
ISBN 9781118688533 (ePDF)
ISBN 9781118688595 (ePub)

Printed in the United States of America

10 9 8 7 6 5 4 3 2 1

For Pamela

For Ahmad and Linda

And for all those around the world who seek to improve democracy

CONTENTS

LIST OF FIGURES, EXHIBITS, AND TABLES

PREFACE

Please Participate in Improving This Book.

To fully capture the variety and ingenuity of public participation today, this book would need to be much longer. It would have to encompass engagement projects and structures in many other fields and issue areas, describe the contributions of people working in many other domains and disciplines, and cover work being done all around the world. Even so, given the pace of innovation, such a book would be out of date five minutes after publication.

Fortunately, because of changes in publishing methods and technologies, this book can, and will, change. We invite you to contribute to this effort by challenging and refining the ideas we have presented here, describing other public issues that have been the basis for engagement efforts, and adding to the examples of public participation on the ground.

You can do so by submitting information about public participation to Participedia, an online network of scholars, practitioners, and democracy innovators that houses hundreds of examples, methods, and organizations relating to public participation around the world (see www.Participedia.net). In addition, please add to this ongoing discussion by contacting us, connecting with us through social media, or by participating in events and exchanges convened by the Program for the Advancement of Research on Conflict and Collaboration (PARCC) at the Syracuse University Maxwell School of Citizenship and Public Affairs and the Deliberative Democracy Consortium (DDC). We welcome your contributions and look forward to continuing the discussion.

— Tina and Matt

ACKNOWLEDGMENTS

We have been influenced over the years by hundreds of practitioners, researchers, technologists, organizers, public officials, and others who care deeply about democracy and who have worked tirelessly to lead, study, organize, and promote participation. This book would not have been possible without their work and their willingness to help us learn from it. Many also gave invaluable comments on drafts of this book, including: Shaun Adamec, Kyle Bozentko, Barbara Brush, Kara Carlisle, Caitlyn Davison, Lew Friedland, Will Friedman, Sandy Heierbacher, Robert Leighninger, Peter Levine, Mike McGrath, Ines Mergel, Alece Montez, Quixada Moore-Vissing, Cynthia Nikitin, Patrick Scully, Karol Soltan, Pamela Swett, and Mary Thompson. We are also grateful to Shawna Rabbas, a graphic designer in the Central New York area, who helped us with most of the figures in this book.

ABOUT THE AUTHORS

Tina Nabatchi (Ph.D., Indiana University-Bloomington, 2007) is an associate professor of public administration and international affairs at the Maxwell School of Citizenship and Public Affairs, Syracuse University, where she also co-directs the Collaborative Governance Initiative for the Program for the Advancement of Research on Conflict and Collaboration (PARCC). Her research focuses on citizen participation, collaborative governance, and conflict resolution. She has published her work in numerous journals, such as *Public Administration Review*, *Journal of Public Administration Research and Theory*, *American Review of Public Administration*, *National Civic Review*, *Conflict Resolution Quarterly*, and the *International Journal of Conflict Management*, among others. Tina has also published several book chapters, monographs, research reports, and white papers. She is the lead editor of *Democracy in Motion: Evaluating the Practice and Impact of Deliberative Civic Engagement* (Oxford University Press, 2012) and co-author of *Collaborative Governance Regimes* (with Kirk Emerson, Georgetown University Press, 2015).

Matt Leighninger is the executive director of the Deliberative Democracy Consortium (DDC), an alliance of the major organizations and leading scholars working in the field of deliberation and public participation. The DDC represents more than fifty foundations, nonprofit organizations, and universities collaborating to support research activities and advance democratic practice, in North America and around the world. Over the last twenty years, Matt has worked with public engagement efforts in more than 100 communities, forty states, and four Canadian provinces. Matt serves on the boards of e-democracy.org, the International Association for Public Participation (IAP2USA), The Democracy Imperative, and the Participatory Budgeting Project, and is a Senior Associate for

Everyday Democracy. He has written for publications such as *The Huffington Post, Chronicle of Philanthropy, The Christian Science Monitor, The National Civic Review, Public Management, Zócalo Public Square, Public Administration Review, School Administrator,* and *Nation's Cities Weekly.* His first book, *The Next Form of Democracy: How Expert Rule Is Giving Way to Shared Governance—and Why Politics Will Never Be the Same,* traces the shifts in the relationship between citizens and government and examines how these trends are reshaping our democracy. Two of his main accomplishments in the last year were leading a working group that produced a model ordinance on public participation and developing a new tool, "Text, Talk, and Act," that combined online and face-to-face participation as part of President Obama's National Dialogue on Mental Health.

Editorial Assistants

Jack Alexander Becker graduated from the Syracuse University Maxwell School of Citizenship and Public Affairs with an MPA degree in the summer of 2014. He has been intimately involved in the field of public deliberation and public engagement: as a student at Colorado State University Center for Public Deliberation, as a research assistant with the Charles F. Kettering Foundation, and in his current position with the Office of Family and Community Engagement for Denver Public Schools.

Emma Ertinger is an MPA candidate at the Maxwell School of Citizenship and Public Affairs at Syracuse University. She worked for New York City Council Member Brad Lander, served as an AmeriCorps member in Brooklyn, and taught English as a Fulbright ETA in Venezuela. She is originally from Liverpool, New York, and received a BA in anthropology and Spanish from Nazareth College.

Suyeon Jo is a Ph.D. student studying public administration at the Maxwell School of Citizenship and Public Affairs, Syracuse University. A native of South Korea, she earned her MPA from the Bush School of Government and Public Service at Texas A&M University. Her research interests include citizen participation, collaborative governance, and public and nonprofit management.

Alvaro A. Salas-Castro is a Ph.D. student studying public administration at the Maxwell School of Citizenship and Public Affairs, Syracuse University. A native of Costa Rica, he earned an MPA degree from Cornell University, as well as a BA in foreign affairs, LLB in law, and MBA in finance, economics, and sustainable development from INCAE Business School. His research interests include citizen participation and collaborative governance.

PART ONE

Participation in a Rapidly Changing Democracy

Citizenship, Outside the Public Square

The problems we face are daunting, and our capacity to address them is remarkable. Climate change, terrorism, financial instability, and other challenges are indeed formidable, but our power to address them is more advanced than ever before.

The greatest element of our improved problem-solving capacity lies in citizens themselves. We enjoy higher levels of education and communication, and we are more committed than ever to the notion that all people deserve certain inalienable rights. Our ability to understand, use, and improve technology is growing by leaps and bounds: everyone, it seems, is a potential scientist, analyst, or inventor. The power of ordinary people, and the ability of government, civil society, and other institutions to unleash that capacity, is the key to our progress as a civilization.

The reality of rising citizen capacity is not, however, a comfortable fact for public leaders. Trapped in systems designed to protect their expertise from citizen interference, besieged by people who no longer believe their data or respect their authority, and faced with hostile constituents at public events, public officials, managers, and other leaders are understandably skeptical about the virtues, capabilities, and good sense of their fellow men and women.

In turn, citizens are skeptical about the virtues, capabilities, and good sense of their public officials. Highly polarized policy debates, the inability of elected leaders to agree on seemingly common-sense measures, and the massive influence of moneyed interests have helped produce the highest levels of citizen distrust in government that we have ever seen.

The official, conventional processes and structures for public participation are almost completely useless for overcoming this divide between citizens and government; in fact, they seem to be making matters worse. In large part, that is because the infrastructure for participation is inefficient and outdated; it does not recognize citizen capacity and it limits our collective problem-solving potential.

To supplement or circumvent this official participation infrastructure, local leaders have devised a host of new processes, formats, and structures for engaging the public. These include intensive face-to-face deliberations, convenient digital tools, and online networks that add dexterity to the power of face-to-face relationships. Many of these innovations not only satisfy the fundamental needs and goals of citizens, but also demonstrate the potential of public participation for making difficult decisions and solving formidable problems. So far, however, they have been pursued primarily on a temporary, ad hoc basis and have not been incorporated into the way that governments and communities operate.

Public participation can help protect our liberties, ensure justice and equality, and improve our quality of life. It is sometimes characterized as the interaction that makes democracy work—but it might be more accurate to say that public participation *is* the democracy in our primarily republican political systems. The greatest challenge we now face is how to transform those systems in ways that allow us to tap citizens' full, democratic, problem-solving potential.

Illuminating that challenge is the purpose of this book. Before we explore the potential of participation (in Chapter 2), we will first examine the new attitudes and capacities people bring to public life. We also describe the existing infrastructure for participation and begin to explore why it typically fails to provide the things that citizens want.

CONFIDENT, FRUSTRATED, CONNECTED, AND LONELY: THE CURIOUS CASE OF THE 21ST CENTURY CITIZEN

"What is public participation?" would seem to be the first question to answer in this book. But there is a more fundamental question: "What do citizens want?" The most common mistake made by people who are trying to engage the public is that they try to facilitate citizen participation without first trying to understand citizens. Understanding citizens is, of course, no easy task. Citizens' attitudes toward community and public life seem full of contradictions.

Public Problem-Solvers, Who Distrust the Official Public Problem-Solvers

People who are not policy experts or public servants are making increasingly sophisticated contributions to the governance and improvement of their communities.

Some of these efforts involve the use of new online tools. Armed with new technologies and previously inaccessible government data, people have mapped crime patterns, assessed zoning policies, developed bus schedule apps, and monitored water quality. Other examples are impressive not for their technological sophistication, but for the audacity and commitment of volunteers. In Kansas, a team of forty-two volunteers worked with state government to complete a twelve-mile water pipeline in a fraction of the time (and cost) it would normally have taken (McGuigan, 2013). More common examples are the numerous street cleanups, neighborhood patrols, and after-school programs conducted by citizen problem-solvers.

Despite the obvious public-spiritedness of these and many other examples, the attitude of citizens toward government and other public institutions is strikingly negative. Trust in government is at an all-time low (Pew, 2013). Voting rates have declined steadily for decades, along with other measures of civic attitudes. One finding of the Knight Foundation's (2010) *Soul of the Community* research was that people who had participated in a conventional public meeting had lower levels of attachment to community than people who had not. Citizens seem more eager to contribute to public problem solving, yet more frustrated with the conventional processes for governance.

Civil in Private, but Not in Public

Another curious contradiction has to do with the state of civil discourse. In public life, incivility has become increasingly common. Rudeness and intolerance are apparent in official public meetings, on newspaper comment threads, and in other public venues. A study of California public managers concluded that "everyone involved . . . had personal experience with—or could relate to descriptions of—instances of the public-acting-badly and civic-engagement-gone-wrong" (Pearce & Pearce, 2010).

And yet, in our private lives, incivility is less obvious. For one thing, it is no longer widely considered acceptable for people to use slurs and stereotypes relating to race, gender, or sexual orientation. While public hearings may be full of angry people and angry words, at least anecdotally it would seem that workplaces, campuses, and other public spaces are not.

Connected—and Lonely

The omnipresence of social media and other online connections contrasts oddly with citizens' sense of social isolation. As of 2013, 73 percent of all adults who went online were users of social networking sites—a percentage that has doubled in the last five years (Duggan & Smith, 2013). Twenty-two percent of American adults use "digital tools to talk to their neighbors and keep informed about community issues" (Smith, 2010).

But at the same time, the number of people expressing loneliness and a lack of social connections has continued to increase. The rate of people who consider themselves "lonely" has doubled since the 1980s, up to 40 percent of all adults. Furthermore, this social isolation seems to have other negative impacts on people's lives, including their health. One study suggests that loneliness is as deadly as cancer and twice as deadly as obesity (Olien, 2013).

These trends may seem contradictory, but they are not. People are mistrustful of, angry at, and unfulfilled by public life, in part because of the public participation opportunities they are (and are not) being offered. The most widely available of these opportunities—voting, attending public hearings, and filing complaints—are, at best, insufficient and, at worst, detrimental.

THE FAILING INFRASTRUCTURE OF THE PUBLIC SQUARE

To realize the full potential of participation, we need to focus on what citizens actually want: problem solving, civility, and community. If we start with these goals in mind, it becomes easier to understand why official avenues for engagement do not appeal to the public.

In Chapter 2, we define participation and its various forms in greater detail and describe how some of those forms are capable of delivering the things that citizens want. For now, we follow the line of our citizen-centered analysis to a definition that does not mention government at all: *Public participation is an umbrella term that describes the activities by which people's concerns, needs, interests, and values are incorporated into decisions and actions on public matters and issues* (see Nabatchi, 2012; Nabatchi & Amsler, 2014; Roberts, 2008). The word "public" in this definition refers to all kinds of people and to all kinds of matters and issues—not just policy decisions and pieces of legislation, but also how people work together to plant trees, clean up vacant lots, or organize activities for children.

Ultimately, public participation is (or, at least, can be) a way for citizens to achieve problem solving, civility, and community. But for these participation activities to take place and for participation to have these impacts and benefits, it must be sustained by a robust participation infrastructure. We define participation infrastructure as: *the laws, processes, institutions, and associations that support regular opportunities for people to connect with each other, solve problems, make decisions, and celebrate community.*

We already have a participation infrastructure, and it occupies a great deal of our time, money, and political capital. But it does not support the kinds of participation we describe above, is not suited to the needs of citizens or officials, and is out of step with the way people live today. This participation infrastructure has several facets:

- **Legal**—At the local, state, and federal levels, we have numerous laws, rules, and regulations that were intended to help citizens monitor government decisions, comment publicly on them, and (in some cases) weigh in through petitions, ballot initiatives, and other forms of direct participation. These laws exert great influence on how participation happens, but in many cases, they are obsolete, unclear, or in conflict with one another (Working Group on Legal Frameworks for Public Participation, 2013; see also PARCC, 2013). At best, the current legal framework is inadequate; at worst, it obstructs and delegitimizes democratic innovation.

- **Governmental**—Most governments have employees tasked with informing and interacting with citizens, either in a particular issue area or by liaising with citizen groups and associations. These staff positions are often occupied by the youngest and most inexperienced employees. Many governments also have commissions and task forces, in areas such as human relations or planning and zoning, which are charged with engaging the public as part of their work. The volunteers serving in these capacities often see their roles as representative, not participatory: they are there to bring the interests and concerns of others to the table, not engage those people directly. Both the employees and the volunteers tend to have only a vague sense of the skills and capacities necessary for productively engaging the public (Lukensmeyer, Goldman, & Stern, 2011).

- **Civic**—There are many formal and informal associations, from civic watchdog organizations to neighborhood and parent groups, that exist, in part, to engage citizens in public affairs. Again, the term "public" should be understood broadly; these public affairs could be the policies being debated by city council or Congress, but they are more often the most immediate citizen priorities and concerns. However, these associations are usually not very participatory or productive. Their leaders are often relatively unrepresentative of the people for whom they claim to speak—and those leaders are unsure of how to bring more people to the table. Even at the grassroots level, these associations function more as fundraising and lobbying organizations than genuinely participatory ones (Leighninger, 2008).

- **Electoral**—Some observers would argue that the electoral process represents another aspect of participation infrastructure, since candidates and parties could engage citizens on policy questions during their campaigns. But for the most part, the two main American parties have not involved their members extensively in platform decisions since the first half of the 20th Century. Some advocates believe that if campaign finance and other electoral reforms were successful, candidates would have greater incentives to engage meaningfully with voters. But right now, electoral campaigns rarely seem to engage citizens, other than to ask them for their votes and their money. So when they vote, citizens are selecting among candidate platforms that they did not help create, may not understand, and largely will not be able to affect after the election (Nabatchi, Becker, & Leighninger, 2015).

- **Educational**—From elementary schools to graduate programs, our educational system has always had the preparation of citizens as part of its core mission. There are many different ways to help people develop the skills and habits of participation, from courses in "civics" to extracurricular leadership programs to public service opportunities. As authorities like Peter Levine (2007, 2013; see also Levine & Youniss, 2009) argue, this wide array of lessons and activities has not been organized into a coherent, comprehensive system of civic education. Meanwhile, our professional graduate programs in public administration, public policy, social work, planning, journalism, and other fields do not adequately provide future public leaders with the skills and knowledge necessary to organize, inform, and evaluate participation (Leighninger, 2011).

Throughout this book, we examine our current participation infrastructure and explain how it fails to meet the needs, desires, and capacities of citizens. We also explore ways to transform it into the participation infrastructure we need—one that can support public participation for 21st Century democracy.

WHERE WE GO FROM HERE

For readers who were looking for new tools and techniques, this book may come as a surprise: they may feel like mechanics in training who have suddenly been confronted by the need for a whole new kind of automobile. Or, to use a more appropriate analogy, readers looking for new ways of interacting with citizens may be challenged by the need to redesign the public square. Furthermore, while there are many established practices and promising experiments in public participation, these elements have rarely been combined in long-term plans or systems. Those who want to redesign and strengthen the infrastructure for public participation often do not know where to start or where to turn for guidance.

We assert that redesigning the public square is neither as abstract nor as difficult as it sounds. This book bridges the far-off visions and the up-close techniques and encourages people to look at their political systems with clear-eyed, hard-headed utopianism. Ultimately, the mission of this book is to help people get more of what they want out of participation, government, and democracy.

Part One of the book lays the foundation for readers' understanding of public participation. Chapter 2 defines participation more explicitly, including its conventional, thin, and thick forms. It also explains how bad participation causes problems and the ways in which good participation can solve them. Chapter 3 examines the (r)evolution of participation and democracy, using a number of snapshots that illustrate particularly salient moments. The chapter concludes with a summary of the current state of our participation infrastructure and briefly suggests ways that it can be strengthened.

Part Two of the book takes a closer look at how participation happens—and how it could happen. The first three chapters of Part Two focus on particular policy areas: Chapter 4 examines education; Chapter 5 focuses on health; and Chapter 6 deals with planning and land use. Chapter 7 describes participation at the state and federal levels of government. Each of these chapters begins by exploring the development of participation in that area. Each then turns to the people involved, including those working in the official settings and the various networks for participation. Next, the chapters explore how the participation infrastructures could be strengthened through six building blocks or overarching categories of participation activities, as well as by incorporating a variety of systemic supports for those building blocks.

Part Three provides more specific guidance on how to strengthen the skills and structures necessary for productive participation. Chapter 8 focuses on participation scenarios and tactics; it is supplemented by the Participation Skills Module, available at www.wiley.com/go/nabatchi. Chapter 9 delves more deeply into how to assemble local participation infrastructure. Chapter 10 concludes the book by summarizing its themes and discussing how the concept of participation in democracy can unite people who have, until now, been working in parallel to one another.

SUMMARY

This chapter set the stage for the rest of the book by arguing that public participation can be a powerful force for solving public problems. In fact, creating more meaningful, productive relationships between people and their public institutions may be a key to the development of democracy and our progress as a civilization. We summarized the main trends in citizen expectations and capacities, and then analyzed how our participation infrastructure fails to meet these needs and goals. Finally, we described how the rest of the book will examine the current state and future potential of public participation.

DISCUSSION QUESTIONS

1. Do you agree that the capacity of citizens to solve problems is more advanced than ever before? Why or why not? Do you have any examples where citizens have contributed to solving social problems?

2. Do you agree with the argument that public leaders and citizens are skeptical about each other's abilities to address problems? Why or why not? If you do agree, what do you think are the causes of this skepticism and how might it be addressed?

3. What do you think are the causes of declining trust in government? What can be done to counteract this problem?

4. Review the "citizen contradictions" discussed in this chapter. Do you identify with any of these contradictions? Can you think of others that were not included in the list?

5. The authors assert that citizens want problem solving, civility, and community. Do you agree? Why or why not? What do you want as a citizen from government?

6. Do you agree that the infrastructure of the public square is failing? In what ways (besides voting) have you engaged in the public square?

7. What do you think is the potential of public participation for repairing the connection between citizens and public leaders? Can it be used to solve problems? What have been your experiences with public participation?

8. Citizens are increasingly using social media and other online tools. Do you think these tools are good or bad? Why? How do you think they can be used to promote public participation?

9. This chapter identifies five facets of the participation infrastructure (legal, governmental, civic, electoral, and educational). Evaluate each facet from your perspective, and suggest ways that each might be improved.

10. Improving public participation will require both new skills and new structures. What might be some of those new skills and new structures?

References

Duggan, Maeve, & Aaron Smith. (2013). *Social media update 2013*. Washington, DC: Pew Research Internet Project. Available at www.pewinternet.org/2013/12/30/social-media-update-2013/.

Knight Foundation. (2010). *Soul of the community 2010. Why people love where they live and why it matters: A national perspective*. Miami, FL: Knight Foundation.

Leighninger, Matt. (2008). *The promise and challenge of neighborhood democracy: Lessons from the intersection of government and community*. Hallettsville, TX: Grassroots Grantmakers.

Leighninger, Matt. (2011). Teaching democracy in public administration. In R.O'Leary, D. Van Slyke, & S. Kim (Eds.), *The future of public administration around the world: The Minnowbrook perspective*, 233–244. Washington, DC: Georgetown University Press.

Levine, Peter. (2007). *The future of democracy: Developing the next generation of American citizens*. Medford, MA: Tufts University Press.

Levine, Peter. (2013). *We are the ones we have been waiting for: The promise of civic renewal in American*. New York, NY: Oxford University Press.

Levine, Peter, & James Youniss (Eds.). 2009. *Engaging young people in civic life*. Nashville, TN: Vanderbilt University Press.

Lukensmeyer, Carolyn, Joe Goldman, and David Stern. (2011). *Assessing public participation in an open government era: A review of federal agency plans*. Washington, DC: IBM Center for the Business of Government.

McGuigan, Patrick B. (2013). A heartland with heart: 42 Kansans get-'er-done. Watchdog .org. Available at http://watchdog.org/117911/heartland-heart-42-kansans-get-er-done/.

Nabatchi, Tina. (2012). *A manager's guide to evaluating citizen participation*. Washington, DC: IBM Center for the Business of Government.

Nabatchi, Tina, & Lisa Blomgren Amsler. (2014). Direct public engagement in local government. *American Review of Public Administration*, 44(4suppl): 63s–88s.

Nabatchi, Tina, Jack Becker, & Matt Leighninger (2015). Using public participation to enhance citizen voice and promote accountability. In J.L. Perry & R. Christensen (Eds.), *Handbook of public administration* (3rd ed.). Hoboken, NJ: John Wiley & Sons.

Olien, Jessica. (2013). Loneliness is deadly. Social isolation kills more people than obesity does—and it's just as stigmatized. Slate.com. Available at www.slate.com/articles/health_and_science/medical_examiner/2013/08/dangers_of_loneliness_social_isolation_is_deadlier_than_obesity.html.

PARCC. (2013). *Priorities for public participation and open government: Recommendations to President Obama.* Syracuse, NY: Program for the Advancement of Research on Conflict and Collaboration.

Pearce, W. Barnett, & Kimberly A. Pearce. (2010). *Aligning the work of government to strengthen the work of citizens: A study of public administrators in local and regional government.* Dayton, OH: Kettering Foundation.

Pew Research Center for the People & the Press. (2013). *Public trust in government: 1958–2013.* Washington, DC: Pew Research Center. Available at www.people-press.org/2013/10/18/trust-in-government-interactive/.

Roberts, Nancy C. (2008). *The age of direct citizen participation.* Armonk, NY: M.E. Sharpe.

Smith, Aaron. (2010). *Neighbors online: How Americans learn about community issues.* Washington, DC: Pew Research Center.

Working Group on Legal Frameworks for Public Participation (Ed.). (2013). *Making public participation legal.* Denver, CO: National Civic League.

Good or Bad? Charming or Tedious? Understanding Public Participation

K nowing how to distinguish "good" participation from "bad" participation is an essential step in improving public life. In most cases, this is a visceral distinction—people know bad participation when they see it—but it is also an intellectual one. The purpose of this chapter is to describe, analyze, and categorize the main forms of engagement so that readers can understand how to judge the quality of participation.

But first, we want to take the moral undertones out of this comparison. "It is absurd to divide people into good and bad," wrote Oscar Wilde (1893). "People are either charming or tedious." We are not trying to stand in judgment of public officials, public employees, and other leaders: many genuinely good people organize, authorize, or facilitate public engagement activities that we would consider bad or downright terrible. But we do want to zero in on the people who matter most in participation: citizens, the (potential) participants. As Wilde's quote suggests, we can learn a great deal about the quality of engagement simply by finding out whether people find these experiences charming or tedious.

After justifying our broad definition of public participation, we describe the three main forms of participation in use today—thick, thin, and conventional—with some of their most charming and tedious properties. We then examine the true costs of bad participation and the benefits of good participation and explain why high-quality engagement has been so difficult to establish and maintain.

DEFINING PUBLIC PARTICIPATION AND EXPLORING ITS MODERN FORMS

Defining public participation is a challenge. The term encompasses a wide array of activities and processes, which makes it confusing both for civil servants who are simply trying to understand their responsibilities and for citizens who may never have attended a public meeting. To understand participation, we must not only define the term, but also explore some of its variations.

The definition we introduced in Chapter 1 is intentionally broad: *Public participation is an umbrella term that describes the activities by which people's concerns, needs, interests, and values are incorporated into decisions and actions on public matters and issues.* In this book, our main focus is on direct forms of participation, in which citizens are personally involved and actively engaged in providing input, making decisions, and solving problems, rather than on indirect forms, in which citizens affect decisions primarily by voting for their representatives or donating money to their preferred candidates and causes (Nabatchi & Amsler, 2014).

Of course, not all direct participation looks alike. It can occur in many different contexts and happen in many different ways. Moreover, the people who organize, support, or take part in these activities may also have many different purposes and goals. Over the last two decades, however, direct participation has coalesced into three main forms—thick, thin, and conventional—each of which encompasses a wide variety of processes and activities that share common features (Sifry, 2014; Zuckerman, 2013). Figure 2.1 shows the variations falling under the umbrella of public participation.

Thick Participation

Thick participation enables large numbers of people, working in small groups (usually five to fifteen per group), to learn, decide, and act. Generally speaking, it is the most meaningful and powerful of the three forms of direct participation, but also the most intensive and time-consuming and the least common.

There is great variety among thick participation processes (see Box 2.1), but perhaps the most significant commonality is the notion of empowering the small group. These processes encourage people to work out what they think and what they want to do in conversation with other participants. The main academic term for this kind of small-group talk is *deliberation*, defined as *a thoughtful, open, and accessible discussion about information, views, experiences, and ideas during which people seek to make a decision or judgment based on facts, data, values, emotions, and*

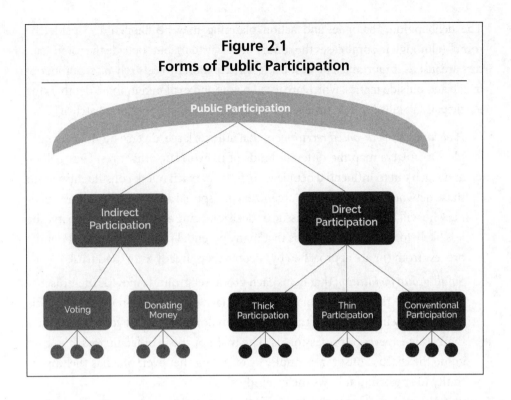

Figure 2.1
Forms of Public Participation

Public Participation

Indirect Participation

Direct Participation

Voting

Donating Money

Thick Participation

Thin Participation

Conventional Participation

other less technical considerations (see Gastil, 2005, 2008; also Bessette, 1980, 1994, 1997; Bohman, 1998; Dryzek, 2000; Elster, 1998; Gastil & Levine, 2005; Gutmann & Thompson, 2004; Habermas, 1984). However, "deliberation" can be hard to use because it is not a very accessible term, and because some scholars define it so narrowly that their visions bear little resemblance to the deliberation that occurs in thick participation practices (Leighninger, 2012 ; see also Lukensmeyer and Torres, 2006).

Thick participation is not all deliberation, either. When looking at how people talk in thick participation processes, scholars also note many instances of dialogue and debate (see Walsh, 2007), and again, the scholarly definitions for each of these types of talk are often very specific. Regardless, for many people, the most important part of the discussion is at the end, when participants get down to brass tacks about what they actually want to do. Though this is a common feature in deliberative processes, it could also be labeled with the simpler term of action planning.

And while the way people talk is important, the other elements of thick participation processes—particularly, how many people take part and whether the people are diverse or similar both in terms of socio-demographic characteristics and political opinions—tend to have a more significant impact on whether they are successful.

The deliberation, dialogue, and action planning may be happening "inside the room" (although in some cases the room may be virtual), but "outside the room" factors are just as important. The best thick participation projects rely on a number of inside and outside tactics, which are listed below and explored in more depth in the Participation Skills Module (available online at www.wiley.com/go/nabatchi).

- *Proactive, network-based recruitment* that attracts large, diverse numbers of people. Organizers map the different kinds of networks to which residents belong and reach out to influential people who, in turn, reach out to constituents within those networks. In many cases, organizers pay special attention to recruiting people who will be affected by the issue or decision being addressed, but who may be less likely to attend. The result is that many potential participants hear about the process from (or are approached by) people they already know and trust.

- *Small-group facilitation* that helps each group set ground rules for their discussion and use the time and materials they have been given. In most cases, this is a relatively light form of facilitation, often done by trained volunteers rather than issue experts or professionals. The main purpose of facilitators is to help guide the discussions, for example, by ensuring that everyone has the opportunity to speak and follows the ground rules.

- A *discussion sequence* that takes participants from sharing experiences to considering views and policy choices to planning for action. The first step in this sequence creates understanding and empathy, the second informs and establishes common ground, and the third helps participants define goals and actions.

- *Issue framing* that describes the main views or policy options on the issue or decision being addressed. Operating foundations and nonprofit organizations such as Everyday Democracy, Public Agenda, and the National Issues Forums Institute, frame national policy issues and produce discussion guides used by local organizers. Groups like MetroQuest have pioneered online formats for issue framing, and many local organizers, including public employees and private consultants, have become adept at framing issues.

- An *action strategy* that helps participants, public officials, and other decision-makers capitalize on the input and energy generated through the process. This work is accomplished in different ways. In some cases, it resembles a volunteer fair, where local organizations help participants connect with specific service opportunities. In other cases, it focuses on fundraising and ensuring that ideas and projects have the in-kind support and financial capital they need to move forward. In still others, it looks more like an advocacy campaign, with participants and public officials working on policy proposals and reaching out to other citizens and officials who are neutral or opposed.

An underappreciated type of thick participation is the category of "serious games" that simulate real-world events to educate users and sometimes solve problems (Lerner, 2014). Although a serious game may be entertaining, amusement is not its primary objective; rather, a serious game is intended to "further government or corporate training, education, health, public policy, and strategic communication objectives" (Zyda, 2005: 26; see also Abt, 1970; Lerner, 2014). Serious games are sometimes used as discrete exercises within thick participation processes. Others are standalone processes that include large numbers of people in deliberation, role-playing, and competition. "Participatory Chinatown" (an immersive 3-D game designed to be part of the master planning process for Boston's Chinatown) and "Community PlanIt" (a local engagement game designed for community planning, learning, and action) are two examples (see www.participatorychinatown.org/ and https://community-planit.org/; see also Phelps, 2011).

Thin Participation

Thin participation activates people as individuals rather than in groups. Before the Internet, signing petitions and filling out surveys were probably the most common kinds of thin participation. Now, just by sending a text or clicking a link, a citizen can sign an e-petition, "like" a cause on Facebook, retweet an opinion, or rank ideas in a crowdsourcing exercise. In just a few minutes, people can contribute to maps and documents, donate money to a project, or give feedback on public problems and services (Patel, Sotsky, Gourley, & Houghton, 2013).

While they participate as individuals, people who take advantage of these opportunities are often motivated by feeling a part of some larger movement or cause. When sufficient numbers of people are involved, thin participation can have real impact (Fung, Gilman, & Shkabatur, 2013). These activities occasionally "go viral," through the vast networking power of the Internet, attracting huge numbers of people and mass media attention.

As compared to thick participation processes, thin participation experiences require shorter time commitments, as well as less intense intellectual and emotional contributions. While the need to absorb information and listen to other

Box 2.1. Thick Participation: What's in a Name?

Some thick participation processes have official names. A few, such as 21st Century Town Hall Meetings™ and Deliberative Polling™, have even been trademarked. Many other thick participation processes use a more generic name, such as "community conversations," and others do not use a name at all. Sometimes, the project itself has a title—for example, "Decatur Next," "Chapel Hill 2020," or "Portsmouth Listens"—but not always. Furthermore, the names tend to describe only the "inside the room" dynamics of these processes, rather than the "outside the room" factors that are so critical to their success.

Chapter 8 describes some of these thick participation processes in greater detail. (For more information, see Gastil and Levine, 2005; Leighninger, 2012.) We list a number of face-to-face and online processes here to illustrate the diversity of thick participation.

Some Face-to-Face Processes for Thick Participation

- Appreciative Inquiry
- Citizen Assemblies
- Citizen Juries
- National Issues Forums
- Open Space
- Participatory Budgeting
- Planning Charrettes
- Serious Games
- Study Circles
- Sustained Dialogue
- World Café

Some Online Platforms and Tools for Thick Participation

- Common Ground for Action
- Dialogue-App
- Engagement HQ
- MetroQuest
- Zilino

participants is built into the structure of thick participation, thin participation opportunities often allow people to skip those steps.

Although it would be easy to recast the thick-thin distinction as face-to-face versus online participation, that would be too simplistic. Some face-to-face participation can be fast, convenient, and thin, while some online engagement is quite thick and intensive. Furthermore, some of the best examples of thick participation use online tools to inform and complement face-to-face processes.

In fact, some online participation opportunities can be as thin, or thick, as the participant wants them to be. A visitor to a crowdsourcing platform can take two minutes to vote for her favorite ideas or spend many hours submitting or commenting on ideas and interacting with other users. People are often drawn to what Mark Headd calls the "3 Bs of open data: bullets (crime statistics), budgets (city expenditures), and buses (public transit schedules)," but in addition to giving citizens the information they need, these platforms also often give people the chance to make comments, engage with civil servants or other citizens, or help gather more data (Nemani, 2014). As these digital activities grow, they will presumably continue to blur the line between thick and thin and allow people to move back and forth between the two more easily.

There is more variety among thin participation activities (see Box 2.2) than among thick or conventional processes. Specifically, thin activities may include opportunities for people to:

- *Affiliate* with a cause;
- *Rank ideas* for solving a problem or improving a community;
- *Donate money* (although we have characterized this as an indirect form of participation, the ease and customization of online "crowdfunding" blurs the line between direct and indirect);
- *Play games* that educate citizens, gather public input, or contribute in some other way to decision-making and problem-solving (see Lerner, 2014); and
- *Provide discrete pieces of data* that help identify community issues, improve public services, or add to public knowledge.

What unites thin participation activities is that individuals are provided with opportunities to express their ideas, opinions, or concerns in a way that requires only a few moments of their time. While thin participation opportunities that take place online can spread more rapidly than their thick counterparts, in most cases they still require the same kind of proactive, network-based recruitment to attract a large, diverse critical mass of people. "The phrase 'If you build it, they will come' definitely does not apply," argues digital strategist Qui Diaz (Leighninger, 2011).

Thin and thick forms of participation have different strengths, but similar shortcomings. Thin participatory innovations often have limited impact because they are isolated products that are seldom incorporated into any larger engagement plan or system. Thick participatory innovations tend to be temporary processes, and they, too, are seldom incorporated into any larger engagement plan or system. Micah Sifry, who covers civic technology as the editor of TechPresident, laments that "thick engagement doesn't 'scale,' and thin engagement doesn't stick" (Leighninger, 2014). One promising direction is to combine the best features of thick and thin participation, especially in ways that are replicable, sustainable, and embedded in communities.

Conventional Participation

Conventional participation processes are older forms of engagement that were developed to uphold order, accountability, and transparency. If thick and thin participation are designed to empower citizens (albeit in different ways), conventional participation is intended to provide citizens with checks on government power.

Conventional participation is the most common form of direct participation because it is entrenched in most of our public institutions and often required by law. Accordingly, official participation is almost always conventional participation (though this need not be the case). Official, however, does not just mean governmental; even in more informal settings such as neighborhood associations and parent-teacher organizations, the participants often use *Robert's Rules of Order* and other trappings of conventional participation.

Conventional participation describes most of the meetings or hearings held by public bodies such as school boards, zoning commissions, city councils, congressional representatives, state and federal agencies, and other government entities. Exhibit 2.1 shows a typical conventional public meeting. Conventional processes generally rely on a number of common procedures (some of which are mandated by law):

- *Advance notification*, typically by putting an announcement on a bulletin board at City Hall, on a government website, or in the local newspaper.
- *An audience-style room setup*, with decision-makers behind a table (often on a dais) at the front of the room and citizens in chairs laid out in rows.
- *A preset agenda* that is strictly followed and that defines the specific topics for discussion. In many cases, issues not on the agenda cannot be raised.
- *Public comment segments*, during which citizens have two to three minutes at an open microphone to address their elected officials. Sometimes, citizens must sign up in advance to speak at such meetings. Other times, they must wait in line for their turns.

It would be easy to say that conventional participation is "bad"—and that because these processes are most often administered by government, that all *official* participation is bad. However, many public officials and employees

Exhibit 2.1
A Conventional Public Meeting

have led, organized, or supported better forms of public participation (both thick and thin). So the role of government does not have to be limited to official participation—and official participation does not necessarily have to be bad. Nevertheless, both citizens and public officials tend be frustrated by conventional participation opportunities. In the following section, we explore the characteristics that, as Oscar Wilde might conclude, make conventional participation tedious.

WHY DOES CONVENTIONAL PARTICIPATION CAUSE PROBLEMS?

While conventional participation processes are intended to uphold public values like transparency, accessibility, and accountability, they generally do not succeed (Nabatchi, Becker, & Leighninger, 2015); poll results indicate that the majority of citizens do not find their governments to be transparent, accessible, or accountable. There are many reasons for this. For one thing, transparent practices do not necessarily lead to broad public awareness or give people the sense that public officials have heard their concerns. But the most basic reason these processes fail is that citizens do not attend. As Mark Funkhouser (2014), the former mayor of Kansas City, Missouri, puts it:

Regular folks have made the calculation that only in extreme circumstances, when they are really scared or angry, is attending a public hearing worth their time. And who can blame them when it seems clear that the game is rigged, the decisions have been made, and they'll probably have to sit through hours of blather before they get their three minutes at the microphone?

As a result, conventional public participation has become more than just an obstacle. These meetings and processes incur a range of costs, from the time and resources needed to organize them to their long-term impacts on public trust and the financial sustainability of public institutions.

All kinds of public leaders have reacted to the shortcomings of conventional participation by organizing more effective and participatory processes. But at least in the United States and other countries of the Global North, leaders typically do this on a case-by-case basis, in reaction to the latest controversy or crisis. Their projects tend to be temporary and limited to a single issue or decision, and, although they offer better processes, they do not change official structures. In her essay, "Participatory Democracy Revisited," Carole Pateman (2012: 10) argues that most examples of public participation today "leave intact the conventional institutional structures and political meaning of 'democracy.'" They do not, in her words, "democratize democracy."

By attempting to bypass conventional participation processes rather than improve them, leaders are simply trying to work around a problem rather than solve it. And conventional participation is indeed a problem, for a number of reasons.

Conventional participation can be harmful to citizens. Conventional participation tends to increase citizens' feelings of inefficacy and powerlessness. It decreases political interest, trust in government, and public-spiritedness, and damages perceptions of government legitimacy and credibility (Irvin & Stansbury, 2004; McComas, 2001; see also Collingwood & Reedy, 2012; Dryzek, 2000; Nabatchi & Amsler, 2014). For example, Katherine McComas (2003a, 2003b) found that in two public meetings about landfills, only 41 to 44 percent of participants were satisfied with the process, only 5 to 8 percent thought their opinions would matter in the final decision, and most left the meetings feeling worse about the situation. Conventional participation may also increase polarization, with people shifting toward more extreme positions. As evidence for this claim, one need only think of the 2009 town hall meetings on health care reform held by members of Congress.

Not surprisingly, fewer and fewer people participate in conventional opportunities (Hock, Anderson, & Potoski, 2012). To give one specific example, nearly 80 percent of all public meetings on how to spend community development block grant (CDBG) funding have an average attendance of fewer than twenty people, and often have no attendees (Handley & Howell-Moroney, 2010). This trend of declining participation is not a sign of citizen apathy, but rather is a rational decision based on a calculation of costs and benefits (Funkhouser, 2014). People have to overcome high transaction costs to attend—they have to expend time and often spend money (e.g., for transportation and childcare), and they have to forgo other activities.

Conventional participation can harm administrators and public officials. Administrators and officials also face high transaction costs for participation (Irvin & Stansbury, 2004). They must organize and prepare for conventional meetings, diverting energy and resources from other aspects of their work.

This is made worse by another problem: it is frustrating, discouraging, and sometimes even dangerous to deal with hostile, uninformed citizens in public meetings. In a personal communication with one of the authors, a California city clerk described council meetings as a "hostage-taking and punishment process." In some tragic cases, this frustration has escalated into actual violence, like the 2008 city council shooting in Kirkwood, Missouri (Davey, 2008). These scary and scarring experiences have contributed to an apparent decline in the number of public participation processes held by government officials, and particularly town halls by members of Congress (Chaddock, 2011; Kroll, 2011; Rupp, 2013).

Conventional participation can harm policy and governance. Many scholars assert that conventional public meetings do not actually involve citizens in decision making in any policy area (Wang, 2001). Moreover, a study of California public managers found that most officials believed public participation actually degraded the quality of decision making and policy implementation (Pearce & Pearce, 2010). Adams (2004: 44) explains that this is, in part, due to the organization and design of such processes:

> Citizens march up to the podium, give their two minute speeches, the presiding official says "thank you very much," and then officials proceed with their business irrespective of the arguments made by citizens. Citizens may speak their minds, but officials do not listen and

usually have their minds made up before the public hearing. Hearings, in this view, are mere democratic rituals that provide a false sense of legitimacy to legislative outcomes: Officials can say they received input from the public, and it can give their decisions the respect afforded to democratic processes, even though citizen input has no impact.

The consequences of conventional participation go far beyond miserable meetings. As the relationship deteriorates between the people and their public institutions, the legitimacy and financial sustainability of governments continue to decline. Many local leaders understand the implications of this shift. They know that the financial pressures facing local governments, school systems, and other public institutions are not just the result of larger economic cycles. "If we think we're going to come out of this recession and expect everything to go back to normal, we've got another thing coming," said Harry Jones, former county executive of Mecklenburg County, North Carolina. "We need to reach out and reframe our relationship with citizens—the people who are the ultimate source of our revenues" (Leighninger, 2013). The attempt to reframe this relationship is at the heart of "good" participation.

WHAT IS "GOOD" PARTICIPATION?

If conventional processes are usually examples of "bad" participation, what do we mean by "good" participation? At the most basic level, *good participation means treating citizens like adults.* An exchange that typifies this trend took place at a public meeting in Lakewood, Colorado, in 2004. The mayor called a meeting of neighborhood and community leaders to better understand how he might balance the city budget. Even though survey results suggested that residents valued local government services, they had repeatedly voted down local sales tax increases meant to maintain the same level of services. Finally, someone at the back of the room said, "Look, mayor, we like you, and we think you work hard, but what we've had here is a parent-child relationship between government and citizens, and what we need is an adult-adult relationship" (Leighninger, 2006: 1).

There are a number of ways in which good participation activities—both thick and thin—can confer the respect, recognition, and responsibility that typify an adult relationship:

- *Providing factual information—as much as people want.* In an era when information—and disinformation—circulates more quickly and widely than ever, providing basic information about public problems, budget expenditures, public services, and other data is an essential component of public participation. Information can be shared in numerous ways, including simple printed handouts, information briefs, infographics, interactive online maps, machine-readable datasets, presentations, discussion and issue guides, and the availability of subject matter experts. Some kinds of participation, such as action research projects (Cunningham & Leighninger, 2011) and online platforms like SeeClickFix, PublicStuff, and Ushahidi, rely on citizens to help gather and analyze the data.

- *Using sound group process techniques.* Process skills and techniques have emerged as a critical factor in the development of public participation. Public leaders have learned, often by trial and error, that thinking carefully about agendas, formats, and facilitation rather than accepting conventional formats—or not thinking through the process at all—can be the difference between success and failure. This is true for both online and face-to-face forms of participation.

- *Giving people a chance to tell their stories.* The chance for people to explain why they care about an issue, and to feel like others hear and understand their story, is the most fundamental missing ingredient in conventional formats. It is probably also what Oscar Wilde would call the most charming aspect of good participation. When people have a chance to relate their experiences, they are much more likely learn from each other, be civil toward one another, form stronger relationships, and make the connection between their individual interests and the public good (Ryfe, 2006). Over the last twenty years, small-group formats that allow this kind of storytelling have been a core component of successful face-to-face participation. With the rise of social media, a different but complementary kind of storytelling has emerged, no longer bound by the constraints of time and space (Gordon, Baldwin-Philippi, & Balestra, 2013).

- *Providing choices.* Although they do so in different ways, both thick and thin forms of participation give people choices. Rather than trying to "sell" participants on a particular policy, these good participation opportunities allow citizens to decide for themselves what they think. In their article on the future of the Internet and politics, Fung, Gilman, and Shkabatur (2013) hypothesize that this practice of giving choices, either in face-to-face settings or online, will be increasingly demanded by citizens—and increasingly granted by public officials.

- *Giving participants a sense of political legitimacy.* In almost every public participation setting, people want to know whether what they say really matters. They often ask for some kind of formal or informal legitimacy—a sense that decision-makers are listening, will use their input in policymaking, and will explain how it had an impact. Participatory budgeting is perhaps the fastest growing form of participation because it goes one step further: built in to the process is the opportunity for participants to vote on how to spend public funds (Ganuza & Baiocchi, 2012; Wampler, 2012). The question of who has a legitimate voice, and what the parameters are for using that voice, looms as one of the largest questions in any adult relationship.

- *Supporting people to take action in a variety of ways.* Participation processes can encourage and support citizens to take action in numerous ways, from clicking a link to joining a task force to cleaning up a park. Some projects result in higher levels of volunteerism. Others direct people toward avenues for further influence on the policymaking process. Still others support the formation of committees and task forces to tackle specific, more advanced assignments. All of these opportunities for action recognize citizens as (adult) problem-solvers, capable of making their own contributions to solving problems.

- *Making participation enjoyable.* Another way in which successful participation treats citizens like adults is by thinking seriously about the value of fun. Because people have many options for how to spend their time, making the experience enjoyable can help encourage and enrich participation. In *Making Democracy Fun*, Josh Lerner (2014) not only documents the increasing use of games in public participation, but also unpacks the ways in which participatory processes can be gratifying to participants.

- *Making participation easy and convenient.* Most adults have many different pressures on their time. They value participation opportunities that fit easily into busy schedules, in addition to the ones that are more powerful and time-consuming. People also value opportunities they can seize at the very moment they are confronted with a public problem or opportunity: for example, the smartphone app that lets Boston residents identify a burned-out streetlight, directing the information straight to the city's public works employees (Schreckinger, 2014).

This final attribute of an adult relationship is often in tension with the rest: there is an obvious tradeoff between convenience and the benefits people receive. Thick forms of participation, which are most likely to treat citizens as adults in other ways, require a greater commitment of time and energy. Thin forms of participation, which usually offer fewer of the other attributes of an adult-adult relationship, are generally the easiest and most convenient.

Finally, it is important to note that the involvement of a large, diverse number of participants is usually a key factor in the success of participation—especially when the process is intended to inform policy. Engaging a critical mass of people maximizes the possibility of non-governmental action by bringing more problem-solvers to the table and distributing the individual benefits of participation to the widest possible number of citizens. In addition, the presence of a critical mass of participants may produce some aspects of the adult-adult relationship. For example, being part of a large cross-section of the community may give people a sense of political legitimacy, even when public officials have been unable or unwilling to confer the expectation that citizen opinions will "matter" in the policymaking process. When it comes to influencing a policy decision, anecdotal evidence suggests that a large, diverse number of participants is critical even when public officials are supportive (Fagotto & Fung, 2009; Friedman, 2006; Leighninger, 2006).

Given the attributes of "good" participation, it is easy to see why conventional processes do not measure up. Table 2.1 assesses each form of participation—thick, thin, and conventional—in terms of treating citizens like adults. Thick participation generally features many of the attributes of an adult-adult relationship, although it is not easy and convenient. Thin participation is easy and convenient and sometimes features the attributes of an adult-adult relationship. Conventional participation offers few of the attributes of an adult relationship, and in most cases it is not particularly easy or convenient. But aside from making people feel better, how does good participation actually solve problems?

HOW DOES GOOD PARTICIPATION SOLVE PROBLEMS?

If conventional participation incurs costs and causes problems, can other forms of participation do better? Can thin and thick participation better address the issues we face in our communities? In Chapter 1, we argued that citizens want civility, community, and problem solving. Can good participation provide what citizens want and what public officials need? A great deal of evidence suggests that it can, and often does; however, that evidence also suggests that the positive

Table 2.1
Forms of Participation and the Attributes of
an Adult-Adult Relationship

Attribute	Thick Participation	Thin Participation	Conventional Participation
Providing information—as much as people want	Yes	Sometimes	Sometimes
Giving people a chance to tell their stories	Yes	Sometimes	No
Presenting a range of policy choices	Yes	Sometimes	No
Giving citizens a sense of political legitimacy	Yes	Sometimes	No
Supporting people to take action in a variety of ways	Yes	Sometimes	No
Using sound group process techniques	Yes	No	No
Making participation enjoyable	Sometimes	Sometimes	No
Making participation easy and convenient	No	Yes	No

benefits of good participation are difficult to sustain (Nabatchi & Amsler, 2014; Nabatchi, Gastil, Weiksner, & Leighninger, 2012).

Participation can create civility. If the essence of successful public participation is treating people like adults, then it should come as no surprise that people act like adults in these settings. And yet public officials and citizens often *are* surprised; their experiences in conventional meetings have been so discouraging that they no longer believe civility in public dialogue is possible. When Tina Nabatchi and Cynthia Farrar (2011) interviewed state legislators and Congressional staffers, they had to explain in detail how productive participation processes worked—and even then, the interviewees treated productive participation as more of a far-fetched hypothetical than something that might happen in real life. Laura Black (2012: 78), a communication scholar, observes:

"What happens in deliberative events is vastly different from politics as usual, and participants often report being pleasantly surprised by their experiences in these events."

The surprising civility in well-structured participation seems to arise from two key elements in an adult-adult relationship: (1) more opportunities to share and digest information and (2) the invitation for people to use stories and personal experiences to explain what they think. As sociologist David Ryfe (2006) explains, storytelling helps participants relate to one another, analyze information they have been given, handle disagreements, and empathize with people who have views and backgrounds different from their own. As a result, the way people talk in successful participation environments is more emotional—including more anger, more sadness, and more humor—than you would expect from highly rational prescriptions for participation and highly theoretical visions of deliberation.

The new relationships fostered through participation do not simply occur among citizens; they also form between citizens and public servants, especially when those public servants are part of the process. This may be one of the reasons why some forms of participation lead to higher levels of trust between citizens and government. People who took part in the CaliforniaSpeaks project on health care reform, which was run by the national nonprofit America*Speaks*, were over 55 percent more likely to agree, after the process, with statements like "We can trust our state's government to do what is right" (Fung, Lee, & Harbage, 2008). In one North Carolina project, "external political efficacy" (the extent to which people feel that government is responsive to their interests) increased by 31 percent (Nabatchi, 2010).

Participation can create community. Given the demonstrated capacity of participation to produce civility and build relationships, it may seem safe to assume that participants can also develop stronger community bonds and networks. But since most participation processes are temporary projects lasting only a few weeks or months, their effects on community may also be short-lived. The link between participation and community is worth exploring, both strategically and empirically, because research demonstrates the extent to which community matters. Strong, ongoing connections between residents, robust relationships between people and institutions, and positive feelings by citizens about the places they live are highly correlated with a range of positive outcomes, from economic development to public health. For example:

- Cities and towns that have higher levels of community attachment have higher rates of economic growth and lower levels of unemployment (Knight Foundation, 2010).
- Neighborhoods where people work together and have higher collective efficacy have lower crime rates (Hurley, 2004; see also Davis, 2013; Sampson, Raudenbush, & Earls, 1997).
- People with stronger relationships to friends and neighbors are at less risk of serious illness and premature death (Olien, 2013). Reflecting on a successful public participation process conducted by the Centers for Disease Control, epidemiologist Roger Bernier speculated that "Democracy is good for your health" (Leighninger, 2006).

More evidence about the link between participation and community has emerged in the Global South, where some countries have established more durable structures for public participation. Scholars have studied the effects of citizen-driven land use planning exercises in India, local health councils in Brazil, ward committees in South Africa, and "co-production" in the Philippines (Spink, Hossain, & Best, 2009). These more sustained forms of participation seem to have stronger impacts on equity, government efficiency, and trust. In a review of longitudinal studies of these and other structures, Tiago Peixoto (n.d.) finds that:

- Participants are more willing to pay taxes (see also Torgler, Schneider, & Schaltegger, 2009).
- Governments are more likely to complete planned projects.
- Public finances are better managed and are less prone to corruption (see also Andersson, Fennell, & Shahrokh, 2011).
- Participants are more trusting of public institutions.
- Public expenditures are more likely to benefit low-income people.
- Poverty is reduced.

In the United States, treating people like adults, occasionally and in an ad hoc way, is helping public leaders deal with crises and make controversial decisions. There is increasing evidence from other countries that treating people like adults, in a more ongoing and systemic way, can unlock a more significant array of benefits.

Participation can solve policymaking and public problems. The evidence on how participation—particularly thick participation—can affect policymaking is more abundant, even in the Global North. Initiated most often by local leaders, these strategies have been used hundreds if not thousands of times to address issues involving land use, crime prevention, education, racism and discrimination, immigration, youth development, budgets, poverty and economic development, and strategic planning. In communities across the United States, participation projects have left their mark on the physical landscape, from the Village Academy in Delray Beach, Florida (Leighninger, 2006), to the Fremont Street Troll in Seattle, which is shown in Exhibit 2.2 (Diers, 2008). One can easily find case studies demonstrating how these processes have affected public policy (Fagotto & Fung, 2009; Friedman, Kadlec, & Birnback, 2007; Leighninger, 2006; Levine & Torres, 2008; see also Participedia.net).

Exhibit 2.2
The Fremont Street Troll in Seattle

Although meaningful public participation has been much more common at the local level, there are some state and federal policy examples in the United States (see Chapter 7). For example, participation initiatives helped shape prison reform legislation in Oklahoma, the Unified New Orleans Plan adopted after Hurricane Katrina (Lukensmeyer, 2007, 2013), and the flu vaccine policy of the Centers for Disease Control. There are additional international examples; in Brazil, policy conferences engaging thousands of people have been used to produce federal policies on a wide variety of issues since 1988 (Pogrebinschi, 2014).

How can participation affect policymaking? A range of anecdotal stories and empirical evaluations suggest some answers:

- *By participating, people become more informed about public issues.* Sometimes the awareness of a key set of facts, coupled with a set of recommendations reflecting this new understanding, can swing the pendulum in a policy debate (Abelson & Gauvin, 2006; Muhlberger, 2006). In research on National Issues Forums in South Dakota, 72 percent of participants reported gaining new insights about issues, 79 percent reported discussing aspects of the problem that they had not considered before, and 37 percent reported thinking differently about the issue (Fagotto & Fung, 2006).

- *Participation can bridge divides.* When participation brings together citizens on different sides of a policy debate, they often find common ground, which can break a legislative deadlock. In a statewide process called "Balancing Justice in Oklahoma," finding common ground helped the state legislature shift from an aggressive prison construction policy to becoming one of the leading states in community corrections (Leighninger, 2006). In the Cleveland Flats section of Cleveland, Ohio, it helped bridge what city councilman Joe Cimperman called a "culture of conflict" over development issues, and led to the "Flats Forward" plan (Leighninger, 2014).

- *Participation increases the accountability of elected officials.* Participation can connect citizens and public officials during the course of an effort, and inspire more communication afterward. For example, after the "CaliforniaSpeaks" process on health care in that state, 40 percent of the 3,500 participants contacted a public official (Fung, Lee, & Harbage, 2008). But when public officials act against the recommendations of citizens who have been mobilized to address a key issue, they often regret it. When the city council of Eugene, Oregon, decided not to embrace the budget recommendations advanced through "Eugene Decisions," one of the first participatory budgeting processes in the United States, citizens rallied against the decision. City council members changed their minds and accepted the recommendations a week later (Weeks, 2000).

In all of these examples, the capacity of the public participation exercise to reach a large number of people played a key role in the policy-affecting capacity of citizens. Informing, reconciling, and empowering people has policy impacts only if it achieves a certain scale; breakthroughs are less likely if disinformation still predominates, if large segments of the community are still in conflict, or if there are only a few voices pressuring their elected representatives.

This kind of critical mass is easiest to achieve at the local level, and yet some observers feel that public participation is the most promising approach—and in some cases, the last hope—of solving global problems like climate change. In the Worldwatch Institute's 2014 *State of the World* report, editors Tom Prugh and Michael Renner (2014: 251) write:

> Deliberative civic engagement has been found to increase citizens' civic skills, involvement, and interest in political issues, with corresponding impacts on policy. Human-authored solutions to sustainability problems seem unlikely to emerge without those—indeed, they may be the only way of deepening the responsiveness of democracies to citizens' wishes and harnessing it to the pursuit of sustainability.

Similarly, Prugh and Renner (2014: 251) decry the "repeatedly disappointing results of the annual high-level international meetings on climate change," and conclude that the "rapid expansion of democracy around the world thus seems to offer the only kernel of hope for breaking the logjam."

Some of the thinner kinds of engagement, in which people spend less time but receive smaller helpings of information, legitimacy, and storytelling, have had significant policy impacts simply through their ability to "go viral," achieving impressive critical mass despite being geographically diffuse. Archon Fung, Hollie Russon Gilman, and Jennifer Shkabatur (2013) point to the Trayvon Martin case, the Kony 2012 controversy, and the defeat of the Stop Online Piracy Act/Protect Intellectual Property Act (SOPA/PIPA) as key examples. In each case, participants only had to click a link to express their support for a particular cause, but they did so in such numbers that they were able to affect decision-makers.

- *Participation can prompt citizen action to solve problems.* Public participation can also solve problems by catalyzing action outside the policy arena, by people who are not public employees and organizations that are not part of government. There are several ways in which participation can support this kind of problem solving.

- *Participation generates new ideas.* Participation creates settings in which people come up with ideas for new activities or initiatives. Researchers studying a project organized by the West Virginia Center for Civic Life were able to quantify this effect: they found that 88 percent of the participants felt that the forums had given them new ideas of possible actions to take (Fagotto & Fung, 2009). Among the thinner forms of participation, online "crowdsourcing" has emerged as a structured process for idea generation. Crowdsourcing allows participants to propose solutions, comment on and add to others' proposals, and rank ideas according to which they like best. Cities like Manor, Texas, have supplemented the process by giving prizes to winning ideas (see generally, Svara & Denhardt, 2010).

- *Participation helps citizens find resources and allies.* A second way in which participation supports nongovernmental problem solving is that it helps citizens find the resources and allies they need (partly by forming relationships with others) to implement their ideas. Participation efforts have brought together citizen problem-solving teams to take on a host of issues. An early example was the construction of a shopping center in a low-income neighborhood in Fort Myers, Florida (Leighninger, 2006). In a large-scale participation process in several Southeastern states called "Turning the Tide on Poverty," 81 percent of the post-survey respondents who had participated in at least four of the five discussion sessions indicated they had joined an action team; over 39 percent of respondents volunteered after participating in three or fewer sessions. Moreover, 15 percent of all the volunteers indicated that this was their first time taking action in the community (Beaulieu & Welborn, 2012).

- *Participation develops new leadership.* Participation also provides spaces where new leaders can emerge. The Horizons project, which has involved people in over 300 towns across seven states in dialogue and action on rural poverty, provides empirical data that go beyond anecdotal stories (see Morehouse, 2009). Over 75 percent of the Horizons communities reported that, after the project, decisions about what happens in the community involve more people, and 77 percent reported that there are now more partnerships among local community organizations. In 39 percent of the communities, more people joined local boards, clubs, and service or other organizations. This leadership development may also encourage more government-initiated problem solving. For example, 34 percent of the Horizons communities reported that people new to leadership roles were elected to public office.

- *Participation encourages public-private collaboration.* There are also many instances in which people inside and outside government work together to solve problems. This is sometimes called the co-creation or co-production of public goods and services, and it, too, is more likely to happen when citizens, public officials, and public employees come together to compare notes, generate ideas, and take action (Spink, Hossain, & Best, 2009). For example, on the island of Kauai, Hawaii, business owners and residents joined forces to repair a bridge to a state park for which the State Department of Land and Natural Resources did not have the finances (Simon, 2009; see also Nabatchi & Mergel, 2010).

Table 2.2
Assumptions and Realities About Public Participation and Citizens

Assumption	Reality
Participation is and should be led by government.	Participation is sometimes organized by government officials, but also may be organized by civil society leaders and regular citizens.
Participation is and should be periodic and temporary.	Some participation opportunities are one-off endeavors; many others are regular but conventional (e.g., monthly school board meetings); and still others are repeatedly triggered by law (e.g., participation under the National Environmental Policy Act). Examples of sustained participation are rarer, but seem to have greater positive effects than temporary processes.
Citizens do not want to actively participate in the work of government.	Citizens increasingly express more desire to engage in public problem solving, and have more capacities and skills to do so.
Citizens do not understand their individual needs and interests, and are likely to give undue weight to personal, rather than public, concerns.	Participation can provide citizens with the information they need to assess their own needs and interests, as well as the needs and interest of others. In doing so, citizens can become more aware of and open to broader public concerns.

WHY BAD PARTICIPATION HAPPENS TO GOOD PEOPLE

Given the wealth of evidence showing the benefits of good participation, why is there still so much bad participation? This question becomes even more puzzling when one realizes that the decision-makers who preside over bad participation are often just as frustrated with it as everyone else.

The most important reason is the argument we introduced in Chapter 1 and flesh out through the rest of this book: our participation infrastructure is inefficient, outdated, and disconnected from the needs, goals, and capacity of citizens. Our current infrastructure is supported by, and works to reinforce, a set of outdated assumptions about participation and about citizens. These assumptions do not align with the realities of democracy and citizenship in the 21st Century. Table 2.2 lays out several of these assumptions and realities (see also Nabatchi, 2012). As a result, good public participation remains an uncommon, often unofficial, usually temporary phenomenon. To sustain more and better participation, we must understand the historic and modern roots of conventional, thick, and thin participation. This is our focus in Chapter 3.

SUMMARY

This chapter centered on the basics of public participation. We defined public participation as the activities by which people's concerns, needs, interests, and values are incorporated into decisions and actions on public matters and issues. Moreover, we distinguished between indirect participation (in which citizens select some kind of representative or intermediary to act for them) and direct participation (in which citizens are personally involved and actively engaged in providing input, making decisions, and solving problems).

Within direct participation, there are three main variations:

- *Thick participation*, in which large, diverse numbers of people engage in small-group discussions about issues, choices, and actions. Generally speaking, it is the most meaningful and powerful of the three forms, but also the most intensive and time-consuming, and the least common.

- *Thin participation*, in which individuals (sometimes in large numbers) indicate preferences, submit ideas, or provide information in fast and convenient ways. While there are face-to-face and telephone opportunities for thin participation, online approaches are proliferating rapidly.

- *Conventional participation*, in which individuals have the chance to submit complaints and briefly address their elected officials at public meetings. Conventional participation is sometimes legally required, although it seldom meets the needs of citizens or public officials. Because these older approaches are entrenched in our public institutions, they also frequently serve as participation models for civic organizations.

We asserted that conventional participation can be harmful to citizens, public officials, and policy and governance. Because it has high time and resources costs and negative impacts on public trust and the legitimacy of public institutions, we described conventional participation as "bad."

We asserted that "good" participation means treating citizens like adults. Good participation processes and activities—both thin and thick—are more successful when they: (1) provide people with information, (2) use sound group process techniques, (3) give people a chance to tell their stories, (4) present a range of policy choices, (5) give participants a sense of political legitimacy, (6) support people to take action in a variety of ways, (7) make participation enjoyable, and (8) make participation convenient. Good participation can have positive impacts on citizens, communities, and governance in many different ways and through many different mechanisms.

Despite the drawbacks of conventional participation, it is more common than thin and thick participation because it is supported by our current participation infrastructure. This infrastructure is based on, and works to reinforce, a set of outdated assumptions about participation and about citizens.

DISCUSSION QUESTIONS

1. Define public participation. Explain the differences between indirect and direct participation.

2. Define conventional, thin, and thick participation. What are the merits and shortcomings of each form? Under what conditions do you think each form works well (and does not)?

3. Discuss your experiences in public participation. Would you categorize your experiences as conventional, thin, or thick? Why? Were your experiences positive or negative? Why?

4. Review the list of online platforms in Box 2.2. Have you used any of these? If so, what were your experiences with them? What are some of the inherent challenges of online engagement?

5. Do you agree with the claims that conventional participation causes problems? Why or why not?

6. Discuss the characteristics of an adult-adult relationship. Do you believe it is important to incorporate these characteristics into public participation? Why or why not? What would you do to integrate these characteristics into public participation?

7. What are the characteristics of "good" participation? Do you agree with the claims about what makes for "good" participation? Why or why not?

8. Do you agree with the claim that "democracy is good for your health"? Why or why not?

9. Do you think the assumptions and realties presented in Table 2.2 are accurate? Why or why not? Does your opinion change if you look at them from the perspective of a public servant?

10. Do you think public participation is more influential at the local, state, or federal level? Why?

References

Abelson, Julia, & Francois-Pierre Gauvin. (2006). *Assessing the impacts of public participation: Concepts, evidence, and policy implications.* Ottawa, Canada: Canadian Policy Research Networks.

Abt, Clark C. (1970). *Serious games.* New York, NY: The Viking Press.

Adams, Brian. (2004). Public meetings and the democratic process. *Public Administration Review, 64*(1): 43–54.

Andersson, Edward, Emily Fennell, & Thea Shahrokh. (2011). *Making the case for public engagement: How to demonstrate the value of consumer input.* London, UK: Involve.

Beaulieu, Bo, & Rachel Welborn. (2012). *Turning the tide on poverty: Measuring and predicting civic engagement success.* Mississippi State, MS: Southern Rural Development Center.

Bessette, Joseph M. (1980). Deliberative democracy: The majority principle in republican government. In R.A. Goldwin & W.A. Schambra (Eds.), *How democratic is the constitution?*, 102–116. Washington, DC: American Enterprise Institute.

Bessette, Joseph M. (1994). *The mild voice of reason*. Chicago, IL: University of Chicago Press.

Bessette, Joseph M. (1997). *The mild voice of reason: Deliberative democracy and American national government*. Chicago, IL: University of Chicago Press.

Black, Laura W. (2012). How people communicate during deliberative events. In T. Nabatchi, J. Gastil, M. Weiksner, & M. Leighninger (Eds.), *Democracy in motion: Evaluating the practice and impact of deliberative civic engagement*, 59–80. New York, NY: Oxford University Press.

Bohman, James. (1998). The coming of age of deliberative democracy. *The Journal of Political Philosophy*, 6(4): 400–425.

Chaddock, Gail Russell. (2011). Congress, spooked by summer town halls, tries job fairs instead. *Christian Science Monitor*. Available at www.csmonitor.com/USA/Politics/2011/0823/Congress-spooked-by-summer-town-halls-tries-jobs-fairs-instead.

Collingwood, Loren, & Justin Reedy. (2012). Listening and responding to criticisms of deliberative civic engagement. In T. Nabatchi, J. Gastil, M. Weiksner, & M. Leighninger (Eds.), *Democracy in motion: Evaluating the practice and impact of deliberative civic engagement*, 233–259. New York, NY: Oxford University Press.

Cunningham, Kiran, & Matt Leighninger. (2011). Research for democracy, and democracy for research. In N. Thomas (Ed.), *Educating for deliberative democracy*, 59–66. San Francisco, CA: Jossey-Bass.

Davey, Monica. (2008). Gunman kills 5 people at city council meeting. *New York Times*. Available at www.nytimes.com/2008/02/08/us/08missouri.html?_r=0.

Davis, Michael. (2013). *The purpose of police*. Video presentation at the Annual Frontiers of Democracy Conference, Jonathan M. Tisch College of Citizenship and Public Service, Tufts University, Medford, MA. Available at http://activecitizen.tufts.edu/demfront/.

Diers, Jim. (2008). *From the ground up: The community's role in addressing street-level social issues*. Calgary, Alberta, Canada: Canada West Foundation.

Dryzek, John S. (2000). *Deliberative democracy and beyond: Liberals, critics, contestations*. Oxford, UK: Oxford University Press.

Elster, Jon (Ed.). (1998). *Deliberative democracy*. Cambridge, MA: Cambridge University Press.

Fagotto, Elena, & Archon Fung. (2006). *Embedded deliberation: entrepreneurs, organizations, and public action*. Boston, MA: Taubman Center for State and Local Government.

Fagotto, Elena, & Archon Fung. (2009). *Sustaining public engagement: Embedded deliberation in local communities*. East Hartford, CT: Everyday Democracy and Kettering Foundation.

Friedman, Will. (2006). Deliberative democracy and the problem of scope. *Journal of Public Deliberation*, 2(1): Article 1.

Friedman, Will, Alison Kadlec, & Lara Birnback. (2007). *Transforming public life: A decade of citizenship engagement in Bridgeport, CT*. New York, NY: Center for Advances in Public Engagement, Public Agenda.

Fung, Archon, Hollie Russon Gilman, & Jennifer Shkabatur. (2013). Six models for the Internet +Politics. *International Studies Review, 15*(1): 30–47.

Fung, Archon, Taeku Lee, & Peter Harbage. (2008). *Public impacts: Evaluating the outcomes of the CaliforniaSpeaks statewide conversation on health care reform.* Available at http://ckgroup.org/wp-content/uploads/2011/05/CaSpks-Eval-Report.pdf.

Funkhouser, Mark. (2014). The failure and promise of public participation. *Governing.* Available at www.governing.com/gov-institute/funkhouser/col-failure-promise-public-participation-government.html.

Ganuza, Ernesto, & Gianpaolo Baiocchi. (2012). The power of ambiguity: How participatory budgeting travels the globe. *Journal of Public Deliberation, 8*(2): Article 8.

Gastil, John. (2008). *Political communication and deliberation.* Thousand Oaks, CA: Sage.

Gastil, John, & Peter Levine (Eds.). (2005). *The deliberative democracy handbook: Strategies for effective civic engagement in the 21st century.* San Francisco, CA: Jossey-Bass.

Gordon, Eric, Jessica Baldwin-Philippi, & Martina Balestra. (2013). *Why we engage: How theories of human behavior contribute to our understanding of civic engagement in a digital era.* Cambridge, MA: Berkman Center for Internet & Society.

Gutmann, Amy, & Dennis Thompson. (2004). *Why deliberative democracy?* Princeton, NJ: Princeton University Press.

Habermas, Jürgen. (1984). *The theory of communicative action, Volume 1* (translation by Thomas McCarthy). Boston, MA: Beacon Press.

Handley, Donna Milam, & Michael Howell-Moroney. (2010). Ordering stakeholder relationships and citizen participation: Evidence from the community development block grant program. *Public Administration Review, 70*(4): 601–609.

Hock, Scott, Sarah Anderson, & Matthew Potoski. (2012). Invitation phone calls increase attendance at civic meetings: Evidence from a field experiment. *Public Administration Review, 73*(2): 221–228.

Hurley, Dan. (2004). Scientist at work—Felton Earls: On crime as science (a neighbor at a time). *New York Times.* Available at www.nytimes.com/2004/01/06/science/scientist-at-work-felton-earls-on-crime-as-science-a-neighbor-at-a-time.html.

Irvin, Renée A., & John Stansbury. (2004). Citizen participation in decision making: Is it worth the effort? *Public Administration Review, 64*(1): 55–65.

Jeynes, William H. (2005). *Parental involvement and student achievement: A meta-analysis.* Cambridge, MA: Harvard Family Research Project.

Knight Foundation. (2010). *Soul of the community 2010. Why people love where they live and why it matters: A national perspective.* Miami, FL: Knight Foundation.

Kroll, Andy. (2011). Congress has an answer for public wrath: Eliminate town halls. *Mother Jones.* Available at www.motherjones.com/mojo/2011/08/paul-ryan-congress-town-hall.

Leighninger, Matt. (2006). *The next form of democracy: How expert rule is giving way to shared governance—and why politics will never be the same.* Nashville, TN: Vanderbilt University Press.

Leighninger, Matt. (2011). Citizenship and governance in a wild, wired world. *National Civic Review, 100*(2): 20–29.

Leighninger, Matt. (2012). Mapping deliberative civic engagement: Pictures from a (r) evolution. In T. Nabatchi, J. Gastil, M. Weiksner, & M. Leighninger (Eds.), *Democracy in motion: Evaluating the practice and impact of deliberative civic engagement*, 19–39. New York, NY: Oxford University Press.

Leighninger, Matt. (2013). Three minutes at the microphone: How outdated citizen participation laws are corroding American democracy. In Working Group on Legal Frameworks for Public Participation (Ed.), *Making public participation legal*, 3–6. Denver, CO: National Civic League.

Leighninger, Matt. (2014). *Infogagement: Citizenship and democracy in the age of connection.* Washington, DC: Philanthropy for Active Civic Engagement.

Lerner, Josh. (2014). *Making democracy fun: How game design can empower citizens and transform politics.* Cambridge, MA: MIT Press.

Levine, Peter, & Lars Hasselblad Torres. (2008). *Where is democracy headed? Research and practice on public deliberation.* Washington, DC: Deliberative Democracy Consortium.

Lukensmeyer, Carolyn J. (2007). Large-scale citizen engagement and the rebuilding of New Orleans: A case study. *National Civic Review, 96*(3): 3–15.

Lukensmeyer, Carolyn J. (2013). *Bringing citizen voices to the table: A guide for public managers.* San Francisco, CA: Jossey-Bass.

Lukensmeyer, Carolyn J., and Lars Hasselblad Torres. (2006). *Public deliberation: A manager's guide to citizen engagement.* Washington, DC: IBM Center for the Business of Government.

McComas, Katherine A. (2001). Theory and practice of public meetings. *Communication Theory, 11*(1): 36–55.

McComas, Katherine A. (2003a). Citizen satisfaction with public meetings used for risk communication. *Journal of Applied Communication Research, 31*(2): 164–184.

McComas, Katherine A. (2003b). Trivial pursuits: Participant views of public meetings. *Journal of Public Relations Research, 15*(2): 91–115.

Morehouse, Diane L. (2009). *Horizons sustained effects: A report on continuing leadership and poverty reduction activities and outcomes in Horizons alumni communities.* Minneapolis, MN: Northwest Area Foundation.

Muhlberger, Peter. (2006). *Report to the Deliberative Democracy Consortium: Building a deliberation measurement toolbox.* Available at www.geocities.com/pmuhl78/abstracts.html#VirtualAgoraReport.

Nabatchi, Tina. (2010). Deliberative democracy and citizenship: In search of the efficacy effect. *Journal of Public Deliberation, 6*(2): Article 8.

Nabatchi, Tina. (2012). *A manager's guide to evaluating citizen participation.* Washington, DC: IBM Center for the Business of Government.

Nabatchi, Tina, & Lisa Blomgren Amsler. (2014). Direct public engagement in local government. *American Review of Public Administration, 44*(4suppl): 63s–88s.

Nabatchi, Tina, Jack Becker, & Matt Leighninger (2015). Using public participation to enhance citizen voice and promote accountability. In J.L. Perry & R. Christensen (Eds.), *Handbook of public administration* (3rd ed.). Hoboken, NJ: John Wiley & Sons.

Nabatchi, Tina, & Cynthia Farrar. (2011). *Bridging the gap between the public and public officials: What do public officials want and need to know about public deliberation?* Washington, DC: Deliberative Democracy Consortium.

Nabatchi, Tina, John Gastil, Michael Weiksner, & Matt Leighninger (Eds.). (2012). *Democracy in motion: Evaluating the practice and impact of deliberative civic engagement.* New York, NY: Oxford University Press.

Nabatchi, Tina, & Ines Mergel. (2010). Participation 2.0: Using Internet and social media technologies to promote distributed democracy and create digital neighborhoods. In J.H. Svara & J. Denhardt (Eds.), *Connected communities: Local governments as partners in citizen engagement and community building*, 80–87. Phoenix, AZ: Alliance for Innovation.

Nemani, Abhi. (2014). *Small (city) pieces, loosely joined: Experiments in stitching together civic technology for local governments.* Available at http://abhinemani.dreamhosters.com/medium-export/Small–City–Pieces–Loosely-Joined-5202fb5a93e3.html.

Olien, Jessica. (2013). Loneliness is deadly. Social isolation kills more people than obesity does—and it's just as stigmatized. *Slate.com.* Available at www.slate.com/articles/health_and_science/medical_examiner/2013/08/dangers_of_loneliness_social_isolation_is_deadlier_than_obesity.html.

Patel, Mayur, Jon Sotsky, Sean Gourley, & Daniel Houghton. (2013). *The emergence of civic tech: Investments in a growing field.* Miami, FL: Knight Foundation.

Pateman, Carole. (2012). Participatory democracy revisited. *Perspectives on Politics, 10*(1): 7–19.

Pearce, W. Barnett, & Kimberly A. Pearce. (2010). *Aligning the work of government to strengthen the work of citizens: A study of public administrators in local and regional government.* Dayton, OH: Kettering Foundation.

Peixoto, Tiago. (n.d.). *The benefits of citizen engagement: A (brief) review of the evidence.* Available at http://democracyspot.net/2012/11/24/the-benefits-of-citizen-engagement-a-brief-review-of-the-evidence/.

Phelps, Andrew. (2011). Community PlanIt turns civic engagement into a game—and the prize is better discourse. *Niemanlab.* Available at www.niemanlab.org/2011/09/community-planit-turns-civic-engagement-into-a-game-and-the-prize-is-better-discourse/.

Pogrebinschi, Thamy. (2014). Turning participation into representation: Innovative policymaking for minority groups in Brazil. In C. Sirianni & J. Girouard (Eds.), *Varieties of civic innovation: Deliberative, collaborative, network, and narrative approaches,* 181–202. Nashville, TN: Vanderbilt University Press.

Prugh, Thomas, & Michael Renner (Eds.). (2014). *State of the world: Governing for sustainability.* Washington, DC: The Worldwatch Institute.

Rupp, Keith Lee. (2013). R.I.P. Town Hall Meeting. *U.S. News and World Report.* Online. Available at www.usnews.com/opinion/blogs/keith-rupp/2013/08/26/why-congress-town-hall-meetings-may-become-history.

Ryfe, David M. (2006). Narrative and deliberation in small group forums. *Journal of Applied Communication Research, 34*(1): 72–93.

Sampson, Robert J., Stephen W. Raudenbush, & Felton Earls. (1997). Neighborhoods and violent crime. *Science,* 277: 918–924.

Schreckinger, Ben. (2014). Boston: There's an app for that. *Politico.* Available at www .politico.com/magazine/story/2014/06/boston-theres-an-app-for-that-107661.html# .VEU1uTMtCP8.

Sifry, Micah. (2014). Civic tech and engagement: Announcing a new series on what makes it "thick." Available at http://techpresident.com/news/25204/civic-tech-and-engagement-announcing-new-series-what-makes-it-thick.

Simon, Mallory. (2009). Island DIY: Kauai residents don't wait for state to repair road. *CNN.com.* Available at http://edition.cnn.com/2009/US/04/09/hawaii.volunteers.re-pair/index.html?iref=topnews.

Spink, Peter K., Naomi Hossain, & Nina J. Best. (2009). Hybrid public action. *Institute of Development Studies Bulletin, 40*(6): 128.

Svara, James H., & Janet Denhardt. (2010). *The connected community: Local government as partners in citizen engagement and community building.* Phoenix, AZ: Alliance for Innovation.

Torgler, Benno, Friedrich Schneider, & Christoph A. Schaltegger. (2009). Local autonomy, tax morale, and the shadow economy. *Public Choice, 144*(1–2): 293–321.

Walsh, Katherine Cramer. (2007). *Talking about race: Community dialogues and the politics of disagreement.* Chicago, IL: University of Chicago Press.

Wampler, Brian. (2012). Participatory budgeting: Core principles and key impacts. *Journal of Public Deliberation, 8*(2): Article 12.

Wang, Xiaohu. (2001). Assessing public participation in US cities. *Public Performance & Management Review, 24*(4): 322–336.

Weeks, Edward C. (2000). The practice of deliberative democracy: Results from four large-scale trials. *Public Administration Review, 60*(4): 360–372.

Wilde, Oscar. (1893). *Lady Windermere's fan.* London, UK: E. Mathews and J. Lane.

Zuckerman, Ethan. (2013). *Beyond the "crisis in civics"—Notes from my 2013 DML Talk.* Available at www.ethanzuckerman.com/blog/2013/03/26/beyond-the-crisis-in-civics-notes-from-my-2013-dml-talk/.

Zyda, Michael. (2005). From visual simulation to virtual reality to games. *Computer, 38*(9): 25–32.

Pictures from a (R)evolution: chapter **THREE** The Fitful Development of Public Participation in the United States

I f we want to anticipate and affect the development of public participation, we need to understand the path it has taken so far. Every effort to engage citizens—from the most ambitious process to the most limited exercise—is part of a compelling, continuing story.

It is, admittedly, a long story: the struggle to define, protect, and sustain citizen participation is as old as civilization itself. This chapter provides a brief synopsis of this history, focusing (as in Chapters 1 and 2) on direct participation, rather than on voting and other forms of indirect participation. Although we begin by examining the roots of participation in the ancient world, the chapter centers on historic episodes in the United States.

The central thread of this story is the way in which informal democratic processes and traditions interact with formal governance structures and systems. People have a natural inclination to band together to solve problems. At many times in our history, and in almost every culture on earth, we see instances in which people do this democratically, in ways that value, enable, and ensure the support of the group as a whole. This habit has rarely, and never fully, been incorporated into our systems of governance, which have often substituted voting and other kinds of indirect participation for the direct involvement of citizens in policy-making and problem solving. Time and again, democratic movements have led to republican reforms, especially in the United States.

Scholars describe the informal processes and formal structures of democratic development in many ways. Some emphasize informal citizen meetings, protests, and processes as examples of "the citizens outdoors," in contrast with the "indoor" formality of government structures and procedures (e.g., Goodwyn, 1976, 1978; see also, Dzur, 2012; Morone, 1990; Schudson, 1998; Wiebe, 1996). Mansuri and Rao (2014) distinguish between the "organic participation" of citizens and civic groups acting independently of government and "induced participation" led by governments and/or by non-governmental organizations acting through the state. Researchers of participation in the Global South, where democratic, participatory developments may be more advanced than in the North, have compared the "invented spaces" of citizens mobilizing to articulate their interests with the "invited spaces" set up by government to accommodate their needs and demands (Cornwell & Schattan Coehlo, 2007; Gaventa, 2006; Görgens & van Donk, 2011; von Lieres, 2007). In their work, these scholars are documenting the quest to create structures that support participatory processes—public spaces where, in the words of Thomas Jefferson (1816), "the voice of the whole people would be fairly, fully, and peaceably expressed, discussed, and decided by the common reason." They also echo Hannah Arendt's (1963) question of why the structure of our democracies "provide a public space only for the representatives of the people, and not for the people themselves."

But although amplifying the "voice of the whole people" in governance is a long, historic struggle, it is not an impossible one. The history of democratic development is one of fitful but steady progress: citizens have, over the broad sweep of time, gained new safeguards for their lives, liberties, and public happiness. As noted in Chapter 1, significant recent trends—the availability of education, changing attitudes toward authority, the rise of the Internet—have shifted how citizens can contribute to governance, and what they expect from it. We should not treat structure and process as opposing and irreconcilable forces, as some sort of "yin" and "yang" in democratic development. In fact, it seems clear that they are two strands of democracy that are stronger when woven together. A wide range of scholarly research and anecdotal experience suggests that, like hardware and software, they need one another.

This chapter traces how these two strands—process and structure—have spooled out from ancient times through the present. Of course, we cannot do justice to the full sweep of this history, even by confining the narrative to the United States. Instead, we provide snapshots of some particularly significant moments, and conclude with an examination of the principal assets and challenges we face today.

THE DEMOCRATIC ROOTS OF PARTICIPATION IN THE ANCIENT WORLD

The history of direct participation in governance is long and varied, and encompasses many different civilizations, time periods, and parts of the world. Many people claim democracy to be a Western invention and trace the origins of popular participation to 5th Century Athens. We do not. Although the historical record is scarce and subject to debate, some evidence suggests that loosely democratic institutions and processes of governance existed centuries, even millennia, before the Athenian experiment (for a discussion, see Robinson, 1997; see Box 3.1 for a discussion about the etymology of democracy).

Although his argument is sometimes challenged, Ronald M. Glassman (1986) speculates that "tribal democracies" or "campfire democracies" existed among the earliest hunter-gatherer societies, particularly in Africa. He acknowledges that early kinship systems were often built around hierarchical criteria such as gender and age, but also asserts that some societies were democratic in that they made decisions through deliberation. These decision-making processes were guided by principles such as the involvement of all tribe members, rules that could be debated and amended, and limits on the exercise of power. These processes were supplemented with formal decision-making structures, most notably the male council, where adult men worked to attain unanimous approval of decisions.

There are more examples of democratic structures in the ancient history of the Middle East. Using Sumerian epic, myth, and historical records, Thorkild Jacobsen (1970 [1943], 1970 [1957]) argued for the existence of "primitive democracy," pointing to city-states in Sumer (in the third millennium BCE) where the king did not hold autocratic power, but rather had to consult with and persuade deliberative councils who possessed final political authority. Other historians describe similar democratic structures and practices in the Hittite Old Kingdom, on the island of Elba, in Syro-Palestinian cities, in Phoenician cities, and among the Israelites of the Biblical Book of Deuteronomy (Robinson, 1997).

Democratic practices may also have been institutionalized in republican polities in India from the 6th to the 4th Century BCE. In these self-governing republics, called *Ganas* (meaning equal) or *Sanghas* (meaning assembly), financial, administrative, judicial, and other major decisions were made by members working and deliberating together (Robinson, 1997; see also Muhlberger, 1998). In some cases, attendance at these deliberative assemblies was open to all free men (rich or poor), but in others, it was limited to the heads of the most important families.

Debate about the democratic elements of these early civilizations continues, in part because of limited direct evidence; however, there is extensive evidence about the functioning of popular government in 5th Century BCE Greece (Robinson, 1997). According to many historians, the Athenian *Ecclesia* is the first written record of direct citizen participation in the work of government. Open to all free male citizens who were at least eighteen years old and had two years of military service, the Ecclesia served as the popular assembly of Athens, where citizens could speak their minds, seek consensus, and make legislative and foreign policy decisions by majority rule. (Women, children, metics or resident aliens, and slaves were banned from participation in the functions of government.) The policymaking power of the Ecclesia was checked by the *Boule*, or the Council of 500, which was comprised of aristocratic representatives chosen by lot. The Boule set the agenda for discussion in the Ecclesia and oversaw many of the day-to-day activities of government administration. Many of these administrative functions were delegated to decision-making bodies staffed by free male citizens serving in a short-term capacity. These positions were also selected by lot to ensure better representation.

Together, these examples demonstrate that popular government has a very long history. In these and other ancient civilizations, citizens were involved in the processes and structures of government, where they made decisions through consultation and debate. Of course, not everyone was authorized to participate, but the issue of inclusion and exclusion is a recurring theme in the history of participation—and a challenge we still face today.

DEMOCRACY IN AMERICA BEFORE COLUMBUS

Turning to the Americas, there is evidence that this conversation about participation was taking place even before the arrival of the first Europeans. The people of the Haudenosaunee Confederacy claim to have established the "oldest living participatory democracy on earth." (Haudenosaunee means "people of the long house"; the French later referred to them as the Iroquois Confederacy.) The Haudenosaunee Confederacy was founded sometime between the years 1090 and 1150 CE (e.g., Grinde, 1992; Grinde & Johansen, 1991; Weatherford, 1988), and continues to this day. It features a federated, horizontal governance structure and a complex system of checks and balances.

The foundation of the Haudenosaunee Confederacy is the Great Law of Peace. Each Nation in the Confederacy runs its own internal affairs with a council of elected delegates, which in turn sends representatives to the Grand Council. The Grand Council makes all major decisions affecting the Nations through deliberation and consensus. Within the Grand Council are the Elder Brothers (Seneca and Mohawk Nations) and the Younger Brothers (Oneida, Cayuga, and Tuscarora Nations). The Onondaga Nation promotes deliberation and consensus-building within the Council. The democratic structures and processes of the Haudenosaunee Confederacy give women substantive and powerful roles. Clan mothers select (and remove) members of the Grand Council, hold their own decision-making councils, speak at men's councils, and often take the initiative in suggesting legislation.

Some historians—and the Haudenosaunee themselves—claim that this Confederacy was a direct model for the United States Constitution (e.g., Grinde, 1992; Grinde & Johansen, 1991). They point out that both are federal systems, featuring checks and balances, and that the two houses of Congress mirror the Elder and Younger Brother Councils. The U.S. system has not, however, had overt processes for consensus building or specific roles for women.

DEMOCRACY AND REPUBLICANISM IN THE FOUNDING OF THE UNITED STATES

While debate continues over the influence of the Haudenosaunee, most historians agree that Ancient Greece provided the example used by the Founding Fathers to promote and legitimize the American experiment. From their writings and speeches to the Classical Revival architecture they used for public buildings, the founders emphasized their ancient, classical, deliberative roots.

The structures of early American democracy were also supported by successful democratic processes, most notably the early New England Town Meetings where free, white, property-owning, adult male community members came together to make policy, budgetary, and other administrative decisions for local government (Bryan, 2003). These meetings, which are in many ways successors to the *Ecclesia* (Roberts, 2008), began in approximately 1620 in what are now the states of Connecticut, Massachusetts, and Rhode Island, and over time expanded to several others.

The primary concern of the Founders was balancing liberty and power to ensure the long-term stability of the political system. The basic question centered on how to protect the liberty of the people from the intrusions of government—but still give government the power needed to conduct public affairs. This question was repeated throughout the constitutional debates, where there was widespread agreement about the dangers and weaknesses of popular, direct democracy and the virtues of republicanism. Some notable quotes reflecting the Founders' views on democracy are in Box 3.2.

Recognizing the potential of citizens to destabilize the new nation, the Founders incorporated barriers to direct public participation in the Constitution. Benjamin Rush (1787) described this shift by saying that although "all the power is derived from the people, they possess it only on the days of their elections. After this, it is the property of their rulers."

Box 3.2. Founders' Views of Popular Democracy

"... democracies have ever been spectacles of turbulence and contention; have ever been found incompatible with personal security, or the rights of property; and have in general been as short in their lives as they have been violent in their deaths."

—James Madison, Federalist No. 10, 1787

"Remember, democracy never lasts long. It soon wastes, exhausts and murders itself. There never was a democracy yet that did not commit suicide."

—John Adams, 1814 letter to John Taylor

"It has been observed that a pure democracy, if it were practicable, would be the most perfect government. Experience has proved that no position is more false than this. The ancient democracies, in which the people themselves deliberated, never possessed one feature of good government. Their very character was tyranny; their figure deformity."

—Alexander Hamilton at a 1788 ratifying convention in Poughkeepsie, New York

The effect of the Constitution on public participation is yet another controversial topic among historians. Some argue that as the locus of official power moved from municipalities to state legislatures and the federal government, the town hall meetings and other arenas for direct participation began to wither. Others point to the many voluntary associations and other "mediating institutions" described by de Tocqueville when he visited the United States in the 1830s and argue that participation moved out of official government and into civil society. Still others claim that the new federal system was essential for economic development and adequate defense and that it was necessary to de-emphasize participation to ensure the prosperity and survival of democracy.

Whatever the effect, the Founders adopted a federal system of majority rule, with shared powers and checks and balances among separate institutions, and allowed for only limited, indirect participation by the citizenry in periodic elections. The result was a set of government structures that favored delay over rapid change, diffused power rather than concentrated it, distrusted executive action rather than strengthened it, and limited participation processes to protect political and administrative structures from an over-active citizenry. These decisions shaped and continue to affect the structures and processes of our current participation infrastructure.

PARTICIPATORY POPULISM IN 19TH CENTURY AMERICA

During the first half of the 19th Century, Americans experienced a broadening of democracy at the state and national levels, but a recession at the local level. Just as voting rights were extended to all white men and the civil service was opened to all educated citizens, participation in local government was pushed into the background. But when the livelihood of farmers was threatened in rural areas and the volume of unattended problems grew in the cities, people formed a variety of voluntary associations to support participation and problem solving (Roberts, 2008).

The Farmer's Alliance, which emerged on the Great Plains during the 1870s and swept across the South in the 1880s, was the largest participatory movement in 19th Century America. The Alliance, which eventually became the Populist Party, provided both economic and political opportunities. It allowed farmers to address a variety of issues, including exploitative credit terms, unfair crop prices, and unfavorable terms of trade. The movement spread quickly, partly because of a network of sympathetic newspapers, a system of traveling lecturers, and meetings that included deliberation, celebration, and socializing. In his classic book, *The Populist Moment*, Lawrence Goodwyn (1978: xvii) describes Populism as "a political, an organizational, and above all, a cultural achievement of the first magnitude" (see also Postel, 2007).

By the time the movement peaked, the Populists were the dominant political force in sixteen states. But though they were able to bridge the enormous cultural divisions left behind by the Civil War, the farmers of the Alliance were unable to forge lasting partnerships with their counterparts in the cities, despite many shared political interests. Goodwyn (1978) argues that the attempt to shift their efforts from a participatory process to an electoral campaign—and specifically the failed presidential candidacy of William Jennings Bryan in 1896—was the last straw for the Populist movement.

By the turn of the 20th Century, a number of participatory activities emerged in cities to confront social problems and articulate the political interests of workers, immigrants, and the poor. For example, unions like the Industrial Workers of the World provided new arenas for workers to articulate their interests (Isserman, 1993), and Jane Addams' Hull House provided a locus for dialogue, education, mobilization, and communal self-help for recent immigrants in urban neighborhoods (Levine, 2012; Mattson, 1998). But like the Populists before them, the unionists and settlement house residents participated in successful processes, but were largely separated from government structures.

THE EXPANSION OF EXPERTISE

At the beginning of the 20th Century, American politics was rife with corruption. Political "machines" and their bosses ruled most of the major cities by dispensing patronage and using racial and ethnic antagonisms to attract residents' support. Inequality was high and business was generally unregulated. The work of "muckraking" journalists, catastrophes like the Triangle Shirtwaist Fire and the Johnstown Flood, and general disgust with big bosses and big business helped produce the Progressive political movement.

Progressives sought to professionalize government, and most aspects of public life, to deal with these problems. Core to the Progressive philosophy was the notion that science and expertise could solve social problems, prevent corruption, and protect citizens. Progressivism birthed most of the "public professions" that still survive today, including planning, social work, and public administration.

Ballot initiatives and referenda were institutionalized in some states, giving citizens the chance to vote on selected policy issues. However, outside the ballot box, the Progressive movement raised new legal and philosophical barriers between citizens and public decision making and problem solving (Sirianni & Girouard, 2012). Henceforth, government would treat citizens occasionally as advisors, but rarely as problem-solvers.

As participatory processes for addressing social problems became increasingly separate from governmental structures, voluntary citizen groups emerged to deal with a wide range of issues, from city planning, to environmental improvement, to slum eradication (Day, 1997; Roberts, 2008). Simultaneously, urban reformers began to promote "home rule" laws that created a zone of action insulated from state legislative interference and the potential of corruption (Barron, 2003; Nabatchi & Amsler, 2014). One approach to home rule, known as the reformist social view, recognized the political nature of municipal decisions and the role of the public in making those decisions (Barron, 2003). Nevertheless, with the exception of the occasional lay planning commission, participation was largely relegated to voluntary action.

For the most part, the Great Depression and the "New Deal" continued the trend of treating citizens as advisors rather than as actors. The Roosevelt Administration birthed a large-scale administrative apparatus at the federal and state levels, including dozens of new agencies and at least 100 new offices. Many New Deal initiatives, such as the Works Progress Administration and the Civilian Conservation Corps, gave meaningful work opportunities to unemployed people and enabled large numbers of "citizen actors" to build schools, paint murals, establish parks, and make other contributions to the civic infrastructure of the 20th Century (R. Leighninger, 2007). But the federal government never really made the connection between citizen labor and citizen participation in government.

At the federal level, the work of New Deal administrative agencies prompted the passage of the federal Administrative Procedure Act (APA) in 1946, creating the first major building block in the current legal infrastructure for participation. The APA enabled a form of direct public participation by requiring opportunities for notice and comment in rulemaking; this was the most prominent and influential ratification of the role of citizens as advisors to the experts and technocrats in government. Today, the APA and its state-level counterparts still shape many of the approaches to, and requirements for, participation in federal policymaking (Bingham, 2010; Nabatchi & Amsler, 2014).

Beginning in the late 1940s, the practice of "urban renewal" further illustrated the need for public participation and the inadequacy of the infrastructure to support it. At the end of the decade, Congress passed the Housing Act of 1949, which required local government agencies to hold public hearings on redevelopment plans for "blighted" neighborhoods. While this is an instance of "formal, legislatively mandated participation" (Day, 1997: 423), "most cities responded by creating a citywide advisory committee composed of leading citizens with little or no representation from the neighborhoods affected by urban renewal" (Hallman, 1972: 421; see also Stenberg, 1972). Participation was therefore limited to "blue-ribbon" citizens—most people (and indeed those who were most affected by urban problems) were excluded from the opportunity to provide input. Federal laws added to the structural elements of participation but paid little attention to effective, inclusive processes (Sirianni & Girouard, 2012, citing Fullilove, 2004; Gans, 1962; Jacobs, 1961).

PARTICIPATION IN THE WAR ON POVERTY

In the 1960s, the combination of social turbulence, the civil rights movement, and "a new generation of thought about the participatory rights of citizens in a democracy" (Aleshire, 1972: 428) led the federal government to take a more ambitious—and controversial—role in promoting public participation, mainly at the local level. President Lyndon B. Johnson's "Great Society" program (commonly referred to as the "War on Poverty") launched a series of social reforms aimed at eliminating poverty and racial injustice in cities, partly through participation.

The momentum for strengthening direct participation came in part from legislative victories guaranteeing indirect participation. The Civil Rights Act of 1964 and the Voting Rights Act of 1965 provided for universal suffrage: all American adults gained the right to vote and vote freely, without literacy tests, poll taxes, or other impediments (see Keyssar, 2000). Once these rights were established, civil rights leaders began to shift the discussion from the right to vote to an examination of "direct participation by the citizenry in day-to-day activities of the state" (Stewart, 1976: 1).

The War on Poverty programs also reflected a "realization that the natural forces of the economy would not produce the good life for all Americans" and that "if a sense of community could be created, the chances of dealing with social problems would be greatly increased" (Aleshire, 1972: 429). The result was a boom of federally financed citizen participation in a number of issue areas, but most famously in Community Action Agencies and the Model Cities Program.

Community Action Agencies (CAAs) were created by the Economic Opportunity Act (EOA) of 1964 (see Boone, 1972). They received federal funding but were operated by nonprofit organizations that were not under the control of local governments. CAAs were given three tasks: the provision of services, the mobilization of public and private resources, and the achievement of "maximum feasible participation of residents of the areas and members of the groups served" (Title II, Part A, Section 202 (a)(3)). With this dramatic, justifying language, CAAs had the potential to be structures that sustained effective processes for participation (Sirianni & Friedland, 2001), but they were almost immediately controversial, sparking debate that continues today. Approximately 1,000 Community Action Agencies still operate across the nation (see www.communityactionpartnership. com/). We focus on two main points of contention: the role of low-income residents and the nature of the processes within the CAA structures.

The most prominent critic of CAAs was Senator Daniel Patrick Moynihan (1969), who later derided the program as "maximum feasible misunderstanding." One of his main arguments was that low-income residents were simply not capable of participating in public decision making. "It may be that the poor are never 'ready' to assume power in an advanced society," Moynihan concluded. His critique turned into a widely accepted nostrum that "the poor cannot be trusted to behave responsibly in the governmental process" (Berry, Portney, & Thomson, 1993: 30). Other observers countered, then and now, that this critique was simply an attempt to muzzle new leaders who had emerged through the civil rights and black power movements. Nevertheless, "Unfair as it was, this perception became the historical reality" (Berry, Portney, & Thomson, 1993: 30).

While the CAAs were, especially in their initial stages, caught up in the conflicts between new and existing urban regimes, some observers feel that this was simply an unavoidable (and ultimately healthy) phase, rather than a sign that some citizens were incapable of citizenship. Carmen Sirianni and Jennifer Girouard (2012) write that "Community Action may often have appeared to have been captured by the dynamics of political and racial struggle. At the grassroots level, however, it was almost always much more, and poor people demonstrated time and again that they were primarily interested in participating pragmatically to solve problems in their communities."

The second point of contention deals with whether CAAs as structures had any of the participation processes they really needed. As Moynihan pointed out, Congress and the Administration were vague about what "maximum feasible participation" really meant. In practice, the most common form of participation in CAAs was not terribly participatory: residents of low-income neighborhoods had representatives on the boards that governed the CAAs. In their book, *The Rebirth of Urban Democracy*, Berry, Portney, and Thomson (1993: 31) hypothesize that this happened partly because board makeup was easier to measure: "Representation on boards [was] a bureaucratically convenient indicator of whether the poor were participating." The authors argue that, except in a few cases, there were almost no processes that would allow other neighborhood residents to participate in the work of the CAAs. In contrast, Sirianni and Girouard (2012) claim that successful processes were indeed developed after an initial phase of "conflict and confrontation." In any case, there seems to be little evidence for Moynihan's charge that the CAAs of the 1960s were "an excess of participatory democracy." In fact, Berry and his coauthors (1993: 34) claim the opposite, calling the original CAAs "restrained exercises in representative democracy."

The controversy around "maximum feasible participation," the complaints of local governments, and the worries about nonprofits that were not politically accountable led to the Demonstration Cities and Metropolitan Development Act of 1966, which is perhaps best known for establishing the Model Cities Program. While the legislation once again called for "widespread citizen participation" (Section 103(a)(2)), the implementation of the program was crafted "to limit, rather than maximize, participation of the poor" (Strange, 1972: 656). While the Community Action Programs made city control optional, the Model Cities Program returned power to local officials, giving them "ultimate responsibility for the development of programs and, more importantly, the expenditure of significantly large amounts of money" (Strange, 1972: 656; see also Hallman, 1972). What followed was a difficult, sometimes contentious, negotiation in scores of cities as citizens, public officials, and other leaders talked and sometimes fought about how to distribute federal resources. One outcome of these discussions was the first wave of neighborhood council systems, which institutionalized resident participation in community and local decision making. Another was the spread of Community Development Corporations as an alternative conduit for federal and foundation aid to neighborhoods (Sirianni & Girouard, 2012, citing Corburn, 2009; Deitrick & Ellis, 2004; Lee, 2005; Shutkin, 2000; Sirianni & Sofer, 2011; Stoutland, 1999).

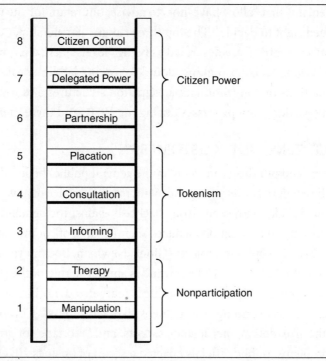

Figure 3.1
Arnstein's "Ladder of Participation"

8	Citizen Control	⎫
7	Delegated Power	⎬ Citizen Power
6	Partnership	⎭
5	Placation	⎫
4	Consultation	⎬ Tokenism
3	Informing	⎭
2	Therapy	⎫
1	Manipulation	⎬ Nonparticipation

Source: Arnstein, Sherry R. (1969). A Ladder of Citizen Participation. *Journal of the American Planning Association, 35*(4): 216–224.

None of these forays into participation were helped much by the ways in which the governments of the 1960s defined and implemented the term. One of the earliest and most influential critics was Sherry Arnstein, who was chief advisor on citizen participation to the Department of Housing and Urban Development (Sirianni & Girouard, 2012). In 1969, Arnstein published an influential article, "A Ladder of Participation," in an attempt to clarify the roles and levels of authority given to citizens and government in a participatory process. She argued that "citizen participation is a categorical term for citizen power. It is . . . the redistribution of power that enables the have-not citizens, presently excluded from the political and economic processes, to be deliberately included in the future" (1969: 216). Arnstein's ladder, reproduced in Figure 3.1, has eight rungs. The bottom two rungs, "manipulation" and "therapy," are labeled "non-participation," where the goal is to "enable powerholders to 'educate' or 'cure' the participants." The middle three rungs, "informing," "consultation," and "placation," are described as forms of "tokenism" that "allow have-nots to advise, but retain for the powerholders the continued right to decide." The top three rungs, "partnership," "delegated power," and "citizen control," are described as being "levels of citizen power with increasing degrees of decision-making clout." Arnstein's ladder speaks directly both to the limitations of conventional participation structures and to the difficulties in defining participation processes during the 1970s and thereafter.

NOT CITIZENS, BUT "CUSTOMERS"

Politicians and pundits (and many in the general public) believed the War on Poverty to be a failure at everything except increasing the size of government. Thus, the following decades witnessed strong backlash against the demands of activists, and governments and foundations reduced their funding of community organizing and community development projects (Gittell, Newman, Bockmeyer, & Lindsay, 1998).

During the 1970s and 1980s, attitudes about the role of the public sector were dominated by neoclassical economics, marketized notions of efficiency, and language about "running government like a business." Complaints flourished about the size, delays, inefficiencies, costs, and "red tape" of government. To fix these problems, public officials enacted a series of business-like reforms to make bureaucracy more streamlined, entrepreneurial, customer-driven, and results-oriented, including Total Quality Management, Reinventing Government, and the general methods of New Public Management.

Ironically, some of these reforms gave rank-and-file public employees a greater voice in how to increase organizational productivity (Cohen & Brand, 1993). They involved techniques such as facilitated small-group discussions that mirror successful public participation tactics. Like some of their counterparts in private companies, some government employees gained at least a small degree of democratic control within the workplace.

The relationship between government and citizens, however, was, if anything, less democratic. During the 1980s, the new buzzwords for citizens became "stakeholders" and "customers." Successful governing meant satisfying people's immediate desires on a transaction-by-transaction basis, not engaging them in public decision making or problem solving. The use of surveys was expanded as a tool for gathering public input. Government would be serving the public interest, went the theory, if it could meet the "narrowly defined self-interests of many individuals" (de Leon & Denhardt, 2000: 89). If people could renew their driver's licenses and apply for building permits more quickly and easily, they would be more satisfied with government than if public officials engaged them in highway safety decisions or comprehensive land use planning. But not all observers, then or now, agreed that "reinventing" governments would make the public sector more trusted or admired. The "self-interest assumption," wrote Linda de Leon and Robert Denhardt (2000: 89), "entails a rejection of democratic citizenship, civic engagement, and the public interest."

In an attempt to meet the needs of citizen-customers, policy and decision making became even more dominated by experts who analyzed "hard" data at the expense of public judgment, opinion, and understanding (Yankelovich, 1991). Although not completely dismantled, many of the structures for direct participation built during the 1960s were severely weakened, and the processes for participation were largely overlooked.

NOT IN MY BACK YARD (OR SCHOOL, OR NEIGHBORHOOD)

During the 1990s, the tables began to turn against the experts. The cracks in conventional participation structures became more apparent, and cultural deference to expert authority waned. With few meaningful opportunities to express themselves, citizens began to overwhelm local government systems, in some cases bringing the policymaking process to a screeching halt. When controversial decisions were being discussed or announced, people packed the meeting rooms and council chambers of school boards, planning commissions, and city councils; when controversial decisions were not on the table, the public was largely absent (Leighninger, 2006).

The issues that provoked these outbursts tended to be ones that were closest to people's direct interests: land use decisions having to do with development, landfills, affordable housing, and other kinds of construction; school decisions relating to redistricting, school safety, bond issues, standards, and superintendent hiring; and policing decisions on how officers should be deployed or disciplined. State and federal agencies were not immune: those with local decisions to make, such as agencies dealing with environmental preservation, housing, and transportation, faced angry crowds whenever a controversy arose. Public officials and civil servants used the term NIMBY—for Not in My Back Yard—to describe what they perceived to be the selfish, short-sighted reactions of their constituents (www.planetizen.com/node/152; see also King, Feltey, & Susel, 1998).

These incidents were mostly isolated from one another; citizens did not come together in a larger movement, as they had done to promote Populism or civil rights. Nevertheless, NIMBY conflicts were, and are, remarkable in the sheer diversity of the people involved. They are also remarkable in the consistency of their demands. Finding that the conventional avenues for participation did not deliver the needed influence or impact, all kinds of people—urban and rural, rich and poor, students and seniors, people of different racial and ethnic backgrounds—came (and continue to come) together to voice their desire for more control over their neighborhoods, schools, and communities.

The desire for control was also apparent in the origins of one of the most significant types of public participation to emerge in the late 20th Century: Participatory Budgeting (PB). Pioneered in the city of Porto Alegre, Brazil, in 1989, PB was a reaction not just to expert government, but also to corrupt and authoritarian government (Abers, 1998; Wampler, 2012). Once the Worker's Party gained control in municipal elections, PB was developed as a way to engage residents in decision making about how the city budget should be spent. PB in Porto Alegre and many other South American cities has reached a critical mass of participation not yet seen in the Global North: tens of thousands of people take part annually, in face-to-face assemblies, online balloting, and celebratory events. PB has proliferated around the world in the last two decades and is currently spreading rapidly in the United States. We return to a discussion of PB in Chapter 10.

WHY CAN'T WE ALL JUST GET ALONG? (AND, IS THAT ENOUGH?)

As tension between citizens and government rose in the 1990s, a separate but related tension was also increasing: friction along the lines of racial and cultural differences. One catalyst for participation on issues of race was the violent aftermath of the 1992 Rodney King verdict in Los Angeles. The civil disturbances in L.A. made productive participation seem not just desirable, but critical. And public officials recognized that interaction between citizens and government was only part of the solution: people of different backgrounds had to talk with one another about their race-related perceptions, biases, and beliefs. This was a different kind of mandate for public participation (Dalton, 1995; Potapchuk, 2001), one that required more than conventional processes.

After the Rodney King incident, and then the O.J. Simpson verdict, public participation initiatives on race swept the nation, involving hundreds and sometimes thousands of citizens in forums, trainings, workshops, and small-group dialogues (DuBois & Hutson, 1997; Shapiro, 2002; Walsh, 2007). Big cities were not the only venues: some of the most influential programs were initiated in smaller cities like Lima, Ohio, Fort Myers, Florida, and Springfield, Illinois (Leighninger, 2006). In most cases, these participatory processes were of the thick variety: they involved proactive recruitment through community networks, gave people a chance to tell their stories, allowed for deliberation about views and options, and created opportunities to move from talk to action. Many local leaders became experts on recruiting citizens and designing productive meetings. In this way, race-based challenges helped propel improvements in public participation.

In most cases, these projects were successful at easing racial tensions. The most basic reason for this—and one of the earliest lessons learned by practitioners, not just for participation on race but also for many other issues—was the value of introductory sessions that allowed people to talk about their backgrounds and experiences. By first finding out more about one another as people, participants were able to build the trust and candor necessary for dealing with less comfortable subjects.

But while many of these efforts focused purely on increasing dialogue, many others led directly to action. Rodney King's question, "Can't we all just get along?" was a basic plea for tolerance, but once citizens begin to talk about race, they usually go much further than that, addressing complex issues of institutional racism as well as simpler forms of prejudice. For many participants—especially those who were people of color—dialogue and understanding were not enough. So public participation on race led to action at a variety of levels, from cultural celebrations, to after-school programs, to government hiring and training policies, and more (Leighninger, 2006, 2009).

By the end of the 20th century, these and other participatory experiments had produced a rich and vast knowledge about better processes for participation. However, most of these initiatives took place outside of official governmental structures, and little attention was paid to developing the participation infrastructure necessary to sustain them.

PARTICIPATORY TACTICS ON THE 2008 CAMPAIGN TRAIL, BUT NOT THE WHITE HOUSE

Driven by race, land use, education, and other issues, new participatory tactics continued to develop in the 2000s; however, participation remained a largely local phenomenon. Although there were a few efforts at "good" state- and nation-wide participation, these tended to be demonstration projects—attempts to show that citizens could grapple with federal issues—rather than processes that had a discernible policy impact. And though political candidates had often used the rhetoric of participation in their election bids, none had successfully incorporated participation strategies in the way they ran for office.

Barack Obama's 2008 presidential bid was a breakthrough, perhaps the first major instance of a more participatory kind of campaign. Obama's campaign speeches were full of civic language: "I won't just ask for your vote as a candidate; I will ask for your service and your active citizenship when I am president of the United States. This will not be a call issued in one speech or program; this will be a cause of my presidency." In addition to the rhetoric, the organizing tactics used by the Obama campaign mirrored some of the main principles evident in successful participation initiatives:

- *Mobilizing large numbers through proactive, network-based recruitment.* In the United States, political campaigns have traditionally relied on television advertising and media relations as a primary means of reaching voters. Like its predecessors, the Obama campaign spent huge amounts of money on TV ads, but it also deployed an unprecedented number of organizers—estimated at more than three million—to reach people directly, both face-to-face and online. Just like their counterparts in the participation field, these organizers mapped networks, targeted particular groups for outreach, created connections to leaders in those networks, and supported those leaders as they reached out to their constituents.
- *Giving people a chance to tell their stories.* Marshall Ganz, the former community organizer and current Harvard lecturer, embedded storytelling into his training for Obama's field organizers. Training participants shared the "Story of Self," then formulated a "Story of Us," and then began working on a "Story of Now." Obama campaigners then used a wide variety of formats, including house parties, Facebook groups, phone calls, online chats, and door-knocking campaigns to allow people to tell their stories. Most of these formats were interactive, allowing participants to talk with one another, and with representatives of the campaign itself, about a wide range of topics. Peter Levine (2013: 156) argues that:

> . . . the campaign was structured in ways that reflected Obama's civic philosophy. Volunteers were encouraged and taught to share their stories, to discuss social problems, to listen as well as mobilize, and to develop their

own plans. There was a rich discussion online as well as face-to-face. His deliberative style was particularly attractive to young, college-educated volunteers, who felt deeply empowered and who played a significant role in the election's outcomes, especially in the Iowa Caucuses.

- *Giving people different ways to take action.* Traditionally, American presidential campaigns have focused on convincing people to contribute money and to vote. The Obama campaign was intent on giving people more ways to act on behalf of the campaign—from encouraging online networking, to soliciting comments on the candidate's policy positions, to recruiting campaign volunteers in a much more proactive way. For the first time, unpaid supporters did more than just stuff envelopes and canvass voters: many Obama volunteers took on highly sophisticated technological jobs, and some of them managed teams that included scores or even hundreds of other volunteers.

It is worth pointing out that these tactics are not inherently progressive or left-leaning; the Republican Party has since adopted some of the same ideas. In the United Kingdom, both the Labour Party and the Conservative Party have used some of these tactics, and both parties have tried to portray themselves as the champions of democratic decentralization and citizen control. Prime Minister David Cameron's vision of a "Big Society" could be considered the most developed conservative prescription for democratic governance (Peterson, 2010).

But while the 2008 Obama Campaign used the language and some thin and thick participation tactics to win the White House, the 2008–2014 Obama Administration has largely ignored them (Levine, 2010). In Chapter 7, we describe the current state of public participation at the federal level, including Obama's "Open Government" efforts. For now, suffice to say that, while the Administration has promoted some degree of thin participation, it has not taken meaningful steps to increase thick participation by citizens in federal policymaking (Nabatchi, 2014; PARCC, 2013), and despite the rhetoric, participation under the Obama Administration has, for the most part, remained conventional.

BIGGER GOVERNANCE THROUGH TECHNOLOGY

In the 2010s, technology has offered yet more possibilities for participation, both thick and thin. As Eric Gordon, Jessica Baldwin-Philippi, and Martina Balestra put it in *Why We Engage* (2013), technology has already changed the "how" of public participation, and is now beginning to change the "who" and the "why."

Online technologies have affected citizenship and participation in two phases: the effects of the first major phase are now apparent, but the effects of the second are just starting to take hold. In the first phase, the Internet helped to empower individuals. It gave people who have some degree of interest and capacity (roughly speaking, this means some combination of education level, confidence, and access to and familiarity with technology) a much greater ability to find the information, resources, and allies they need to make an impact on issues or public decisions they care about. Using online tools along with face-to-face organizing, these people can be either more productive or more disruptive in policymaking arenas (Leighninger, 2011a, 2011b).

The second phase of change is empowering groups, not just individuals. Social media platforms have made it much easier to build and maintain interactive networks of people, with far greater levels of electoral power, financial resources, and collective problem-solving capacity. Not all of these connections are digital; in fact, online communication seems to make people more interested in meeting face-to-face (Hampton, Goulet, Her, & Rainie, 2009). If anything, the line between online and face-to-face relationships seems to be getting blurrier (Gordon, Baldwin-Philippi, & Balestra, 2013; Gordon, Schirra, & Hollander, 2011).

Many of these online communities center on shared interests that have little to do with where the participants live. But one of the fastest growing forms of online networking is based on geographic ties. Neighborhood and school-based online forums have spread dramatically, starting with simple listservs, then Facebook groups, then slightly more sophisticated platforms promoted by nonprofit groups (such as e-democracy.org, localocracy, and Front Porch Forum) and an increasing array of for-profit enterprises. (One sign of the potential profitability of these networks was the investment of $100 million in venture capital in one of the first neighborhood networking for-profits, NextDoor.)

One key to the growth of these platforms is that they allow people to meet their social needs, not just engage in political discussions. Members of these online forums may talk about what the school board did, or what the mayor said, but they also ask questions like "Who has a plumber they can recommend?" "Has anyone seen my lost cat?" or "When is the neighborhood barbecue?" A woman in Minnesota who was baking lasagna for a memorial service realized she had eight trays of lasagna but only one oven. An hour after posting her appeal on the neighborhood network, seven neighbors had offered their ovens. People stay involved in these virtual spaces for many reasons: they are convenient, they allow for interaction, they deepen and complement face-to-face relationships, they are adaptable by the participants, and they give people a powerful sense of membership. In other words, they combine some of the best features of thick and thin forms of participation.

As these interest- or geography-based online networks continue to grow and proliferate, it is becoming increasingly difficult to run for office, make a policy decision, or develop a community plan without them. At the same time, the practice of public participation, which mainly has been initiated by formal leaders, is becoming more and more of a two-way street, with a wide variety of informal leaders and active citizens using social media to mobilize their peers and engage their public officials. Because these networks can be sustained far more easily than the organizing efforts of the past, they give citizens and public leaders the opportunity to build a more durable infrastructure for public participation. However, although technology has made governance bigger than it used to be, many digital divides still exist.

A FINAL SNAPSHOT: THE CURRENT STATE OF OUR PARTICIPATION INFRASTRUCTURE

The snapshots from our brief trip through the history of democracy and participation should be encouraging, partly because they offer evidence that:

1. Democracy is not a static, unchanging edifice, but rather a creation that continually evolves and can be improved.
2. Direct participation is a universal human impulse, not a capacity that is confined to any one civilization, culture, or regime.
3. Citizens are capable of deliberation, problem solving, and self-governance.

However, it is also true that the development of democracy and participation has left us with a political system that has not (yet) combined durable structures with successful processes for direct participation. The challenge we now face is how to incorporate these two elements—the hardware and software of democracy—in the building of robust, sustainable participation infrastructure.

The notion of strengthening our participation infrastructure for 21st Century democracy can be intimidating, conjuring up visions of major reforms and financial expenditures. However, while not easy, it need not be so scary. Strengthening our participation infrastructure requires focusing on three major elements:

(1) empowering and activating leaders and networks, (2) assembling participation building blocks; and (3) providing systemic supports.

Empowering and Activating Leaders and Networks

We already have many different kinds of participation leaders and a wide variety of social and civic networks; we only need to further empower and activate them. Participation leaders include elected officials (e.g., mayors, city council members, school board members, and legislative representatives); other public servants (e.g., city managers, school superintendents, police chiefs, planners, librarians, human relations directors, and government agency staff); civic leaders (e.g., directors and staff at community foundations and nonprofit organizations; faculty, staff, and students at colleges and universities; community organizers; policy advocates; civic technologists and civic hackers; and neighborhood association leaders); and participation professionals (e.g., solo consultants or those in private or non-profit organizations) (Leighninger, 2012; see also Carcasson, 2008; Lee & Polletta, 2009). These participation leaders and their organizations play a variety of roles. They serve as *conveners* (those responsible for a participation effort), *organizers* (those who coordinate logistics and other on-the-ground aspects of participation), and as *funders* (those who provide financial resources). There is often substantial overlap between these roles, and the same organization or set of people often handles all three responsibilities.

A wide variety of networks for participation also exist, including schools, colleges, and universities; businesses; nonprofit organizations and foundations; community organizing groups; youth groups; social service agencies; unions; media; and homeowner and neighborhood associations, among many others. Understanding and activating these and other networks is critical, not just for improving temporary participation processes, but also for strengthening our participation infrastructure.

Assembling Participation Building Blocks

As we have noted, numerous public participation opportunities already exist; thus, strengthening our participation infrastructure does not mean starting from scratch or reinventing the wheel. However, it does require taking stock of what is already happening and making choices about how to improve and expand those efforts. In particular, it requires assembling six overarching categories or building blocks of a robust, sustainable participation infrastructure. In Chapters 4 through 7, we describe how the building blocks are essential to participation in education, health, land use, and the work of state and federal government. For now, we simply list them and offer examples in parentheses:

1. Disseminating Information (websites; social media networks; dashboards and apps; serious games)
2. Gathering Input and Data (crowdsourcing; websites and apps; surveys, polls, interviews, and focus groups)
3. Discussing and Connecting (wired, welcoming buildings; online networks and forums; social events)
4. Enabling Small-Scale Decision Making (conferences or teams comprised of officials and citizens; deliberative processes)
5. Enabling Large-Scale Decision Making (deliberative processes; task forces; advisory boards)
6. Encouraging Public Work (volunteer coordination; crowdfunding and mini-grants; apps and platforms for teams and tasks)

Providing Systemic Supports

In addition to these activities, a stronger participation infrastructure requires systemic supports that enable people to take on new roles, connect different activities to one another, and institutionalize and sustain their efforts. Included among the many needed systemic supports are incentives for participation leaders, opportunities for training and skill development, adequate financial and other resources, clear policies and procedures, and reliable evaluation measures and benchmarks.

These three aspects of the participation infrastructure—empowering people and networks, using participation building blocks, and incorporating systemic supports—are illustrated in Part Two of the book. We further unpack them in Part Three.

SUMMARY

In this chapter, we argued that people have an innate desire to participate in decision making and problem solving. Over time, public institutions have been designed, adapted, or overhauled in reaction to this participation impulse—sometimes in ways that were intended to support and enable it, sometimes in ways that were intended to channel and control it. To illustrate this desire and the institutional responses to it, we used a series of historical snapshots, culminating in an examination of our current situation.

While the snapshots provide insight into the (r)evolution of democracy and participation, they also reveal that our political system that has not (yet) combined durable structures with successful processes for direct participation. Bringing together the hardware and software of democracy—the structures and the processes—is the critical challenge we face in the next phase of our history. To do so, we must build a stronger participation infrastructure by empowering a variety of participation leaders and activating a variety of networks, assembling the building blocks of participation activities, and incorporating myriad systemic supports.

DISCUSSION QUESTIONS

1. The title of this chapter suggests that development of public participation in the United States has been a "(r)evolution" and "fitful." What do the authors mean by these terms? Do you agree with their assessment? Why or why not?

2. The authors trace the roots of democracy and participation to ancient eras. Do you believe democracy and participation are stronger now or then? Why?

3. What were the Founders' views on democracy and participation? Why did they want to limit direct participation in government? Do you agree or disagree with their views? Why?

4. Compare the views on participation in the Populist and Progressive Eras. With which view do you agree more, and why?

5. One goal of the War on Poverty was to change the nature of participation, particularly in urban areas. Do you think the War on Poverty was successful in achieving this goal? Why or why not?

6. Compare and contrast the views on participation in the 1970s, 1980s, and 1990s. How did perceptions about citizens and public participation change during those eras?

7. In what ways did the Obama campaign incorporate greater participation? Do you think future campaigns will use more participation as a result? Why or why not?

8. Which three historical eras do you think had the greatest impact on direct public participation in the United States? Justify your selections.

9. Explain the three elements of building a stronger participation infrastructure. Do you think the authors missed any critical elements?

10. What do democracy and participation mean to you? If you are not from the United States, how does the experience of participation in your country compare to the American experience?

References

Abers, Rebecca. (1998). Learning democratic practice: Distributing government resources through popular participation in Porto Alegre, Brazil. In M. Douglass & J. Friedmann (Eds.), *Cities for citizens: Planning and the rise of civil society in a global age*, 39–66. Hoboken, NJ: John Wiley & Sons.

Aleshire, Robert A. (1972). Power to the people: An assessment of the community action and model cities experience. *Public Administration Review*, *32*(Special Issue): 428–443.

Arendt, Hannah. (1963). *On revolution*. New York, NY: The Viking Press.

Arnstein, Sherry R. (1969). A ladder of citizen participation. *Journal of the American Planning Association*, *35*(4): 216–224.

Barron, David J. (2003). Reclaiming home rule. *Harvard Law Review*, 116: 2255–2386.

Berry, Jeffrey M., Portney, Kent E., & Thomson, Ken. (1993). *The rebirth of urban democracy*. Washington, DC: Brookings Institution Press.

Bingham, Lisa Blomgren. (2010). The next generation of administrative law: Building the legal infrastructure for collaborative governance. *Wisconsin Law Review*, *10*: 297–356.

Boone, Richard W. (1972). Reflections on citizen participation and the Economic Opportunity Act. *Public Administration Review*, *32*(Special Issue): 444–456.

Bryan, Frank M. (2003). *Real democracy: The New England town meeting and how it works*. Chicago, IL: University of Chicago Press.

Carcasson, Martin. (2008). *Democracy's hubs: College and university centers as platforms for deliberative practice*. Dayton, OH: Kettering Foundation.

Cohen, Steven, & Ronald Brand. (1993). *Total quality management in government: A practical guide for the real world*. San Francisco, CA: Jossey-Bass.

Cornwell, Andrea, & Vera Schattan Coehlo. (2007). *Spaces for change? The politics of participation in new democratic arenas*. London, UK: Zed Books Ltd.

Dalton, Harlon. (1995). *Racial healing: confronting the fear between Blacks and Whites*. New York, NY: Doubleday.

Day, Diane. (1997). Citizen participation in the planning process: An essentially contested concept? *Journal of Planning Literature*, *11*(3): 421–434.

de Leon, Linda, & Robert Denhardt. (2000). The political theory of reinvention. *Public Administration Review, 60*(2): 89–97.

DuBois, Paul Martin, & Jonathan J. Hutson. (1997). *Bridging the racial divide: A report on dialogue in America.* Hadley, MA: Common Wealth Printing.

Dzur, Albert. (2012). *Punishment, participatory democracy, and the jury.* New York, NY: Oxford University Press.

Fagotto, Elena, & Archon Fung. (2009). *Sustaining public engagement: Embedded deliberation in local communities.* East Hartford, CT: Everyday Democracy and Kettering Foundation.

Fullilove, M.T. (2004). *Root shock: How tearing up city neighborhoods hurts America, and what we can do about it.* New York, NY: Random House.

Gans, Herbert J. (1962). *The urban villagers: Group and class in the life of Italian-Americans.* New York, NY: Free Press of Glencoe.

Gaventa, John. (2006). Finding the spaces for change. *IDS Bulletin, 37*(6): 23–33.

Gittell, Marilyn, Kathe Newman, Janice Bockmeyer, & Robert Lindsay. (1998). Expanding civic opportunity: Urban empowerment zones. *Urban Affairs Review, 33*(4): 530–558.

Glassman, Ronald M. (1986). *Democracy and despotism in primitive societies: A neo-Weberian approach to political theory.* Port Washington, NY: Associated Faculty Press.

Goodwyn, Lawrence. (1976). *Democratic promise: The populist movement in America.* New York, NY: Oxford University Press.

Goodwyn, Lawrence. (1978). *The populist moment: A short history of the agrarian revolt in America.* New York, NY: Oxford University Press.

Gordon, Eric, Jessica Baldwin-Philippi, & Martina Balestra. (2013). *Why we engage: How theories of human behavior contribute to our understanding of civic engagement in a digital era.* Cambridge, MA: Berkman Center for Internet & Society.

Gordon, Eric, Steven Schirra, & Justin Hollander. (2011). Immersive planning: A conceptual model for designing public participation with new technologies. *Environment and Planning B: Planning and Design, 38*(3): 505–519.

Görgens, Tristan, & Mirjam van Donk. (2011). *Exploring the potential for "networked spaces" to foster communities of practice during the participatory upgrading of informal settlements.* Cape Town, South Africa: Isandla Institute.

Grinde, Donald A. (1992). Iroquoian political concept and the genesis of American government. In J. Barreiro (Ed.), *Indian roots of American democracy,* 47–66. Ithaca, NY: Akwe:kon Press of Cornell University.

Grinde, Donald A., & Bruce E. Johansen. (1991). *Exemplar of liberty: Native America and the evolution of democracy.* Los Angeles, CA: UCLA American Indian Studies Center.

Hallman, Howard W. (1972). Federally financed citizen participation. *Public Administration Review, 32*(Special Issue): 421–427.

Hampton, Keith, Lauren Sessions Goulet, Eun Ja Her, & Lee Rainie. (2009). *Social isolation and new technology.* Washington, DC: Pew Research Center, Internet & American Life Project.

Isserman, Maurice. (1993). *If I had a hammer: The death of the old left and the birth of the new left*. Chicago, IL: University of Illinois Press.

Jacobs, Jane. (1961). *The death and life of great American cities*. New York, NY: Random House.

Jacobsen, Thorkild. (1970) [1957]. Early political development in Mesopotamia. In W.L. Moran (Ed.), *Toward the image of Tammuz and other essays on Mesopotamian history and culture*, 132–156. Cambridge, MA: Harvard University Press.

Jacobsen, Thorkild. (1970) [1943]. Primitive democracy in ancient Mesopotamia. In W.L. Moran (Ed.), *Toward the image of Tammuz and other essays on Mesopotamian history and culture*, 157–170. Cambridge, MA: Harvard University Press.

Jefferson, Thomas. (1816). Letter from Thomas Jefferson to Samuel Kercheval, Monticello, July 12, 1816. Available at www.constitution.org/tj/ltr/1816/ltr_18160712_kercheval.html.

Keyssar, Alexander. (2000). *The right to vote: The contested history of democracy in the United States*. New York, NY: Basic Books.

King, Cheryl Simrell, Kathryn M. Feltey, & Bridget O'Neill Susel. (1998). The question of participation: Toward authentic public participation in public administration. *Public Administration Review, 58*(4): 317–326.

Lee, Caroline, & Francesca Polletta. (2009). *The 2009 dialogue and deliberation practitioners survey: What is the state of the field?* Easton, PA: Lafayette College. Available at http://sites.lafayette.edu/ddps/.

Leighninger, Matt. (2006). *The next form of democracy: How expert rule is giving way to shared governance—and why politics will never be the same*. Nashville, TN: Vanderbilt University Press.

Leighninger, Matt. (2009). *Democracy, growing up: The shifts that reshaped local politics and foreshadowed the 2008 presidential election*. New York, NY: Public Agenda.

Leighninger, Matt. (2011a). Citizenship and governance in a wild, wired world. *National Civic Review, 100*(2): 20–29.

Leighninger, Matt. (2011b). *Using online tools to engage—and be engaged by—the public*. Washington, DC: IBM Center for the Business of Government.

Leighninger, Matt. (2012). Mapping deliberative civic engagement: Pictures from a (r)evolution. In T. Nabatchi, J. Gastil, M. Weiksner, and M. Leighninger (Eds.), *Democracy in motion: Evaluating the practice and impact of deliberative civic engagement*, 19–39. New York, NY: Oxford University Press.

Leighninger, Robert. (2007). *Long-range public investment: The forgotten legacy of the New Deal*. Columbia, SC: University of South Carolina Press.

Levine, Peter. (2010). The path not taken (so far): Civic engagement for reform. *Huffington Post*. Available at www.huffingtonpost.com/peter-levine/the-path-not-taken-so-far_b_437317.html.

Levine, Peter. (2012). A new Hull House? The monumental challenge of service-learning and community engagement. In D.W. Butin & S. Seider (Eds.), *The engaged campus:*

Certificates, minors, and majors as the new community engagement, 171–176. New York, NY: Palgrave/Macmillan.

Levine, Peter. (2013). *We are the ones we have been waiting for: The promise of civic renewal in America.* New York, NY: Oxford University Press.

Mansuri, Ghazala, & Vijayendra Rao. (2014). The challenge of promoting civic participation in poor countries. In P. Levine & K. Soltan (Eds.), *Civic studies,* 59–72. Washington, DC: Bringing Theory to Practice.

Mattson, Kevin. (1998). *Creating a democratic public: The struggle for urban participatory democracy during the Progressive era.* University Park, PA: Pennsylvania State University Press.

Morone, James. (1990). *The democratic wish: Popular participation and the limits of American government.* New York, NY: Basic Books.

Moynihan, Daniel P. (1969). *Maximum feasible misunderstanding: Community action in the War on Poverty.* New York, NY: The Free Press.

Muhlberger, Steve. (1998). *Democracy in ancient India.* Available at www.infinityfoundation.com/mandala/h_es/h_es_muhlb_democra_frameset.htm.

Nabatchi, Tina. (2014). *Open government? Check. Public participation? Not yet.* Available at http://conflictandcollaboration.wordpress.com/2013/12/20/open-government-check-public-participation-not-yet/.

Nabatchi, Tina, & Lisa Blomgren Amsler. (2014). Direct public engagement in local government. *American Review of Public Administration,* 44(4suppl): 63s–88s.

PARCC. (2013). *Priorities for public participation and open government: Recommendations to President Obama.* Syracuse, NY: Program for the Advancement of Research on Conflict and Collaboration.

Peterson, Pete. (2010). Cameron's "Big Society" and its discontents. *Front Porch Forum.* Available at www.frontporchrepublic.com/2010/04/camerons-big-society-and-its-discontents/.

Pitkin, Hanna F., & Sara M. Schumer. (1994). On participation. *Kettering Review,* summer: 327–352.

Postel, Charles. (2007). *The populist vision.* New York, NY: Oxford University Press.

Potapchuk, Maggie. (2001). *Steps toward an inclusive community.* Washington, DC: Joint Center for Political & Economic Studies.

Roberts, Nancy C. (2008). Direct citizen participation: Challenges and dilemmas. In N.C. Roberts, *The age of direct citizen participation,* 3–17. Armonk, NY: M.E. Sharpe

Robinson, Eric W. (1997). *The first democracies: Early popular government outside Athens.* Stuttgart, Germany: Franz Steiner.

Rush, Benjamin. (1787). *Address to the people of the United States.* Available at http://teachingamericanhistory.org/library/document/address-to-the-people-of-the-united-states/.

Schudson, Michael. (1998). *The good citizen: A history of American civic life.* New York, NY: The Free Press.

Shapiro, Ilana. (2002). *Training for racial equity and inclusion: A guide to selected programs.* Washington, DC: The Aspen Institute.

Sirianni, Carmen, & Lewis Friedland. (2001). *Civic innovation in America: Community empowerment, public policy, and the movement for civic renewal.* Berkeley, CA: University of California Press.

Sirianni, Carmen, & Jennifer Girouard. (2012). The civics of urban planning. In R. Weber & R. Crane (Eds.), *The Oxford handbook of urban planning,* 669–690. New York, NY: Oxford University Press.

Sissa, Giulia. (2012). Democracy: A Persian invention? *Mètis: Anthropologies des mondes grecs anciens, 10*: 227–261.

Stenberg, Carl W. (1972). Citizens and the administrative state: From participation to power. *Public Administration Review, 32*(3): 190–198.

Stewart, William H. (1976). *Citizen participation in public administration.* Birmingham, AL: Bureau of Public Administration University of Alabama.

Strange, John H. (1972). Citizen participation in community action and model cities programs. *Public Administration Review, 32*(Special Issue): 655–669.

von Lieres, Bettina. (2007). Social movements, HIV/AIDS politics and new deliberative spaces in South Africa. Unpublished manuscript.

Walsh, Katherine Cramer. (2007). *Talking about race: Community dialogues and the politics of disagreement.* Chicago, IL: University of Chicago Press.

Wampler, Brian. (2012). Participatory budgeting: Core principles and key impacts. *Journal of Public Deliberation, 8*(2): Article 12.

Weatherford, Jack. (1988). *Indian givers: How the Indians of the Americas transformed the world.* New York, NY: Crown Publishers.

Wiebe, R.H. (1995). *Self-rule: A cultural history of American democracy.* Chicago, IL: University of Chicago Press.

Yankelovich, Daniel. (1991). *Coming to public judgment: Making democracy work in a complex world.* Syracuse, NY: Syracuse University Press.

PART TWO

Participation in Action

Participation in Education

E ducation is fundamental to participation and democracy for one simple reason: people care about kids. The way we educate young people is a subject of intense hope and concern for many of us, regardless of whether we are parents ourselves. But that is only the most direct way in which education matters to participation, and participation matters to education.

1. We look to our education systems as the training grounds for future citizens, giving students the skills, knowledge, and experiences they need to be members of a democracy.

2. Creating an environment in which their children can thrive is a tremendously compelling incentive for parents. For many people, it is the primary motivation pulling them into public life—an onramp or even a precondition for their participation in other issues.

3. As physical spaces, schools can be natural hubs for community; they are sometimes used for public meetings and other gatherings.

4. In many places, the school system is the largest employer and represents the largest expenditure of tax revenues; a school budget decision may be the most significant public finance issue faced by a community.

5. In addition to being the leaders of tomorrow, young people can be effective leaders today—students can be participants not only in improving their own education, but in other aspects of public life.

In sum, education provides several of the most common answers to why and where people participate and has an important influence on how they participate.

Participation in education encompasses a wide variety of activities, from discussions on school bond issues to parents talking with their children about schoolwork. Participation can occur in school, at home, online, or in other community settings; it can be part of the official processes for decision making or the informal rhythms of daily life; it can be conventional and paternalistic or it can be productive and egalitarian; it can be thick or thin. The word "engagement" is used more often in education than "participation," but what people mean by the term is the same. The more formal, official kinds of participation tend to get the headlines, but the informal ones may have the greatest impact on student success. For example, the involvement of parents and other family members in student learning is directly linked to higher test scores and other measures of academic achievement (Hill & Tyson, 2009; Jeynes 2005, 2007; McRae, 2012; Willems & Gonzalez-DeHass, 2012).

So can participation help adults help kids? (And can it help kids help adults?) The short answer is yes—and in the following section, we describe a number of ways in which this happens. But the long answer is that participation in education happens sporadically and inefficiently, partly because conventional activities still predominate, and partly because family engagement and all the other effective forms of participation are almost always pursued separately from one another, in ways that center more on the needs of the institution than on those of the citizen. Moreover, although participation is most effective and efficient when it is part of an overall strategy, very few school districts or communities have such a plan.

In this chapter, we describe how participation in education has developed, including the motivations for it and the successful tactics that have emerged. We assess the most common settings and networks for participation and list some questions to help readers evaluate their own communities and school systems. Finally, we provide a framework for thinking about how to strengthen the participation infrastructure for education.

THE DEVELOPMENT OF PARTICIPATION IN EDUCATION

For at least twenty years, a range of school reform advocates, public officials, parent leaders, and educators have championed many different kinds of participation, for a variety of reasons. As a result, participation in education has developed along separate, parallel paths, in the service of goals that are clearly related but seldom treated that way. These goals include promoting family engagement in student learning; making redistricting and school closure decisions; explaining school standards and test scores; making school funding decisions; closing achievement gaps among students of different racial groups; and ensuring school safety. Despite their different forms and goals, the best examples of participation in education embody an adult-adult relationship between educators and parents (and in some cases, students).

Family Engagement in Student Learning

School reform advocates such as James Comer (1986) and Joyce Epstein (2011) have been perhaps the most prominent voices promoting the role of parents, families, and communities in child development (Cutler, 2000). According to the 2010 *Beyond Random Acts* report of the National Policy Forum for Family, School, and Community Engagement, research "repeatedly correlates family engagement with student achievement" (Weiss, Lopez, & Rosenberg, 2010). Family engagement also gives students better attitudes toward learning (Fantuzzo, McWayne, Perry, & Childs, 2004), produces better social skills and fewer disciplinary problems (Caspe & Lopez, 2006), and leads to lower drop-out rates and higher graduation rates (Bridgeland, DiIulio, & Morison, 2006).

On the surface, family engagement may seem like a question of good parenting rather than public participation. But like all forms of public participation, family engagement is predicated on the relationship between the individual and the institution. Comer, Epstein, and many others argue that family engagement is largely dependent on how teachers and schools interact with parents. "When schools and communities support sustained family engagement—including transitions from preschool to school and from one grade level to the next—students benefit" (Weiss, Lopez, & Rosenberg, 2010: 6; see also Dauber & Epstein, 1989). Parents are more likely to become involved in their children's education when they have a clear understanding of their roles, are confident about their ability to help, and feel invited by educators—especially teachers—to take part (Hoover-Dempsey, Walker, & Sandler, 2005; Lloyd-Smith & Baron, 2010).

The traditional approach to building family engagement is the parent-teacher conference, but these meetings often embrace the dynamics of conventional participation: they are short, superficial, privilege the expert role of the teacher, and serve mainly as a chance to air complaints rather an opportunity to develop plans. These meetings are particularly inadequate for low-income parents, those with lower levels of education, those who are not native English speakers, and parents of color (Gonzalez-DeHass & Willems, 2003).

More energetic advocates of family engagement have pursued tactics like after-school programs, parent workshops, and student-centered learning plans with goals set jointly by families and teachers. They also use online tools that allow parents to track students' progress (Weiss, Lopez, & Rosenberg, 2010). Looking more closely at projects that have deployed these tactics, it would appear that they embody some of the key characteristics of good participation—of "treating people like adults." They provide families with more information on what students are learning and how they can learn more effectively; give them more opportunities for two-way communication with educators (including more chances to tell their stories); offer more choices about what and how students want to learn; and provide opportunities to take action.

Another education reform idea, "student-centered learning," has taken this line of thinking one step further. Schools that embrace this approach find ways to make learning more personalized (with learning plans and portfolios developed by students) and more competency-based (with benchmarks based on skills that all students must master) (Chaltain, 2014; see also http://edglossary. org/). Students are given more ways to take ownership of their education and more opportunities to learn outside the traditional classroom (NMEF, 2014). Summarizing the research, Patricia Willems and Alyssa Gonzalez-DeHass (2012: 12) report that "When students are given choices, it feeds an innate need for autonomy, and they are more likely to feel a sense of ownership, empowerment, and enjoyment in their learning; they are more likely to be intrinsically motivated and satisfied with instruction." In this type of participation, the students are treated more like adults and given more information and more choices, in a setting in which educators and parents can help guide their decisions.

Other forms of participation in education are more immediately recognizable as such, mainly because they are initiated by school boards and school administrators and focus on potentially divisive public decisions.

Redistricting, School Closures, and Funding

Many participation efforts focus on the logistical and financial decisions related to school funding, redistricting, and the prospect of school closures. When school boards decide to close schools, they often face angry crowds of parents, students, and other residents. In most cases, these meetings follow a conventional format, in which school leaders present their findings and take questions from the audience. "Most parents see local public schools as important community institutions and viscerally reject the idea that closing schools—even those that are persistently low-performing—is a good way to improve accountability in education," reports Jean Johnson of Public Agenda (2013: 14).

Some districts have created parent task forces and advisory boards and organized more deliberative kinds of public meetings to make and explain these decisions. Others have tried to seek public input and support for bond issues and other financial measures that often underlie the decisions about buildings and staffing. Still others, like the school systems in Omaha, Nebraska, Iowa City, Iowa, and the District of Columbia, have used online platforms like Mindmixer to solicit ideas and comments about policies relating to budgets, school boundaries, and school choice, and to create strategic plans. These engagement efforts seem to be more successful when they begin early in the district's decision-making process and when they adopt formats that allow people to analyze the information, ask questions, and discuss possible responses, usually in small groups (Fagotto & Fung, 2009; Leighninger, 2006). As with successful examples of family engagement, the "adult-adult" opportunities for participants to speak, use information, and exercise choice seem to be especially valuable.

Some participation efforts on funding and redistricting questions also encourage people to come up with new ideas and devote time to implementing them. For example, when the Cincinnati Public Schools proposed a bond issue in 2002, their plan allowed parents and other neighbors to select the architects to work on their new or renovated schools (Frey, 2014). The bond issue passed and the schools now function as "community learning centers" that are open to the neighborhood and include a range of social services for students and families.

School Standards and Testing

Participation in education has also been affected by school accountability measures, exemplified by the federal "No Child Left Behind" law and the Common Core State Standards. Some observers have welcomed the increased attention to test scores, arguing that it aids engagement by providing more information to parents and the community. Others say that "high-stakes testing" focuses attention on the wrong things, leads to unfairly negative perceptions of schools, and pushes educators into a "bunker mentality" that encourages autocratic management styles rather than public participation (Henig, 2011). In an in-depth study of one school system, Tina Trujillo (2013) described how "performance-based accountability pressures led school board members to abandon public discussions in favor of closed-door decision making." Jean Johnson argues that opposition to

Common Core has risen because reformers "didn't go through an inclusive process" in developing it. "Common Core is a case in point in how important it is to build deliberative democracy into reform and to have those deliberative discussions as a policy develops, not to count on messaging and public relations after the fact" (Becker, 2014).

In some districts, school boards and administrators organize meetings to help citizens interpret test scores and other sources of data. Whether these participation efforts succeed seems to depend on a community's ability to develop more "independent capacity to generate, interpret, and analyze data" (Henig, 2011)—in other words, on the extent to which parents and citizens trust and can use the information and feel that educators are treating them like adults.

Achievement Gaps

Issues that relate to racial and cultural differences in education, such as achievement gaps in test scores between students of color and white students, have inspired other kinds of participation initiatives. Some districts have held forums to discuss the racial distribution of test scores or racial segregation within their school systems.

A few, such as the Montgomery County, Maryland, school system, have sustained long-term programs that engage parents, educators, and students in dialogue on issues of race and difference (Orland, 2007). The circles brought to light prejudice and other challenges that minority students and parents face. Teachers and school administrators gained awareness of racial barriers and learned about ways to create a more inclusive school environment. Actions included hiring special outreach coordinators and encouraging minority students to join more challenging classes. The dialogues also helped build trust among participants, spurred collaboration and volunteering, and boosted the participation of minority parents (Fagotto & Fung, 2009: 2). The achievement gap in the Montgomery County schools has narrowed significantly since the program began, although this progress has stalled in the last two years (Bonner-Thompkins, 2014; Childress, Doyle, & Thomas, 2009).

Compared to other examples of participation in education, projects that aim to address the achievement gap focus even more on enabling participants to tell their stories. Connecting on this level helps parents and teachers strengthen their relationships, change their attitudes and behavior, and build their skills and knowledge (Orland, 2007).

School Safety and Bullying

As a focus for participation, school safety is often addressed at the school or district level. Many schools operate programs intended to reduce bullying and the risk of violence among students. Some of these projects involve parents, police officers, and other community members.

When school shootings and other violent incidents grab the headlines, principals and district-level leaders sometimes reach out to parents and other community members to review safety procedures, consider new policies, and enlist volunteers to help as school monitors and in other roles. A wave of these kinds of participation efforts occurred after the December 2012 Sandy Hook shooting in Newtown, Connecticut (NSPRA, 2013).

Other participation efforts take a broader view of safety and attempt to address neighborhood and community issues such as poverty, substance abuse, guns, and mental health. One example is the project in Colorado's Sheridan School District, which involved the police department, city council, and school board as partners in a "joint working committee to develop ways to determine, prioritize, and address the problems of crime, poverty, and community viability" (Colorado Association of School Boards, 2003). In addition to providing information and opportunities to tell stories, a common feature of participation efforts on school safety is that they tap into the capacity of parents, students, and other people to take action, from changing their personal behavior to engaging in volunteer or advocacy roles in the community.

Table 4.1 lists the main education issues and priorities that have inspired attempts at public participation. It also summarizes the features of successful participation—which embody aspects of an adult-adult relationship between citizens and educators—that have emerged in these different contexts. For example, people organizing family engagement projects have found it critical to provide information, give participants the chance to tell their stories, give them choices about student learning, and help them take action. On issues relating to redistricting and school finance, giving participants the sense that their input matters—that they have "legitimacy" in the eyes of school leaders—has been important.

The table also suggests that school systems most often interact with citizens in the situations of greatest pain and controversy. In fact, many instances of public engagement in education could be characterized as "Band-Aid" attempts to address the symptoms of larger problems that have been caused, or at least exacerbated, by a lack of productive participation. Local friction around testing and standards reflects a lack of engagement and public consensus at the state and

Table 4.1
How Aspects of the Adult-Adult Relationship Emerged in Response to Common Education Issues

Common Education Issues	Characteristics of Treating People Like Adults				
	Provide Information	Give People a Chance to Tell Stories	Provide Choices	Give Sense of Political Legitimacy	Support People to Take Action
Family Engagement in Student Learning	X	X	X		X
Finance and Budgeting	X		X	X	X
Redistricting and Closures	X	X	X	X	
Standards and Testing	X			X	
Achievement Gaps	X	X	X	X	X
Safety and Bullying	X	X			X

federal levels (Berry & Herrington, 2013); school closures may be caused by a lack of participation and agreement on school budgets and finances; school safety breakdowns expose a lack of attention to the larger community factors that drive crime and violence. The absence of participation even influences the decisions parents make about which schools their children should attend: one of the factors parents consider is how much control they will have over the schooling their children receive. The appeal of charter schools and private schools may be based, to a large extent, on the sense that parents will have more say in what happens within those schools (Wohlstetter & Chau, 2004). These special schools could be considered Band-Aid solutions of their own: they provide parents who have the capacity to look for other options with a larger degree of control and participation, while failing to address that lack of choice in mainstream schools.

Meanwhile, the more formal avenues for participation are still largely disconnected from family engagement programs and the more direct ways in which people can help kids. A 2010 report of the Harvard Family Research Project concludes, "Family and community engagement is siloed into disparate programs that are disconnected from instructional practice and school turnaround strategies. This state of 'random acts of family involvement' has to give way to systemic and sustained approaches" (Weiss, Lopez, & Rosenberg, 2010: 1).

Some of the participation processes and techniques used in education are successful at reaching their goals, even in situations of high conflict or entrenched inequities—Band-Aids can be quite useful, after all. But for the most part, the more successful processes and interactions happen "outside the system," that is, outside of the official processes for school decision making and problem solving. In the next sections, we examine the official avenues for participation inside the system, describe the networks that interact in and outside the system, and offer some questions to help readers assess the state of participation in their communities.

OFFICIAL SETTINGS FOR PARTICIPATION IN EDUCATION

Most school systems maintain a range of official settings for participation at the district, school, and classroom levels, from public comment periods at school board meetings, to advisory committees, school councils, and parent-teacher meetings (see Figure 4.1). Numerous participation leaders operate within these existing settings, including school administrators, teachers, support staff, school board officials, parents, and students.

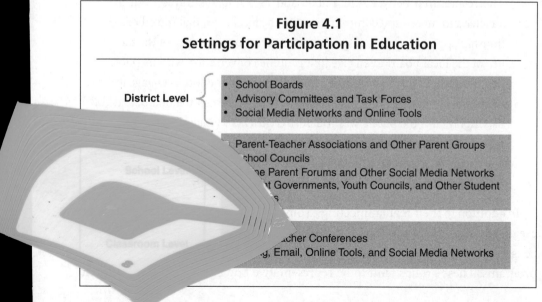

Figure 4.1
Settings for Participation in Education

District Level
- School Boards
- Advisory Committees and Task Forces
- Social Media Networks and Online Tools

- Parent-Teacher Associations and Other Parent Groups
- ̇hool Councils
- ̇e Parent Forums and Other Social Media Networks
- ̇t Governments, Youth Councils, and Other Student

- ̇cher Conferences
- ̇g, Email, Online Tools, and Social Media Networks

District Level

Legally and politically, the organizations that bear the greatest responsibility for ensuring participation at the district level are school boards. In fact, some advocates claim that engagement is the most fundamental role of school boards, and the one that justifies their continued existence in an increasingly professionalized education system. For example, a study conducted by the Colorado Association of School Boards (2003) argues that:

> The development of large, professionally run school systems, or, some might say, the delegation of the management of public education to our professionals, has left not just the public but the publicly elected local representatives in our local communities on the sidelines. The one role for which locally elected school boards are uniquely suited, and the one for which education professionals are at best ill-suited, is engagement with local school communities.

The most common participation format used by school boards, however, is the public comment section of school board meetings. These sessions typically follow the standard format of public meetings, in which citizens have two to three minutes at an open microphone to address the board. The Colorado study cited above found that boards that went beyond this conventional process enjoyed better relationships with parents and community members:

> The relationship between the public and its schools is frayed even in smaller and more rural communities. On the local level, that frayed relationship appears in many respects to be a direct consequence of the failure of the local board to engage in a genuine conversation with its publics. However, if the board made a good faith and fair effort to engage its publics on a broad set of issues, the relationship between the board, and its schools, and the public was much strengthened. Finally, not surprisingly, the most profound impact on the relationship between the schools and their publics occurred if the community engagement effort was sustained over time. (Colorado Association of School Boards, 2003)

In addition to their regular meetings, some school boards and superintendents create advisory committees or task forces that include parents and other citizens to address key issues such as transportation, bullying, or special education programs. These groups tend to be representative bodies that bring some of the perspectives of parents and others to bear, without actually engaging large numbers of people.

Many school districts now make active use of social media networks and other online tools to reach parents, although they generally use them for one-way transmission of information rather than more interactive or deliberative forms of participation. Most districts have their own Twitter and Facebook presences, and some use texting platforms to send reminders or notices to participants. Districts also use "robocall" systems for similar purposes. A few have created more tailored online services that help citizens find the information they want in ways that help them understand and make choices. The "DiscoverBPS" app in Boston is one such example (see Box 4.1).

School Level

At the school level, there are a number of official settings for participation by parents. These parent groups mainly differ in the level of official authority they are given by the school system.

Box 4.1. Case Study

"Discover BPS," Boston, Massachusetts

In 2011, the *Boston Globe* ran an exposé on how difficult it was for parents to figure out which public schools their children were eligible to attend. The city's Office of New Urban Mechanics, working with Code for America Fellows, created an app called "DiscoverBPS" that determines the available schools based on location, admissions quotas, and other factors. The app also provides parents with test scores, historical admissions data, transportation options, and other information on the available schools. School Superintendent Carol Johnson says that DiscoverBPS has "changed the way [the School Department] relates to parents." Two years later, parents and administrators in the district had also found common ground on a new assignment system to determine which schools would be available to which students.

Links

http://beyondtransparency.org/chapters/part-1/open-data-and-open-discource-at-boston-public-schools/

www.politico.com/magazine/story/2014/06/boston-theres-an-app-for-that-107661_Page3.html#.U6iV57H5fxA

www.nytimes.com/2013/03/13/education/no-division-required-in-this-school-problem.html?pagewanted=1&_r=1

The Parent-Teacher Association (PTA) continues to be the most common vehicle for parent involvement at the school level. Many PTAs and other parent groups primarily focus on fundraising and coordinating volunteer activities, such as tutoring programs, award ceremonies, and school safety measures. They also may play a significant advisory role for school principals and teachers, although this is generally an informal relationship.

Some school boards have established local school councils to be the management team at each school. School councils are official, elected bodies that make school-level decisions and district-level recommendations. In a few cases, these councils have a say in school budget decisions and have the authority to hire and fire principals. One example is the Chicago Public Schools, where local school councils were established by state law in 1988. Political scientist Archon Fung (2003, 2006) argues that the councils have been "avenues of popular participation and control" for thousands of Chicagoans. At their inception, critics charged that the councils would create new possibilities for corruption in the system. While those fears have proved unfounded, enthusiasm for the system has waned over the years, with fewer and fewer people choosing to run for school council positions (Sanchez, 2014).

Some PTAs, school councils, and other parent groups have been highly successful at boosting parent volunteerism, creating a welcoming climate at school, encouraging collaboration among parents and educators, and advocating for the school and school system in city-wide or state-level policy debates. Too often, however, parent groups fall short of their potential because they rely on a small set of people and a format that does not encourage or support broader, more diverse participation. In part, this is because recruitment is done primarily through flyers, emails, announcements, and other one-way messages. Meetings tend to be small—unless a controversy has arisen—and discussion typically occurs as a whole-group conversation. Some groups use *Robert's Rules of Order* to structure their proceedings. As a result, "Attendance at school councils [and other parent group meetings] tends to stagnate, dominated by the same circles of powerful parents from year to year" (McRae, 2012).

An increasing number of schools now have online parent forums and social media networks of some kind, including listservs and Facebook groups, which facilitate communication among parents and disseminate announcements from PTAs, schools, and the school district. Most of these online networks have been set up by parent groups or individual parents, although some principals and teachers have become active contributors.

Finally, there are also participation settings for students at the school level, although these arenas vary tremendously in the kind of engagement they support. Many student governments are fairly superficial bodies with no orientation to decision making or problem solving, but some allow students to give input to administrators and parents on certain issues. A few schools have developed systems that engage the majority of their students in governance decisions ranging from food services to attendance policies (Berman, 2004). For example, when the school system in Kuna, Idaho, was building a new high school, students worked directly with the architect to design the cafeteria and other parts of the building (Leighninger, 2006). The experience of Park Forest Elementary School in State College, Pennsylvania, shows that even younger students can be productive citizens: fifth-graders lead "All School Gatherings" that engage kids on all kinds of issues facing the school (Dzur, 2013). Even though these examples are clearly outliers, almost every high school has some sort of student government, as well as a student body that is highly networked through texting and social media. For communities that want to support higher levels of participation by students, these are intriguing civic assets.

Some local governments have provided a similar opportunity for youth participation by establishing youth councils. These groups are advisory bodies that provide input to city councils and other groups, mainly on issues that are important to young people but outside the purview of the school system. They are also intended to "make a powerful statement to all young people and adult residents that youth are full and valued members of the community" (NLC, 2002: 3). Most youth councils—both inside and outside schools—are relatively small and engage only a handful of students. A few, however, are linked to student governments and many other kinds of student groups and serve as hubs for much broader systems of youth engagement (Carlson, 2010).

Classroom Level

The parent-teacher conference is the traditional format for parents' participation at the classroom level. The meetings are typically short (about twenty minutes or less) and occur once or twice per year—with the first meeting midway through the semester, often after the first report card or progress report, rather than at the beginning of the year. Again, an increasing number of teachers use text, email, apps, and social media networks to interact with parents between meetings, although some school districts discourage this practice and others prohibit teachers from giving out their email addresses.

Some schools that have embraced the philosophy of student-centered learning feature students more prominently in these family-teacher interactions at the classroom level. For example, at Pittsfield Middle-High School in New Hampshire, student-led conferences have replaced traditional parent-teacher conferences, allowing students to take the lead role in presentations that articulate academic, personal, and social growth (NMEF, 2014).

In sum, every school district maintains a wide array of official settings for engagement in education. Embedded within these official settings are a wide array of participation leaders—from school administrators and teachers to parents and students. There are inspiring examples, from Colorado to New Hampshire, of official avenues that treat parents—and sometimes students—as adults. But in the vast majority of education settings, the default participation format is conventional and the default interaction paternalistic. The consequences of these formats and interactions are evident in parent attitudes. In her report analyzing the results of focus groups with parents and educators in six states, Jean Johnson (2013: 19) of Public Agenda writes, "Getting more data—and having more transparent policies regarding school metrics—may be helpful, but what leaps out in direct conversations with parents is their hunger for two-way communications and for a personal relationship with the educators in their schools."

STRENGTHENING THE INFRASTRUCTURE: LEADERS AND NETWORKS FOR PARTICIPATION IN EDUCATION

Describing the official settings is only one way of assessing the state of participation in a school system. Another way to begin strengthening the infrastructure for engagement in education is by paying attention to the full range of leaders and networks.

In most places, a wide variety of constituencies have played an active role in education, often outside the conventional interactions between parents and teachers, or between citizens and administrators. Understanding these connections is critical for improving participation, whether in temporary attempts to engage citizens or more structural changes to the system (Sanders, 2012). "Attempts to modify formal structures in support of greater collaboration, shared leadership and decision-making require changes in existing social relationships," write Alan Daly and Kara Finnegan (2012: 26).

Figure 4.2 shows some of the other common networks that can be activated for participation in education. For example, in some school districts, the business community has produced reports, plans, scholarship programs, and other

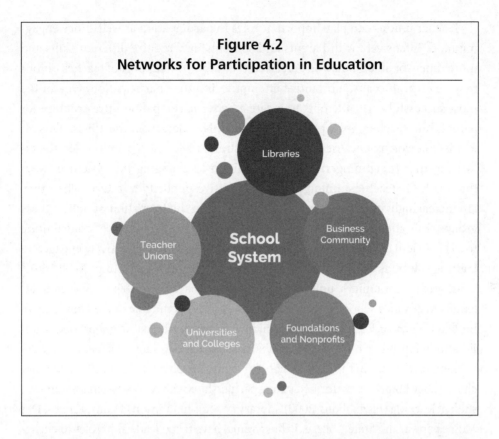

Figure 4.2
Networks for Participation in Education

Libraries

Teacher Unions

School System

Business Community

Universities and Colleges

Foundations and Nonprofits

initiatives that influence school systems. In other cities, community organizing groups have been the primary drivers of school reform efforts (Lin & Keevil, 2014). Youth groups, social service agencies, and other nonprofit organizations may also be key parts of the picture.

Foundations have also played a key role in public participation in some school districts. This is particularly true of Local Education Funds (LEFs), nonprofit organizations that raise private dollars to complement existing school budgets. Some LEFs have engaged parents and other residents in deliberative discussions on school policy questions. Reporting on that work, Brenda Turnbull (2006: 36) writes: "When LEFs tried to shape their initial work around specific policy prescriptions, they did not gain broad-based community support for those policies. . . . technical specifics of data and policy were not the key factors in engaging the public . . . instead the political dynamics of participation and influence were more significant." As an LEF director in Mobile, Alabama, put it, "This is not rocket science, it's political science" (Turnbull, 2006: 36).

Teacher unions can play important roles in participation as well. Since engaging more intensively with parents and students may require different skills and more time—or at least may be perceived that way—the support of teacher unions may be critical to any substantive attempt to improve participation. One of the most successful early attempts to create a better participation infrastructure for parents and teachers took place in Plainfield, New Jersey, in the 1990s. This effort is noteworthy because school administrators and teacher unions led the effort together (Leighninger, 2006). In addition to changing the system in ways that work for teachers, unions can gain positive publicity at a time when they are increasingly under attack. "By participating in the formation of policy, these groups shift attention away from the rhetoric that accuses them of contributing to the problem of low student achievement to being viewed as actively engaged in crafting solutions to raise student achievement" (Jacobsen & Young, 2013: 166).

In some communities, universities and colleges have been deeply involved in attempts to advance school reform ideas. One example is the role of the University of Buffalo Center for Urban Studies in building the Perry Choice Neighborhood Mini-Education Pipeline, a multi-sector collaborative intended to support a "democratic devolution revolution" in the Buffalo schools (Taylor, McGlynn, & Luter, 2013). In other cities, public libraries have formed strong partnerships with school systems to improve student learning (Fitzgibbons, 2000). Library systems in Johnson County, Kansas, Des Moines, Iowa, and State College, Pennsylvania, have taken leadership roles in engaging large numbers of citizens on education and other issues (Kranich, 2012).

Discovering and responding to the motivations and interests of the people in these and other networks is a critical step toward creating a broader, more supportive framework for participation. These constituencies may be fully committed to the success of students, but beyond that basic, shared interest, they may have very different assumptions about how educational success should be achieved and what kinds of outcomes are most beneficial to the community. This conversation can help communities rethink the school "system" as something that is bigger than students, teachers, and principals. In a personal communication with the authors, Shaun Adamec of the Nellie Mae Education Foundation argued that "Policymakers, community members, parents, business leaders, etc., should also characterize the 'system,' and part of an engagement strategy is helping community members realize that."

The networks of interested constituencies and the official settings for engagement are two key elements of the "political science" of participation in education. Box 4.2 provides a set of questions that can be used to help readers assess their

Box 4.2. Assessing the State of Participation in a School System

Any attempt to overhaul public participation in a school system should begin with some basic research on the current opportunities for engagement, both inside and outside the system, and the other contextual factors that may be critical to the relationships among parents, students, and educators. Here are some questions to consider:

- What kinds of participation opportunities are available for parents and other citizens in the school or school district?

- How effective are the public meetings and other official interactions between citizens and district leaders, such as the superintendent and school board?

- How effective are the public meetings and other official interactions between citizens and school leaders, such as the principal?

- Do the people who work on participation efforts reflect and represent the full diversity of the parents or community?

- How well are parent-teacher associations, school councils, and other parent groups functioning?

- Are there segments of the community that historically have been ignored or excluded?

- In what ways are recent immigrants connected, or disconnected, from the rest of the school community?

- What are some of the key networks and constituencies when it comes to education issues in the community?

- How well are young leaders supported, and is their potential being tapped effectively?

- How are social media being used to connect with parents and the community?

- Is school data available online, and how effectively does it complement and inform public participation?

- How much is the school system spending—in money and/or in staff time—on public participation annually?

- How are participation activities and initiatives evaluated and assessed?

- What are the legal mandates and restrictions on public participation?

- Do teachers, administrators, and staff have the skills, cultural awareness, and organizational support to work productively with citizens?

own districts. By answering these questions and developing their own analyses, engagement leaders will have a better sense of how to strengthen their participation infrastructure.

STRENGTHENING THE INFRASTRUCTURE: BUILDING BLOCKS FOR PARTICIPATION IN EDUCATION

"Infrastructure" can be an intimidating word, and implementing systemic reforms can be difficult, even when no one is happy with the way the system is currently working. So a logical next step in strengthening participation infrastructure might be to ask: What are the "bricks" or building blocks that would help make a school system participatory, vibrant, and strong? Specifically, what kinds of participation activities could be beneficial, or even essential, to improving education? What official (and unofficial) settings could provide the logical homes for such activities? And how could leaders in those settings carry out the activities? Below—and summarized in Figure 4.3—are six overarching categories of participation activities, including disseminating information, gathering input and data, discussing and connecting, enabling student and family decision making, enabling community decision making, and encouraging public work. For each building block, we identify a list of relevant settings and participation tools or vehicles that can be used.

Three overarching points are worth considering. First, each of the six building blocks is necessary, at least to some extent, in any successful participation infrastructure. At first blush, this might seem overwhelming. However, many of the settings and tools for these activities already exist, at least to some degree, in every school district. For example, most, if not all, schools have websites and use social media, hold regular social events, and have parent-teacher conferences, Parent Teacher Associations, and school boards. Thus, strengthening participation infrastructure does not always mean creating something *new*. In the following discussion, we suggest numerous ways in which existing participation settings and tools can be improved, as well as ways new tools and approaches can be employed. The options provided should be seen as a menu to help school systems make informed choices.

Second, some of these settings, like parent groups and school boards, are central and versatile—they could potentially play a vital role in all six activities. In general, however, we mention each only once, under the activity to which it is likely to contribute the most. But for most of the parents,

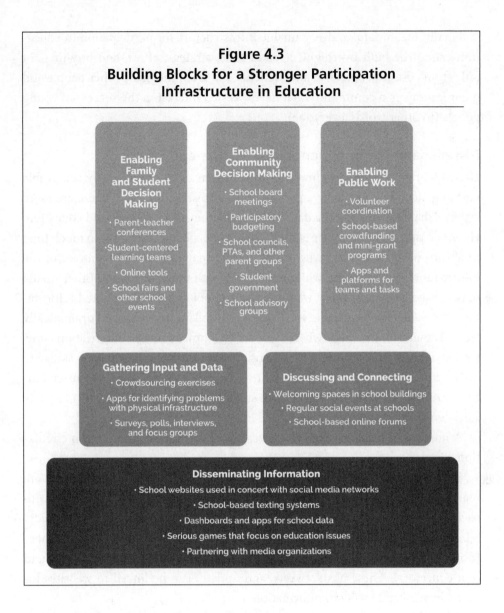

Figure 4.3
Building Blocks for a Stronger Participation Infrastructure in Education

Enabling Family and Student Decision Making
- Parent-teacher conferences
- Student-centered learning teams
- Online tools
- School fairs and other school events

Enabling Community Decision Making
- School board meetings
- Participatory budgeting
- School councils, PTAs, and other parent groups
- Student government
- School advisory groups

Enabling Public Work
- Volunteer coordination
- School-based crowdfunding and mini-grant programs
- Apps and platforms for teams and tasks

Gathering Input and Data
- Crowdsourcing exercises
- Apps for identifying problems with physical infrastructure
- Surveys, polls, interviews, and focus groups

Discussing and Connecting
- Welcoming spaces in school buildings
- Regular social events at schools
- School-based online forums

Disseminating Information
- School websites used in concert with social media networks
- School-based texting systems
- Dashboards and apps for school data
- Serious games that focus on education issues
- Partnering with media organizations

school officials, and other participation leaders in charge of these existing settings, supporting participation more effectively will require changes—sometimes significant ones—in the way they operate and how they think about engagement. We offer a more in-depth examination of participatory tactics and skills in Chapter 8 and in the Participation Skills Module available at www.wiley.com/go/nabatchi.

Finally, meaningful and sustainable infrastructure for participation in education cannot be built overnight. It takes time, strategy, effort, and buy-in—not only from educators, parents, and students, but from the many other people and organizations in a community that have a vested interest in the success of young people (in other words, everyone).

Disseminating Information About Schools and Education

Disseminating information may seem like the most basic and easily achievable building block in a productive participation infrastructure, since there are more avenues than ever for sharing data and information about schools and education. However, that overabundance is itself a challenge; people have only so much time to absorb what they read or hear and may or may not trust the sources of the information. Furthermore, while interacting with newspapers and other media outlets used to be a primary way in which school systems distributed information, the media landscape and the field of journalism have changed dramatically (see Chapter 10). In an age when there are five times more public relations professionals than paid reporters (Williams, 2014), and when journalistic skills are distributed more widely in society, school systems need more ways to reach citizens directly. While media relations are still important, schools can no longer rely solely on media organizations to be the intermediaries.

A number of participation vehicles can help meet these information circulation needs.

School websites used in concert with social media networks. While websites are mainly used for the one-way provision of information, they can be coupled with social media to make the experience at least somewhat interactive. Social media seems to work best for news, announcements, and simple questions or exchanges (not just between educators and parents, but among all kinds of educators and non-educators). These posts, tweets, and updates can be linked to websites for more detailed and in-depth information.

School-based texting networks. Texts are far more likely to be read than email messages or notices sent through the mail (Roggio, 2013). Online platforms like the ones created by Textizen, Mobile Commons, and OneCounts allow educators to set up text networks for sharing information. Teachers can broadcast texts to the parents of all their students, notifying them of an upcoming test, and parents can text back any questions they have; principals and superintendents can broadcast texts about snow days, emergencies, or upcoming events. Some platforms also allow administrators to conduct polls or organize crowdsourcing exercises through texts.

Dashboards and apps for school data. Some school systems use online dashboards to display data on various measures of student success. The first generation of these dashboards showed aggregate data for the entire school or student population; a second wave of this work has produced individualized dashboards for students.

Serious games that focus on education issues. Instead of overwhelming people with information, games create artificial contexts in which they players can put that information to use (Lerner, 2014: 62). While there are not currently many examples of serious games for participation in education, games that exist in other settings could be easily adapted.

Partnering with media organizations. Even though newspapers and other traditional media outlets may have less capacity to cover public education, the changes in the media landscape may be opening up new opportunities. Some newspapers have decided that supporting public deliberation is part of their core journalistic mission, and they have tailored their coverage so that it both informs citizens and makes them aware of participation opportunities. The Portsmouth, New Hampshire, *Herald* and its involvement in Portsmouth Listens is one example (Ames, 2012).

Gathering Input and Data

In addition to the data that educators can provide to the community, the community can provide valuable data to educators. Many participation vehicles can be used to collect input and data on school challenges and opportunities.

Crowdsourcing exercises to gather ideas for improving schools. Some school systems have used online tools to tap the wisdom of the crowd. For example, the Poway Unified School District in California asked community members to generate and vote on ideas for improving school safety. "The site generated more than 10,000 page views, about 500 comments, and nearly 1,000 votes on 97 new ideas proposed. At the end of the project, the district had a top-10 list of winning ideas to pursue that came from employees as varied as a school counselor, an afterschool program supervisor, and a bus driver" (Davis, 2013). The district has devoted $600,000 to fund the winning ideas, including a "K-12 comprehensive school-counseling and student-services support system in the district."

Apps for reporting problems with physical infrastructure. Like many local governments, school systems are starting to use apps that allow people to report problems like graffiti, broken playground equipment, and other damage to school facilities (Thibodeau, 2012). These apps enable parents, students, teachers, and other community members to bolster the inspection and reporting responsibilities of school maintenance employees.

Surveys, polls, interviews, and focus groups. Opinion surveys or polls, interviews, and focus groups can help principals, superintendents, and school boards gain a better sense of what parents and community members want. Interviews can be used to gather input and data from parents or students who have been particularly affected by an issue such as bullying. Likewise, focus groups can be used to convene people—across and within all the networks for education—who are affected by an issue, or to generate new ideas for improvements in areas such as family engagement and student opportunities.

Discussing and Connecting

The social aspects of participation are often overlooked, but they are critical for establishing the kinds of relationships that communities need to improve the quality of education. An evaluation of "First 5 LA," an initiative that has engaged thousands of Los Angelenos in supporting the learning and health of young children, underscored the value of social ties. "By promoting a sense of belonging, engagement activities help establish social ties that bring people together based upon their commonalities. They enhance interdependencies and mutually beneficial interaction of the family and community members" (First 5 LA, 2010: 39). There seemed to be particularly strong effects from regular social events that involve the whole family. "When all family members are engaged, benefits to young children and parents often increase and last" (First 5 LA, 2010: 104).

The First 5 LA experience provides a more detailed, concrete look at the way that education and social capital reinforce one another and support earlier research that showed the link between student achievement and social capital at the district level (e.g., Friedman, Gutnick, & Danzberger, 1999). Schools can support the social life of a community more naturally than just about any other institution; they are civic assets that can be hubs for discussion and connection.

Welcoming spaces within school buildings. Physically, school systems provide spaces of all kinds—from auditoriums to classrooms to gymnasiums—in buildings that are generally easy to access. They have libraries and computer centers that can connect people online. They have facilities for preparing and serving food and rooms and playgrounds that are ideal for child care. For many, these spaces have an emotional pull: people are drawn to schools because they are drawn to kids and want to see what students are learning and doing.

There are often legal and logistical impediments to using schools as hubs for discussing and connecting. For example, school boards are often wary of the insurance liabilities involved with having facilities open after school hours. It is also true that many adults do not feel comfortable going to schools, either because of cultural barriers or simply because they did not have positive school experiences when they were young. Nevertheless, school systems can transform spaces within their buildings to be more welcoming and can use those spaces to help people connect and discuss issues in education.

Regular social events at schools. Many schools already capitalize on their capacity for supporting social connections between parents by holding barbeques, sporting events, concerts, plays, and other events. In many cases, however, these events serve mainly to connect parents—few educators (other than those actively involved in the event) and few adults (other than those related to the students) attend. These social events are usually not linked to other engagement processes and activities.

It is not difficult to add other participatory elements—serious games, small-group discussions, one-on-one interviews—to social events, and vice versa. Many models exist, from the Jane Addams School of Democracy in St. Paul, Minnesota to the use of "parent cafés" by First 5 LA. "Early on, it was a struggle to recruit parents to attend stand-alone sessions, but participation steadily increased as [youth leaders] began targeting outreach to existing groups of parents affiliated with local community-based organizations and schools. As parents experienced cafés for themselves, word of mouth became a very effective tool for promotion" (First 5 LA, 2010: 45). A common success factor of these events is that they are regular: weekly in the case of the parent cafés, and twice a month for the Jane Addams School. "The simple act of providing a consistent day of the week and convenient space for parents to share their concerns and problem solve together can go far toward helping families build informal support networks" (First 5 LA, 2010: 106).

School-based online forums. Finally, school-based online forums provide another arena that schools can tap to build and sustain social connections and discussions. Whether they take the form of email lists, listservs, social media groups, or more elaborate forums, these online spaces serve to circulate information, help people coordinate face-to-face events, and continue policy discussions in a more convenient, ongoing way. These forums need not be limited to parents, students, and educators; they can also be used to start building connections to the many networks involved in education, such as libraries, universities, and businesses.

Enabling Family and Student Decision Making

People want choices, and the choices they care most about are generally the ones that will have the greatest impact on their lives and those of their children. When students and parents have the opportunity to make those choices, with the input and guidance of educators, using information they trust, they take greater ownership of other aspects of the education system (Epstein, 2011; Willems & Gonzalez-DeHass, 2012). It can also help them make better and wiser choices, which in turn may have positive impacts on schools and school systems. Ultimately, this ability to make smart decisions depends on the strength of the relationship between families and educators.

Some of the minor, day-to-day choices made by families and students are appropriate for thin participation, while the major ones require the greater interaction characteristic of thick participation. But overall, the convenience and information-disseminating capacity of thin participation and the relationship- and knowledge-building power of thick participation is an effective combination for supporting decision making about individual student and family issues. In Chapter 8, we provide more detailed information about thick and thin participation tactics. Here, we identify a number of participation vehicles that can be used to enable and improve family and student decision making.

Parent-teacher conferences. Families, students, and educators face many day-to-day choices about what students should learn, how they should learn it, how to measure their progress, and what to do in difficult situations. Many families (and students) would like a greater role in these choices—in some cases, the chance to make the choice themselves and, in others, the chance to give input to educators. The parent-teacher conference is by far the most common opportunity for these exchanges.

There are many ways to improve the standard format for parent-teacher conferences. Holding the first parent-teacher conference early in the year (rather than a short conversation at a "meet the teacher" night) can give teachers more information about the strengths, weaknesses, and learning styles of each student and affirm the parents' role as the primary educator for their children. Emails and text messages can be helpful for supplementing the face-to-face meetings. Some districts have also brought parents together in other combinations than the standard parent-teacher conference (see Box 4.3 for an exemplary approach used in the Creighton School District in Arizona).

Improving parent-teacher interactions ought to be a shared endeavor: school administrators and parent groups can hold workshops at the beginning of the year to help teachers and parents decide on the most effective strategies (PTA, 2009).

Student-centered learning teams. As noted above, students sometimes want more say in day-to-day decisions about education issues about what and how they learn, which classes to take, and how to prepare for life after graduation. These decisions also benefit from the input of parents, teachers, aides, guidance counselors, school social workers, and others. Student-centered learning teams are vehicles that can be used to help bring greater coherence, focus, and purpose to the decisions students make about their education.

Online tools for tracking student progress. Some schools use personalized dashboards, protected by passwords and other security measures, that allow families to monitor the academic progress of their students. Parents and students can use

---

Box 4.3. Case Study

Academic Parent-Teacher Teams in the Creighton School District, Arizona

The Creighton Elementary School District organizes Academic Parent-Teacher Teams as an alternative to the traditional parent-teacher conference. Each year, three group meetings are held for all parents. During these meetings, parents receive aggregate student performance data, along with the data for their own children. This data is used to help parents set student academic goals, interpret assessment data, and understand each child's standing in relation to the entire class. Teachers model reading and math skills during the sessions, and parents practice these skills before applying them at home. Parents also participate in one individual parent-teacher meeting to review performance data. Administrators report that teachers were at first hesitant to coach parents, but now welcome them as teaching partners. Parent attendance averages 92 percent, higher than in regular conferences. Maria Paredes (2010), the director of Community Education, claims that the parent-teacher teams focus on purposeful communication that demands parents' engagement and measurable accountability (see also Weiss, Lopez, & Rosenberg, 2010).

Links

www.hfrp.org/CreightonAPPT

www.creightonschools.org/apps/pages/index.jsp?uREC_ID=180085&type=d&pREC_ID=374885

---

these dashboards to obtain important information about attendance, behavior, course overviews, and individual learning plans and ongoing and completed activities, projects, and tasks.

School fairs and other avenues. Families also need to make more significant decisions about the education of their children, such as which school to attend (or even in which district to live). These decisions are complicated by the growing diversity of education opportunities, including traditional public schools, charter schools, magnet schools, and cyber schools, as well as specific academic programs (such as International Baccalaureate programs or Advanced Placement classes). When confronted with such choices, families need information to guide their decisions.

Sometimes, this information can come from thin participatory opportunities, such as websites and school fairs. Often, however, families want more advice and information than can be provided in these forums; PTAs, parent groups, and parent-teacher conferences can serve that need. Families also can benefit from in-depth discussions with teachers, school counselors, social workers, and administrators. Smartphone-based apps like DiscoverBPS (see Box 4.1) can deliver customized information in response to data provided by the user.

Enabling Community Decision Making on Education Issues

The infrastructure for participation in a school system would be inadequate if it failed to help the district address major policy decisions and develop long-term strategic plans. Because they are likely the most visible and high-stakes examples of participation, opportunities to make community decisions about education have an important impact on the legitimacy of engagement overall.

Making potentially controversial decisions in a productive way generally requires the use of thick, deliberative processes that bring large, diverse numbers of people together to establish common ground. In turn, large-scale deliberation is more likely to succeed when other forms of participation are taking place—where social capital is high, data are trusted and readily available, and families are part of day-to-day decisions about education. Although some school systems have used thick participatory processes, these processes are far less common than the other activities described in this section. In Chapter 8, we offer more information about thick participation tactics; here, we simply note some common and emerging educational settings into which these processes can be incorporated.

School board meetings. School boards can incorporate deliberative elements into their regular monthly meetings by establishing a section of the agenda in which board members and attendees engage in small-group discussions on an important topic (see Box 6.5 about "Revamping the Public Meeting" in Chapter 6). School-based online forums, social media networks, and other online tools can be used to ascertain the "hot topics" that people might want to address in future meetings. School leaders will be better able to attract a broad array of people, including adults who do not have children in school, if they work with other local institutions and organizations, such as those in the various networks listed in Figure 4.2.

Annual participatory budgeting processes for district budgets. Participatory Budgeting (or PB) deserves special mention here because it is commonly implemented as an official, annual practice (we provide more details about PB in Chapters 8 and 10). School systems around the world have used PB to involve people in allocating portions of the school budget (Schugurensky, 2014). Full-fledged PB processes can support information dissemination, input-gathering, discussion and connection, and public work in addition to community decision-making.

School councils and parent associations. Councils, PTAs, and other parent groups can partner with school boards and other district-level organizations on community-wide engagement processes. They can also organize their own school-level processes, and incorporate participatory strategies into their regular meetings (see Box 4.4). This sort of role for parent groups can heighten their standing among parents and other community members by giving more people a chance to contribute. An advantage that school-level parent groups bring to this work is the way in which they can combine deliberative opportunities with social events. Again, working with organizations outside the school—neighborhood associations, local businesses, faith communities, and other groups—can help broaden the outreach and impact of the process.

Student governments and youth councils. Student governments and youth councils can also be effective organizers of deliberative processes. They are particularly well-suited for engaging students on important school policy issues such as safety and bullying. Not only does deliberation in youth councils play an educational role for young people, but it also cultivates many important skills (such as students' capacity to mobilize people and facilitate and lead small-group discussions) and attitudes (such as a sense of voice and political efficacy). Many of the tips offered in Box 4.4 for parent groups can also be applied to youth groups.

School task forces and advisory committees. Task forces and advisory committees can help collect and analyze data, with the goal of developing options or alternatives for broader discussion. The efficacy of these participation mechanisms increases when they are representative bodies that bring together the perspectives of diverse stakeholders, such as parents, educators, administrators, and other community members. In certain situations, committee members can become participation leaders in their own right, helping to bring larger numbers of people to the table around a particularly important topic or decision.

Encouraging Public Work

Finally, a successful participation infrastructure would encourage parents, students, and other community members to expend time, energy, and sweat equity in ways that will improve the quality of education. In addition to its impact on schools, this sort of collaboration to accomplish public goals—what Harry Boyte and Nan Kari (1996) have called "public work"—seems to have beneficial impacts

---

Box 4.4. Making Parent Groups More Participatory

There are many options for making parent organizations more participatory, powerful, and fun:

- Make the meetings more social and kid-friendly.

- Meet weekly instead of monthly.

- Recruit extensively (especially at the beginning of the school year), paying special attention to networks of people who have not typically been engaged.

- Start an online forum focused on that school.

- Partner with other organizations nearby.

- Organize some kind of whole-group action project every semester (and recruit extensively for it).

- Come to an agreement with the principal about roles and responsibilities.

- No talking heads at the meetings—feature small-group discussion, games, and other participatory exercises.

For more information, see PTA (2009).

---

for the people involved, as we described in Chapter 2. Furthermore, it attracts parents and other community members who care most about "getting their hands dirty" and producing visible results (Mathews, 2006).

Within the context of education, typical public work activities include tutoring programs; mentoring, internship, and apprenticeship opportunities; assisting with sports, music, drama, and other extracurricular activities; walking young children to and from school; constructing, cleaning, and maintaining playgrounds, athletic fields, and other facilities; and monitoring school properties to help keep students safe. A variety of participation vehicles can assist with cultivating public work for education.

Volunteer coordination. Many educators, parents, and students have led or coordinated projects that recruited large numbers of volunteers to accomplish a task; others have set up ongoing roles for volunteers as tutors, mentors, monitors, and coaches. In some cases, volunteer coordination is done outside of the school and school system, for example, by parent groups or booster clubs, while in other cases, schools and school systems maintain a volunteer coordinator position and program. In both cases, there are a growing number of apps and platforms that make recruiting, tracking, and managing education volunteers easier.

School-based crowdfunding and mini-grant programs. Small amounts of money can leverage large contributions of volunteer time and labor. School systems can use crowdfunding and mini-grants to seed and support problem-solving efforts proposed by students, parent groups, and others in the community. A growing number of online platforms and digital applications—like Citizinvestor—enable volunteers to attract donations online.

Apps and platforms for teams and tasks. Some aspects of doing public work in education are project-based and require the coordination of teams and tasks. The management of such projects is becoming easier, particularly because of apps and platforms that allow this work to be done online and in a decentralized way. A number of online platforms, such as PublicStuff, ChangeByUs, and Shareabouts, enable people to map problems and tasks, develop solutions, and attract the involvement of other citizens (see Chapter 8). These tools have been used mainly to coordinate neighborhood improvements, but they could be employed in ways that benefit schools. Other online tools, like CivicEvolution, guide small teams through a process of information-gathering, planning, and collaborative action to implement an idea (Hartz-Karp & Sullivan, 2014).

STRENGTHENING THE INFRASTRUCTURE: SYSTEMIC SUPPORTS FOR PARTICIPATION IN EDUCATION

Some combination of the building blocks described above would create a stronger participation infrastructure for schools. But to make these tools and activities work properly, communities also need systemic supports that enable people to take on new roles, connect the different building blocks to one another, and institutionalize participation in the regular functioning of schools and school districts. As noted in the First 5 LA report (2010: 39):

> Rather than one-time support, effective engagement approaches focus on sustaining parent involvement and work intentionally to overcome the tendency toward episodic participation. Mutual recognition, trust, and reciprocity are more likely to develop between parents, staff, and other community leaders. Sustained participation in community-building efforts is more likely to strengthen the voices of parents and other residents in their community's civic and political institutions.

So what systemic supports would help make a participation infrastructure sustainable, strong, and resilient? We go into greater detail on this topic in Part Three. Here, we simply identify some of the most critical supports for education, including training and skill development, professional incentives, policies and procedures, and funding and budgeting.

Training and Skill Development

Becoming a more participatory school system may require a fundamental shift in educator skills and attitudes. A 1999 report from Public Agenda asserts that "The way school systems and citizens typically operate is antithetical to community dialogue and school-community collaboration" (Friedman, Gutnick, & Danzberger, 1999: 47). More than fifteen years later, many educators and parents would argue that the same ways of working are still prevalent in districts today.

Many of the needed attitudinal changes and skill development can come through training. Unfortunately, the overall "lack of preparation, administrative support, and resources offered teachers presents a rather bleak picture in terms of the support teachers have in facilitating parental involvement" (Gonzalez-DeHass & Willems, 2003: 96). Training in these skills should be part of the curriculum at teachers' colleges and other degree-granting and accreditation programs, and should be offered as stand-alone workshops and seminars. These kinds of workshops and seminars can also be offered for parent and community leaders—and if educators and non-educators go through these skill development sessions together, the training program may have the added benefit of building relationships and collaboration among the people who will be supporting public participation. In the Participation Skills Module, we discuss participation skills in more depth and identify numerous avenues for obtaining training.

Professional Incentives for Educators and Other Participation Leaders

People need skills, but they also need incentives. For the most part, educators are not rewarded for being good at public participation; how teachers interact with parents or how administrators interact with the public is seldom incorporated directly into the rubric for calculating pay raises, promotions, or other modes of professional advancement. School systems could uphold public participation as a job priority for teachers and administrators so that performance review processes assess how well educators are engaging parents and other community members. This structural change would require educators (and community members) to define what they mean by participation, identify the particular kinds of engagement that are important to each job position, and have ways to measure the quantity and quality of that engagement.

But not all participation leaders have to be educators: the participation infrastructure for education could also feature parents and students as leaders, as well as people from libraries, universities, nonprofit organizations, local governments, and myriad other networks engaged in education. Incentives should be devised for these potential participation leaders. It is important to note that not all incentives need be monetary; non-monetary incentives, such as recognition, awards, and forms of authority and legitimacy, can also be effective.

Policies and Procedures

School districts should establish policies and procedures that provide clarity and transparency about different aspects of participation and decision making. To effectively coordinate the kinds of participation activities described in the previous section, educators and other community members should designate who is responsible for each activity. This is particularly true because of the varied, disparate nature of potential participation leaders: the people supporting participation may be working in different parts of the school system, in other organizations in the community, or in unpaid but significant volunteer roles.

To make productive participation part of the regular school routine, districts also must establish who is accountable for supporting it. The participation responsibilities of each staff position or elected leader—and those of organizations such as PTAs, school councils, advisory commissions, and youth councils—should be established in school system policies and procedures, and in some cases in local ordinances.

Similarly, citizens want to know how much influence and authority their input will have on school district decisions. If the expectations of participants do not match those of administrators, elected officials, or other leaders, a well-intentioned engagement effort can quickly go off the rails. Charts like the IAP2 Spectrum (see Chapter 8) can be helpful for clarifying—or, in some cases, negotiating—the role that a participation process will play in the policymaking arena. Again, these expectations should be sanctioned in the district's policies, procedures, and laws.

Funding and Budgeting

For school administrators and other educators, reading a long list of potential participation activities can bring on sticker shock. Some might argue that, even if parents and other community leaders pitch in, the financial cost to the school system of maintaining such a wide array of participation opportunities is prohibitive. However, others might argue that participation is the key to sustaining or growing the pool of financial resources available to school districts—because the resources will be coming (or not) from participating parents and community members.

In either case, two points are worth noting. First, "When school systems go into financial crisis mode, the budgets for communications and engagement often get cut first," says Rich Bagin, director of the National School Public Relations Association. "But doing that often prevents the district from ever getting out of the crisis. Basically what they are doing is eating their seed corn." Simply put: engagement is necessary for financial stability. Second, the costs of this participation infrastructure need not be huge. In fact, research shows that the costs of most participation projects are relatively small (Lee & Polletta, 2009). Moreover, most school systems already offer a range of settings and use a range of tools and activities for participation. Thus, upgrading the quality of participation does not necessarily require significant new outlays of financial resources.

SUMMARY

The potential for public participation on education may be greater than for any other issue. The school system is a large institutional presence in almost every community, and education often attracts more attention, allegiance, and concern than any other public issue. Public participation in education has been shaped by a number of separate but related priorities, including family involvement in student learning, finances and budgeting, redistricting and closures, standards and testing, achievement gaps, and safety and bullying.

We know that participation in education can produce a wide variety of benefits, from better school policymaking to the success of individual students. However, despite the fact that most school systems support a wide array of engagement avenues and arenas, the inadequacy of that infrastructure—and the processes used within it—has prevented most communities from capitalizing on the potential of public participation in education.

In this chapter, we provided a number of suggestions about how to strengthen the participation infrastructure for education. Specifically, we asserted that participation in education can be improved if:

1. *Leaders and networks for participation are activated and empowered.* Most school systems have a range of official settings for participation at the district, school, and classroom levels, and within these settings are numerous participation leaders, from school administrators, teachers, and support staff, to school board officials, parents, students, and others. Most communities also have a wide variety of networks and constituencies that can play an active role in education, including universities and colleges, foundations and nonprofits, the business community, teacher unions, and libraries. Activating and empowering leaders in these settings and networks can go a long way toward creating a broader, more supportive framework for participation in education.

2. *The six building blocks of participation activities are put into place.* Most schools and school systems already undertake a number of activities related to disseminating information, gathering input and data, discussing and connecting, enabling student and family decision making, enabling community decision making, and encouraging public work. However, these activities often use conventional approaches and are not well connected to each other. The infrastructure for participation in education can

be strengthened if schools and school systems incorporate a wide variety of thin and thick participation tools and vehicles in these activities.

3. *Systemic supports are used to make participation sustainable, strong, and resilient.* To help people to take on new roles, and to institutionalize participation in the regular functioning of schools and school districts, several systemic supports are needed, including training and skill development, professional incentives, policies and procedures, and funding and budgeting.

While these three tasks may seem overwhelming, strengthening the infrastructure for participation need not be. As noted above and throughout this chapter, much of what is needed already exists—at least to some extent—in every school system. Thus, the most important step is simply for communities and school systems to take stock of their existing assets, consider the kinds of participation activities they want to foster and support, and make changes to enable the education system to operate in more democratic ways.

DISCUSSION QUESTIONS

1. Review the common education issues listed in Table 4.1. Which issue or issues do you think are most important? Which do you think can be addressed effectively through public participation? Why?

2. Summarize the current official settings for participation in education at each level (district, school, and classroom). How can participation at each level be improved?

3. What role do you think students can and should play in participation at the district, school, and classroom levels? Justify your ideas.

4. Who are (or should be) the key actors in participation in education? What are (or should be) each actor's role in participation? Do those roles vary depending on the level (i.e., district, school, or classroom) at which participation is happening?

5. What should be the role of colleges, universities, and nonprofit organizations in enabling effective participation in education?

6. Use the questions in Box 4.2 to assess the state of participation in your local school system.

7. Review the six building blocks for a stronger participation infra-structure in education (Figure 4.3). Which are (or were) present in your school system? Were the activities conventional, thin, or thick? Which opportunities would you have liked to have had or would like to see now, and why?

8. What are the benefits and drawbacks of using school facilities for public participation? Do the schools in your community have a place-making function? If so, how? If not, why?

9. How does technology encourage participation in education? What are the advantages and disadvantages of integrating technology such as social media or online dashboards in education?

10. What kinds of skills, training, and incentives do you think would work best to support participation in education? Why?

References

Ames, Steven. (2012). *Stewarding the future of our communities*. Shelburne, VT: Orton Family Foundation.

Becker, Jack. (2014). Understanding the public: Lessons from Public Agenda's Jean Johnson. *KF News*. Available at http://kettering.org/kfnews/understanding-the-public/.

Berman, Sheldon H. (2004). Teaching civics: A call to action. *Principal Leadership*, 5(1): 16–20.

Berry, Kimberly, & Carolyn Herrington. (2013). States and their struggles with NCLB: Does the Obama blueprint get it right? *Peabody Journal of Education*, 86(3): 272–290.

Bonner-Thompkins, Elaine. (2014). *Performance of Montgomery County public schools' high schools—A FY 2014 update*. Rockville, MD: Montgomery County Office of Legislative Oversight.

Boyte, Harry C. (2013). Reinventing citizenship as public work: Civic learning for the working world. In D.W. Brown & D. Witte (Eds.), *Higher education exchange*, 14–27. Dayton, OH: Kettering Foundation.

Boyte, Harry C., & Nan Kari.(1996). *Building America: The democratic promise of public work*. Philadelphia, PA: Temple University Press.

Bridgeland, John M., John J. DiIulio, & Karen Burke Morison. (2006). *The silent epidemic: Perspectives of high school dropouts*. Washington, DC: Civic Enterprises.

Carlson, Cindy. (2010). *Authentic youth civic engagement*. Washington, DC: National League of Cities.

Caspe, Margaret, & M. Elena Lopez, (2006). *Lessons from family-strengthening interventions: Learning from evidence-based practice*. Cambridge, MA: Harvard Family Research Project.

Chaltain, Sam. (2014). Summer, once a time for reflection, now the time for radical re-design. *Huffington Post*. Available at www.huffingtonpost.com/sam-chaltain/summer-once-a-time-for-re_b_5626743.html.

Childress, Stacey M., Denis P. Doyle, & David A. Thomas. (2009). *Leading for equity: The pursuit of excellence in the Montgomery County Public Schools*. Cambridge, MA: Harvard Education Press.

Colorado Association of School Boards. (2003). *Public engagement in five Colorado school communities: Report to the Kettering Foundation*. Denver, CO: Colorado Association of School Boards.

Comer, James. (1986). Parent participation in the schools. *Phi Delta Kappan*, 67: 442–446.

Cutler, William. (2000). *Parents and schools: The 150-year struggle for control in American education*. Chicago, IL: University of Chicago Press.

Daly, Alan J., & Kara S. Finnegan. (2012). The social side of district change. *District Administration*, 48(7): 26–31.

Dauber, Susan L. & Joyce L. Epstein. (1989). *Parent attitudes and practices of parent involvement in inner-city elementary and middle schools*. Baltimore, MD: The Johns Hopkins University Center for Social Organization of Schools.

Davis, Michelle R. (2013). K-12 districts, groups turn to mobile "crowdsourcing" to solve problems. *Digital Directions*. Available at www.edweek.org/dd/articles/2013/06/12/03mobile-crowd.h06.html.

Dzur, Albert W. (2013). Trench democracy in schools: An interview with principal Donnan Stoicovy. *Boston Review*. Available at www.bostonreview.net/blog-us/albert-w-dzur-trench-democracy-schools-interview-principal-donnan-stoicovy.

Epstein, Joyce. (2011). *School, family, and community partnerships: Preparing educators and improving schools* (2nd ed.). Boulder, CO: Westview Press.

Fagotto, Elena, & Archon Fung. (2009). *Sustaining public engagement: Embedded deliberation in local communities*. East Hartford, CT: Everyday Democracy and Kettering Foundation.

Fantuzzo, John, Christine McWayne, Marlo A. Perry, & Stephanie Childs. (2004). Multiple dimensions of family involvement and their relations to behavioral and learning competencies for urban, low-income children. *School Psychology Review*, 33(4): 467–480.

First 5 LA. (2010). *Partnerships for families: Stories and lessons from Los Angeles communities*. Los Angeles, CA: First 5 LA. Available at www.cssp.org/publications/child-welfare/partnerships-for-families-stories-and-lessons-from-los-angeles-communities-2010.pdf.

Fitzgibbons, Shirley. (2000). School and public library relationships: essential ingredients in implementing educational reforms and improving student learning. *School Library Media Research*, 3: 1–66.

Frey, Susan. (2014). Nonprofit and for-profit partners help Cincinnati transform its failing schools. *EdSource*. Available at http://edsource.org/2014/nonprofit-and-for-profit-partners-help-cincinnati-transform-its-failing-schools/63548#.VDFF4Ra9bRc.

Friedman, Will, Aviva Gutnick, & Jackie Danzberger. (1999). *Public engagement in education*. New York, NY: Public Agenda.

Fung, Archon. (2004). *Empowered participation: Reinventing urban democracy*. Princeton, NJ: Princeton University Press.

Fung, Archon, & Erik Olin Wright (Eds.). (2003). *Deepening democracy: Institutional innovations in empowered participatory governance*. London: Verso Press.

Gonzalez-DeHass, Alyssa R., & Patricia P. Willems. (2003). Examining the underutilization of parent involvement in the schools. *School Community Journal, 13*(1): 85–99.

Hartz-Karp, Janette, & Brian Sullivan. (2014). The unfulfilled promise of online deliberation. *Journal of Public Deliberation, 10*(1): Article 16.

Henig, Jeffrey. (2011). The contemporary context of public engagement. In M. Orr & J. Rogers (Eds.), *Public engagement for public education: Joining forces to revitalize democracy and equalize schools*, 52–85. Stanford, CA: Stanford University Press.

Henry Louis Taylor, Jr., Linda McGlynn, & D. Gavin Luter. (2013). Neighborhoods matter: The role of universities in the school reform neighborhood development movement. *Peabody Journal of Education, 88*(5): 541–563.

Hill, Nancy E., & Diana F. Tyson. (2009). Parental involvement in middle school: A meta-analytic assessment of the strategies that promote achievement. *Developmental Psychology, 45*(3): 730–763

Hoover-Dempsey, Kathleen V., Joan M.T. Walker, & Howard M. Sandler. (2005). Parents' motivations for involvement in their children's education. In E.N. Patrikakou, R.P. Weisberg, S. Redding, & H.J. Walberg (Eds.), *School-family partnerships for children's success*, 40–56. New York, NY: Teachers College Press.

Jacobsen, Rebecca, & Tamara V. Young. (2013). The new politics of accountability: Research in retrospect and prospect. *Educational Policy, 27*(2): 155–169.

Jeynes, William H. (2005). A meta-analysis of the relation of parental involvement to urban elementary school student academic achievement. *Urban Education, 40*(3): 237–269.

Jeynes, William H. (2007). The relationship between parental involvement and urban secondary school student academic achievement: A meta-analysis. *Urban Education, 42*(1): 82–110.

Johnson, Jean. (2013). *Will it be on the test? How leaders and parents think about accountability in public schools*. Dayton, OH: Kettering Foundation and Public Agenda.

Kranich, Nancy. (2012). Libraries and civic engagement. In D. Bogart (Ed.), *Library and book trade almanac*, 75–97. Medford, NJ: Information Today.

Lee, Caroline, & Francesca Polletta. (2009). *The 2009 dialogue and deliberation practitioners survey: What is the state of the field?* Easton, PA: Lafayette College. Available at http://sites.lafayette.edu/ddps/.

Leighninger, Matt. (2006). *The next form of democracy: How expert rule is giving way to shared governance—and why politics will never be the same*. Nashville, TN: Vanderbilt University Press.

Lerner, Josh. (2014). *Making democracy fun: How game design can empower citizens and transform politics*. Cambridge, MA: MIT Press.

Lin, Charrissa, & Christopher Keevil. (2014). Performing effective advocacy. *Stanford Social Innovation Review Blog.* Available at www.ssireview.org/blog/entry/performing_effective_advocacy.

Lloyd-Smith, Laura, & Mark Baron. (2010). Beyond conferences: Attitudes of high school administrators toward parental involvement in one small Midwestern state. *School Community Journal, 20*(2): 23–44.

Mathews, David. (2006). *Reclaiming public education by reclaiming our democracy.* Dayton, OH: Kettering Foundation Press.

McRae, Dan. (2012). Parent engagement: School councils are not enough. *The Quest for Improved Student Achievement: A Journal of Educational Inquiry and Practice.* Available at https://www.yrdsb.ca/Programs/PLT/Quest/Journal/2012-Parent-Engagement-School-Councils-are-Not-Enough.pdf.

NLC. (2002). *Promoting youth participation: Action kit for municipal leaders.* Washington, DC: National League of Cities, Institute for Youth, Education, and Families.

NMEF. (2014). *Student-centered learning in action.* Quincy, MA: Nellie Mae Education Foundation.

National School Public Relations Association (NSPRA). (2013). *Responding to the Newtown Tragedy.* Available at https://www.nspra.org/files/docs/NSPRAEngagementGuide ForSchoolSafety.pdf.

Orland, Catherine Brenner. (2007). *Teachers, study circles and the racial achievement gap: How one dialogue and action program helped teachers integrate the competencies of an effective multicultural educator.* Brattleboro, VT: School for International Training.

Paredes, Maria C. (2010). Academic parent-teacher teams: reorganizing parent-teacher conferences around data. *Fine Newsletter, 2*(3). Cambridge, MA: Harvard Family Research Project.

PTA. (2009). *PTA national standards for family-school partnerships: An implementation guide.* Alexandria, VA: National PTA.

Roggio, Armando. (2013). Text messaging effective for retailers. *Practical Ecommerce.* Available at www.practicalecommerce.com/articles/4139-Text-Messaging-Effective-for-Retailers-.

Sanchez, Melissa. (2014). See who won the LSC elections. *Catalyst Chicago.* Available at www.catalyst-chicago.org/notebook/2014/04/24/65883/see-who-won-lsc-elections.

Sanders, Mavis. (2012). Achieving scale at the district level. *Educational Administration Quarterly, 48*(154).

Schugurensky, Daniel. (2014). *Evaluating participatory budgeting: Five dimensions.* Paper presented at the Third International Conference on Participatory Budgeting in North America. Oakland, California, September 25–27.

Taylor, Henry Louis, Jr., Linda McGlynn, & D. Gavin Luter. (2013). Neighborhoods matter: The role of universities in the school reform neighborhood development movement. *Peabody Journal of Education, 88*(5): 541–563.

Thibodeau, Patrick. (2012). L.A. schools use mobile app to report maintenance problems. *Computerworld.* Available at www.computerworld.com/article/2502147/mobile-apps/l-a–schools-use-mobile-app-to-report-maintenance-problems.html.

Trujillo, Tina. (2013). The disproportionate erosion of local control: Urban school boards, high-stakes accountability, and democracy. *Education Policy, 27*(2): 334–359.

Turnbull, Brenda. (2006). *Citizen mobilization and community institutions: The public education network's policy initiatives.* Washington, DC: Policy Studies Associates.

Warren, Mark. (2014). Public schools as centers for building social capital in urban communities: A case study of the Logan Square Neighborhood Association in Chicago. In K.L. Patterson & R.M. Silverman (Eds.), *Schools and urban revitalization: Rethinking institutions and community development,* 167–184. New York, NY: Routledge.

Weiss, Heather B., M. Elena Lopez, & Heidi Rosenberg. (2010). *Beyond random acts: Family, school, and community engagement as an integral part of education reform.* Cambridge, MA: Harvard Family Research Project.

Willems, Patricia P., & Alyssa R. Gonzalez-DeHass. (2012). School-community partnerships: Using authentic contexts to academically motivate students. *School Community Journal, 22*(2): 9–30.

Williams, Alex T. (2014). *The growing pay gap between journalism and public relations.* Washington, DC: Pew Research Center. Available at www.pewresearch.org/fact-tank/2014/08/11/the-growing-pay-gap-between-journalism-and-public-relations/.

Wohlstetter, Priscilla, & Derrick Chau. (2004). Does autonomy matter? Implementing research-based practices in charter and other public schools. In K.E. Bulkley & P. Wohlstetter (Eds.), *Taking account of charter schools: What's happened and what's next?,* 53–71. New York, NY: Teachers College Press.

Participation in Health

People care about their health. Issues relating to health are fundamental to democracy and participation, for several reasons:

1. Every one of us has experiences, hopes, and concerns when it comes to our own health and that of our loved ones; health is an issue that literally affects everyone.

2. Indicators of public health are interwoven with and strongly linked to a variety of other social and economic indicators; healthy communities are likely to be socially and economically vigorous, and vice versa.

3. In the United States, health care reform has been a contentious, high-stakes, high-profile policy issue for decades.

4. There is a substantial local and state health care infrastructure, providing a range of services to citizens and (at least potentially) a wide range of opportunities for citizens to participate in decisions that affect them.

Advocates of "healthy communities" make the connection between health and democracy, and health and place, even more explicitly. "The growing capacity to innovate and successfully solve problems via collaborative action," writes Tyler Norris (2014: 4), "presents the greatest potential for improving the health of people and place and revitalizing participatory democracy in the process."

Health is also a field in which experts have been particularly dominant: from the number-crunching health policy analyst to the authoritative family doctor, health professionals have been trained to believe in the primacy of their knowledge and training (CAH, 2014). As research has emerged showing the benefits of changing that relationship, and engaging people both as "patients" and as citizens, public participation has become a significant priority and a significant challenge for the field (CAH, 2014; Rubio-Cortés & McGrath, 2014).

In this chapter, we examine the ways in which participation has developed in health arenas ranging from individual doctor-patient interactions to large-scale, deliberative planning processes. These trends have affected both personal health and public health, a broader term that encompasses the many behaviors, risk factors, and social issues that affect a population. We connect the common impulses in those different setting and describe how communities can tap into health networks, revitalize official settings for health decision making, and strengthen their infrastructure for participation on health issues.

THE DEVELOPMENT OF PARTICIPATION IN HEALTH

On issues like education and land use, the need for public participation has been a key part of the rhetoric, if not always part of the practice. In health, both the rhetoric and practice of participation have developed slowly and subtly. Personal health in America has a conceptual foundation that emphasizes the expertise of doctors and scientists over the need for input from patients or citizens.

Public health has shifted, however, driven both by scholarly research and by the new capacities and expectations of citizens. The field has moved toward ways of working that provide meaningful participation opportunities for patients and citizens—opportunities that encourage the elements of an "adult-adult" relationship. This is particularly evident in the five main areas in which participation in health has developed: messaging and healthy behavior, the "healthy communities" movement, mapping inequities in health, engaging citizens in health policy making, and patient engagement and patient-centered care.

Messaging and Healthy Behavior

The notion that expertise and professionalization could improve public health was a hallmark of the Progressive movement in the early 20th Century. Progressive journalists like Upton Sinclair, Lincoln Steffens, and Jacob Riis deplored the health conditions they observed in workplaces, neighborhoods, and schools. Reformers presented science and administration as the most powerful answers to these public dilemmas (Rubio-Cortés & McGrath, 2014).

Starting in the second half of the century, researchers began to uncover a much broader picture of the factors affecting public health. "As scientific studies during the 1950s and 1960s began to uncover startling connections between behaviors—tobacco smoking and diet—and dramatic increases in leading chronic killers—heart disease, stroke, and cancer—the need for communitywide action and grassroots leadership in public health became impossible to ignore" (McGinnis & Robinson, 2014: 10). A number of public officials and other leaders began to assert that "community wellness" was not just a smarter approach to health, but a "social obligation" (McGinnis & Robinson, 2014). The Surgeon General's 1979 "Healthy People" report underscored the "feasibility and necessity of community action." This shift in analysis emphasized the importance of environment, networks, and civic infrastructure. In addition to providing information, it also led to a greater appreciation of citizens' personal experiences and ability to take action—setting the stage for an adult-adult approach to participation.

At first, the emerging evidence about social determinants led health care professionals to use one-way messages intended to persuade people to change their behavior. These kinds of messages, about the dangers of smoking, obesity, drunk driving, substance abuse, reckless sexual behavior, and other threats to public health, are still common today. They have been joined by one-way messages about the importance to health of family and friendship networks. For example, a major communications campaign of the Substance Abuse and Mental Health Services Agency reminds us "What a Difference a Friend Makes." The public health campaign of the California Endowment uses the slogan "Health Happens Here," underneath pictures of a father and daughter hugging and young cyclists on a bike path (Standish & Ross, 2014).

The "Healthy Communities" Movement

Starting in the late 1980s and early 1990s, a variety of organizations and thinkers came together to achieve what they called "healthy communities." More explicitly than ever, advocates argued that health was determined by a wide array of community factors and could be improved by communities working together (Pittman, 2014). Above all, they felt, those determinants could be affected by how people related to their fellow community members and the places where they lived. "To create and sustain health, people need, and are naturally wired to thrive in, places where there is an authentic sense of community and connection to place" (Roulier, 2014: 8).

At various points, the healthy communities movement has received key support from the federal government. A 1988 collaboration between the U.S. Public Health Service and the National Civic League helped broaden the work beyond partnerships between hospitals and local governments (Sirianni & Friedland,

2001). From 2001 through 2005, the Healthy Communities Access Program of the Department of Health and Human Services provided assistance to communities and health care providers to develop integrated health care delivery systems and coordinated services for individuals who were uninsured or underinsured. This program spawned 193 healthy community coalitions that provided access to care for over 500,000 uninsured individuals (Crump, 2014: 64).

The organizations championing healthy communities believed that public participation was a key to affecting this wide array of social conditions. Gloria Rubio-Cortés and Mike McGrath (2014: 16) of the National Civic League assert "From the beginning, the term 'healthy communities' carried a double meaning. It referred to community health in the primary definition of physical and mental well-being, freedom from disease, and the like, but also suggested a broader set of values and principles related to the way communities make decisions and address challenges." Broad, diverse leadership has repeatedly been identified as a top success factor in these projects. In addition, research shows that "residents must be engaged from the outset. They have invaluable insights for every phase of the work" (Twiss, Kleinman, & Hafey, 2014: 22).

How have these initiatives engaged residents? The most common participation vehicle has been comprehensive local health planning. Many healthy community initiatives began their work by organizing participatory processes in which large, diverse numbers of people examined different health challenges, decided which issues to tackle, and produced a plan for allocating community resources according to health needs. "Working with a shared vision as a starting point has been a staple practice for most healthy community efforts," reports Monte Roulier (2014: 4), citing examples in Scranton, Pennsylvania, Greenville, South Carolina, and Omaha, Nebraska. Some of these planning efforts centered on issues that contribute to health; for example, a healthy community initiative in Colorado's Roaring Fork Valley led to the creation of a regional transit authority and a heavily used bus system (Larson, Christian, Olson, Hicks, & Sweeney, 2002).

Communities have used a number of other participation vehicles to inform and extend the work done in face-to-face planning sessions. In developing a health plan for Polk County, Iowa:

> Five town hall meetings were convened throughout the community for public input. Using a community dialogue process, over 650 county residents shared what they thought were the most pressing

concerns. This level of engagement was deepened even further for the Healthy Polk 2020 plan. Through participation in an online survey, responding to a telephone interview, or attending a community conversation, over 2,300 people identified potential community priorities. After this list was narrowed to "measurable" priorities, 150 Polk County residents convened on a midwinter Saturday morning for a traditional Iowa-style community caucus to choose the final ten priorities that serve as our current agenda. (Miles-Polka, Frantsvog, & Kozin, 2014: 22)

In some communities, there have been successive cycles of healthy community visioning, carried out over many years. In others, the initial plan either languished or continued as a bundle of loosely connected health initiatives that no longer engaged citizens in planning or policymaking. The most common ongoing format for participation in decision making is a resident advisory board or committee that provides input to the institutional partners in the healthy community coalition. But regardless of whether they continue to involve large numbers of citizens in making policy choices, nearly all of these projects provide information and opportunities for people to talk about their personal experiences and empower people to take action on their own health, as well as on community health priorities.

The data on the results of healthy communities are in many cases dramatic. In twenty years of work in Polk County, for example, there have been decreases in infant mortality, teen smoking and drinking, and exposure to lead and increases in dental health, breastfeeding, and the percentage of people with health insurance (Miles-Polka, Frantsvog, & Kozin, 2014). Other communities have documented and quantified decreases in obesity (Cheadle, Rauzon, & Schwartz, 2014), violence (Davis, 2014), and chronic diseases and conditions (Mikkelsen, Cohen, & Frankowski, 2014). A summary of the outcomes of the California Healthy Cities and Communities program points to:

> Increased fruit and vegetable consumption, decreases in prevalence of adult and youth obesity, improved academic scores as a result of intergenerational tutoring, development of quality-of-life indices that guided policy development and resource allocation, and incorporation of health elements into general plans. Health-promoting public policies, from tobacco control to healthier food access, have passed in hundreds of jurisdictions. Innumerable physical improvements—for

example, community gardens, improved walkways, and bike lanes—
have made communities safer and more livable for residents across
the life span. (Twiss, Kleinman, & Hafey 2014: 21)

Mapping Inequities in Health

The healthy communities movement continues to emphasize data and find new
ways of using it—and inequality is always apparent in that data. The fact that there
are health disparities between different groups of people, correlated with income,
race, ethnicity, and other factors, has been a driving force in public health for a
century. On many indicators, the health of people of color in the United States is
comparable to that of the populations of developing nations (Galloway-Gilliam,
2014; Manchanda, 2013). Practices like Community-Based Participatory Research
(CBPR) emerged during the 1990s to track and counteract these disparities.

In the last decade, researchers and health advocates have used Geographic
Information Systems (GIS) and other online tools to map health outcomes and
show how inequities play out in communities. "Increasingly, research is confirm-
ing what many of us intrinsically understood: that your zip code is a powerful
predictor of how healthy you are and how long you are likely to live. In fact,
there may be as much as fifteen to twenty-five years' difference in life expectancy
between neighborhoods in the same city" (Standish & Ross, 2014: 31). Reflecting on his work at a clinic in South Central Los Angeles, Dr. Rishi Manchanda
explains the dilemma: "Patients with chronic conditions like diabetes and high
blood pressure can't take my advice to exercise, because they don't have a park or
feel unsafe going to the park. They can't take my advice to eat healthier, because
they lack access to healthy food stores. They can't live a healthy life despite my
best recommendations" (http://activecitizen.tufts.edu/blog/2008/12/01/citizen-
doctor-helps-patients-find-their-civic-voice/).

This concern about inequalities in health has impacted how healthy community initiatives conduct participation. Demographic diversity is a high priority in
recruiting for coalitions, steering committees, advisory groups, and other bodies.
There is also a habit of "ongoing introspection" about how initiatives are functioning, including a sensitivity to cultural differences and a concentration on "who's
benefiting or being adversely impacted" (Twiss, Kleinman, & Hafey, 2014: 23).

Most recently, the concern over inequalities and the development of technology
have turned mapping from an expert-driven exercise to one that is more participatory and planning-oriented. For example, the Quad Cities collaborative in Illinois and

Iowa has worked on the problem of "food deserts," areas where it is difficult to find fresh, affordable fruits and vegetables. They used a web-based mapping utility to:

> combine and correlate locally collected data (from grocery stores and food pantries) with other relevant publicly available data on a broad range of focal areas, such as schools, poverty, and the retail food environment. The result is a web-based map that allows the entire community to identify neighborhoods and areas in greatest need of healthy and affordable food outlets. (Roulier, 2014: 5)

Even more than in other areas of health participation, the work to address inequities is driven by increased access to data, the ability of citizens to contribute to that data, and technological changes that help people visualize and track efforts and activities.

Engaging Citizens in Health Policymaking

Some attempts to conduct public participation on questions of health policy were motivated by the division and controversy regarding health care reform. The most well-known example—and one that has done tremendous damage to the field of public participation in the United States—is the series of "town hall meetings" held by Members of Congress in the summer of 2009. Other public participation initiatives on health care reform, such as America*Speaks*' 2007 "California Speaks" project (see Chapter 7) and 2005 "Tough Choices in Healthcare" project in Maine, were more civil and productive and even led to some policy and service changes (Lukensmeyer, 2013).

Beyond reform, some participation initiatives have focused on specific aspects of health policy. Two large-scale public participation efforts, both conducted by federal agencies, stand out. Both combine some of the local, holistic concerns of the healthy communities movement with opportunities to influence federal policymaking. They also embodied several aspects of an adult-adult relationship, including providing people with information, a chance to tell stories, policy choices, and a sense of political legitimacy.

First, the Centers for Disease Control and Prevention, which arguably has the best participation track record of any federal agency, has organized a number of ambitious projects, including the Public Engagement Pilot Project on Pandemic Influenza (PEPPPI) in 2005 (Liburd, Giles, & Jack, 2014). PEPPPI engaged citizens, academics, non-governmental organizations, health care providers, industry representatives, and local, state, and federal governmental officials in deliberations about how to allocate flu vaccines in the event of a major pandemic. The question had both ethical and technical components: in the early days of an outbreak, when there are always limited vaccine supplies, who should be immunized? The purpose of the PEPPPI project was twofold: (1) to evaluate a new mechanism for engaging the public on vaccine policy decisions and (2) to better inform a pending government decision by providing a ranked list of immunization goals (Bernier, 2014).

Second, the Substance Abuse and Mental Health Services Administration (SAMHSA) played a key role in the National Dialogue on Mental Health, launched by President Obama in June 2013, which includes a wide range of public participation opportunities under the banner of "Creating Community Solutions" (CCS). The goal of CCS was to help local leaders all over the country engage residents in deliberation and problem solving in mental health. As of March 2015, more than 10,000 people in more than 200 communities had taken part in these discussions. In six targeted metropolitan areas, coalitions led by local officials convened large-scale processes to develop action plans for strengthening mental health. In each of these sites, local foundations and other sources contributed up to $200,000 for implementation. Decisions made by local and state mental health agencies, nonprofits, and SAMHSA were influenced by these local, citizen-driven CCS plans. CCS also featured a new format for participation, "Text, Talk, and Act," a nationwide, text-enabled, face-to-face discussion on mental health (see Box 7.5 in Chapter 7).

Patient Engagement and Patient-Centered Care

A final area of public participation in health looks not to large-scale engagement for community and policy changes, but rather to individual-level engagement for improved health outcomes. Over the last several years, two major trends have emerged in this realm: patient engagement and patient-centered care, both of which call for increased participation of individual patients in health care decisions. As Dr. Charles Safran noted in his 2004 testimony before the House Ways and Means Committee: "Patients are the most underutilized resource" in American health care. "Patients want to be involved, and they can be involved" (http:// waysandmeans.house.gov/media/transcript/9897.html).

The desire to engage people in their own health care is prompted, at least in part, by technological advances (CAH, 2014). The growing use of out-patient surgeries and the continually expanding array of medications, particularly for chronic conditions, require patients and families to manage increasingly complex treatment programs. In turn, this growing complexity has led to changes in how health care professionals think about the role of patients. Whereas health care providers used to expect "compliance" from people, they now increasingly expect "engagement" (Oldenburg, 2014).

Conceptually, the need to engage patients in health mirrors the desire to engage families in student learning (see Chapter 4). In both cases, the system has acknowledged the capacity of non-professionals and is struggling to activate and accommodate them. This new thinking even challenges the term "patient." As one physician put it, "Few or no people I have met define or refer to themselves as patients. They understand that a patient is less than a whole person, is less than what they are. I would prefer thinking of 'people' engaged in their health and health care" (CAH, 2014: 10). These attempts to break free of the "language of passivity" and "reimagine the patient relationship" (Oldenburg, 2014) are part of the shift to an adult-adult relationship in participation. In successful patient engagement and patient-centered care, this means providing information and the opportunity to tell stories, make choices, and take action.

Although it is not always clearly defined, patient engagement is generally considered to be a package of "actions individuals must take to obtain the greatest benefit from the health care services available to them" (CAH, 2010: 7). These include finding and organizing health care, communicating with health care professionals, making treatment decisions, participating in treatment, obtaining preventive care, and planning for the end of life. New technologies, such as remote monitoring of blood pressure, apps for tracking asthma and for cardiac rehabilitation, and "patient portals" that allow people to communicate with their health care providers, are stretching the boundaries of patient engagement (Sharp & Tritle, 2014).

The related concept of "patient-centered care" could be considered a step beyond patient engagement. At first, the idea was simply that doctors should treat patients as more than a "bundle of symptoms." But the concept has evolved and expanded so that patient-centeredness "is defined 'through the patient's eyes' and in a broader societal context" (Millenson, 2012: 7). Today, patient-centeredness means that people have the right to "care that incorporates the values of transparency, individualization, recognition, respect, dignity and choice in all matters"—language that has been written into the Medicare regulations of the Affordable Care Act (Millenson, 2012: 8). This increases patients' economic power (because the costs of care are transparent) and ability to make informed decisions (because they have evidence about the tradeoffs of different treatment options). In short, patients are not simply engaged in their care, they have autonomy over it.

One of the main ways hospitals and other health institutions have implemented patient-centered care is by recruiting people to serve as "Patient-Family Advisors." These volunteer roles are occupied by people who are not health professionals, but who interact with practitioners and patients, and can influence decision making at many levels within the institution (HPOE, 2013). Advocates of patient-centered practices point to research showing that they lead to lower costs and better results on a wide range of health problems, from diabetes and cancer to avoidable treatment errors and emergency room delays (Nicolato, 2013).

There are many conceptual links among messaging and healthy behaviors, the healthy communities movement, concerns over health disparities and inequities, citizen involvement in health policymaking, and the move toward patient engagement and patient-centered care. But despite inspired efforts to engage citizens, we still lack a coherent, comprehensive infrastructure for public participation in health. The field, however, may be moving in that direction. In their interviews with stakeholders, the Center for Advancing Health (CAH, 2014: 9) found that people "spoke of multiple levels of engagement," including the individual level (e.g., "what people do day in and day out"), interpersonal level (e.g., "how individuals interact with their clinicians"), and institutional level (e.g., how "people are involved in improving health care").

Table 5.1 summarizes how these different impulses toward public participation in health have encouraged aspects of an adult-adult relationship between the individual and the institution. Because health is such a personal issue, it makes sense that giving people opportunities to tell their stories is a core component of all participation efforts. Because health is also a technical issue, it stands to reason that providing information is essential. Health participation efforts vary more in the other aspects of an adult-adult relationship, for example, whether they provide people with choices, offer a sense of political legitimacy, and support people to take action.

In the next sections, we take stock of the official settings and networks for participation in health and offer some questions to help readers assess the state of health participation in their communities.

Table 5.1
How Aspects of the Adult-Adult Relationship Emerged in Response to Common Health Issues

Common Education Issues	Characteristics of Treating People Like Adults				
	Provide Information	Give People a Chance to Tell Stories	Provide Choices	Give Sense of Political Legitimacy	Support People to Take Action
Messaging and Encouraging Healthy Behaviors	X	X			X
Healthy Communities Initiatives	X	X			X
Mapping Health Inequities	X	X			
Health Policy Making	X	X	X	X	
Patient Engagement and Patient-Centered Care	X	X	X		X

OFFICIAL SETTINGS FOR PARTICIPATION IN HEALTH

For the average citizen who wants to participate in decision making and problem solving on issues of health, it is often hard to know where to go. There is not a familiar pattern of official public meetings like the ones held by school boards, planning and zoning commissions, and city councils. Because the key institutions span the public, private, and nonprofit sectors, it is often unclear which organization is responsible for which issues or aspects of personal and public health. And while people interested in planning issues might attend a neighborhood association meeting and concerned parents might reach out to their school's Parent-Teacher Association, there are no obvious corollaries for these groups in the health domain. There are, however, examples in other countries, such as Local Health Information Networks in Ontario and local health councils in Brazil (Schattan Coehlo, Cornwell, & Shankland, 2012).

Meanwhile, health care professionals who are advocates of patient engagement and patient-centered care often feel like their institutions are still not hospitable to those concepts. "The health care system doesn't make patient engagement easy," laments a Center for Advancing Health report (CAH, 2014: 12). However, with the advent of the Affordable Care Act, colloquially known as "Obamacare," there are new openings for embedding participation in health systems.

While not always obvious, official settings for participation in health can be found at the community, hospital/clinic, and patient/citizen levels, and include things such as Accountable Care Organizations, Patient Engagement Committees, and apps and other online tools (see Figure 5.1).

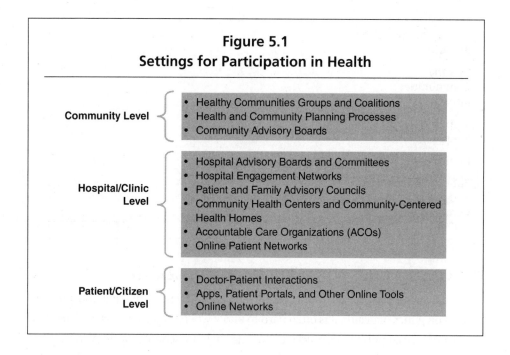

Figure 5.1
Settings for Participation in Health

Community Level
- Healthy Communities Groups and Coalitions
- Health and Community Planning Processes
- Community Advisory Boards

Hospital/Clinic Level
- Hospital Advisory Boards and Committees
- Hospital Engagement Networks
- Patient and Family Advisory Councils
- Community Health Centers and Community-Centered Health Homes
- Accountable Care Organizations (ACOs)
- Online Patient Networks

Patient/Citizen Level
- Doctor-Patient Interactions
- Apps, Patient Portals, and Other Online Tools
- Online Networks

Community Level

Opportunities for participation in health do not always exist at the community level, although this may be slowly changing. In places that have healthy community initiatives, meetings and planning processes sometimes occur. Similarly, some communities develop plans that include health as a priority issue. Sometimes, these planning processes are either open to the public or have a public participation component.

Perhaps the most common ongoing opportunities for public participation in health at the community level are advisory boards, which are sometimes incorporated in healthy community initiatives or other public health projects. Partly due to concerns about equity and health disparities, these are usually highly representative bodies, with members from a variety of backgrounds. However, these committees generally have the same small "r" republican characteristics as advisory boards on other issues: they may bring people representing the most commonly held interests and concerns to the policymaking table, but do not directly engage large numbers of citizens.

Hospital/Clinic Level

Many health care organizations, from hospitals to health centers, have advisory boards and committees that allow for patient and family engagement. In some cases, these boards and committees are connected to Hospital Engagement Networks (HENs), whereas in others, they stand alone. There is great breadth in the functions of such boards, committees, and HENs. Among their many purposes are to engage patients and families in: policy and program development, implementation, and evaluation; health care facility design; professional education; ethics issues; the selection of potential employees; safety and quality improvement; and the delivery of care (HAP, 2013).

Many hospitals have discovered that patient and family advisory councils can help the organization improve the design and delivery of care and services (HAP, 2013). This has been especially true for community health centers, organizations that provide community-oriented primary care, particularly in low-income areas. As of 2013, they served more than twenty-two million people in over 9,000 locations (Fukuzawa, 2013). Community health centers are successful, in part because they generate "greater connectivity and social capital," when they involve "community members as authentic partners" (Fukuzawa, 2013: 59). A few communities have taken this notion a step further by creating "Community-Centered Health Homes" (CCHHs) that work to translate "high-priority medical conditions into active involvement in community advocacy and change" (Mikkelsen, Cohen, & Frankowski, 2014: 57).

Accountable Care Organizations (ACOs), established by the Affordable Care Act, also provide an avenue for participation in health. As organizations and health care providers, ACOs agree to be accountable for the quality, cost, and overall care of patients, by coordinating services and addressing many different aspects of health, including population health management and an emphasis on prevention (American Academy of Pediatrics, 2011; Fukuzawa, 2013). As of June

2014, there were 626 ACOs across the United States. Of these, 329 had government contracts, 210 had commercial contracts, and seventy-four had both government and commercial contracts (Petersen, Gardner, Tu, & Muhlestein, 2014).

Participation is built into the mission of ACOs. Medicare's ACO requirements direct these organizations to implement patient-centered care in numerous ways:

> The *governance-level requirements* require the ACO's governing body to promote patient-centered care; the patient's voice in the boardroom can shape how care is delivered in the exam room. *Quality improvement activities* address the actual care provided. This includes ensuring that evidence-based medicine has a patient-centric focus, producing internal quality and cost reports related to patient-centered care and using data to manage population health. Requirements related to *individual level patient-clinician interactions* include promoting the active participation of patients and their families in medical decision making, taking into account factors such as race, gender, sexual orientation, disability and income status. (Millenson, 2012: 2)

It remains to be seen how ACOs will operate. Some critics are concerned that they will continue the pattern of emphasizing treatment over prevention, while others doubt the impact they will have on the landscape for public participation (Manchanda, 2013). Nevertheless, ACOs do seem to have some of the legal and structural elements necessary to become official settings for public participation in health.

Finally, at both the hospital/clinic level and the patient/citizen level, online networks are being used to facilitate communication about health and health care. Some of these networks are small, focusing on a particular health facility; others are much larger, with members from all over the world, centering on a particular disease or condition.

Patient/Citizen Level

By far the most common setting for participation in health—and the one almost never treated as such—is the direct interaction between patients and health care professionals. Traditionally, these health care professionals included doctors and nurses, but today, many other caregivers may be instrumental, from nutritionists, social workers, and physical therapists to the "patient-family advisors" now deployed by many ACOs (Millenson, 2012). The level of trust, transparency, and informed decision making in these relationships seems to have a significant impact on health outcomes.

This communication between health care professionals and patients is also extending beyond the traditional office appointment. A wide variety of apps, patient portals, and other online tools are being used to record patient histories, track vital signs, and monitor conditions so that information is readily available as part of an exchange that can happen "asynchronously"—whenever is convenient for the patient and the doctor—rather than in real time. As noted above, online networks are increasingly being used to connect people to health care facilities and professionals, as well as to others that share a particular disease or condition.

In sum, the variety of official settings for participation in health is growing at the community, hospital/clinic, and patient/citizen levels. Within these official settings are a wide array of potential participation leaders—from doctors, nurses, and other health care professionals to patients, families, and advocates. Participation in these official settings is often a new development. Continuing to develop this infrastructure will be critical to giving both citizens and health officials what they want and need. In the next section, we explore ways to further activate and empower people as leaders for participation in health.

STRENGTHENING THE INFRASTRUCTURE: LEADERS AND NETWORKS FOR PARTICIPATION IN HEALTH

Strengthening the infrastructure for participation in health requires paying attention to the people—to the potential leaders of participation. These participation leaders need not be limited to health care providers and consumers. Many different networks and constituencies have a vested interest in health, and many communities have a strong track record in helping different groups work together. But while there are partnerships among people inside and outside health institutions, the inside-the-institution thinking about the role of patients does not seem well connected to the outward view of creating healthy communities. A second challenge is sustaining strong relationships among local networks and the state- and federal-level agencies and foundations that are trying to support them.

Because health behaviors "are shaped by the environments in which people live, work, learn, and play" (Krieger, 2014: 31), the healthy communities movement has, from the start, tapped into many different networks and constituencies. These initiatives require a "multisectoral approach . . . to accomplish change on this scale" (Ridini, Sprong, & Foley, 2014: 35). Such approaches have encompassed the traditional health care institutions, including hospitals,

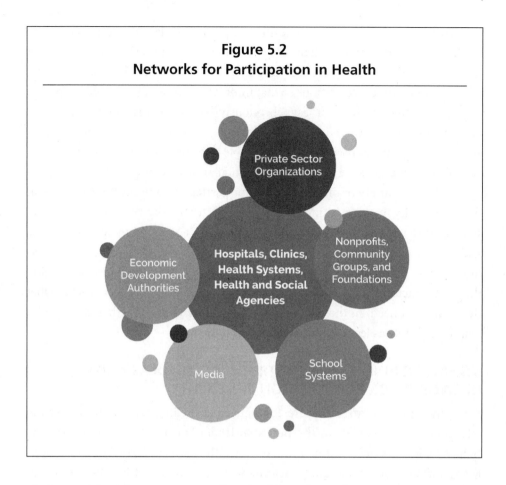

Figure 5.2
Networks for Participation in Health

clinics, and health systems, as well as health and social service agencies. They have also, as shown in Figure 5.2, included non-health-specific organizations such as community-based nonprofit organizations, neighborhood and faith-based groups, foundations, and private philanthropy; school systems; economic development authorities and chambers of commerce; and media. Private sector organizations have also been partners in community health initiatives (Norris, 2014), including grocery stores, restaurants, hotels, and insurance companies (Soler, 2014).

State health departments have played a catalytic role in bringing these networks together. State-level foundations and other philanthropic organizations have also been very active. But the relationship between local networks and statewide sponsoring organizations can be difficult to navigate. Lisa Hershey (2014: 30) reports that in California's Convergence Initiative:

Roots are planted deeply in community, in the people on the ground, and in history and experience of the multisector, multifaceted strategies and social movements that came before. One strength is that policies grown from the ground up have a better chance of creating communities where everyone can participate and prosper. A challenge is that community issues and funder priorities do not always align; relationships are built on trust and history, and when investments shift prematurely from the community perspective, trust is broken.

Because of the holistic nature of their goals and the coalition-building pattern they have already established, the people trying to expand public participation in health are well-positioned to do more and better multisectoral work. Thus, activating and empowering the participation leaders embedded in these and other networks will be critical to the development of health participation. Box 5.1 provides a set of questions that can be used to help assess the relationships among these networks, as well as the state of participation, in a community.

The final sections of this chapter explore more concrete actions that officials and participation leaders can take to strengthen the participation infrastructure in health.

STRENGTHENING THE INFRASTRUCTURE: BUILDING BLOCKS FOR PARTICIPATION IN HEALTH

For the last two decades, public participation in health issues has been driven by data and by local leaders and health practitioners determined to act on that data. In the healthy communities movement, this "boundary-crossing civic leadership" has produced "complementary benefits for collective impact" (Norris, 2014: 7–8). In the push for patient engagement and patient-centered care, health care professionals have produced sophisticated arrangements to better facilitate participation with patients (Nicolato, 2013). However, in most places, participation in health continues to be carried out by fragile coalitions and through isolated practices, often working against the current of health institutions and professions.

Tyler Norris (2014: 8) warns that the power of data to inspire participation has its limits, and works best "when applied in locales with enough civic infrastructure (collaborative skills, effective decision-making processes, and trust relationships) to drive informed action." Steve Ridini and his colleagues (2014: 35) agree

Box 5.1. Assessing the State of Health Participation in a Community

Any attempt to overhaul public participation in health should begin with some basic research on the current opportunities for engagement, both inside and outside health care systems, and the other contextual factors that may be critical to the relationships among patients, doctors, and administrators. Here are some questions to consider:

1. What kinds of participation opportunities are available within the traditional health institutions, such as hospitals, clinics, health systems, and health and social service agencies?

2. Is there a "healthy community" initiative in the area?

3. Do the people working on participation efforts reflect and represent the full diversity of the people affected?

4. Is there an accountable care organization (ACO) or a community health center in the area?

5. Are there segments of the community that historically have been ignored or excluded when it comes to health issues?

6. In what ways are recent immigrants connected, or disconnected, when it comes to health issues?

7. What are some of the key networks and constituencies when it comes to health issues in the community?

8. Is local health data available online, and how effectively does it complement and inform public participation?

9. How much are health organizations spending—in money and/or in staff time—on public participation annually?

10. How are participation activities and initiatives evaluated and assessed?

11. What are the legal mandates and restrictions on public participation?

12. Do health professionals have the skills, cultural awareness, and organizational support to work productively with citizens?

that thinking more carefully about this infrastructure—including the diffusion of principles and skills and the sustainability of systems and coalitions—is the next step for the healthy communities movement. And some of the pioneers of patient engagement have sounded similar themes about the need to recast "systems," "processes," and "procedures" to support partnerships among patients, caregivers, and the community (Oldenburg, 2014).

What would such an infrastructure for health participation look like? This section, summarized in Figure 5.3, paints that picture by returning to the six overarching building blocks of participation activities: disseminating information, gathering input and data, discussing and connecting, enabling patient and family decision making, enabling community decision making, and encouraging public work. For each building block, we identify a list of relevant settings and participation tools or vehicles that can be used. As with education (Chapter 4) and land use (Chapter 6), some of the settings and tools for these broad categories

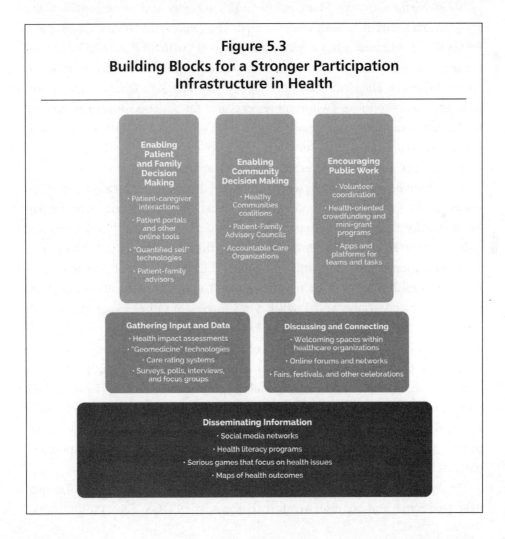

Figure 5.3
Building Blocks for a Stronger Participation Infrastructure in Health

Enabling Patient and Family Decision Making
· Patient-caregiver interactions
· Patient portals and other online tools
· "Quantified self" technologies
· Patient-family advisors

Enabling Community Decision Making
· Healthy Communities coalitions
· Patient-Family Advisory Councils
· Accountable Care Organizations

Encouraging Public Work
· Volunteer coordination
· Health-oriented crowdfunding and mini-grant programs
· Apps and platforms for teams and tasks

Gathering Input and Data
· Health impact assessments
· "Geomedicine" technologies
· Care rating systems
· Surveys, polls, interviews, and focus groups

Discussing and Connecting
· Welcoming spaces within healthcare organizations
· Online forums and networks
· Fairs, festivals, and other celebrations

Disseminating Information
· Social media networks
· Health literacy programs
· Serious games that focus on health issues
· Maps of health outcomes

of participation activities already exist and simply need to be improved, whereas others need to be developed.

Disseminating Information About Health

Fifty years ago, the primary concern of health officials was to adequately inform people about the dangers posed by smoking, drinking, obesity, and other health risks. Now, the sheer volume of information available about public health is staggering, and the greater challenge may be to ensure that people understand the context and personal relevance of information they receive. A number of participation vehicles can be used to help people access and absorb health data.

Social media networks. Many public health agencies and some providers use social media to circulate health information. The Centers for Disease Control and Prevention, for example, has a network of 420,000 Twitter followers (Oza, 2014). Some health organizations use tweets and updates to generate discussion with and among followers. The Healthcare Hashtag project (www.symplur.com/healthcare-hashtags/) seeks to make Twitter more accessible for patients, providers, and the health care community as a whole; from the website, one can learn where health conversations are taking place, discover who to follow within a particular specialty or disease area, and see what health care topics are trending in real time.

Health literacy programs. Research indicates that health information is often presented in ways that are not usable by most Americans and that the gap between information and understanding is linked to poor health outcomes and rising costs (HHS, 2010). Attempts to address the challenge focus both on how the information is presented and on people's ability to absorb it. In some communities, health literacy is being incorporated into adult education offerings, public library programs, and English for Speakers of Other Languages classes (HHS, 2010). For example, the Adult Learning Center, the New York City Office of the Mayor, the Harvard School of Public Health, the Literacy Assistance Center, and the Harlem Hospital Center piloted a health literacy study circle that infuses health literacy skills into an adult education curriculum. Through their participation, many adult students acquired health insurance and became more knowledgeable about specific health issues and services. At the same time, health professionals became more culturally and linguistically attuned to the needs of patients (HHS, 2010).

Serious games that focus on health issues. A number of health organizations have used games and exercises to inform citizens. The CDC's "Solve the Outbreak" app-based game and "Zombie Pandemic" comic book series help people start thinking about disease prevention and emergency preparedness (Parcell, 2013). In "The Last Straw!," a game developed by professors at the University of Toronto, players navigate the impacts of the social determinants of health (Coulson, 2014). These kinds of games can spread understanding of health issues, sometimes on a large scale.

Maps of health outcomes. Geographically representing health assets and challenges allows people to understand variations in health issues among different areas and segments of the population. The Quad Cities "food deserts" map is one example (www.arcgis.com/home/item.html?id=100f5f2a8403490e976669765f08f666). In Cincinnati, a map of child asthma attacks showed a strong correlation with building code violations, allowing a hospital and the legal aid society to pressure landlords to improve housing conditions and ensure that asthma triggers were addressed (Mikkelsen, Cohen, & Frankowski, 2014: 58).

Of course, just receiving information about health does not mean people will automatically adopt healthy behaviors or work to overcome community health challenges. Whether people move from information to action is frequently dependent on relationships—with family members, neighbors, health care providers, and other community members. Of the vehicles described above, social media networks may be the best for building and maintaining those relationships, but some of the participation activities described below hold greater potential.

Gathering Input and Data

Just as there are numerous new opportunities for people to receive data, there are also numerous ways for them to generate it. This input can be valuable for large-scale community planning and for individual decisions made by caregivers and citizens. Many tools for this work exist.

Health impact assessments. Pioneered by Rajiv Bhatia of the San Francisco Department of Public Health, health impact assessments are now widely used to gauge policy decisions in all kinds of issue areas, such as housing, transportation, and land use (Roudman, 2014). The process gathers and uses data to determine how a decision will affect various populations broken down by demographic groups. Health impact assessments move through a sequence of phases, each of which provides opportunities for participation, including screening, scoping, assessing health effects, recommending mitigations and alternatives, reporting and communication, and monitoring (Bhatia, 2011).

"Geomedicine" technologies. Geographic information system (GIS) technologies are now ubiquitous in smartphones, laptops, and other electronic devices. When applied to health issues, the use of GIS to collect data is sometimes called "geomedicine" (Davenhall, 2012). "Geomedicine has the potential to reveal patterns of social and environmental health risks within neighborhoods," says Rishi Manchanda (2013). "For instance, I've seen a clinic use geomedicine to determine that patients with poorly controlled diabetes lived in more remote, hard-to-reach areas compared with those with well-controlled diabetes. Now the clinic proactively allocates more outreach and support services to patients in remote areas." For an example of how geomedicine technologies are being used to fight asthma, see Box 5.2.

Care rating systems. Giving patients more opportunities to rate their care, from overall standards to individual visits, not only enables them to clarify their expectations, but also provides more information to caregivers and consumers. "Federal and state governments and private insurers are also starting to use newer performance measures that encourage clinics to become patient-centered medical

---

Box 5.2. Case Study
Asthmapolis—Geomedicine in Action

Louisville, Kentucky, has a large population of individuals with breathing disorders such as asthma and COPD. To combat the problem, the city partnered with Propeller Health in 2012 to launch a demonstration project called "Asthmapolis." The overarching goals of the project were to identify patients who need more help controlling their disease and identify community-wide asthma triggers that can be improved or eliminated.

As part of the program, 500 asthmatic residents were provided with "smart inhalers." When residents used the inhalers, sensors sent information on their place and the time to the patient's physician and city officials, who then used the data to generate "heat maps" of emergency asthma attacks.

With the help of data analysts at IBM, public health officials compared the trends against a variety of potential causes—including air quality, pollen outbreaks, and traffic congestion—to strategize interventions in the most at-risk areas. The project has since expanded into other geomedicine areas. For example, the city plans to deploy bike-mounted sensors to monitor air quality along routes frequented by children during the summer.

Link

http://propellerhealth.com/

---

homes, rating providers on how well they provide continuity and coordinate patient care" (Manchanda, 2013). Using input from rating systems may prompt lower-performing organizations to improve.

Surveys, polls, interviews, and focus groups. Surveys, polls, and focus groups can help communities and health care providers gain a better sense of what is needed and desired in terms of health. Surveys and polls can be used to help understand the health obstacles faced by community residents. Interviews can be used to gather input and data from patients and families who are affected by health-related issues or by a particular disease. Focus groups can be used to convene people affected by an issue or to generate new ideas about tackling a particular problem.

Discussing and Connecting

The relationships people build in social settings can be helpful—and are often essential—to the participation activities described in this section. Relationships help people absorb information, make decisions, mobilize around important issues and policies, and take action. Their effect on positive health outcomes is so clear in the research that some public health agencies promote the building of peer networks (for example, the "what a difference a friend makes" campaign of the Substance Abuse and Mental Health Administration) without explicitly connecting those relationships to input-gathering, policymaking, or public work. These connections may be particularly valuable when it comes to health topics that people are reluctant to talk about in more public arenas. "Problems of substance abuse, depression, and stress-related conditions, coping with dementia, and health disparities among population groups cannot be reversed by keeping them behind the closed doors of the afflicted," argue McGinnis and Robinson (2014: 12).

Social connections are also critical when it comes to improving health outcomes for very young children. Parents benefit from regular, convenient opportunities to compare notes and gain knowledge on child health, from prenatal care and immunizations to chemical exposures and recognizing danger signs. The weekly events organized as part of the "First 5 LA" health and education initiative (discussed in Chapter 4) help people learn, decide, influence, and act. These social occasions also reduce stigma and feelings of isolation, increase health interactions, and cultivate reciprocal, supportive relationships (First 5 LA, 2010).

The importance of discussing and connecting can also be demonstrated at a biological level. The experience of face-to-face conversation has positive impacts on brain chemistry (Lewis, Amini, & Lannon, 2000). Our bodies are wired for the most immediate, interpersonal forms of participation, and exercising those faculties can make us healthier. Within the health arena, there are several specific examples of building this kind of interaction into broader participation strategies:

Welcoming spaces within health care organizations. Some health care organizations have spaces—auditoriums, boardrooms, and waiting rooms—that could be used as welcoming spaces where people can come together to discuss and connect on health issues. All of these spaces have seating, and many have wi-fi access; they need only be opened and transformed to serve as physical hubs for community discussion and connection.

Online forums and networks. Some hospitals, clinics, substance abuse networks, and other groups encourage online forums and networks that connect people who have similar conditions or concerns. For example, the PatientsLikeMe online social community has over 200,000 members (Sarasohn-Kahn, 2014). These (often global) peer-to-peer health care networks provide ways to "tap into our instincts to gather together, help other people, and be helped ourselves" (Fox, 2011: 4).

Fairs, festivals, and other celebrations. A staple of the healthy communities movement, fairs, festivals, and other celebrations can build connections and inform people about conditions, services, and opportunities to become involved. There are, of course, many other existing settings where people spend time discussing and connecting. Most of these opportunities are not explicitly related to health (or education, or land use, or any other public issue). In these cases, the question is how to introduce health topics, information, and policy questions in ways that are enjoyable, educational, and empowering.

Enabling Patient and Family Decision Making

Being able to make decisions about health is the central element of patient engagement. This goes beyond the choices about care offered by doctors and other health practitioners; it also means having the confidence and motivation to make small but significant day-to-day decisions about diet, exercise, medications, and risky behaviors. This broader autonomy over health could be considered the difference between passive patients and active citizens. Once again, many settings exist to enable patient and family decision making; however, the interactions within these settings often need to be improved or "democratized."

Patient-caregiver interactions. The concepts of patient engagement and patient-centered care suggest, and in some cases produce, fundamental changes in how people interact with health care professionals. Some providers give patients more opportunities to articulate their "values and convictions" at the beginning of the relationship; others use surveys to track how patients feel about their care; some deploy registered nurses as "health coaches"; and others use "shadowing" programs to better understand the patient experience (Millenson, 2012). For some caregivers, this shift also means paying more attention to questions of race, gender, and other cultural differences, both in terms of patient relationships and the composition of the health care workforce (Manchanda, 2013; Millenson, 2012).

How doctors relate to patients is also dependent on their position within the health care system, which is changing with the implementation of the Affordable Care Act. Most ACOs are headed by physicians and designed, in part, to make primary care physicians the "quarterbacks" of the system (Nicolato, 2013). In this capacity, doctors are being encouraged to take a more holistic view of patient health, including the key social determinants that affect them. Rishi Manchanda (2013) calls physicians who look for and treat the sources of health problems, not just symptoms, "upstream doctors."

Patient portals and other online tools. Rapid developments in online tools and technologies are enabling changes in the patient-caregiver relationship that can improve decision making. For example, patient portals that are linked to the person's electronic medical records allow people to communicate with caregivers in a way that is both convenient and data-driven. Secure messaging systems are being used to create a more reliable and immediate connection between people and health care professionals.

"Quantified self" technologies. Another way to support better decision making by patients and families is to give them more information in ways that are connected to their daily lives. Here again, a wave of technological innovations has created new opportunities. One indicator of this proliferation: over 20,000 health and medical apps are available on Apple's app store (Sarasohn-Kahn, 2014). These mobile apps and wearable sensors allow people to collect data on their health and the factors that impact it, from air quality to caloric intake, heart rates, and time spent exercising. By using these technologies, patients are not only gathering data that they (and their caregivers) can analyze, but are also taking more ownership of their health and the social determinants that affect it (Manchanda, 2013). For an example of using technology to help citizens and health providers, see Box 5.3 on the Healthy Shopper Rewards Program.

> **Box 5.3. Case Study**
> **The Healthy Shopper Rewards Program**
>
> With support from the Lerner Center for Public Health Promotion at Syracuse University, St. Joseph's Hospital Health Center (a community health clinic in an economically depressed area of Syracuse, New York) and Nojaim Brothers Supermarket (a family-owned grocery store in the same area) have partnered to promote public health through the Healthy Shopper Rewards Program.
>
> The program uses a new nutrition-scoring index for the supermarket, where items receive a score of 1 to 100 based on their nutritional value, with healthy foods receiving the highest scores. The scores help customers make smarter choices without having to examine food labels and serve as incentives for healthy shopping. Shoppers can sign up for the Rewards Program and use the collected points they earn for items such as a YMCA membership or a bicycle.
>
> Customers can opt to have their shopping records transferred to physicians at St. Joseph's new Primary Care Center–West, who can then review the records and make suggestions on eating plans to improve the patient's health. Doctors can even write "prescriptions" for vegetables, thus allowing at least some of the cost to be offset by the Lerner Center.
>
> "The goal of this project is to improve the health of the community by enabling and empowering residents to make healthier choices about the food they eat," said Dr. Tom Dennison, the Lerner Center's director. "Using data to help people make decisions about what to buy and eat coupled with the primary care setting has enormous potential to impact population health."
>
> **Link**
>
> http://lernercenter.syr.edu/projects/Healthy-Shopper-Rewards.html

Patient-family advisors. Health care organizations, particularly hospitals and health clinics, are creating patient-family advisor positions to help with individual-level decision making. Advisors assist patients and families with a wide variety of issues, such as coordinating care, monitoring health, and navigating health care services and treatments. Patient-family advisors also can have roles in community decision making, which we describe in the next section.

Enabling Community Decision Making

This category of participation in health is where the micro-level focus on patient-centered care connects with the macro-level goals of the healthy communities movement. There is great potential in combining the official settings within hospitals, clinics, and accountable care organizations with the boundary-crossing coalitions and participatory planning practices of healthy communities initiatives. Joint projects would help bridge the key differences between the approaches to decision making that have sprung from patient engagement and those that have emerged from the healthy communities movement: the former assumes that action and change originate from inside health care institutions, while the latter emphasizes the potential for action and change outside them. Accepting and encouraging both avenues for change may make for more robust innovations in health participation.

Healthy communities coalitions. In the proliferation of community health centers and the consolidation of healthy communities coalitions, there may be new opportunities for maintaining durable arenas for public participation in health. David Fukuzawa (2013: 59-60) observes that:

> Around the country, health care systems are moving to create upstream, collective impact structures that are multisectoral, community centered, disparity reducing, and focused on improving population health while not sacrificing patient care quality. We believe that these are the elements of a community-centered health system, which includes medicine, public health, and community partners, all holding each other accountable within a partnership structure for achieving greater community health and well-being. . . . this suggests new frameworks and structures for communities to engage in building healthy communities.

Compared to issues like education or land use, the institutional relationships between health organizations are not as clear or consistent from one place to the next, and the landscape of participation in health seems to be in a period of transition. This presents new challenges and opportunities for health participation. Convened by healthy communities coalitions, in partnership with patient-advisory councils and ACOs, citizens could help decide how these institutional relationships ought to work and how people can be productively engaged over the long term.

Patient-family advisory councils. Hospitals and clinics that have fully embraced patient-centered care have found many ways to incorporate citizens into decision making. "The voice of the patient and family is everywhere in the institution," says the chief operating officer of the Dana-Farber Cancer Center, which has 400 patient-family advisors participating in its regular operations. "They teach us and teach us everyday things that we don't know" (IFCC, 2004: 3). These patient-family advisory councils usually, but not always, consist of volunteers with a particular interest in health issues. They "help shape virtually every aspect of the organization, including safety and quality improvement, facility design, and the hospital's management priorities" (Millenson, 2012: 12). They influence hospital policies and practices; take part in faculty programs in which they help train students and staff and help interview potential hires; and help plan new centers, programs, and capital projects (IFCC, 2004). Box 5.4 suggests ideas for upgrading advisory councils and other kinds of advisory bodies.

Encouraging Public Work

Volunteer coordination. As in education, volunteers can be a tremendous asset in health. Not only can they serve in hospitals, clinics, and health centers as patient and family resources, but they can also assist communities in dealing with incidents of public health significance. For example, communities can use volunteers to help plan for emergency preparedness and to coordinate emergency responses and recovery, through functions such as helping with hospital surge capacity and capability needs; organizing alternate care sites, facilities, or dispensing points; managing shelters and centers; and providing first aid, mass triage, or other screening needs. The U.S. Department of Health and Human Services, Centers for Disease Control has produced guides on volunteer coordination and management for public health, including reports such as *Ethical Guidance for Public Health Emergency Preparedness and Response* (Jennings & Arras, 2012) and *Public Health Preparedness Capabilities: National Standards for State and Local Planning* (CDC, 2011).

Health-based crowdfunding and mini-grant programs. Small amounts of money can leverage large contributions of volunteer time and labor. Mini-grant programs can seed and support problem-solving efforts in a wide variety of health areas; for example, in Ithaca, New York, mini-grants are being used to support community gardens, recreation trails, and fun runs (Clement, 2014). Similarly, crowdfunding efforts can support a variety of health innovations and practices (Diana, 2014). A growing number of crowdfunding sites and platforms, such as Citizinvestor, can be used to help support a wide range of community health projects.

Apps and platforms for teams and tasks. Much of what constitutes "public work" in health is project-based and involves the coordination of various teams and tasks. Apps and platforms for team and task management are proliferating, making project coordination easier, more decentralized, and online. As we describe in Chapter 8, a number of online platforms allow users to map problems and tasks, develop solutions, and attract other citizens to help. Other online tools listed in Chapter 8, such as CivicEvolution and Community Tool Box Workstations,

Box 5.4. Upgrading Citizen Advisory Boards

Advisory boards are common in many different aspects of public life. They go by many different names, such as steering committees, councils, or action teams. In health care, they may also be called family advisory councils or community task forces. The basic role of these groups has been to represent citizen interests to official decision-makers. However, the appeal of this representative function has waned. In some cases, their legitimacy is questioned by other citizens, who often bypass the advisory groups to bring their concerns directly to the official decision-makers (Leighninger, 2006). To take on more productive roles in public participation, advisory boards can:

- **Ensure that they reflect the full diversity of the community.** This is significant not just because a diverse board can represent a diverse array of interests, but because those board members will be better able to recruit and interact with a broader swath of the population.

- **Establish clear expectations about their role and authority.** The specifics of their official capacity must be clear to board members, public officials, and citizens. Tools like the IAP2 Spectrum of Public Participation (see Chapter 8) can help boards understand and publicize how they will operate. Board members and public officials should develop, or review and adapt, a charter that codifies this understanding of their roles.

- **Engage citizens directly, not just represent their interests.** Advisory boards can bring people to the table, not only by recruiting them for large-scale processes and events, but by using interviews, open houses, meeting-in-a-box tools, and listening sessions to engage people "where they are."

- **Tap the full interactive capacity of online tools.** Some advisory boards use online tools for transparency by releasing their meeting minutes, publicizing their decisions and recommendations, and/or notifying citizens of upcoming meetings. A smaller number use Twitter hashtags, Facebook groups, online surveys, or online forums. These more interactive efforts can help advisory board members get input on citizen ideas and concerns.

- **Advise and oversee evaluation and measurement.** Evaluation and assessment practices can help advisory boards monitor the performance of a health care effort or system, and demonstrate strengths and gaps to the broader community (Manchanda, 2013; Millenson, 2012).

- **Use effective group process techniques.** The default mode for advisory board meetings is a basic agenda, presentations by staff, and free-for-all discussion. The "facilitator" role is sometimes played by a public employee who acts more as an information provider than a custodian of the process. As with other formats for participation, advisory boards are more effective if they enable members to set their own ground rules, share experiences, and use other group process techniques (see Participation Skills Module).

are designed to help small groups work together to implement action ideas. In general, these tools take the analytical power of data gathering and mapping, and add functions that support citizen action (Hartz-Karp & Sullivan, 2014).

STRENGTHENING THE INFRASTRUCTURE: SYSTEMIC SUPPORTS FOR PARTICIPATION IN HEALTH

Fulfilling the potential of health participation requires not just the six building blocks discussed above, but also a variety of systemic supports that empower participation leaders, connect the blocks to one another, and otherwise institutionalize participation in health. Some of the most critical supports for health are training and skill development, professional incentives, policies and procedures, and funding and budgeting.

Training and Skill Development

As we noted earlier in this chapter, many participation leaders, both inside and outside health institutions, have helped create and sustain public participation efforts on health issues. But they are a distinct minority among their peers, and so the first challenge in expanding health participation is simply to expand the number of participation leaders in the field. The second challenge, and perhaps a far more difficult one, is to empower health care providers to discard, once and for all, the undemocratic attitudes that have prevailed in their field for decades.

Organizations like the National Physicians Alliance have noted the power inequalities in the doctor-patient relationship, especially when other demographic factors—race, gender, income, age, level of education—are factored in. "Clinicians who share a cultural background with their patients may bring important insights to their care," says Rishi Manchanda (2013), "but the makeup of the medical professions still doesn't match the diversity of the U.S. population." This creates a dynamic that affects not only the quality of the health care patients receive, but also the way in which both doctors and patients participate in public life. "Advocacy and civic participation on behalf of the patient and society are core elements of medical professionalism," but there is an "overemphasis on professional *advocacy for* patients rather than on *civic engagement with* patients," resulting in a "limited civic voice" for both groups (Manchanda & Silver-Isenstadt, 2010: 50).

To help shift these assumptions and change the nature of patient-provider interactions, training and skill development can be valuable. As Monte Roulier (2014: 7) points out, the need for collaboration requires skills that are not common in the health domain. "Collaboration within and across coalition teams requires substantial support: facilitation; communication through meetings, notes, notices, and updated action plans; research to determine proven strategies; evaluation to establish the baseline and identify gaps; and convening meetings." These participatory skills should be part of the curriculum in medical schools and hospital administration programs, and should be offered as standalone workshops and seminars for mid-career health practitioners and potential participation leaders in health networks.

Professional Incentives for Health Practitioners and Other Participation Leaders

Health participation can also be advanced through professional incentives. When health practitioners and other leaders understand how they are expected to engage patients and citizens, and are rewarded professionally for doing so, participation becomes a more common part of their routine, and the routine of health institutions. This structural change requires health professionals and community members to define participation, identify the particular kinds of engagement that are important to each job position, and have ways to measure the quantity and quality of that engagement.

Many participation leaders in health will come from non-governmental organizations and citizen groups, and they, too, need incentives for their work. A number of non-monetary incentives, such as recognition, awards, and forms of authority and legitimacy, can be used to inspire these leaders.

Policies and Procedures

Because many key health decisions are made by private or nonprofit organizations rather than governments, and because participation in health is often organized by cross-sector coalitions rather than by single institutions, the legal framework for participation has not played as prominent a role in health as in other issues. This may change as participation becomes more visible and more clearly identified as a form of civic engagement in health reform efforts. In any case, thinking through the policies and procedures for health participation, particularly within organizations, can be constructive because it promotes transparency, awareness, and shared expectations (Roulier, 2014).

Funding and Budgeting

Some of the financial support necessary for growing participation is available through the Affordable Care Act and its associated Medicare rules. Under these rules, ACOs "must measure and manage four specific domains of patient-centeredness: patient care/caregiver experience; care coordination/patient safety; preventative health; and at-risk populations. If they score at least 70 percent on each domain's measures and meet other requirements, they share any money they save on care with the government. If they fail to meet the threshold, they risk being expelled from the program" (Millenson, 2012: 20). A key to local efforts to access this funding will be to articulate a plan for health participation that meets the federal guidelines and also taps the local capacity of foundations, corporations, and other sources.

SUMMARY

The potential for public participation in health is large and growing. Health care is critical to our lives and has become an increasingly prominent political and economic issue. In the United States, participation in health has developed in five main arenas: messaging and healthy behavior, the "healthy communities" movement, mapping inequities in health, engaging citizens in health policy making, and patient engagement and patient-centered care. Within these and other arenas, research shows that participation in health can produce a wide variety of benefits for individuals and communities. However, the official settings that support participation are few, but evolving.

We provided a number of suggestions about how to strengthen the participation infrastructure for health. Specifically, we asserted that participation in health can be improved if:

1. *Leaders and networks for participation are activated and empowered.* Although not always obvious or well-established, most communities have official settings for participation in health at the community, hospital/clinic, and patient/citizen levels. Within these official settings are numerous potential participation leaders, including a wide variety of health care providers and consumers. In addition to these official settings and potential leaders, most communities have a range of networks and constituents

that can play an active role. Activating and empowering leaders in these settings and networks can go a long way toward creating a broader, more supportive framework for participation in health.

2. *The six building blocks of participation activities are put into place.* Some health care institutions and communities undertake a number of activities related to disseminating information, gathering input and data, discussing and connecting, enabling patient and family decision making, enabling community decision making, and encouraging public work. However, in most places, participation in health continues to be carried out in isolation or by fragile coalitions. The infrastructure for participation in health can be strengthened if health care institutions and communities incorporate and connect a wide variety of thin and thick participation tools or vehicles into these activities.

3. *Systemic supports are used to make participation sustainable, strong, and resilient.* To help people to take on new roles, connect the different building blocks to one another, and institutionalize participation in the regular functioning of health institutions and communities, several systemic supports are needed, including training and skill development, professional incentives, policies and procedures, and funding and budgeting. Integrating such systemic supports will strengthen the official settings, leaders and networks, and participation activities in health.

To achieve the benefits of participation in health, communities should take stock of the current picture of engagement, consider the kinds of participation activities they want to foster and support, and make changes (both inside and outside of health care systems) that will enable more democratic interactions among health care providers, patients, families, and community members.

DISCUSSION QUESTIONS

1. Review the common health issues listed in Table 5.1. Which are the most important? Which do you think are best addressed through public participation? Why?

2. Summarize the current official settings for participation in health at each level (community, hospital/clinic, and patient/citizen). How can participation at each level be improved?

(continued)

(*continued*)

3. Who are (or should be) the key actors in participation in health? What are (or should be) each actor's role in participation? Do those roles vary depending on the level (community, hospital/clinic, and patient/citizen) at which participation is happening?

4. Define patient compliance, patient engagement, and patient-centered care. How do they differ in terms of participation?

5. Use the questions in Box 5.1 to assess the state of health participation in your community.

6. Consider your own experience as a patient, and review the six building blocks for a stronger participation infrastructure (Figure 5.3). Which building blocks were present? Were the participation opportunities conventional, thin, or thick? Which opportunities would you have liked to have had or would like to see now, and why?

7. What are the benefits and drawbacks of using health facilities for public participation? Do the health institutions in your community have a place-making function? If so, how? If not, why?

8. Do you think that technology can encourage participation in health? What are the advantages and disadvantages of integrating technology such as social media or online dashboards in health?

9. What kinds of skills, training, and incentives do you think would work best to support participation in health? Why?

10. What are the major public health issues in your community? How could public participation be used to address these issues?

References

American Academy of Pediatrics. (2011). Accountable care organizations and pediatricians: Evaluation and engagement. *AAP Professional Resources*. Available at www.aap.org/en-us/professional-resources/practice-support/Pages/Accountable-Care-Organizations-and-Pediatricians-Evaluation-and-Engagement.aspx.

Bernier, Roger. (2014). Lessons learned from implementing a multi-year, multi-project public engagement initiative to better inform governmental public health policy decisions. *Journal of Participatory Medicine*, 6: e8.

Bhatia, Rajiv. (2011). *Land use regulation and environmental health impact assessment: Current practices*. San Francisco, CA: Department of Public Health.

Center for Advancing Health (CAH). (2010). *Snapshot of people's engagement in their health care*. Washington, DC: Center for Advancing Health.

Center for Advancing Health (CAH). (2014). *Here to stay: What health care leaders say about patient engagement*. Washington, DC: Center for Advancing Health.

Centers for Disease Control and Prevention (CDC). (2011). *Public health preparedness capabilities: National Standards for State and local planning*. Washington, DC: U.S. Department of Health and Human Services.

Cheadle, Allen, Suzanne Rauzon, & Pamela M. Schwartz. (2014). Community-level obesity prevention initiatives: Impact and lessons learned. *National Civic Review*, *103*(1): 35–39.

Clement, Katherine. (2014). Mini-grants promote community health. *Ithaca.com*. Available at www.ithaca.com/news/mini-grants-promote-community-health/article_144950c2-c0c6-11e3-acae-0019bb2963f4.html.

Coulson, Andrew. (2014). The gamification of community engagement. *CommsGo-Digital*. Available at www.commsgodigital.com.au/2014/01/gamification-in-community-engagement-offline/.

Crump, Regan. (2014). What can federal officials do to support healthy communities? *National Civic Review*, *103*(1): 63–65.

Davenhall, Bill. (2012). *Geomedicine: Geography and personal health*. Redlands, CA: Ersi.

Davis, Rachel A. (2014). Preventing urban violence to save lives and foster healthy communities. *National Civic Review*, *103*(1): 55–56.

Diana, Alison. (2014). Crowdfunding the next healthcare hit. *Information Week*. Available at www.informationweek.com/healthcare/leadership/crowdfunding-the-next-healthcare-hit/d/d-id/1141654.

First 5 LA. (2010). *Partnerships for families: Stories and lessons from Los Angeles communities*. Los Angeles, CA: First 5 LA. Available at www.cssp.org/publications/child-welfare/partnerships-for-families-stories-and-lessons-from-los-angeles-communities-2010.pdf.

Fox, Susannah.(2011). *Peer-to-peer health care*. Washington, DC: Pew Research Center's Internet & American Life Project.

Fukuzawa, David D. (2013). Achieving healthy communities through community-centered health systems. *National Civic Review*, *102*(4): 57–60.

Galloway-Gilliam, Lark. (2014). Racial and ethnic approaches to community health. *National Civic Review*, *102*(4): 46–48.

HAP. (2013). *Patient- and family-centered care: A key element in improving quality, safety, perception of care, and care outcomes*. Harrisburg, PA: The Hospital and Healthsystem Association of Pennsylvania.

Hartz-Karp, Janette, & Brian Sullivan. (2014). The unfulfilled promise of online deliberation. *Journal of Public Deliberation*, *10*(1): Article 16.

Hershey, Lisa. (2014). People, places, partnerships at the heart of success in California's building a movement of movements. *National Civic Review*, *102*(4): 29–30.

HHS. (2010). *National action plan to improve health literacy*. Washington, DC: U.S. Department of Health and Human Services, Office of Disease Prevention and Health Promotion.

HPOE. (2013). *A leadership resource for patient and family engagement strategies*. Chicago, IL: Health Research & Educational Trust.

Institute of Medicine. (2001). *Crossing the quality chasm: A new health system for the 21st century*. Washington, DC: National Academy Press.

IFCC. (2004). *Strategies for leadership. Advancing the practice of patient- and family-centered care*. Washington, DC: Institute for Family-Centered Care.

Jennings, Bruce, & John Arras. (2012). *Ethical guidance for public health emergency preparedness and response: Highlighting ethics and values in a vital public health service*. Washington, DC: Ethics Subcommittee, Advisory Committee to the Director, Centers for Disease Control and Prevention. Available at www.cdc.gov/od/science/integrity/phethics/ESdocuments.htm.

Krieger, James W. (2014). Policy and systems change to build health communities in King County, Washington. *National Civic Review, 102*(4): 31–34.

Larson, Carl, Alison Christian, Linda Olson, Darrin Hicks, & Catherine Sweeney. (2002). *Colorado Healthy Communities Initiative: Ten years later*. Denver, CO: The Colorado Trust.

Leighninger, Matt. (2006). *The next form of democracy: How expert rule is giving way to shared governance—and why politics will never be the same*. Nashville, TN: Vanderbilt University Press.

Lewis, Thomas, Fari Amini, & Richard Lannon. (2000). *A general theory of love*. New York, NY: Random House.

Liburd, Leandris C., Wayne Giles, & Leonard Jack, Jr. (2014). Health equity: The cornerstone of a healthy community. *National Civic Review, 102*(4): 52–54.

Lukensmeyer, Carolyn J. (2013). *Bringing citizen voices to the table: A guide for public managers*. San Francisco, CA: Jossey-Bass.

Manchanda, Rishi. (2013). *The upstream doctors: Medical innovators track sickness to its source*. New York, NY: Ted Books.

Manchanda, Rishi, & Jean Silver-Isenstadt. (2010). A prescription for a healthier democracy: The role of health care in civic participation. *National Civic Review, 99*(2): 48–53.

McGinnis, J. Michael, & Elizabeth L. Robinson. (2014). Place matters: Health and healthy communities at twenty-five. *National Civic Review, 102*(4): 10–13.

Mikkelsen, Leslie, Larry Cohen, & Sonya Frankowski. (2014). Community-centered health homes: Engaging health care in building healthy communities. *National Civic Review, 103*(1): 57–59.

Miles-Polka, Becky, Chris Frantsvog, & Rick Kozin. (2014). Healthy Polk 2000 to healthy Polk 2020: What a long, strange trip it has been. *National Civic Review, 103*(1): 21–24.

Millenson, Michael L. (2012). *Building patient-centeredness in the real world: The engaged patient and the accountable care organization*. Washington, DC: Health Quality Advisors with the National Partnership for Women & Families.

Nicolato, Courtney. (2013). Supporting ACO success with meaningful patient engagement. *Becker's Hospital Review*. Available at www.beckershospitalreview.com/

accountable-care-organizations/supporting-aco-success-with-meaningful-patient-en-
gagement.html.

Norris, Tyler. (2014). Healthy communities at twenty-five: Participatory democracy and
the prospect for American renewal. *National Civic Review, 102*(4): 4–9.

Oldenburg, J. (2014, January). From compliance to engagement: Reimagining the patient
relationship. *EngagingPatients.org*. Available at www.engagingpatients.org/redesigning-
patient-care/compliance-engagement-reimagining-patient-relationship/.

Oza, Priyanka R. (2014). Social media for public health professionals. *Talk Public Health*.
Available at http://talkpublichealth.wordpress.com/2014/02/25/social-media-for-pub-
lic-health-professionals/.

Parcell, Jacob. (2013). New outbreaks (but no zombies) on CDC's Solve the Outbreak. *Dig-
italgov*. Available at www.digitalgov.gov/2013/10/31/new-outbreaks-but-no-zombies-
on-cdcs-solve-the-outbreak/.

Petersen, Matthew, Paul Gardner, Tianna Tu, & David Muhlestein. (2014). *Growth and
dispersion of accountable care organizations: June 2014 update*. Washington, DC: Leavitt
Partners, LLC.

Pittman, Mary. (2014). Leadership for the public's health: Legacy of the healthy communities movement. *National Civic Review, 102*(4): 17–19.

Ridini, Steve, Shari Sprong, & Judith Foley. (2014). Building healthy communities in Massachusetts: Key ingredients and lessons learned. *National Civic Review, 102*(4): 34–36.

Roudman, Sam. (2014). Innovator's dilemma: How SF's Rajiv Bhatia pioneered open health
data and ruffled feathers. *Techpresident*. Available at http://techpresident.com/news/24720/
innovators-dilemma-how-rajiv-bhatia-pioneered-health-data-and-ruffled-feathers.

Roulier, Monte. (2014). Place-based practices shape the healthy communities movement.
National Civic Review, 103(1): 4–8.

Rubio-Cortés, Gloria, & Michael McGrath. (2014). Role of the National Civic League in
healthy communities. *National Civic Review, 102*(4): 14–16.

Sarasohn-Kahn, Jane. (2014). *The wisdom of patients: Health care meets online social
media*. Oakland, CA: California HealthCare Foundation.

Schattan Coelho, Vera P., Andrea Cornwall, & Alex Shankland. (2012). Taking a seat on
Brazil's health councils. *OpenDemocracy*. Available at https://www.opendemocracy.
net/andrea-cornwall-vera-schattan-p-coelho-alex-shankland/taking-seat-on-brazils-
health-councils.

Sharp, John, & Brad Tritle. (2014). Five models of patient engagement demonstrate value.
Healthcare Information and Management Systems Society (HIMSS). Available at http://
blog.himss.org/2014/04/11/five-models-of-patient-engagement-demonstrate-value/.

Sirianni, Carmen, & Lewis Friedland. (2001). *Civic innovation in America: Community
empowerment, public policy, and the movement for civic renewal*. Berkeley, CA: University of California Press.

Soler, Lawrence A. (2014). Importance of the private sector in creating healthier communities. *National Civic Review, 102*(4): 49–51.

Standish, Marion B., & Robert K. Ross. (2014). Transforming communities for health: The California endowment. *National Civic Review*, 102(4): 31–33.

Twiss, Joan M., Tanya Kleinman, & Joseph M. Hafey. (2014). California healthy cities and communities: Twenty-five years of cultivating community and advancing a movement. *National Civic Review*, 102(4): 20–25.

Participation in Planning and Land Use

People care about their homes and neighborhoods. Decisions about planning, land use, and the "built environment" are often hot topics for public participation, for several reasons:

1. People care about the safety, convenience, beauty, and charm of the places where they live and want to influence decisions and plans that will have an impact on those qualities.

2. Buying a home is the most significant financial investment most people make, and protecting the property value of that investment is a powerful motivator for involvement in public life.

3. The outcomes of land use decisions are often highly visible; the fact that people can see the impact, or lack of impact, of their participation raises the stakes considerably.

4. The level of residents' attachment to where they live seems to have a significant impact on economic vitality and other aspects of community success.

5. Land use is an area where technology, particularly in the form of smartphones, mapping platforms, and visualization software, is having an outsized impact on citizens' demand and capacity for participation.

6. In most places, there are public institutions and grassroots groups that deal with land use issues; although these entities often fail to host effective engagement, they are at least latent elements of a stronger participation infrastructure.

At a basic and perhaps even instinctual level, people seek control over their immediate surroundings. Summarizing the latest research on the "science of cities," Michael Mehaffy (2014) writes that "Cities perform best when they offer some control of spatial structure to residents." Whether residents feel that sense of control, and how they reconcile their concerns and desires with those of planners, developers, public officials, neighbors, and other citizens, has a huge impact on how they feel about politics, government, and community.

This struggle for control is often highly contentious. Public participation in land use, more than on any other issue, is driven by conflict between citizens and government. Planning and zoning decisions often produce the most spectacular instances of bad participation, featuring screaming residents and glowering public officials at meetings that last late into the night. These tense encounters embody the head-on collision between expert governance and active citizenship.

In light of these bad experiences, planners, civic activists, and participation practitioners have developed a variety of tactics and techniques to make planning more participatory and to take some of the steam out of those tense public meetings. There is now a diverse array of strategies for better participation—perhaps more than for any other issue—including many new online tools. But these techniques are rarely official practice. And most of the neighborhood and homeowners associations that aim to engage citizens in planning have not been up to the task, instead falling into the familiar patterns of conventional participation. In short, the ways to do planning more effectively have not yet been incorporated into the public arenas for participation in planning and land use.

This chapter helps bridge the gap between participatory practice and official practice in land use. We trace the development of participation in planning and describe the most common settings and networks for engagement. We also suggest ways to renovate the participation infrastructure for planning and land use by focusing on the building blocks of participation activities and systemic supports.

THE DEVELOPMENT OF PARTICIPATION IN PLANNING AND LAND USE

The struggle to move from a paternalistic dynamic to a more adult-adult relationship has been more conspicuous in land use than in most other issues. Bit by bit, from one confrontation to the next, citizens in many communities have achieved greater degrees of influence in planning and zoning processes and more opportunities to make their own contributions.

The system of land use decision making does not, however, give residents the sense of control most of them desire—so many people search for that control through their housing decisions. People who have the opportunity to buy a house or rent an apartment in a different community tend to take it, relocating to "tidier, more homogeneous places that look tamer and easier to handle" (Leighninger, 2006: 75; see also Bishop, 2009). Without sufficient opportunities to take part in public governance, people are exercising their options for private governance.

The current trend in many places is to make communities more environmentally friendly, art-filled, and attractive, typified by former New York City Mayor Michael Bloomberg's claim that the city is a "luxury product" (Kotkin, 2011). But while residents may value these changes, Mehaffy (2014) warns that they do not necessarily satisfy people's need to influence their surroundings.

This need for control over our immediate surroundings has had a huge impact on our political geography, helping to produce a landscape of homogeneous, partisan settlements, highly transient populations, areas of distress alternating with areas of gentrification, and development that is economically and environmentally unsustainable. Judged in this light, the development of participation in land use is a race in which engagement practices and structures are struggling to catch up with citizen expectations.

But the question of when and how public participation is useful in planning is not straightforward. There is broad support for the general idea of involving residents in land use decisions, but some express doubts about the practicalities of making participation work. This is partly because people often associate "participation" with the conventional processes of public hearings and planning commissions—settings that in most cases are not participatory at all. But it is also because the more intensive forms of participation vary widely and are applied in different contexts for different reasons. One scholar summarizing the literature on participatory planning quipped that "making generalizations about the effectiveness of citizen participation" is like "comparing apples to aardvarks" (Day, 1997: 422).

Despite the diversity of participatory planning approaches and contexts, it is possible to generalize about their success by examining four main activities: major zoning decisions, community visioning, community development planning, and prioritizing public services. In each of these areas, elements of an adult-adult relationship between citizens and government have emerged, albeit slowly, and rarely to their full potential.

Major Zoning Decisions

The collision course between planners and residents started at least fifty years ago with the rise of "urban renewal." In that era, most residents had very little say in zoning decisions, and planners like Robert Moses, the legendary "master builder" of New York City from the 1930 to the 1960s, built highways and bulldozed neighborhoods with relative impunity. These decisions had particularly devastating impacts on low-income communities of color. "The result was not just a net loss of low-income housing, and increased racial segregation, but also the decimation of once vibrant communities rich in civic relationships and social capital" (Sirianni & Girouard, 2012: 669).

Although the authority of planners has been checked in many ways since the era of unbridled urban renewal, those plans and decisions left physical wounds in many cities. Surveying the physical geography of Bridgeport, Connecticut, planner Paul Fontaine described the highways surrounding downtown as a "noose" that has slowly strangled the community for decades (American Institute of Architects, 2010: 13). In the 1990s, Boston, Massachusetts, removed its own noose by burying an interstate highway beneath its downtown: this "Big Dig" was the most expensive construction project in human history (Stern, 2003).

The antithesis of Robert Moses was Jane Jacobs (1961), who, in *The Death and Life of Great American Cities,* debunked many of the assumptions made by the planning experts of the day. Opposition to urban renewal contributed to the rise of community organizing and other strategies for citizen mobilization (Gordon, Schirra, & Hollander, 2011). One legacy of this work was the importance of "relational organizing" and other tactics that have since become integral to public participation.

Arguments for resident control over zoning and the built environment have become more forceful and extensive. The "right to the city," first asserted by the sociologist Henri Lefebvre in 1968, frames the ability to shape, create, and govern our physical surroundings as a collective human right (Harvey, 2008; Lefebvre 1996). It upholds the ability of citizens to "access, occupy and use space, and create new space that meets people's needs" (Brown & Kristiansen, 2009: 15). The right to the city has also been an important theoretical underpinning of democratic innovation in the Global South (LogoLink, 2014).

By focusing on leading figures like Moses and Jacobs, we risk oversimplifying struggles about land use and glossing over the good intentions and unexamined assumptions of people on both sides of the meeting room. The reality was much more complicated—and has become even more complex.

Nevertheless, simplistic characterizations and insulting stereotypes are still common in planning and zoning. Public officials and planners often use the acronym "NIMBY" (Not in My Back Yard) to describe the willingness of citizens to push back against planning and development decisions they do not like. Similar acronyms include CAVE (Citizens Against Virtually Everything) and BANANA (Build Absolutely Nothing Anywhere Near Anything) (www.planetizen.com/node/152). In turn, residents often deride planners as mindless bureaucrats, real estate developers as shameless profiteers, and public officials as self-serving politicians with developers' hands in their pockets. Large institutional landlords like universities, hospitals, and state and federal government agencies are also subject to derision; for example, Columbia University has frequently been called the "largest slumlord in Manhattan."

To avoid the collisions and go past the stereotypes, planners, public officials, community organizers, and other leaders have developed thick forms of participation that bring people together to make zoning and/or community design decisions. Some, like planning charrettes and "placemaking" workshops, focus on a relatively limited geographic space—a public square, a park, or a housing development—and encourage creative thinking (Kent, 2013; Lennertz & Lutzenhiser, 2006). Others present participants with information and options about resource allocation, land use permitting, or public transportation. Both often use digital tools, including "geographic information systems, computer aided design, planning support systems, virtual environments, and digital games," to "immerse" citizens in ways that help them understand the challenges, implications, and possibilities of different land use options (Gordon, Schirra, & Hollander, 2011: 505). A common feature of all these thick approaches is that they treat participants more like adults—particularly by providing more information and choices and, in many cases, giving a sense of political legitimacy by sending a clear message that people's ideas are valued.

Community and Neighborhood Visioning

Another impulse driving the development of participation in planning is a somewhat broader desire to help people envision and build the communities they want. Like the healthy communities movement described in Chapter 5, the people who pioneered community visioning took a holistic view of how residents' relationships with place could improve quality of life. (This is no coincidence, since the National Civic League was heavily involved in supporting the growth of both healthy communities and community visioning.) The rationale for visioning can be summed up by Jane Jacobs' (1961: 13) famous statement: "Cities have the capability of providing something for everybody, only because, and only when, they are created by everybody."

Visioning processes usually provide thick participation opportunities that often address other public issues in addition to land use. They typically encompass a wide range of community stakeholders and public priorities. Although sometimes used in neighborhoods, visioning projects are more likely to be city-wide or cover an entire metro region, and they typically last for several months (Ames, 1998; Moore, Longo, & Palmer, 1999; NCL, 2000; for examples of several thick participation processes in planning at the local, county, regional, and state levels, see Lukensmeyer, 2013). These processes sometimes engage very large numbers of people. Joel Mills (2011) of the American Institute of Architects writes:

> Philadelphia's process to create a Civic Vision for the Delaware Riverfront, led by Penn Praxis, involved over 4,000 residents. Envision Utah engaged 20,000 residents in a two-year regional visioning process on growth, and Chattanooga Stand attracted more than 26,000 participants in the "largest survey-based visioning campaign" in the world.

Visioning efforts provide not only information, but also opportunities for people to share their stories and talk about why they care about their communities. Some visioning efforts also encourage and support citizens to take action to help realize their visions by planting trees, painting murals, or building playgrounds (Diers, 2008; Leighninger, 2006). In some cases, therefore, this type of participation in land use taps into all the main aspects of an adult-adult relationship between individuals and institutions.

Some communities, like Decatur, Georgia, have kept their civic momentum and further tapped citizen capacity by offering people more intensive opportunities to help develop, implement, and monitor community plans. Others have made visioning a routine activity that happens at regular intervals. But most visioning efforts are temporary processes, and plans often gather dust on shelves without having any real impact on the community. In part, this may be because those communities lack the kind of participation infrastructure that would keep citizens informed about how the vision is being used and keep people accountable to one another for the commitments they make.

Participation that treats citizens like adults can overcome divisions between planners, public officials, and residents, but unless the participation is sustained, relationships and trust will often erode quickly. This goes both ways: residents begin to suspect their input and time was wasted by land use decision-makers, and decision-makers begin to doubt residents' willingness to take care of their homes and the public spaces in their neighborhoods.

Community Development Planning

A third strand in land use participation is the practice of planning for the development, or redevelopment, of neighborhoods and communities that are considered to be "distressed," "underserved," or otherwise "at risk." In many cases, a key focus is deciding how to allocate funding from local, state, or federal governments and/or philanthropic sources. This form of participation can therefore combine the specifics of engagement in zoning decisions with the breadth of community visioning.

From the beginning, there have been concerns about the power differential and the marginalization of low-income residents in community development. Charts like the "ladder of participation" devised by Sherry Arnstein in 1969 (see Figure 3.1 in Chapter 3), and the "Spectrum of Public Participation" created by the International Association for Public Participation (IAP2, 2007; see Figure 8.1 in Chapter 8), were intended to help planners and citizens negotiate and clarify how much "say" residents would have, and at which stages of the process. However, the responses to these charts among planners, and the ways they approach participation, vary widely (Gordon, Schirra, & Hollander, 2011).

Concerns about other public issues also fuel participation in community development planning. One is public safety: when people feel a greater degree of ownership for their physical surroundings, they act in ways that make those places safer. Jane Jacobs (1961) first pointed this out when she observed that the physical layout and social connections in some neighborhoods made them safer because there were always many "eyes on the street." Criminologists, architects, and sociologists have developed this basic idea into Crime Prevention Through Environmental Design (Newman, 1996), a philosophy used extensively in planning today (www.cpted.net/). Newer theories of policing emphasize this connection between people and place and uphold the role of police officers in supporting participation in neighborhoods. Describing the work of his department, Police Chief Michael Davis of Brooklyn Park, Minnesota, says:

This is more sophisticated than community policing, which is defined as merely working with the community....this is activating, working alongside, promoting and in some cases prodding the community to come together. Our role is to reduce the dependency on law enforcement, increase our interdependency on one another, and promote this thing we call democracy. (https://www.youtube.com/watch?v=uw1scT1HvAY)

Another argument makes the link between participation, people's sense of place, and economic growth. The Knight Foundation's *Soul of the Community* research (2010) suggests that residents' feelings of "community attachment" to their city or town has a major impact on economic growth and vitality. Breaking this down further, the study suggests that, in most cases, the primary drivers of attachment are "aesthetics" (whether the community looks the way people want it to), "social offerings" (whether the community has interesting things to do), and "openness" (whether the community is welcoming to a wide variety of people).

The most successful examples of participation in community development planning demonstrate the elements of an adult-adult relationship between residents and decision-makers. Citizens are presented with information, choices, and a range of ways to take action. Officials establish clear expectations and cultivate a sense of political legitimacy by sending the message that people's input is valued.

Reporting Problems and Prioritizing Improvements

The most recent additions to the participatory planning toolbox are online tools that allow people to raise concerns, gather data, and suggest ideas to improve their physical surroundings. SeeClickFix and its British equivalent, FixMyStreet, were the first well-known examples of this thinner form of participation. Many of them rely on the GIS capacity of smartphones to allow people to connect a comment or complaint with a specific location. These tools harness the power of citizens to be intelligent sensors of the world around them, giving them the chance to report problems—such as potholes, water leaks, broken streetlights, graffiti, extensive litter—and then prioritize which ones should be fixed first (Ganapati, 2010; Leighninger, 2011). Platforms like PublicStuff and ChangeByUs take this approach a step further by enabling people to form teams to clean up vacant lots, take care of graffiti, or work on other community projects.

Some "participatory GIS" platforms enable users to map their neighborhoods and communities, pooling information on a wide range of physical and civic assets and problems (Sirianni & Girouard, 2012). Examples include the "OaklandWiki" application of LocalWiki and the "Tidepools" project in Red Hook, Brooklyn. However, the opportunity to relate their hopes and concerns about the built environment through mapping is more than just an information exchange. Projects like Tidepools, which "merge digital and physical community spaces," seem to build the connections and pride of place that help communities seize opportunities and overcome challenges. The wireless and relational network established by Tidepools helped Red Hook residents overcome Superstorm Sandy (http://oti.newamerica.net/blogposts/2013/case_study_red_hook_initiative_wifi_tidepools-78575; www.forbes.com/sites/deannazandt/2012/11/10/what-sandy-has-taught-us-about-technology-relief-and-resilience/). To help other communities create similar maps, the Urban Institute has created an adaptable "Community Platform" that overlays census and other data on unemployment rates, housing costs, health insurance coverage, and other information for each neighborhood (http://nccs.urban.org/Community-Platform.cfm).

For residents who want a more direct way of accessing, understanding, and providing input on public services, a related set of tools has emerged. Local government telephone hotlines—411 for general information, 311 for non-emergency assistance, and 211 for social services—have been augmented by online (and sometimes texting) platforms that allow people to submit questions or requests on everything from waste collection to homeless shelters and building inspections (Black & Neyestani, 2014; Nemani, 2014a, 2014b; Toderian & Glover, 2014; see Box 6.1 for examples of these local government assistance portals). New platforms, such as Heartgov, enable residents to start dialogues with public officials and other citizens about issues—like affordable housing—that go beyond public service questions and requests (McKenzie, 2014).

Abhi Nemani, the chief data officer for the City of Los Angeles, argues that one of the major opportunities—and challenges—facing this burgeoning field of "civic technology" is finding ways to connect different participation opportunities. He reasons that people who sign up to take care of a fire hydrant might also want to give input on public safety issues, and that residents who join local government social media networks might also attend a public meeting. He calls for a "civic upsell" strategy:

> Something as simple as a sign-up box opens up the door for future conversations between government and the citizen or stakeholder. Particularly in informational or transparency websites, these kinds of engagement tactics seem essential. When all a citizen can do is find

Box 6.1. Examples of Online Platforms for Assistance

211 (for connecting to social services):

- Aunt Bertha
- Purple Binder
- Ohana
- Connect Chicago

311 (for non-emergency assistance)

- SeeClickFix
- PublicStuff
- Sport Reporter
- Service Tracker
- Open311Mobile

411 (for general information):

- CityAnswers
- MindMixer
- OSQA

For more information, see Nemani (2014b).

out information or access data on a site, you're missing a rare opportunity to turn their interest into action. (Nemani, 2014c)

The wealth of tools provided by the boom in technology feature two critical aspects of the adult-adult relationship in participation in planning and land use: providing people with information and giving them ways to express their preferences. If communities heed Nemani's call to help people move from one participation opportunity to another, they will support even more aspects of an adult-adult relationship.

Table 6.1 lists the four main planning and land use activities that have inspired public participation. It summarizes the features of successful participation that have emerged over time in these different contexts. For example, providing information, providing choices, and giving a sense of legitimacy have become key elements of successful participation on major zoning decisions. For prioritizing public services, providing information and choices has been the baseline. In successful visioning and community development planning, all five aspects of an adult-adult relationship are usually evident.

Table 6.1
How Aspects of the Adult-Adult Relationship Emerged in Response to Common Planning and Land Use Issues

Common Education Issues	Characteristics of Treating People Like Adults				
	Provide Information	Give People a Chance to Tell Stories	Provide Choices	Give Sense of Political Legitimacy	Support People to Take Action
Major Zoning Decisions	X		X	X	
Community/ Neighborhood Visioning	X	X	X	X	X
Community Development Planning	X	X	X	X	X
Reporting Problems and Prioritizing Improvements	X		X		

As these areas of planning and land use developed, they helped flesh out and reinforce the rationale for broader public participation. Many planners, public officials, and citizens now advocate public participation as a practical, judicious, and ethical imperative. Specifically, they argue that participation results in better plans and decisions because it brings citizens' knowledge and preferences into the mix, builds broader public support for land use plans and decisions, and is appropriate and fair because people have a right to help shape the places where they live (Amsler, 2008; Potter, 2013).

These four forms of participation are not mutually exclusive—they could be combined as part of a single, overarching strategy—but in most cases they have been pursued separately. For the most part, these techniques, processes, and tools are applied unevenly, sporadically, and without any real consensus on how they fit in the larger picture of public participation. In the next section, we describe the official settings for participation in planning and land use.

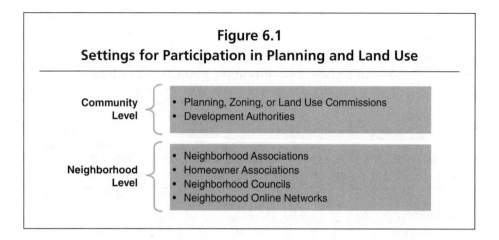

Figure 6.1
Settings for Participation in Planning and Land Use

Community Level
- Planning, Zoning, or Land Use Commissions
- Development Authorities

Neighborhood Level
- Neighborhood Associations
- Homeowner Associations
- Neighborhood Councils
- Neighborhood Online Networks

OFFICIAL SETTINGS FOR PARTICIPATION IN PLANNING AND LAND USE

There are a number of official settings for participation in planning at the community and neighborhood levels, such as zoning commissions, development authorities, and neighborhood associations (see Figure 6.1). Numerous participation leaders operate within these settings, from government planners, commissioners, and other officials, to developers, to residents. Unlike in education and health, there are few opportunities for family or individual participation in planning and land use. Figure 6.1 is therefore one level shorter than its counterparts in Chapters 4 and 5.

Community Level

Almost every city and town has a planning, zoning, or land use commission that makes or reviews land use decisions. Members, who may be elected or appointed, are charged with representing the interests of residents and ensuring transparency in decision making. These commissions typically hold monthly meetings for general decisions, along with special hearings and meetings devoted to specific decisions. Commissions can, and sometimes do, use many of the participatory strategies discussed in the previous section. However, the default (and most common) format for these meetings is conventional: a developer or planner gives a presentation and then takes questions and comments, which are usually given in short increments at an open microphone. The work of planning and zoning commissions is often guided by a comprehensive plan, more commonly referred to as a "comp plan." In some cases, the process of creating a comp plan includes a public participation component, although these too often follow conventional formats.

This routine makes it very difficult to realize the goals and values of participation in planning and does not reflect the characteristics of an adult-adult relationship.

> The public hearing, and its staid approach to information dissemination and dialogue, has become the butt of its own joke. Boring, contentious, geriatric, and filled with the same participants again and again, it composes the image too often associated with the democratic process and the day-to-day dealings of urban planning. (Gordon, Schirra, & Hollander 2011: 506)

Development authorities are government-owned corporations, often created to manage a single project or fund "which the city or county determines is best managed outside of its traditional bureaucracy and lines of authority" (Reich, Crawshaw-Lewis, & Gregory, 2004). This may be a time-limited task, such as allocating a large federal grant for local improvements, although in some states, development authorities are a permanent part of the institutional framework. These entities encounter some of the same participation problems faced by planning commissions. Temporary authorities often face the added challenge that they have less standing in the community and are not well-known to residents. Development authorities that are regional in scope also have to engage citizens who live in different jurisdictions and may have less of an attachment to their metro area than to their city or neighborhood. Nevertheless, development authorities in places like Buckhannon, West Virginia (see Box 6.4), and Decatur, Georgia, have played leading roles in successful engagement processes.

A common dynamic at work in these settings is a communication lag that plagues decision making on controversial topics. When commission members announce that they will consider a particular development project or a request for a zoning variance, the message may take weeks or months to move through the networks of people and organizations that might be affected. At the first few meetings relating to the plan, the level of awareness—and therefore the turnout—is often low, leading commissioners to assume that residents approve or are simply indifferent. Meanwhile, the commission, local government, and developers may invest considerable time and monetary resources on the proposed project—lining up financing, conducting environmental impact assessments, working with engineers and architects, and negotiating with the people who own adjacent property. By the time all these investments have been made and the backhoes are poised to break ground, awareness of the plan has finally filtered out through the community and a crowd of citizens turns out to oppose it. If the commission members vote to halt the project, they waste all the time and money that has been invested so far; if they decide to go ahead over community objections, they erode the trust and goodwill between citizens and government.

Neighborhood Level

Most communities also have grassroots groups that can—and sometimes do—ease these communication gaps and work productively with planners, land use commissions, and developers. There are three main kinds of organizations: neighborhood associations, homeowner associations, and neighborhood councils. A fourth setting, the neighborhood online forum (see following section), is sometimes part of these organizations, but can also operate separately from them.

Neighborhood associations vary dramatically from place to place, but most are voluntary groups of residents who are trying to improve or preserve the quality of life in their neighborhood. These associations are more common in larger cities, particularly in the older, more established sections where the boundaries and physical characteristics of the area are easy to define. (There are also many resident groups in smaller cities and towns that operate like neighborhood associations but use a different name, partly because "neighborhood" has an urban connotation.) Neighborhood associations organize social activities, conduct street and park clean-ups, coordinate playground building, tree planting, and other improvement projects, and advocate on behalf of neighborhood residents in city-level policymaking arenas. Recognizing their value for building social capital and volunteerism, many cities aid and support neighborhood associations by establishing small-grant programs for neighborhood improvement projects, offering leadership training, and assigning planners, police officers, and other city employees to work directly with them (Diers, 2008; Leighninger, 2009; McCabe, 2010).

Homeowner associations (HOAs) are mandatory membership groups, typically set up by real estate developers, to ensure the maintenance of common areas in housing developments and subdivisions. They started appearing in the 1970s and are now common. In many developments, homeowners are required to join the HOA and must abide by its rules and practices. Members typically pay a regular fee for the maintenance of green spaces, swimming pools, golf courses, tennis courts, or other common areas and sometimes also pay a fee for services like trash collection, security, lighting, and drainage. Legally, most HOAs are nonprofit organizations governed by an elected board of directors. They can be small, governing just a few houses, or as large as a small city, with tens of thousands of members. "HOAs do so many of the things that cities do, including holding elections, that they have been called private governments" (McCabe, 2010:113).

Neighborhood councils represent another, more unusual, setting for participation on land use issues. These elected bodies play an official role, either voting or advisory, on local government policies, budgets, and/or services, particularly those most relevant to the neighborhood. ("Neighborhood councils" is a catch-all phrase. In Dayton, Ohio, they are referred to as Priority Boards, while in Atlanta, Georgia, they are called Neighborhood Planning Units, and in Seattle, Washington, District Councils.) These groups are funded and staffed in different ways. In some cases, neighborhood councils receive city funding to hire their own staff; in other places, city employees provide administrative assistance. The first wave of these councils emerged in the 1970s as part of the War on Poverty (Berry, Portney, & Thomson, 1993). A second wave arose in the early 2000s, in a more diverse array of communities, including smaller towns and major cities (Leighninger, 2009).

A common issue with many neighborhood associations, HOAs, and neighborhood councils is that they operate like miniature city councils, with elected leadership, conventional meeting formats, and an inability or unwillingness to engage large, diverse numbers of neighborhood residents. Many also fall into the tired routines of conventional meeting management techniques, such as *Robert's Rules of Order*. In the case of neighborhood councils, these traits may be legally mandated if the council plays a role in policymaking. For the most part, these are small "r" republican structures trying to fulfill small "d" democratic missions.

There is logic to the official settings for land use decision making at the community and neighborhood levels. Together, they are supposed to:

1. Work proactively by crafting and periodically revising comprehensive plans for the community as a whole, and for each neighborhood;
2. Keep open the lines of communication between government and citizens; and
3. React to development proposals as they arise, partly by comparing proposals to comprehensive plans.

However, this logic does not always play out. Comp plans rarely live on in the minds of ordinary people, even in those rare cases where they had a hand in developing them. Thus, neighborhood associations are generally unable to keep the public informed or mobilized. When a controversial proposal emerges, conventional formats are poor environments for helping people understand the issues or sort out their interests, and conflict often ensues.

STRENGTHENING THE INFRASTRUCTURE: LEADERS AND NETWORKS FOR PARTICIPATION IN PLANNING

As noted above, a wide variety of participation leaders operate in the official settings of planning and land use. The most active participants in land use decision-making are local elected officials, professional planners, and citizen representatives in neighborhood associations, HOAs, and neighborhood councils. But several other networks should be included in any discussion of how to improve land use participation: developers, large institutional landowners such as universities and hospitals, local online networks, and civic technologists (see Figure 6.2). People in each of these networks can be activated and empowered as participation leaders.

Developers are often treated like an enemy, if they are mentioned at all, in articles about planning. There are reasons for this; developers are sometimes able to advance their commercial and financial interests over other interests, such as environmental protection or community cohesion. However, developers have played key roles in some of the most celebrated examples of participatory planning. For example, developer Stanley Kwok is often credited with having played

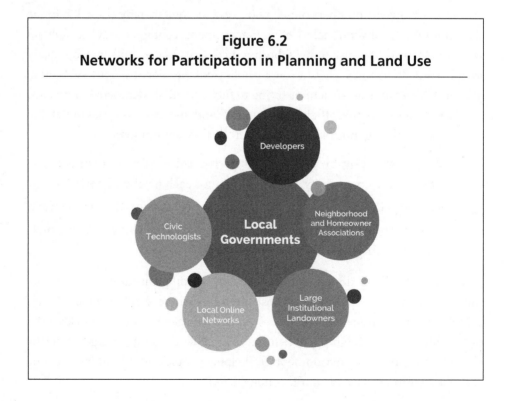

Figure 6.2
Networks for Participation in Planning and Land Use

a key role in Vancouver's rise to being one of the world's most desirable cities in which to live and work (Kiger, 2014).

In many communities, large nonprofit and private institutions, such as universities and hospitals, are major landowners. Like developers, these institutions have the power and sometimes the tacit authority to make significant land use decisions. Moreover, they have their own interests and their own history of cooperation (or noncooperation) with citizens. Some have engaged residents to make decisions related to the buildings and property they own, although these are usually conventional processes.

Neighborhood online forums are the fastest-growing networks for participation in land use; sometimes they emerge as a complement to neighborhood and homeowner associations, and sometimes as a competitor. Some of these "hyperlocal" networks are simply email listservs or Facebook groups, while others are more sophisticated platforms, such as the ones set up by the nonprofit organization e-democracy.org or by for-profit groups like NextDoor (Leighninger, 2011). All of these networks combine the convenience of online communication with the power of face-to-face relationships—even if they do not interact at some sort of meeting, the participants may bump into one another periodically in the grocery store or on a soccer field. According to the Pew *Neighbors Online* report (Smith, 2010: 2), 20 percent of American adults (and 27 percent of American Internet users) were using "digital tools to talk to their neighbors and keep informed about community issues" as of 2010. That number has certainly increased since then; in 2014, over 25 percent of all American neighborhoods had a NextDoor network with at least ten participants (Popper, 2014). In these hyperlocal forums, the ongoing discussions combine the political—"When is the planning and zoning commission meeting?"—with the social—"Who has a plumber they can recommend?" "Has anyone seen my lost cat?" This range of incentives to participate seems to be a key reason for the rapid growth of neighborhood online forums.

The civic technologists who started many of these online forums, and have contributed countless new apps and tools for planning, represent their own network for participation. Some local governments, particularly in cities like Boston and Philadelphia, have worked more intensively with their civic tech communities through events like the Boston Open Data Innovation Summit and OpenDataPhilly (Hoene, Kingsley, & Leighninger, 2013).

Attempts to rethink the official settings for participation in planning and land use should consider ways to bring these networks into the picture. Box 6.2 provides a set of questions that can be used to help clarify that picture, and assess the state of participation in planning and land use within a community.

Box 6.2. Assessing the State of Planning and Land Use Participation in a Community

Any attempt to overhaul public participation in land use should begin with some basic research on the current opportunities for engagement, both inside and outside planning processes, and the other contextual factors that may be critical to the relationships among planners, residents, and public officials. Here are some questions to consider:

1. What kinds of participation opportunities are available for residents in planning and zoning processes?

2. How effective are the official public meetings on land use decisions?

3. Do the people working on participation efforts reflect and represent the full diversity of the people affected?

4. Are there segments of the community that historically have been ignored or excluded when it comes to land use issues?

5. In what ways are recent immigrants connected, or disconnected, when it comes to land use issues?

6. What are some of the key networks and constituencies when it comes to land use issues in the community?

7. How well are neighborhood associations, homeowners' associations, and other grassroots groups functioning?

8. Are there neighborhood online networks? How well are they functioning?

9. How effectively do public officials and employees use social media to connect with residents?

10. Are planning, development, and crime data available online? How effectively does the data complement and inform public participation?

11. How much is local government spending—in money and/or in staff time—on public participation in land use issues annually?

12. How are participation activities and initiatives evaluated and assessed?

13. What are the legal mandates and restrictions on public participation?

14. Do planners and other public employees working on land use issues have the skills, cultural awareness, and organizational support to work productively with citizens?

STRENGTHENING THE INFRASTRUCTURE: BUILDING BLOCKS FOR PARTICIPATION IN PLANNING

In 2009, economist Elinor Ostrom won the Nobel Prize for her research showing that assets like parks, pasture land, and irrigation systems can be managed more efficiently and effectively by citizen networks than by governments or corporations. When the network establishes its own "rules, norms, traditions, or processes that limit the asset's use and/or cause people to replenish it," the asset or resource is more likely to be sustained and preserved (Levine, 2010). Like the research described earlier on crime prevention and economic vitality, Ostrom's findings remind us that, when people take ownership of place, there are a variety of positive effects.

Looking at planning through this larger lens makes the narrow, conventional focus on zoning and developments seem myopic. The ultimate goal of participation in planning and land use should be to strengthen the relationship between people and place and to change the way citizens affect—and are affected by—their physical surroundings. This can happen through the settings and tools that fall under the six main building blocks of a participation infrastructure, including disseminating information, gathering input and data, discussing and connecting, enabling neighborhood decision making, enabling community decision making, and encouraging public work. These six building blocks, with relevant settings, vehicles, and tools, are summarized in Figure 6.3.

As noted previously, individual choices and decisions are not as prominent in land use participation as they are with education and health. (Families and individuals do have choices to make when it comes to land use, but those choices play out primarily in the real estate market, as people look for homes in neighborhoods and communities that fit their civic and other expectations.) Thus, Figure 6.3 is slightly different from its counterparts in the two previous chapters. Here, neighborhood-level decision making refers to places within a town or city, whereas community-level decision making refers to the entire town or city.

However, planning and land use are similar to education and health in that many arenas, tools, programs, staff positions, nonprofit groups, and other civic assets already exist. Thus, some of the settings we discuss below simply need to be upgraded from conventional participation. Again, the first and most significant step in strengthening the infrastructure for participation in planning and land use is to begin thinking of these opportunities as a system and to develop a plan for improving it.

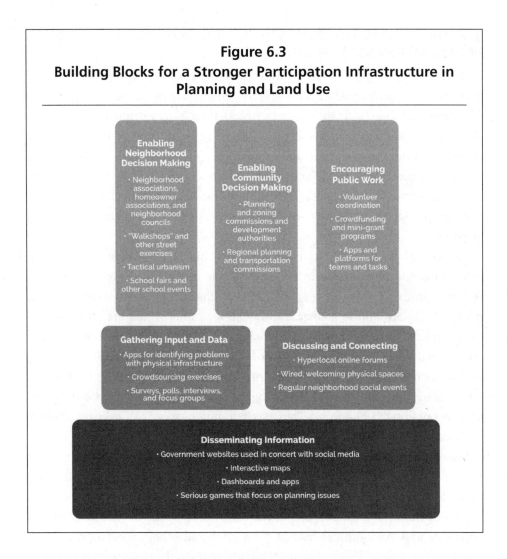

Figure 6.3
Building Blocks for a Stronger Participation Infrastructure in Planning and Land Use

Enabling Neighborhood Decision Making
· Neighborhood associations, homeowner associations, and neighborhood councils
· "Walkshops" and other street exercises
· Tactical urbanism
· School fairs and other school events

Enabling Community Decision Making
· Planning and zoning commissions and development authorities
· Regional planning and transportation commissions

Encouraging Public Work
· Volunteer coordination
· Crowdfunding and mini-grant programs
· Apps and platforms for teams and tasks

Gathering Input and Data
· Apps for identifying problems with physical infrastructure
· Crowdsourcing exercises
· Surveys, polls, interviews, and focus groups

Discussing and Connecting
· Hyperlocal online forums
· Wired, welcoming physical spaces
· Regular neighborhood social events

Disseminating Information
· Government websites used in concert with social media
· Interactive maps
· Dashboards and apps
· Serious games that focus on planning issues

Disseminating Information About Planning and Land Use

Even though there are more ways than ever to disseminate planning information, communication lags are still common. This is partly because planners, public officials, and others are inadequately connected with the neighborhoods and social platforms residents use to receive and absorb information. But it is also because the messages about development proposals, applications for zoning variances, comprehensive plans, and other planning questions tend to be transmitted in ways that are non-interactive, inconvenient, and difficult to understand. There are a number of ways to circulate planning information more effectively. Many of these information tools already exist in communities, while others can be built easily.

Government websites used in concert with social media networks. Some local governments and planning departments use a combination of traditional websites with social media to reach residents in more proactive, interactive ways. Social media seems to work best for news, announcements, and simple questions or exchanges; these posts, tweets, and updates can be linked to websites for more detailed and in-depth information. One study of government in Seattle, Louisville, and Chicago found that social media—and Twitter in particular—were effective not only at distributing information but also for compelling citizens to post comments and look for additional information. In a few cases where public officials and employees were more active at commenting and responding, the result was a more interactive exchange between citizens and government (Mossberger, Wu, & Crawford, 2013; see also Mergel, 2013).

Interactive maps. Online maps provide an engaging way to display geographic and other information. With a few clicks, people can quickly grasp what is happening or what is being proposed, and with a few more, they can find information on the implications of the proposed or forthcoming changes. For example, the Envisioning Development website provides teaching tools about land use and urban development in New York City. Designed by a nonprofit called the Center for Urban Pedagogy, the online and face-to-face tools help New Yorkers navigate the arcane Uniform Land Use Review Procedure, which governs all land use decisions in the city. One of the tools is an interactive neighborhood-by-neighborhood map that shows median income, income distribution, and average rents for a range of apartment sizes (Leighninger, 2011). Maps that allow people to add information about their surroundings, such as those supported by the OpenStreetMaps or LocalWiki platforms, combine information dissemination with citizen-driven data-gathering.

Dashboards and apps for community and neighborhood data. Online dashboards are now being used in some cities to display many kinds of data, from air pollution and crime rates to traffic levels and poverty. These kinds of resources are easy to grasp and well-suited for helping people track community trends. Since data are increasingly geo-located, this information can be easily made more specific to where people live. Clay Johnson, an early civic tech pioneer, envisions dashboards that give people data on their neighborhood in addition to their city or town (CEOs for Cities, 2010). Using the same kinds of increasingly open government data, other technologists have built apps that help users track everything from bus service to trash collection.

Serious games that focus on planning issues. The gamification of planning has been described as "a rich sharing of information at the least, and collaborative accelerated development at its best" (Coulson, 2014). Offline board or role-playing games have been used for decades to help people understand their physical environments. In the Global South, serious games have become a critical strand in democratic innovation (Lerner, 2014). In the last ten years, the number and variety of online games has increased dramatically, developed by organizations like ICivics, Bang the Table, and the Engagement Game Lab.

By giving players control of an environment that is simulated—yet in many cases based on real data—games allow residents to test how different development options will play out. They can be used by individuals playing alone or by people who play in groups and then discuss what happened. The games developed by Eric Gordon's Engagement Game Lab, which include Participatory Chinatown (about a Boston neighborhood) and Detroit 24/7 (see Box 6.3), combine the strengths of thick and thin participation. These tools and activities grab people's attention; the next step, to repeat Abhi Nemani's (2014c) "civic upsell" argument, is to attract people to other opportunities. This thinking about how to meet citizens' interests can connect different elements in a participation infrastructure.

Box 6.3. Case Study
"Detroit 24/7," Detroit, Michigan

As part of a 2012 citywide planning process, over 1,000 Detroiters participated in an online game during which they gave input about the future of their city. Developed by Emerson College professor Eric Gordon, "Community PlanIt turns planning into a story, structured through simple interactions and game mechanics, and invites the public to shape the narrative." It can be played remotely or by people who get together in face-to-face settings and talk while they play. The "Detroit 24/7" rendition of the game lasted for three weeks; players had to tackle a specific mission each week. The game elicited more than 8,400 comments from people about their experiences with the city and how they could be improved.

Links

http://placeofsocialmedia.com/blog/2012/06/11/229/

https://communityplanit.org/

Gathering Input and Data

The chances for a civic upsell between information dissemination and gathering input and data are particularly obvious, mainly because so many of these participation opportunities happen online. The smartest strategy may be to use a variety of avenues and to ensure that respondents can remain in the loop. For example, Vancouver and several surrounding cities have launched "online consultation platforms that allow citizens to sign up once, provide a bit of background about themselves, and receive regular invitations to provide opinions—online or in person—on important civic issues as they arise" (Toderian & Glover, 2014).

Apps for identifying public problems and prioritizing public services. The "participatory GIS" platforms described above give people the chance to report problems that public employees need to know about. "DC 311," in Washington, D.C., is a well-known example (Leighninger, 2011). Other apps allow residents to prioritize problems and organize citizen-driven efforts to fix them.

Crowdsourcing exercises that generate ideas for community improvement. Also called "ideation," crowdsourcing platforms allow participants to propose, refine, and vote on ideas. In some instances, proposal development is primarily citizen-driven, while in others public employees and other experts help people hone their proposals. The small city of Manor, Texas, was one of the first to adopt this approach. In their program, citizens who proposed winning ideas received "Innobucks" redeemable for prizes like a Police Department T-shirt, a gift certificate at a local restaurant, or a chance to serve as "mayor for a day" (Leighninger, 2011).

Surveys, polls, interviews, and focus groups. Many other new and old information-gathering techniques, which can be pursued online or off, help planners and other land use decision-makers understand what citizens want. Among these tools are surveys, polls, interviews, and focus groups. Surveys and polls are better able to tap the perspectives of large numbers of residents, while interviews and focus groups are better for "drilling down" to the details on those perspectives.

Discussing and Connecting

We seem to have more ways of belonging to community, and more potential communities to join, than ever before—but the community of people who live near us, in the same neighborhood, subdivision, housing complex, or small town, will always be critical. The "social capital" of geographic communities affects many other aspects of public life. In his book *Bowling Alone*, Robert Putnam (2000) emphasized the importance of "mediating institutions" and asked, "What will be the Kiwanis Club of the 21st Century?"

Neighborhood online forums. These forums might be the most likely answer so far to Putnam's question. Interestingly, the most important factor in the success of these hyperlocal online networks is one that also applies offline: recruitment. Steve Clift of e-democracy.org, an organization that supports neighborhood online forums in Minnesota and around the world, recommends that anyone trying to start an online forum first gather 100 email addresses (see http://forums.e-democracy.org/support/newforum/; see also the Participation Skills Module, available at www.wiley.com/go/nabatchi). With that kind of critical mass, a forum can become self-sustaining without a great deal of effort from the moderator—but the initial phase of recruiting those 100 participants and ensuring that they have a positive experience is critical.

Wired, welcoming physical spaces. As we noted in previous chapters, community centers, libraries, schools, and other public buildings can aid the development of opportunities for discussing and connecting on land use issues. Of course, organizing and recruitment are still critical—people will not discuss and connect simply because a community center exists—but having a public space that people want to go to can make those tasks somewhat easier.

Regular neighborhood social events. Bringing people together for fun and engaging events is perhaps the most fundamental way to encourage discussion, connection, and strong social capital. Examples like the weekly "Meet and Eat" lunches in Buckhannon, West Virginia (see Box 6.4), illustrate how those opportunities can connect people to other ways of participating in public life. The Buckhannon experience also demonstrates the value of regular gatherings in making participation both enjoyable and routine.

Other creative examples of facilitating discussion and connection rely on sports, the arts, or other cultural assets that draw attendance. The Detroit City Futbol League is an 800-person, twenty-eight-neighborhood league that uses soccer to bring together a diverse array of neighbors, not only to play sports, but also to socialize and take part in volunteer activities that highlight Detroit's unique and historic communities (Hoene, Kingsley, & Leighninger, 2013).

Enabling Neighborhood Decision Making

Neighborhood decision making is particularly notable because, in many cases, it is the point where "top-down" efforts by government to engage citizens meet

Box 6.4. Case Study
"Create Buckhannon," Buckhannon, West Virginia

Every week since 2009, residents of Buckhannon, a small West Virginia town, have gathered at a local restaurant to eat lunch and shape the future of their community. At these "Meet and Eat" gatherings, they use a process (inspired by "open space technology" (see www.openspaceworld.org/) to break into groups: placards showing discussion topics are placed on each table, with some blank placards for people who want to propose new topics, and participants choose a table based on their interests. These discussions have triggered public action: participants developed and implemented plans for a park, a weekly summer music festival and market, a city plan, various downtown improvements, and safe biking and walking routes. "We've had sixty people, and we've had four people at the meeting. Usually, it will be about twenty-five," says facilitator C.J. Rylands. "We just keep meeting. That's the important thing." Participants pay $5 for the meal. Public officials such as the sheriff and Upshur County Development Director are frequent participants.

Links

http://trythiswv.com/have-a-community-conversation/

For information about the "norms" or ground rules used for the discussions, see http://trythiswv.com/wp-content/uploads/2013/10/CBuckNorms.pdf

"bottom-up" grassroots organizing and mobilization. This intersection between 20th Century institutions and 21st Century citizens is rife with both conflict and innovation. The participants at a national meeting on "neighborhood governance," many of whom had worked either as grassroots organizers or as local government employees, concluded that:

> The most promising arenas for public life would be ones that were created jointly, or at least had enthusiastic support, by both community leaders and neighborhood residents. "Basically, we need something in between traditional city council meetings and happenstance barbershop talk," said one participant. (Leighninger, 2009: 15)

Several participation vehicles can fill this void.

Neighborhood associations, homeowner associations, and neighborhood councils. These neighborhood structures typically develop around some common or shared interest, for example, property maintenance and values, historic preservation, crime prevention, or supporting young people. Most residents care about multiple priorities, but neighborhood groups often narrow their support by focusing on only one or two priorities.

While these localized associations play a role in decision making and problem solving on multiple issues, land use and planning questions are often their bread-and-butter concerns. However, these groups face several difficulties that can limit their ability to effectively impact neighborhood decisions. First, and perhaps most importantly, they tend to follow conventional participation models. Recruitment efforts are typically minimal, which means the usual suspects turn out again and again, and meetings lack diversity and a critical mass. The meetings also tend to be dry and boring, with meaningful discussion often limited by *Robert's Rules of Order*. People are seldom provided with opportunities to share information and stories, let alone to make choices or take action. In short, the meetings of most neighborhood groups fail to give people what they want and do not embody the characteristics of an adult-adult relationship.

Second, these groups vary widely in the level of governmental legitimacy they receive. For example, as compared to HOAs and neighborhood associations, neighborhood council systems have institutionalized legitimacy because an official public body gives them a formal role on certain kinds of decisions and policies. Regardless of the level of legitimacy bestowed by government, residents need to know that their work is valued by public officials and other community leaders. People are almost always more likely to participate—and continue participating over time—if they think their input will have some impact on public issues and decisions.

To make the fusion of top-down and bottom-up participation successful, both government and neighborhood structures need to be renovated. They require: more process and recruitment skills; joint "ownership" by neighborhood leaders, public officials and employees, and representatives of other community organizations; and ways to track and support the use of "democratic practices" in neighborhoods (Leighninger, 2009). Box 6.5 provides several recommendations for revitalizing and improving neighborhood groups. Box 6.6 provides ways to improve conventional public meetings.

"Walkshops" and other street exercises. Many different processes and exercises get residents out on the street to better understand, discuss, and make decisions about the built environment. These "block walks," "walkshops," and other street exercises

Box 6.5. Revitalizing a Neighborhood Group

The groups that serve as the "ground floor" for local democracy on land use issues can be revitalized in a number of ways:

- **Surface and reconcile core interests.** A key step in founding and renewing neighborhood groups is giving people a chance to articulate their hopes and concerns in a way that helps them understand one another and unite around common goals.

- **Develop a plan for staffing.** Running a neighborhood group is time-consuming, and staffing is generally under-resourced. Most neighborhood groups are run by volunteers, although some are staffed or supported by nonprofit organizations or public employees. All of these options can work, if there is a well-thought-out plan for staffing.

- **Recruit extensively.** Generating a critical mass is central to effecting change. Recruitment efforts should pay special attention to the networks of people who have not typically been engaged.

- **Partner with others.** Joining forces with other area organizations can help give a neighborhood group the critical mass and gravitas it needs to effect change. Establishing a hyperlocal online forum—or connecting with one that already exists—can also help generate broader participation.

- **Make meetings participatory.** Instead of "talking heads," meetings should feature small-group discussion, games, and other engaging exercises.

- **Make meetings more social, kid-friendly, frequent, and fun.** People will participate if the experience allows them to interact with friends and bring their kids, and if it involves or recognizes young adults. Food and refreshments, as well as entertainment such as music, art, or drama, can also improve meetings.

- **Meet more often.** If people value the experience, they will make time for it.

- **Act as well as meet.** Organizing some kind of whole-group public work project every year (and recruiting extensively for it) can be a particularly effective strategy.

can be incorporated as a regular part of the neighborhood decision-making routine (Kent, 2013; Nedland, 2013; Wates, 2000). As Toderian and Glover (2014) write:

> The "walkshop" is more than just a neighborhood tour—it's a moving conversation, educated and stimulated by looking around. Typically on foot or bike, walkshops allow community members and planners

to better understand their neighborhood together; to document community assets; and to showcase and discuss new and ongoing initiatives.

Tactical urbanism. Tactical urbanism embraces "small-scale, short-term interventions meant to inspire long-term change" (Lydon, Bartman, Woudstra, & Khawarzad, 2011; Pfeifer, 2013). It emphasizes social capital and citizen-government collaboration and encourages residents to contribute ideas and their own time, energy, and "sweat equity" needed to help implement them. Most examples of tactical urbanism are temporary efforts, initiated either by citizens or planners, which emerge organically as people recognize challenges or opportunities in the built environment and are inspired to tackle them. However, they could be used more consistently to foster neighborhood decision making. Regular appeals to residents for creative ideas, streamlined processes for permitting and zoning, and making space in official planning processes are all promising ways to support tactical urbanism (Pfeifer, 2013).

Enabling Community Decision Making

The city or town level is where citizens move from the most immediate, visible problems they face—What kind of development will be allowed near my house? When will the street be repaved?—to the broader questions of what kind of place they want to live in—What is being done to protect green space? How can multimodal transportation be integrated into the community? As noted above, there are many official settings for decision making. There are also many different kinds of participatory processes, including visioning efforts, charrettes, placemaking workshops, and crowdsourcing exercises.

But improving public engagement in land use is more than just a matter of pressuring planners to use more participatory techniques. Realizing the potential of participation also requires making it something for which communities plan. This can be done, for example, through processes that enable citizens and public officials to work out how people want to be engaged on land use issues in the future. What lessons from the temporary efforts, which often feature productive thick and thin participation strategies, can be applied to the ways that planning and zoning happens on an ongoing basis? Can residents envision a more livable community—and also a more successfully democratic one? Many participation vehicles can be used to drive this kind of thinking and to institutionalize participation in planning.

Planning and zoning commissions and development authorities. The work of land use commissions and development authorities can become more participatory in a number of ways. First and foremost, their regular meetings can be improved through changes in the agendas, venues, and facilitation practices (see Box 6.6 for tips on revamping public meetings). Second, commissions could instigate regular comprehensive planning processes and comp plan updates that not only help residents set priorities, but also offer them options for routine, ongoing participation. Third, commissions could interact regularly with residents through neighborhood and homeowner associations, hyperlocal online forms, and other networks to anticipate issues and concerns.

Regional planning and transportation commissions. Although our political jurisdictions at the local level are confined to cities and towns, many key challenges and opportunities in planning and land use are actually regional: they affect an entire metropolitan area and require efforts that are coordinated across jurisdictional lines. Because most participation efforts engage people in the issues facing their city or town, they may miss or minimize the need for regional planning. In the last two decades, regional planning commissions have emerged to facilitate collaboration among local officials and other regional stakeholders, but they have not typically been hubs for public participation. Bill Barnes, formerly of the National League of Cities, argues that regions need to establish a common public discourse, built on the acknowledgement that "cities have common challenges, functions, and purposes" (Barnes, 2012; see also Barnes & Ledebur, 1998). To do this, regional commissions could adopt many of the same democratic practices as planning and zoning commissions: introducing changes to their regular meetings, initiating participatory regional visioning processes, and helping to weave a stronger web of online and face-to-face forums for citizens.

Encouraging Public Work

Countless residents have helped improve their neighborhoods and communities by planting trees, cleaning up streets and vacant lots, establishing community gardens and urban farms, removing graffiti, painting murals and "traffic calming" circles, cleaning up rivers and streams, building playgrounds, and pitching in on many other kinds of volunteer efforts. These forms of public work have positive impacts on neighborhoods, communities, and residents.

Coordinating these efforts is the main focus of many neighborhood and homeowners' associations. Neighborhood leaders might capitalize on their potential to connect residents and to make an impact on decision making by connecting

Box 6.6. Revamping the Public Meeting

Conventional public meetings can work more smoothly when they use strategies to make those meetings more participatory, transparent, and effective (and when a community has other opportunities for thin and thick participation). Public officials can:

- **Adopt a small-group format for some topics.** Depending on state and local law, small-group formats can be used as part of the main meeting or as a separate session before or after the formal proceedings. Randomly assign individuals to groups of five to twelve people; provide discussion questions relevant to the issue under consideration; ask for volunteer group facilitators (offer basic training periodically so that some attendees have these skills); and ask people to introduce themselves and explain why they care about the issue. (See the Participation Skills Module for more information.) Public officials can take part or simply observe, although active participation is usually more valuable.

- **Hold the meetings in places other than city hall.** Allow different community groups and institutions to host these meetings, and invite them to recruit attendees from their networks.

- **Televise the meetings and allow people to participate online or by phone.** Televised community conversations can reach a broad audience, and participation can be increased by allowing questions, comments, or poll responses to be given by phone, social media, or text message. Crowdsourcing techniques can be used to prioritize questions and comments.

- **Change the room layout.** Changing the physical setup so that public officials are not removed from citizens sends an important signal about the value of public participation.

- **Use a moderator.** A skilled moderator, who is trusted and respected by all parties, can facilitate and improve the interactions between board or council members and the public by ensuring that conflicts are addressed productively and all voices are heard.

- **Frame issues broadly and provide information.** Policy decisions are often framed in very narrow terms, without an adequate description of the data, assumptions, and broad goals that brought the public body to the particular decision. Without this background information, citizens (and sometimes public officials and employees) can lose sight of what is being decided and why. Make this information available online and at the meeting.

- **Make clear what kinds of participation are needed in which situations.** Adopt a framework that helps public officials decide when an issue requires a broader, more intensive, more participatory process before a final decision is made. If this framework is itself produced through some sort of public participation process, it will help set clearer expectations for how people will be involved in governance. One potential model is the "What's Next, Alexandria" process in Alexandria, Virginia, which produced a civic engagement handbook.

- **Follow up and report back.** Public boards and councils should always report on how citizen input was used, the reasons behind officials' decisions, and the ways that people can become involved with the issue in the future. This should be done in a range of ways, including social media, other online tools, and face-to-face meetings.

For more information, see Amsler (2005); City of Alexandria (2014); Fung (2010); Gurwitt (2013); and Toderian and Glover (2014).

volunteer campaigns to the other five blocks of participation activities. Tracking and quantifying how much time residents spend improving their built environment can also help neighborhood leaders negotiate with public officials and other stakeholders. There are several ways to encourage and augment public work around planning and land use.

Crowdfunding and mini-grant programs. As we noted in the chapters on education and health, small amounts of money can leverage large contributions of volunteer time and labor. The organizations that exist in the planning and land use arena—from governmental bodies such as planning and zoning commissions to citizen-driven groups like neighborhood councils and homeowner associations—can use mini-grants to seed and support problem solving or community improvement efforts. Crowdsourcing is also growing as a tool with which to fund local land use initiatives, particularly those with a "green" or "eco-friendly" twist. For example, WeTheTrees helps people fund their permaculture, sustainability, and activism projects, and Naturfunding focuses on crowdfunding for environmental initiatives.

Apps and platforms for teams and tasks. Many of the community projects and initiatives undertaken in the name of land use require the coordination of teams and tasks. Again, many of the same software tools, apps, and platforms used for volunteer coordination and project management in education and health can also be used in land use. Some of these are mapping and task coordination platforms like PublicStuff, ChangeByUs, and Shareabouts. Another example is SnowCrew, which helps cities respond to snowstorms: volunteers can sign up to shovel out driveways and sidewalks (or public amenities, like fire hydrants) for residents who are elderly or disabled. Other online tools, such as Community Tool Box Workstations and CivicEvolution, can help small teams coordinate and collaborate.

As communities work to activate participation leaders and strengthen the buildings blocks of their participation infrastructure for planning and land use, they also need to focus on integrating a variety of supports into the existing systems. We discuss these systemic supports in the final section of this chapter.

STRENGTHENING THE INFRASTRUCTURE: SYSTEMIC SUPPORTS FOR PARTICIPATION IN PLANNING

To make local democracy work, the activities in the building blocks described above must be supported by a system that prepares and rewards people for being involved in participation on planning and land use issues. While citizens, public officials, planners, and other participation leaders will continue to find new ways to engage their neighbors, these innovations will rarely survive to reach their full potential if they are left on their own. Ethan Kent (2013) of the Project for Public Spaces writes that "If the ultimate goal of governance, urban institutions, and development is to make places, communities, and regions more prosperous, civilized, and attractive for all people, then government processes need to change to reflect that goal." In Part Three of this book, we delve into this topic in more depth, but several critical supports are worth mentioning here.

Training and Skill Development

The field of planning and land use is full of participation leaders who develop bold and interesting visions for how the built environment ought to look. In some cases, these leaders succeed in realizing those visions, often because they are able to describe them persuasively or because they are good at negotiation. These skills are valuable, but planners, neighborhood leaders, and other people involved in land use issues also need skills for recruitment, communication, process design, and other aspects of participation (see the Participation Skills Module for more information about these skills). Some cities provide training that also serves to connect neighborhood leaders to one another and to public employees in ways that build relationships and communities of practice (Leighninger, 2009). Numerous individuals and nonprofit organizations also provide these kinds of training.

Professional Incentives for Planners and Other Participation Leaders

Success in public participation could be incorporated into the formula for pay raises, promotions, and other modes of professional advancement for planners and other land use officials. As in other fields, this structural change requires planners, community members, and public officials to define participation, identify the particular kinds of engagement that are important to each job position, and have ways to measure the quantity and quality of that engagement. Of course, the participation infrastructure for land use could also feature practitioners who are employed by neighborhood organizations, corporations, universities, school systems, and other institutions. For these positions, definitions and measures of participation could also be incorporated into professional incentive structures.

Many participation leaders in planning and land use will come from nongovernmental (and often non-"official") organizations, and they, too, need incentives for their work. A number of non-monetary incentives, such as recognition, awards, and forms of authority and legitimacy, can be devised to inspire these leaders.

Policies and Procedures

How local governments conduct public meetings, and interact with citizens generally, is a matter of local and state law—and in most cases, the laws are unclear and out-of-date (Working Group on Legal Frameworks for Public Participation, 2013). Changing from conventional formats to more productive thick and thin processes may require a revision, or at least a clearer interpretation, of the local legal framework. Neighborhood councils may also be subject to local ordinances and state laws, since they may receive public funds or have formal public roles. But even volunteer and nonprofit groups need clarity, legal and procedural, in their relationships with decision-makers and the policymaking process. When and how will they be involved by policymakers, on what kinds of issues—and how should they best express neighborhood ideas and concerns to policymakers?

Funding and Budgeting

It is ironic that public participation in planning is sometimes dismissed as too expensive, since land use is an issue where the lack of effective engagement often leads to cost overruns, construction delays, and lost investments by governments and developers. But in addition to simply recognizing the economic value of participation, communities should also take stock of the way this work is funded. Typically, planning departments, developers, and other interested groups treat each new planning decision as a separate topic for participation and spend staff time and money on a discrete set of events, websites, or other activities. Connecting and strengthening the infrastructure for participation might be a more efficient investment. Communities that have neighborhood groups, hyperlocal online forums, and comprehensive plans that convene and represent large numbers of people (to name just a few potential elements) will be better equipped to make difficult land use decisions.

SUMMARY

There is great potential for public participation in planning and land use. People care about their homes, their neighborhoods, and the quality of their built environment. Participation in land use and planning has developed around four main areas: major zoning decisions, community visioning, community development planning, and prioritizing public services. Within each of these areas, research shows that good participation can produce a wide variety of benefits. Driven by the conflicts between citizens and government that conventional public participation cannot handle, planners and other leaders have created thick and thin forms of engagement that tend to be more successful. However, conventional processes still dominate in most communities.

In this chapter, we provided a number of suggestions about how to strengthen the participation infrastructure for planning and land use. Specifically, we asserted that participation can be improved if:

1. *Leaders and networks for participation are activated and empowered.* Most communities have official settings for participation, and numerous potential participation leaders, at both the community and neighborhood levels. In addition, most communities have a range of networks and constituents that can play an active role. Activating and empowering leaders in these settings and networks can go a long way toward creating a broader, more supportive framework for participation in planning and land use.

2. *The six building blocks of participation activities are put into place.* Most communities already undertake a number of activities related to disseminating information, gathering input and data, discussing and connecting, enabling neighborhood decision making, enabling community decision making, and encouraging public work. However, in most places, these activities are designed with conventional formats and are not well connected with one another. The infrastructure for participation in planning and land use can be strengthened if communities incorporate a wider variety of thin and thick participation tools or vehicles into the picture.

3. *Systemic supports are used to make participation sustainable, strong, and resilient.* To help people take on new roles, connect the different building blocks to one another, and institutionalize participation in the regular functioning of planning and land use activities, communities and institutions need to develop several systemic supports, including training and skill development, professional incentives, policies and procedures, and funding and budgeting.

While this may seem to set a high bar for public participation in planning and land use, it need not be insurmountable. To achieve the benefits of participation planning and land use, communities should take stock of the current picture of engagement, consider the kinds of participation activities they want to foster and support, and make changes within and outside of their institutions to give people a stronger role in the governance of their neighborhoods and communities.

DISCUSSION QUESTIONS

1. Review the common planning and land use issues listed in Table 6.1. Which are the most important? Which do you think are best addressed through public participation? Why?

2. Summarize the current official settings for planning and land use at the neighborhood and community levels. How can participation at these levels be improved?

3. Who are (or should be) the key actors in participation in planning and land use? What is (or should be) each actor's role in participation? Do those roles vary depending on whether participation is happening at the neighborhood or community level?

4. Define NIMBY, CAVE, and BANANA. What do you believe are the effects of these terms on participation in planning and land use?

5. Use the questions in Box 6.2 to assess the state of land use participation in your community.

6. Review the six building blocks for a stronger participation infrastructure in planning and land use (Figure 6.3). Which building blocks are present in your neighborhood or community? Are the

(continued)

(continued)

participation opportunities conventional, thin, or thick? Which opportunities would you like to see?

7. Does your neighborhood or community have "welcoming spaces" for participation? How are such spaces used, and how can they be better used?

8. Box 6.6 provides a list of suggestions for revamping the public meeting. What other changes would you like to see in public meetings and forums?

9. What kinds of skills, training, and incentives do you think would work best to support participation in planning and land use? Why?

10. What are the major planning and land use issues in your community? How could public participation be used to address these issues?

References

American Institute of Architects. (2010). *Bridgeport, CT SDAT [Sustainable Design Action Team]*. Washington, DC: American Institute of Architects.

Ames, Steven C. (1998). *A guide to community visioning*. Portland, OR: Oregon Visions Project, Oregon Chapter of the American Planning Association.

Amsler, Terry. (2005). Getting the most out of public meetings. Sacramento, CA: Institute for Local Government. Available at www.ca-ilg.org/sites/main/files/file-attachments/2005_-_gettin_the_most_out_of_public_hearings.pdf.

Amsler, Terry. (2008). Involving the public in city planning. *Western City*. Available at www.westerncity.com/pdfs/Civic_Partnership_Standalone_Final.pdf.

Arnstein, Sherry R. (1969). A ladder of citizen participation. *Journal of the American Planning Association*, 35(4): 216–224.

Barnes, William. (2012). *Emerging issues: Can local democracy save national democracy?* Washington, DC: National League of Cities. Available at www.nlc.org/media-center/news-search/emerging-issues-can-local-democracy-save-national-democracy.

Barnes, William, & Larry Ledebur. (1998). *The new regional economies: The U.S. common market and the global economy*. Thousand Oaks, CA: Sage.

Berry, Jeffrey M., Kent E. Portney, & Ken Thomson. (1993). *The rebirth of urban democracy*. Washington, DC: Brookings Institution Press.

Bishop, Bill. (2009). *The big sort: Why the clustering of like-minded America is tearing us apart*. Boston, MA: Mariner Books.

Black, Alissa, & Bita Neyestani. (2014). *Public pathways: A guide to online engagement tools for local governments*. Washington, DC: New America Foundation.

Brown, Alison, & Annali Kristiansen. (2009). *Urban policies and the right to the city: Rights, responsibilities and citizenship*. New York, NY: UNESCO.

CEOs for Cities. (2010). *We can engage in a robust public life*. Available at http://5000plus. net.au/assets/6508a19a39d2895092c3d2c5f94f301bfa3a8209/ceos-for-cities_we_can_ engage_in_a_robust_public_life.pdf.

City of Alexandria. (2014). *Alexandria's handbook for civic engagement*. Alexandria, VA. Available at https://www.alexandriava.gov/uploadedFiles/special/CivicEngagement/ web_boxes/WNA%20HANDBOOK%20FINAL%20reduced_3_2014.pdf.

Coulson, Andrew. (2014). The gamification of community engagement. *CommsGoDigital*. Available at www.commsgodigital.com.au/2014/01/gamification-in-community- engagement-offline/.

Day, Diane. (1997). Citizen participation in the planning process: An essentially contested concept? *Journal of Planning Literature, 11*(3): 421–434.

Diers, Jim. (2008). *From the ground up: Community's role in addressing street level social issues*. Calgary, Canada: Canada West Foundation.

Fung, Archon. (2010). How to hold a town hall meeting. *Capitol Ideas*. Available at www. csg.org/pubs/capitolideas/mar_apr_2010/pdfs_mar/CI_Mar2010.pdf.

Ganapati, Sukumar. (2010). *Using geographic information systems to increase citizen engagement*. Washington, DC: IBM Center for the Business of Government.

Gordon, Eric, Steven Schirra, & Justin Hollander. (2011). Immersive planning: A conceptual model for designing public participation with new technologies. *Environment and Planning B: Planning and Design, 38*(3): 505–519.

Gurwitt, Rob. (2013). How technology is changing citizen engagement in Austin. *Government Technology*. Available at www.govtech.com/local/how-technology-is-changing- citizen-engagement-in-austin.html.

Harvey, David. (2008). The right to the city. *New Left Review, 53*: 23–40.

Hoene, Christopher, Christopher Kingsley, & Matthew Leighninger. (2013). *Bright spots in community engagement: Case studies of U.S. communities creating greater civic participation from the bottom up*. Washington, DC: National League of Cities.

International Association for Public Participation. (2007). *IAP2 spectrum of public participation*. Thornton, CO: International Association for Public Participation. Available at http://iap2. affiniscape.com/associations/4748/files/IAP2%20Spectrum_vertical.pdf.

Jacobs, Jane. (1961). *The death and life of great American cities*. New York, NY: Random House.

Kent, Ethan. (2013). *What if governments focused on creating great places to live and work?* New York, NY: Project for Public Spaces. Available at www.pps.org/reference/toward- place-governance-civic-infrastructure-placemaking/.

Kiger, Patrick J. (2014). How Vancouver invented itself. *Urban Land*. Available at http://urbanland.uli.org/development-business/how-vancouver-invented-itself/.

Knight Foundation. (2010). *Soul of the community 2010. Why people love where they live and why it matters: A national perspective*. Miami, FL: Knight Foundation.

Kotkin, Joel. (2011). The demise of the luxury city. *Forbes.com*. Available at www.forbes.com/sites/joelkotkin/2011/09/20/the-demise-of-the-luxury-city/.

Lefebvre, Henri. (1996). Right to the city, English translation of 1968 text. In E. Kofman & E. Lebas (Eds. and translators), *Writings on cities*, 14759. Oxford, England: Blackwell Publishing.

Leighninger, Matt. (2006). *The next form of democracy: How expert rule is giving way to shared governance—and why politics will never be the same*. Nashville, TN: Vanderbilt University Press.

Leighninger, Matt. (2009). *The promise and challenge of neighborhood democracy: Lessons from the intersection of government and community*. Austin, TX: Grassroots Grantmakers.

Leighninger, Matt. (2011). *Using online tools to engage—and be engaged by—the public*. Washington, DC: IBM Center for the Business of Government.

Lennertz, Bill, & Aarin Lutzenhiser. (2006). *The charrette handbook: The essential guide for accelerated, collaborative community planning*. Chicago, IL: American Planning Association.

Lerner, Josh. (2014). *Making democracy fun: How game design can empower citizens and transform politics*. Cambridge, MA: MIT Press.

Levine, Peter. (2010). *How a community can own a resource*. Available at www.peterlevine.ws/mt/archives/2010/07/how-a-community.html.

LogoLink. (2014). *The right to citizen participation at the local level*. São Paulo, Brazil: LogoLink.

Lukensmeyer, Carolyn J. (2013). *Bringing citizen voices to the table: A guide for public managers*. San Francisco, CA: Jossey-Bass.

Lydon, Mike, Dan Bartman, Ronald Woudstra, & Aurash Khawarzad. (2011). *Tactical urbanism: Short-term action, long-term change* (Vol. 1). New York, NY: The Street Plans Collaborative.

McCabe, Barbara. (2010). Neighborhood and homeowner associations. In. J. H. Svara & J. Denhardt (Eds.), *Connected communities: Local governments as partners in citizen engagement and community building*, 112–114. Phoenix, AZ: Alliance for Innovation.

McKenzie, Jessica. (2014). In Brooklyn, testing a texting platform that connects locals, representatives & community leaders. *Tech President*. Available at http://techpresident.com/news/25184/brooklyn-testing-texting-platform-connects-locals-representatives-community-leaders.

Mehaffy, Michael. (2014). 5 key themes emerging from the "new science of cities." *City-Lab*. Available at www.citylab.com/design/2014/09/5-key-themes-emerging-from-the-new-science-of-cities/380233/.

Mergel, Ines. (2013). *Social media in the public sector: A guide to participation, collabora-tion, and transparency in the networked world.* San Francisco, CA: Jossey-Bass.

Mills, Joel. (2011). Urban planning's civic dividend. *Planetizen.* Available at www.planeti-zen.com/node/47902.

Moore, Carl M., Gianni Longo, & Patsy Palmer. (1999). Visioning. In L. Susskind, S. McKearnan, & J. Thomas-Larmer (Eds.), *The consensus building handbook*, 557–590. Thousand Oaks, CA: Sage.

Mossberger, Karen, Yonghong Wu, & Jared Crawford. (2013). Connecting citizens and local governments? Social media and interactivity in major U.S. cities. *Government In-formation Quarterly, 30*(4): 351–358.

Nabatchi, Tina. (2012). Putting the "public" back in public values research: Designing public participation to identify and respond to public values. *Public Administration Review, 72*(5), 699–708.

NCL. (2000). *The community visioning and strategic planning handbook.* Denver, CO: Na-tional Civic League.

Nedland, Marcia. (2013). 7 keys to aligning strategies for neighborhood change. *Stable Communities.* Available at www.stablecommunities.org/blog_03-18-13.

Nemani, Abhi. (2014a.) Let's build some infrastructure to make things matter even more. Available at https://medium.com/@abhinemani/lets-build-some-infrastructure-to-make-things-matter-even-more-ca7102d92b01.

Nemani, Abhi. (2014b). Small (city) pieces, loosely joined. Available at https://medium.com/@abhinemani/small-city-pieces-loosely-joined-5202fb5a93e3.

Nemani, Abhi. (2014c). Turning civic service into a call-to-action. *Government Execu-tive.* Available at www.govexec.com/state-local/2014/08/ahbi-nemani-civic-interest-action/90695/.

Newman, Oscar. (1996). *Creating defensible space.* Washington, DC: U.S. Depart-ment of Housing and Urban Development, Office of Policy Development and Research.

Pfeifer, Laura. (2013). *The planner's guide to tactical urbanism.* Montreal, Canada. Avail-able at http://reginaurbanecology.files.wordpress.com/2013/10/tuguide1.pdf.

Popper, Ben. (2014). The anti-Facebook: One in four American neighborhoods are now using this private social network. *The Verge.* Available at www.theverge.com/2014/8/18/6030393/nextdoor-private-social-network-40000-neighborhoods.

Potter, Gwen. (2013). *Public participation in planning as urban citizenship: Contrasting two conceptualizations of citizenship in Toronto's ward 2.* Available at http://fes.yorku.ca/node/41004.

Putnam, Robert. (2000). *Bowling alone: The collapse and revival of American community.* New York, NY: Simon & Schuster.

Reich, Jay, Stacey Crawshaw-Lewis, & Deanna Gregory. (2004). *Public development authorities.* Seattle, WA: Municipal Research and Services Center (MRSC). Available at https://www.mrsc.org/artdocmisc/PDA-IB516.pdf.

Sirianni, Carmen, & Jennifer Girouard. (2012). The civics of urban planning. In R. Weber & R. Crane (Eds.), *The Oxford handbook of urban planning*, 669–690. New York, NY: Oxford University Press.

Smith, Aaron. (2010). *Neighbors online*. Washington, DC: Pew Internet & American Life Project.

Stern, Seth. (2003). $14.6 billion later, Boston's Big Dig wraps up. *The Christian Science Monitor*. Available at www.csmonitor.com/2003/1219/p02s01-ussc.html.

Toderian, Brent, & Jillian Glover. (2014). 10 lessons in more engaging citizen engagement. *Planetizen*. Available at www.planetizen.com/node/67656.

Wates, Nick. (2000). *The community planning handbook: How people can shape their cities, towns and villages in any part of the world*. London, UK: Earthscan.

Working Group on Legal Frameworks for Public Participation. (2013). *Making public participation legal*. Denver, CO: National Civic League.

Participation in State and Federal Government

People care about what happens in their state capitals and Washington, D.C. Public participation in state and federal government is important to people because:

- State and federal policies affect local decisions on all kinds of issues. State and federal laws help define how city councils, school boards, and other community decision-makers can operate; state and federal governments have jurisdiction over land and facilities that are important to communities, including many forests and parks, highways and subways, waste cleanups and brownfields, reservoirs and watersheds, and military bases and historic properties.

- State and federal policies affect us directly, on issues ranging from health care to gun control and immigration to Social Security.

- Even when they do not affect us directly, we care about many of these policies because they reflect who we are. We identify with our nation and states, and we have a stake in the actions they take and the values they represent.

- We have reached a level of distrust in state and federal government that is unparalleled in our history. In addition to making governance more difficult, the poor relationships between people and policymakers may have other negative effects on our society.

At the most fundamental level, participation in state and federal government is important simply because people want it: in poll responses, people favor laws and policies that would support and institutionalize public engagement (NCoC, 2008). This desire probably reflects the reasons given in the bulleted list above, but it may also signify the demand for a different, more adult-adult, relationship between citizens and their state and federal governments.

Some political candidates have picked up on this desire and have made citizenship and participation a common refrain in their campaign rhetoric. In recent years, presidential candidates from both major parties have spoken in vague but inspiring ways about the new roles they see citizens playing in our democracy. Republican John McCain (2001) championed the "brave and determined energies" of citizens "mobilized and empowered by national government." Democrat John Edwards called for the creation of "Citizen Congresses" in which millions of Americans would participate in deliberations about critical policy issues (Bingham, 2007; Gastil, 2007). Republican Lamar Alexander's (1995) campaign slogan was "The people know what to do."

In his speech announcing that he would seek the Democratic nomination for president in 2008, Barack Obama (2007) struck a deep chord, saying: "This campaign has to be about reclaiming the meaning of citizenship, restoring our sense of common purpose, and realizing that few obstacles can withstand the power of millions of voices calling for change." In most of his campaign speeches (and even after his election), Obama called for "active citizenship" (Katz, Barris, & Jain, 2013). In May 2008, he declared:

> We must use all available technologies and methods to open up the federal government, creating a new level of transparency to change the way business is conducted in Washington, and giving Americans the chance to participate in government deliberations and decision making in ways that were not possible only a few years ago. (Katz, Barris, & Jain, 2013)

(For more about the participatory tactics Obama used on the campaign trail, see Chapter 3).

For the most part, however, the changes we have seen at the federal and state levels have centered on information dissemination. The "chance to participate in government deliberations and decision making" has not materialized. Lofty campaign rhetoric has not translated into meaningful participatory governance.

These unfulfilled promises have made Americans even more dissatisfied with political processes and institutions. National polls conducted in 2014 show that only 15 percent of Americans approve of the way Congress is handling its job (Breitman, 2014), and only 13 percent believe the government can be trusted to do what is right always or most of the time (Steinhauser, 2014). Trust in state governments is higher, but it too has declined, with seven states now showing average levels of trust below 50 percent (Jones, 2014). "The number who trust the government . . . has sunk so low that it is hard to remember that there was ever a time when Americans routinely trusted the government," said CNN Polling Director Keating Holland (Steinhauser, 2014).

But while expanding public participation seems a promising way to reverse these trends, understanding how to do so is not easy. There are, of course, many differences between state and federal government, as well as tremendous variations among the fifty state governments. Within those governments, one could examine participation within and across the branches, as well as within and across the numerous departments, agencies, bureaus, offices, and other administrative units. This diversity means that the term "public participation" is applied to a wide and often confusing array of government activities, reflecting highly disparate goals and assumptions about citizens. In addition to the challenges created by the sheer size and diversity of state and federal governments, there are obstacles to and confusion about how to "scale up" the strategies and successes of local participation to the state and federal levels.

This chapter attempts to cut through the confusion, offering strategies for improving participation at the state and federal levels. However, by necessity, this is a broad-brush approach; we cannot deal separately with every government, agency, department, and program. Instead, we explain the main forces driving the development of participation in state and federal government, describe some of the official settings for engagement, and suggest ways to strengthen the infrastructure for participation. While some of the same motivations for engaging the public are evident across governments, the dynamics of participation in the legislative branch are somewhat different from those in administrative agencies; therefore, we look at each area separately.

THE DEVELOPMENT OF PARTICIPATION IN THE LEGISLATIVE BRANCH

Citizen anger has been a continual force in the development of public participation by legislators. At both the state and federal levels, legislators have experienced hostile exchanges with passionate constituents at highly charged conventional public meetings. In a few cases, these interactions have inspired public officials and other organizations to experiment with more deliberative ways of working, but more often, they have led to the use of less participatory, more controlled forms of engagement.

Civil society organizations and other groups outside of government sometimes convene thick and thin participation processes at the state or national level; in these cases, legislators may be involved but are not in charge. Some of these processes have achieved considerable success. However, most suffer from two challenges: (1) problems of scale and (2) lack of connection to policymakers and policy processes. Thicker forms of participation have channeled citizen anger productively, but not often at the scale needed to influence public policy, while the thinner forms have scaled more easily, but not always in a manner that is meaningful for either legislators or participants.

The "Mad and Angry Folks"

In interviews with state and federal legislators for their research on *Bridging the Gap Between Public Officials and the Public*, Tina Nabatchi and Cynthia Farrar (2011) found that, although some view participation as a job requirement ("a necessary part of the game") and essential for their political survival, most are also leery of its risks. One state legislator captured a common sentiment by saying: "There's a perception right now that the only people that would show up to an opportunity to engage their legislator are going to be the mad and angry folks" (Nabatchi & Farrar, 2011: 8). At both the state and federal levels, legislators

> doubted the motivation and willingness of citizens to participate
> ...were fearful of being attacked by angry, partisan, and uninformed
> citizens; were apprehensive of cultivating critics, being caught off
> guard, or subjected to negative press coverage; and worried that
> such processes would be "hijacked" or "commandeered" by orga-
> nized interests. They argued that deliberation was not politically
> feasible and expedient because they are forced to cater to the loud-
> est and most extreme voices and the people with money to finance
> campaigns. They felt trapped in and saw fellow legislators as cor-
> rupted by a legislative system that is itself not civil and deliberative.
> (Nabatchi & Farrar, 2011: ii).

When asked about public participation, one of the first connections legislators make is to the ill-fated "town hall meetings" on health care reform held in the summer of 2009. These meetings mainly consisted of presentations by the Member of Congress, followed by a question-and-answer session with attendees. Recruitment was done primarily through the mass media, which meant that organized groups like the Tea Party were able to pack the meetings with their followers. These sessions were not facilitated, reasoned, deliberative, or productive, and interactions were generally between angry participants and their elected officials, rather than among participants (Kraushaar & Lerer, 2009; Levine, 2013; Lukensmeyer, 2013). Few if any elements of an adult-adult relationship were evident in these meetings.

For many Members of Congress, as well as for state legislators, those meetings were simply a higher-profile version of the same sorts of dysfunctional dynamics they had experienced on other issues. In any case, 2009 may have been a watershed moment: many journalists report that public participation efforts by Members of Congress, and particularly those that involve face-to-face events, have fallen steadily since then (e.g., Kroll, 2011; Rupp, 2013). Not only is there a declining number of town hall meetings held by members of Congress on both sides of the aisle, but Congressional offices are also reportedly going to greater lengths to conceal when and where the meetings take place (Peters, 2013), or arranging meetings in which they give a talk, but do not take questions (Zeleny, 2010).

In contrast, there appears to be growing use of thin participation mechanisms, particularly those that use one-way communication (such as static websites, newsletters, and direct mailings) or limited two-way communication (such as social media, opinion surveys, and polls). For example, Nabatchi and Farrar (2011) found that many legislators, especially at the federal level, use "telephone town halls" (also referred to as tele-town halls). Tele-town halls use software that allows legislators to conduct live telephone forums with hundreds or even thousands of constituents simultaneously. On the one hand, tele-town halls provide a remedy for several problems with traditional face-to-face town halls: they are less resource-intensive, do not require large organizing and logistics efforts, and reach large numbers of people in a short time (and often those who otherwise would not be engaged). They are especially attractive to legislators representing large or rural districts. On the other hand, tele-town halls perpetuate many of the problems with conventional participation: constituents have to get in a queue to ask a question or make a comment and do not have the opportunity to discuss issues in any depth. Perhaps more problematic is that staffers can control the conversations for the legislator. One interviewee reported that the tele-town hall interface allows staffers to strategically select among constituents: "We don't want to talk to Fred, because we know Fred's question is going to be on immigration and . . . that's the last thing I want to talk about" so Fred is skipped in the queue (Nabatchi & Farrar, 2011: 29).

When Other Organizations Convene, Legislators (Sometimes) Listen

Although legislators may be increasingly reluctant to lead participation processes, some express curiosity and occasionally even support for projects convened by organizations outside government. These settings are less risky for legislators. For both the officials and the convening organizations, they offer at least a chance of reducing partisanship and rancor, reaching informed policy recommendations, and generating the broad support necessary for implementing those ideas.

A handful of thick participation processes have been organized at the national level by organizations outside government. The 2008 National Citizens' Technology Forum, organized by the Center for Nanotechnology in Society at Arizona State University, was a series of online and face-to-face meetings across the United States. The goal was to develop citizen recommendations for dealing with new technologies such as nanotechnology, biotechnology, information technologies, and cognitive science. The meetings occurred in six different locations across the United States and involved a total of seventy-four participants who reflected local and national demographics. A final report about the recommendations was presented to a group of U.S. policymakers, researchers, and media at a meeting in Washington, D.C. While organizers had hoped that the recommendations would influence future government policy, their effect has been minimal (for more information, see Hamlett, Cobb, & Guston 2008; see also http://participedia.net/en/cases/national-citizens-technology-forum-usa).

Our Budget, Our Economy (OBOE), organized by America*Speaks*, was a 21st Century Town Meeting held in nineteen communities across the United States, with more than 3,500 individuals who comprised a relatively representative set of participants, both demographically and ideologically. An additional thirty-eight community conversations were organized by volunteers, but may not have had a representative set of participants. The purpose of OBOE was to devise possible solutions to America's long-term fiscal challenges, particularly the national debt. Independent evaluations suggest that participants were able to set aside their ideological views and work toward the common goal of fiscal responsibility and debt reduction. Input from the event was presented to President Obama's National Commission on Fiscal Responsibility and Reform and the Senate and House Budget Committees, as well as other congressional offices and caucuses. The final Commission report included recommendations that drew from OBOE data (Lukensmeyer, 2013; for more information, see Esterling, Fung, & Lee, 2010; http://participedia.net/en/cases/our-budget-our-economy-united-states).

Early examples of statewide participatory processes organized by civil society include "Balancing Justice in Oklahoma" in 1996, which led to a reform of the state's corrections system, and "Healthy Choices Oregon" in 1988, which led to changes in that state's health care system (Leighninger, 2006). A more recent example is the 2007 "CaliforniaSpeaks" project, which was organized by a national nonprofit organization, America*Speaks*. CaliforniaSpeaks brought together a demographically representative sample of nearly 3,500 Californians for an all-day, non-partisan conversation on health care reform. Several state elected officials joined participants at the meeting, including Governor Arnold Schwarzenegger and leaders from the state senate and state assembly. During the process, participants were given neutral, objective information about the issues so that they could develop priorities for statewide health care reform, which were then presented in a report shared with legislators. Independent evaluations show that participants stayed involved in the issue after the process, that policymakers valued the process, and that the legislative proposals moved closer to the public's priorities (Fung & Lee, 2008; Fung, Lee, & Harbage, 2008; Lukensmeyer, 2013).

Other projects at the state level have engaged smaller, demographically representative sets of people, often selected through a random-sample process. For example, the New Jersey Peoples' Tax Assembly of 2003, organized by the New Jersey Coalition for the Public Good, provided recommendations to the legislature for reforming the state's tax system. The Assembly consisted of 100 citizens, a demographic microcosm of the New Jersey population. Facilitators compiled notes from the discussions, which were used along with other materials to produce a final report on the Assembly's findings. The report was provided to the New Jersey Legislature in a set of special hearings and presented at press conferences. However, beyond the creation of a website and the release of several reports, it is unclear whether or how this event affected state legislators' views and decisions on state tax policy (for more information, see Public Agenda with the New Jersey Coalition for the Public Good, 2003; see also http://participedia.net/en/cases/let-people-speak-new-jersey-citizens-tax-assembly-new-jersey-usa).

Another example is the Oregon Citizens' Initiative Review (CIR), which has been used since 2011 to support informed, deliberative evaluation of state ballot initiatives. The CIR empanels twenty to thirty randomly selected and demographically balanced voters from across the state who receive information about the ballot measure and hear directly from experts and advocates. After their deliberations, the panel writes a "Citizens' Statement" that includes key findings, arguments for and against the measure, points of agreement reached by the panel, and a brief comment on the CIR process. The "Citizens' Statement" is published in the statewide voters' pamphlet. The CIR process, which is supported by Oregon state law, has been used to evaluate initiatives on casinos, genetically modified food, education funding, marijuana legalization, and election reform. In their evaluation of the process, John Gastil and Katie Knobloch (2011) found that Oregonians who read the CIR recommendations were likely to follow them—and that on some ballot initiatives, enough of those voters read the pamphlet that it had an effect on whether the measure passed (for more information see http://healthydemocracy.org/citizens-initiative-review/).

The Challenge of Scale and Policy Connection

All of the examples above illustrate the challenges of scaling thick participation for the state and national levels and making appropriate, meaningful connections to policymakers and the policy process. Few of the examples met those challenges. The New Jersey Tax Assembly and Citizens' Technology Forum did not create a critical mass of citizens relative to the scale of the jurisdiction and did not connect to legislators. CaliforniaSpeaks, Balancing Justice in Oklahoma, Healthy Choices Oregon, and to some extent OBOE were at least somewhat successful because they generated a reasonable critical mass and connected to policymakers. The Oregon CIR, which is intended to inform voters rather than legislators, has succeeded to the extent that the outcomes of the process were known to Oregonians.

Thinner kinds of participation processes may be easier to "scale up," but legislators often find it difficult to interpret them. For example, special interest groups often encourage their members to send emails to their legislators, using text that has been provided by the special interest group. Legislators and their staffers often doubt that these kinds of appeals represent the genuine concerns of citizens. "A focus on the large numbers that can be mobilized by electronic means is seen by some legislators as the equivalent of governing by opinion poll, and as both a cause and a consequence of a polarized political environment" (Nabatchi & Farrar, 2011: 10).

Because of their bad participation experiences with conventional participation and their uncertainty over online engagement, legislators have a hard time envisioning more productive forms of participation. Most of them do not have direct experiences with processes that confer the respect, recognition, and responsibility that typify an adult relationship. Instead, legislators are accustomed to the parent-child dynamic between government and citizens. According to Nabatchi and Farrar (2011), legislators express deep skepticism that more productive kinds of engagement are even possible.

Indeed, for at least some legislators, public participation seems to have transitioned from a potential asset to a potential target. One state legislator said, "The more people you get engaged, the more critics you could be breeding. And a lot of my colleagues would say, 'I'd rather keep them in the dark'" (Nabatchi & Farrar, 2011: 14). Some members of Congress have also become increasingly vocal critics of attempts by federal agencies to engage the public. The Centers for Disease Control, an agency that has been unusually active in public participation, has ramped down this work because of language that has been put in its budget allocation by Congress (Dudley, Leighninger, & Gniady, 2014). Hank Topper, a former staffer at the Environmental Protection Agency (EPA), attests that this is becoming a common challenge for agencies: "The Congressional dynamic has a bigger impact on whether agencies do participation than what happens inside the agency. Some Congresspeople treat any expansion of participation as an expansion of the federal government."

THE DEVELOPMENT OF PARTICIPATION IN THE ADMINISTRATIVE REALM

In comparison with their colleagues in the legislative branch, the people working on the administrative side of state and federal government are subject to many legal requirements when they conduct public participation. This legal framework for participation is a hodgepodge of laws and regulations, some decades old. In many cases, these laws require participation without fully defining it; in a few instances, they specifically prescribe how participation must be conducted. In both the laws and in the way that agencies conduct participation, two very different visions of "the public" are evident. In some cases, the public is a set of residents who are concerned about a state or federal decision; in others, the public is a set of experts who are being asked for their input on policy.

The most recent development in participation at the federal level is the Open Government Directive, which set out to make agencies more transparent, collaborative, and participatory. (Similar initiatives have been announced in some states.) However, even among the most successful open government projects, the emphasis has been on informing citizens, gathering data from them, and supporting volunteerism, rather than on giving people a wider array of public choices or a meaningful say in policymaking. The Open Government Directive has led to yet another vision of the public.

The Legal Framework for Participation

As Bingham (2010) notes, the phrase "public participation" appears in the U.S. Code over 200 times and in the U.S. Code of Federal Regulations over 1,000 times. Although few scholars have assessed state laws governing public participation (for an exception, see Piotrowski & Borry, 2010), all fifty states have such laws on the books. For example, public participation at the state level is addressed in state general legislation on administrative procedure, freedom of information and public records, and open public meetings. Specific mandates for public participation at the state level also appear in laws on land use and planning, transportation, elections, budgeting, education, and others (Nabatchi & Amsler, 2014).

Because the term "public participation" (and its variations) is used frequently but defined rarely in laws and regulations, administrators are often confused about when and how to engage the public. Moreover, although the laws do not necessarily prohibit using non-conventional forms of participation, they also do not explicitly allow for it. This leads to administrative concerns about whether particular processes are legal. A recent report, *Priorities for Public Participation and Open Government: Recommendations to President Obama* (PARCC, 2013: 6), notes:

> the laws regulating participation are in tension with the functionality and mission of agencies, as well as with the purposes and goals of participation, and the current legal framework leaves public officials and staff wondering whether the best practices in participation are in fact supported—or even allowed—by the law.

Consequently, administrators know they are authorized and obligated to use public participation, but rarely reach beyond the minimum standards for compliance (Bingham, 2010; Nabatchi & Amsler, 2014). For example, Christian Freitag's (2010: 117, 226) research on public participation under the National Environmental Policy Act finds that officials in the U.S. Forest Service (USFS) generally see participation "as a means to the end of adhering to legal requirements" and "not as an end in itself."

Other laws have a greater effect on how participation is conducted. These include, among others, the Federal Advisory Committee Act (FACA) of 1972 (which governs the establishment, operations, and activities of advisory committees), the

Paperwork Reduction Act (PRA) of 1980 (which regulates the paperwork burden the federal government can impose on private businesses and citizens), and Section 508 of the Rehabilitation Act as amended by the Workforce Investment Act of 1998 (which sets out requirements for use of electronic and information technology). These regulations have become steadily more controversial, and agency staffers increasingly shy away from procedures and requirements they see as unnecessarily bureaucratic.

Finally, the legal framework is complicated by the fact that different laws reflect different assumptions about who and what constitutes "the public." Some laws seem to assume that citizens are non-expert residents who deserve the opportunity to gain information and lodge complaints about public decisions. Other laws seem to encourage "stakeholder" rather than "citizen" participation. For example, the people drawn into advisory committees or other meetings are often scientific or policy experts working for universities, advocacy organizations, trade associations, and other groups that have a stake in the issue being discussed. Both visions of citizenship are evident in the laws and practices of federal and state governments.

"Outside Pressure" and the "Potentially Concerned Public"

A telling term—the "potentially concerned public"—appears in several pieces of legislation that include participation requirements. The most common formats are public hearings, advisory committees, and public comment periods (lasting anywhere from 15 to 180 days during which citizens can submit statements on pending rules and legislation. Unfortunately, although these conventional processes allow "potentially concerned" citizens to raise questions, they do little to quell frustrations.

Having experienced the inability of conventional participation to deal with citizen frustration, some agencies have pioneered more intensive, interactive engagement processes. In personal communications with the authors, Hank Topper, a former EPA staffer, asserted that the "outside pressure" exerted by concerned citizens has produced some of the more innovative forms of public participation. "It is almost impossible for a federal agency to push real participatory work on its own," Topper says. "The only way it can happen is in certain circumstances where there is outside pressure, or if there is a gap where nothing exists—like the lack of a regional natural resources management infrastructure. There just has to be demand for participation from below." This has been particularly true in situations in which state and federal agencies are working on issues of local concern, such as transportation planning, environmental cleanups, and natural resource management.

In some cases, this outside pressure has led to processes that helped foster relationships and collaboration between citizens and government, not just to create policy but also to implement it. In their research on the federal government's track record in "Partnering with Communities," Carmen Sirianni and his colleagues (2010) describe how partnerships became a pathway for:

- Overcoming the limitations of command-and-control regulatory tools, so that communities could have a voice in regulation, and problems could be addressed in a more systemic way;
- Enabling citizen knowledge, participatory research, and "street science" to augment and critique expert and professional knowledge; and
- Building legitimacy and support for policy decisions among citizens and organizations outside government.

Surveying programs in the Environmental Protection Agency, Centers for Disease Control and Prevention, Department of Justice, and Department of Housing and Urban Development, Sirianni and his colleagues (2010) report that federal agencies have supported these partnerships in three main ways: funding projects, facilitating network development, and "coproducing" useful tools such as planning guides, resource clearinghouses, training curricula, and measurement protocols.

Citizens' desire to influence state and federal decision making, particularly when it directly affects their neighborhoods and communities, continues to produce both tension and innovation in participation. Agencies might be more likely to succeed in this work if the laws on potentially concerned citizens were reshaped to reflect the lessons learned by agency staffers about how to address and channel outside pressure.

The "Best Brains Available"

A very different strand in the development of state and federal participation is also apparent in both law and practice. For some agencies, establishing conduits for expert input through advisory committees has long fallen squarely within the definition of public participation (see Chapter 3)—and for many agencies, it remains their main form of engagement. In 1970, the House Committee on Government Operations reviewed the role and effectiveness of federal advisory committees (H.R. REP. NO. 91-1731, at 4 (1970)). They justified the use of advisory committees as "a means by which the best brains and experience available in all fields of business, society, government and the professions can be made available to the Federal Government at little cost."

But later in that decade, critics asserted that advisory committees could be "improperly captured by special interests" (Bull, 2011: 3), and that their work ought to be fully visible to the public. Congress therefore passed the Federal Advisory Committee Act (FACA) to promote open meetings, public involvement, and reporting. However, the new law did not necessarily limit the influence of special interests; until 2010, registered lobbyists were eligible to serve on FACA committees (Bull, 2011).

Adhering to FACA is time-intensive work. John Kamensky (2012) of the IBM Center for the Business of Government points out that it often takes at least a year to create an advisory committee. For federal officials who are trying to keep up with the pace of online engagement, this approach to participation seems increasingly antiquated (O'Reilly, 2011). According to a report on FACA chartered by the Administrative Conference of the United States, "The necessity of formally chartering a committee, announcing its meetings, receiving public input, and then holding a public meeting has led many agencies to avoid the formal advisory committee process whenever possible" (Bull, 2011: 54). In other words, agency staffers often try to avoid triggering FACA requirements when conducting participation. Christian Freitag (2010: 127–128) found that USFS staff sometimes "play a role behind the scenes in helping stakeholders organize themselves in order to circumvent the cumbersome FACA requirements."

The Open Government Directive

In this complicated picture of participation in the administrative realm, one recent initiative had the potential to clear up the confusion and reconcile the different visions of the public in federal agencies. The Obama Administration's Open Government Directive (OGD) was intended to clarify, organize, and catalyze public participation. On his first day in office, President Obama issued a memo to all departments arguing that:

> **Government should be participatory**. Public engagement enhances the Government's effectiveness and improves the quality of its decisions. Knowledge is widely dispersed in society, and public officials

benefit from having access to that dispersed knowledge. Executive departments and agencies should offer Americans increased opportunities to participate in policymaking and to provide their Government with the benefits of their collective expertise and information. Executive departments and agencies should also solicit public input on how we can increase and improve opportunities for public participation in Government. (www.whitehouse.gov/the_press_office/ TransparencyandOpenGovernment)

The Open Government Directive, developed by the Office of Management and Budget (OMB) to implement these ideas, set deadlines for action and required agencies to take several steps toward the goal of open government, including: (1) publishing government information online; (2) improving the quality of government information; (3) creating and institutionalizing a culture of open government; and (4) creating an enabling policy framework for open government (www.whitehouse.gov/open/documents/open-government-directive). The OGD also established obligations for transparency, participation, and collaboration that each agency had to meet. Tellingly, the transparency component had eight specific obligations, while the collaboration component had only three, and the participation component only two. (See Box 7.1 for the OGD language about participation in federal agency Open Government Plans.)

On paper, the OGD seemed to hold promise for increasing public participation, and civil society reformers watched closely as agencies began to develop and publish their plans. However, research on agency Open Government Plans suggests that, in most cases, the participation elements have been difficult to develop, understand, and implement. In fact, some of the staffers who are responsible for carrying out public participation projects are not even aware of them (Dudley, Leighninger, & Gniady, 2014; Lukensmeyer, 2013; Lukensmeyer, Goldman, & Stern, 2011). There are at least two possible reasons for this. First, the transparency elements of the OGD are perhaps more easily grasped by agency staffers. As a result, numerous Open Data Initiatives have been launched and expanded across several sectors, including health, energy, climate, education, finance, public safety, and global development (see www.whitehouse.gov/sites/default/files/microsites/ostp/2013opendata .pdf; see also www.whitehouse.gov/administration/eop/ostp/initiatives). Information on these and other issues is available through numerous platforms, such as Data.gov, recovery.gov, USASpending.gov, and foreignassistance.gov. In addition,

Project Open Data, an online public repository, was launched to help share best practices, examples, and software code to assist federal agencies with releasing data. Numerous U.S. states, counties, and cities, as well as nations around the world, have followed suit and launched a data sharing approach to open government (see https://www.data.gov/open-gov/ and www.opengovpartnership.org/).

Second, and perhaps more importantly, the White House has given more attention to data and transparency than to participation. Almost all of the commitments and initiatives listed in the two National Action Plans for Open Government focus on data sharing and transparency (White House, 2011, 2013). One initiative, developing best practices and metrics for public participation, could present a real opportunity to change the nature of citizen voice in the federal government; however, it has seen little movement, despite the efforts of civil society organizations, foundations, and academic researchers. Another promising commitment exemplifies how government could support meaningful local participation. It aims to "promote public participation in community spending decisions" by directing the

Department of Housing and Urban Development to provide technical support to local participatory budgeting processes (White House, 2013). This is perhaps the only commitment in either plan that specifically calls for a deliberative, decision-focused—or "thick"—form of public participation (Nabatchi, 2014).

In short, the OGD has not given Americans "the chance to participate in government deliberations and decision making" that President Obama described. However, because the OGD has encouraged data-sharing, transparency, and technology-driven innovations, it has given the federal government new avenues for tapping into outside expertise.

The Best Brains Online

The OGD has fostered an array of new participation initiatives that feature online tools. This work has been pioneered and advocated by a burgeoning "civic technology" community, many of whom played key roles in the Obama Campaign. Their initiatives capitalize on the ability of tech-savvy citizens to produce new tools, apps, and analyses that have potential to aid policymakers, improve government efficiency, and help people understand and improve public services (Noveck, 2010). Some of these efforts seem to embody the intent of FACA and other laws in that that they aim to tap the expertise of outside stakeholders. However, the population being targeted is different: instead of seeking an established set of the "best brains available" in universities, corporations, and nonprofit organizations, these initiatives have issued a broader call for expertise from the best brains online.

The availability of government data helps fuel many of these tools. Although associations like the Sunlight Foundation and OpentheGovernment.org still use century-old arguments, such as Louis Brandeis' famous statement that "sunlight is the best disinfectant" for eliminating corruption and inefficiency, they also see open data as an opportunity for citizens to become more advanced public problem-solvers. Beth Noveck (2012), a law professor at New York University who served in the White House Office for Science and Technology Policy (OSTP), writes that "open data can provide the raw material to convene informed conversations inside and outside institutions about what's broken, and the empirical foundation for developing solutions together." Noveck (2011) points to a number of contributions made by tech-savvy citizens, including an online edition of the *Federal Register*, a national first responder network for sharing information during disasters, and the "Peer to Patent" initiative that allows citizens to submit "prior art" as part of the federal patent review process.

Federal officials like Todd Park, former chief technology officer, spoke of the democratic potential of "hackathons" and "datapaloozas," events where civic technologists and others collaborate to develop new innovations. The General Services Administration established www.challenge.gov, which awards prizes for innovative new tools and apps developed by citizens. Other examples of thin participation that have emerged under the OGD are the Online National Dialogue on Reforming Government Websites (www.gsa.gov/portal/content/131495), Regulations.gov (which automates the collection of public comments for federal rulemaking), and ExpertNet (which provides an online alternative for engaging expert stakeholders).

The most well-known initiative, the Administration's "We the People" online petition platform, is different from these other approaches in that it encourages thin participation on a truly massive scale (see Box 7.2). Citizens post petitions to the site, and if a certain number of people sign within thirty days—the threshold has been moved several times, from 25,000 to 100,000 signatures—the Administration offers an official response. We the People has certainly provided one avenue for citizen voice. Since the platform's inception, and as of August 2014, more than ten million users had generated over 270,000 petitions, prompting 151 government replies (https://petitions.whitehouse.gov/). However, the connection between input and policymaking has not been so clear. The White House points to "petitions on online piracy legislation and regulating Internet puppy mills that they say have spurred action by the administration" (NPR, 2013), but these outcomes seem minimal compared to the level of participation on the site.

The work with tech-savvy citizens honors their ability to contribute to problem solving; therefore, these tech-driven approaches may represent a more equal and productive partnership between citizens and government than those embodied in conventional approaches to participation. However, these new approaches appeal to a very different "public" than the "potentially concerned" citizens who attend public hearings or the experts invited to sit on federal advisory committees.

No wonder that agency staffers often seem confused and conflicted about public participation. "I'm always being told, by people inside and outside my agency, that I need to interact with the public," said an employee of the Department of Transportation who attended a workshop on participation metrics. "But I'm not sure who my public really is." These questions about who "the public" is, who speaks for the public, and how to reconcile different conceptions of the public, come up again and again in the official settings for state and federal participation.

Box 7.2. "We the People" Want the Death Star

Some of the more unusual ideas proposed on the "We the People" platform have gained a great deal of attention. After President Obama's 2012 reelection victory, over 400,000 people signed petitions asking for their state to secede from the union. There have been popular petitions asking for the deportation of British television commentator Piers Morgan and Canadian pop star Justin Bieber. Over 30,000 people signed what is now known as the "Death Star petition," recommending that the National Aeronautics and Space Administration (NASA) build a planet-destroying satellite like the one in *Star Wars*.

But even fanciful ideas may be beneficial for participation. The White House response to the Death Star petition led about 100,000 people to sign up for regular updates from NASA that tell them when the International Space Station is going to be passing over their town. Micah Sifry (2013) of Personal Democracy Forum argues:

> The Death Star petition gave the White House team a great, viral way to spread useful information about what the government is doing on the science frontier. In fact, whenever someone signs a petition to the White House, they are explicitly giving the Administration permission to write them back. This is perhaps the most important and least-remarked upon aspect of the "We the People" platform. It's two-way.

While We the People petitions may not often lead to policy action, they have the potential to create interactions between citizens and government that are enjoyable and informative. Thus, some observers see We the People as a potential piece of a broader participation infrastructure. J.H. Snider of iSolon.org says that "Petitions are a type of democratic research and development. Like R and D investments, few petitions will pan out, and it may take many years for the payoff. Despite the short-term cost and hassles, they are worth it. They strengthen democracy" (Marks, 2013). Micah Sifry (2013) even goes so far as to say that We the People "is becoming a genuine digital public square capable of gathering the collective attention of millions of Americans."

Links

https://petitions.whitehouse.gov/

https://petitions.whitehouse.gov/response/isnt-petition-response-youre-looking

OFFICIAL SETTINGS FOR PARTICIPATION IN STATE AND FEDERAL GOVERNMENT

The official settings for state and federal participation are an assortment of opportunities, consisting mainly of older, conventional processes and newer, thinner forms of engagement. Considering the sheer size and diversity of our state and federal governments, there are far more official settings than we can possibly describe here. In this section, we identify the most common ones (summarized in Figure 7.1), including those for interacting with legislators, participating in state or federal agency decisions, and participating in local decisions made by state or federal governments.

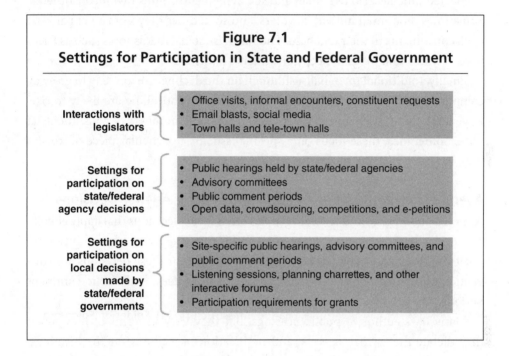

Figure 7.1
Settings for Participation in State and Federal Government

Interactions with legislators
- Office visits, informal encounters, constituent requests
- Email blasts, social media
- Town halls and tele-town halls

Settings for participation on state/federal agency decisions
- Public hearings held by state/federal agencies
- Advisory committees
- Public comment periods
- Open data, crowdsourcing, competitions, and e-petitions

Settings for participation on local decisions made by state/federal governments
- Site-specific public hearings, advisory committees, and public comment periods
- Listening sessions, planning charrettes, and other interactive forums
- Participation requirements for grants

Interactions with Elected Officials

Direct interactions with state and federal officials—particularly elected officials—are (and will continue to be) a common avenue for participation (see Nabatchi & Farrar, 2011). This category of engagement is very broad, and it includes many informal conversations, chance encounters, and visits to the official's district or main office. Both officials and citizens tend to report greater satisfaction with these less formal interactions than with the communication that occurs in conventional participation.

This category also includes an important but often overlooked avenue for participation: constituent requests of their elected officials. Offices of state and federal legislators receive huge numbers of letters, emails, and phone calls from citizens asking questions, expressing comments, and requesting assistance. Many of these appeals deal with situations that would not traditionally be considered within the purview of the official—for example, complaints from renters about their landlords or questions about how to file their taxes. However, staffers in many offices devote a great deal of time to answering or investigating constituent requests. Indeed, "constituent service" is often considered a key to being reelected.

Elected officials also use email and social media to connect with constituents. Sometimes they email individual voters, and sometimes they send an email blast to all constituents in their database. They also use social media tools such as Facebook, Twitter, and blogs to keep constituents informed.

Finally, traditional town halls, although on the decline, are unlikely to go away completely, and tele-town halls and other forms of robocalling are likely to rise. In general, these mechanisms are used to reach large numbers of constituents at once. Sometimes, these focus on a specific issue or a particular piece of legislation, but often they are more general in nature.

Avenues for Participation in State and Federal Agency Decisions

As noted above, state and federal agencies often make decisions that apply equally across smaller jurisdictions. Most of the official participation opportunities explicitly authorized in laws, policies, and regulations for these decisions are conventional, such as public hearings, advisory committees, and public comment periods.

Many laws authorize public hearings, but they vary in terms of how much they dictate the format, agenda, and notification procedures for the meetings. Because they are also ubiquitous at the local level, we discussed the drawbacks of the typical "three-minutes-at-the-microphone" public hearing, as well as the limitations of advisory boards and committees in this and other chapters. For reasons explained elsewhere, these approaches are not particularly satisfying for state and federal agencies, their employees, or citizens, in large part because they do not embody the characteristics of an adult-adult relationship.

Public comment periods are more common at the state and federal levels than at the local level, although they rarely lead to fundamental or controversial changes. Instead, they reflect a process wherein at least some stakeholders have already been consulted and had input. Public comments are increasingly being collected online, for example through platforms such as www.regulations.gov, although this may still have all the features of conventional participation—people simply submit their complaints or comments through a webform or by email, rather than through regular mail.

In addition to conventional processes, numerous thin online participation processes are emerging, such as open data, crowdsourcing, competition, and e-petition websites. These opportunities are useful for sharing and collecting information, and they reflect some characteristics of an adult-adult relationship. They are most likely to reach citizens who are more technologically oriented. Tapping the full potential of these thin online processes may require connecting them to other opportunities for participation.

Avenues for Participation on Local Decisions Made by State and Federal Agencies

In addition to decisions that apply across jurisdictions, state and federal agencies also make numerous decisions that apply to a specific local jurisdiction. In these site-specific cases, the official settings for local participation are more diverse, but still largely conventional.

Many of the official participation avenues mandated by law for local decisions mirror those used for state and federal decisions: public hearings, advisory committees, and public comment periods. That said, there is wide variation among—and even within—agencies' capacity for engagement; thus, there are great differences in how agencies (and their field offices) define and carry out participation. Deborah Dalton, who has coordinated public engagement efforts at the EPA for many years, notes that "each project to some extent has a different conception of public engagement."

Some agencies are developing more interactive ways of engaging the public, in part because agency staffers have reacted to "outside pressure" from citizens, but also because of their own bad experiences with conventional forms of participation. This may be particularly true of the EPA, an agency that makes thousands of local decisions and encounters more angry citizens than perhaps any other federal government body. Suzanne Wells and Helen Duteau of the EPA believe that their agency regularly goes far beyond the legal requirements for participation. In administering the Superfund program, for example, Duteau argues that the agency "goes outside the regulatory box" for engagement (Dudley, Leighninger, & Gniady, 2014). These more productive practices include listening sessions, planning charrettes, one-on-one interviews, and deliberative forums.

Finally, some of the more participation-focused agencies are now requiring stronger engagement practices in proposals for state and federal grants. One example is the Community Challenge Planning Grant program administered by HUD; of the possible 102 points on a proposal's evaluation score, at least fifty-six are related to public participation activities. HUD staffer Kate Dykgraaf observes, "Our program is really different. If you are familiar with the Community Block Grant, it requires two community meetings, and they don't usually collect data to describe their efforts. We (the Economic Resilience program) require grantees to go beyond simple hearings, and they must show engagement plans and how they reach marginalized publics" (Dudley, Leighninger, & Gniady, 2014).

In the following section, we suggest ways to strengthen the infrastructure by activating and empowering the leaders and networks for state and federal participation.

STRENGTHENING THE INFRASTRUCTURE: LEADERS AND NETWORKS FOR PARTICIPATION IN STATE AND FEDERAL GOVERNMENT

Strengthening the infrastructure for participation in state and federal government requires paying attention to the potential leaders of and networks for participation. As suggested above, numerous participation leaders already exist within state and federal government, from legislators to agency officials working in headquarter and field offices. Outside government, there are many different networks with a vested interest in participation at the state and federal levels, and many organizations that have a strong track record of helping different groups work together. For example, Matt Leighninger (2012) has mapped the network of civil society organizations that are engaged in work related to deliberative civic engagement and, in its capacity as the lead evaluator of the National Action Plan for Open Government, Openthegoverment.org has a long list of civil society organizations working in the participation realm. Many foundations, universities and colleges, private sector organizations, and media institutions also have an interest in greater participation at the state and federal levels (see Figure 7.2).

But while there are a handful of partnerships between people inside and outside of state and federal governments, the inside-the-institution thinking about the role of participation does not seem well connected to thinking about people outside the institution. A second challenge is fostering and sustaining stronger relationships among these networks and state- and federal-level agencies.

Figure 7.2
Networks for Participation in State and Federal Government

Private Sector Organizations

Government Officials in Legislatures and Agencies

Civil Society Organizations

Foundations

Media

Universities and Colleges

STRENGTHENING THE INFRASTRUCTURE: BUILDING BLOCKS FOR PARTICIPATION IN STATE AND FEDERAL GOVERNMENT

It is one thing to envision a more participatory neighborhood, town, or city, and quite another to envision a more participatory state or nation. The most successful forms of participation are centered on the hopes and concerns of citizens and based on their willingness to spend time together—solving problems, making decisions, and enjoying one another's company. How are people in one town to connect and deliberate with people in another town, in another state, or on the other side of the country?

This issue of scale has always been a challenge for democratic theorists. Plato asserted that the population limit for a unit of government was 5,040 people (if larger, it would be difficult for everyone to know each other) and Aristotle argued that everyone within a polity should be able to assemble in a single location and hear whoever was speaking (Berry, Portney, & Thomson, 1993: 9). Likewise,

Thomas Jefferson argued that democracy demands an active citizenry, which best takes place in small communities where people can readily grasp issues and where they are closely connected to one another (Friedman, 2006). Today, however, very few political units meet these size requirements. Even if they did, few of our most pressing modern problems respect political and geographic boundaries.

But if public problems are increasingly regional and global, participation remains largely local. Of the thousands of direct participation processes conducted each year, the majority occur in cities, towns, villages, and neighborhoods (Nabatchi & Amsler, 2014). This is because participation initiatives typically require a diverse, critical mass of participants to succeed—as we argued in Chapter 2—and the number of people required to create this diverse, critical mass is smaller at the local level. Recruitment (an issue we discuss further in Chapter 8) is a fundamental factor in successful participation, and both the logistics of recruitment (building a sufficiently large web of relationships so that potential participants are approached by people they already know) and the psychology of recruitment (the perception of citizens that their participation will make an impact) are more conducive at the local level.

Early democratic theorists solved this conceptual challenge by proposing to build from the bottom up. Thomas Jefferson argued that we should "Divide the country into wards," each of them small enough for successful participation, but sufficiently linked to one another that they could function as a nation. To use a different analogy, the physicist Richard Feynman (1959) helped create the field of nanotechnology when he suggested that "there is room at the bottom" for startling innovations; scientists in dozens of fields could take huge leaps by focusing on and experimenting with how particles interacted at the molecular level. In this view of "nanodemocracy," or "microdemocracy," as Luz Santana and Dan Rothstein, directors of the Right Question Institute, call it (http://rightquestion. org/microdemocracy/), a national participation infrastructure consists mainly of thousands of interconnected community infrastructures.

Another way to think about participation at these larger geographic levels is to recognize that we already have some elements of a state and federal infrastructure in place: government already makes considerable investments in helping people become informed, connect with one another, make decisions, and take action. The settings for participation listed in the previous section are the most obvious pieces of that infrastructure, but there are others. For example, in the category of public work, investments such as the Serve America Act support millions of Americans in undertaking service to their communities and country. Thus, some might suggest that we simply need to renovate aspects of the existing infrastructure, such as its legal framework, and connect different elements to one another so that service opportunities, information sources, and decision-making arenas are part of a coherent whole.

Neither of these big-picture visions of participation infrastructure—building from the bottom up or connecting what already exists—is likely to be helpful for state or federal employees who want to support participation on a particular project, decision, or issue. In that context, employees are likely to first ask, "Who is the public?" followed by, "How do we engage that public?" We address these questions in Chapter 8, and examine some of the most likely goals, tools, and tactics for temporary, decision- or planning-specific participation efforts. In this chapter, we stick with the big picture view of building a participation infrastructure at the state and federal levels. We start, as we did in the chapters on education, health, and land use, by exploring the building blocks for meaningful, powerful, and gratifying participation (see Figure 7.3).

Disseminating Information

This is one area where state and federal governments, both in the legislative branch and the administrative realm, have advanced their participation practices in recent years. In large part, they have done this by capitalizing on digital technologies. Many of the vehicles described below are currently being used; however, there is room for expanding and strengthening them.

Platforms for monitoring government spending and decisions. After the federal stimulus package was passed in 2009 and 2010, citizens were able to monitor how the money was spent through recovery.gov. Other examples of these online monitoring platforms include USASpending.gov and foreignassistance.gov. Citizens seem to value these information sources, and they may increasingly expect and even demand them. Of course, these platforms do not by themselves lead to increased trust in or approval of government, either because not enough people visit these sites or because what they see does not encourage them. For example, despite the presence of recovery.gov, respondents to a national poll said they believed that 50 cents of each stimulus dollar had been wasted (Levine, 2013: 157).

Social media networks. Some state and federal legislators and agencies use social media not just to engage citizens temporarily, but to maintain those connections over time—so that people interested in space exploration, environmental concerns, public health threats, or other issues can remain informed and aware of

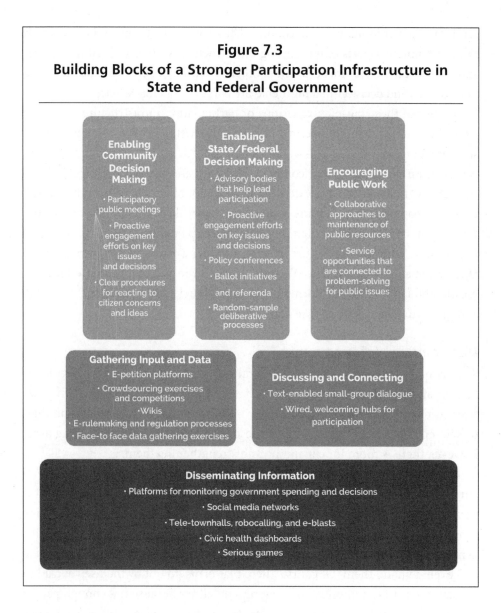

Figure 7.3
Building Blocks of a Stronger Participation Infrastructure in State and Federal Government

Enabling Community Decision Making
· Participatory public meetings
· Proactive engagement efforts on key issues and decisions
· Clear procedures for reacting to citizen concerns and ideas

Enabling State/Federal Decision Making
· Advisory bodies that help lead participation
· Proactive engagement efforts on key issues and decisions
· Policy conferences
· Ballot initiatives and referenda
· Random-sample deliberative processes

Encouraging Public Work
· Collaborative approaches to maintenance of public resources
· Service opportunities that are connected to problem-solving for public issues

Gathering Input and Data
· E-petition platforms
· Crowdsourcing exercises and competitions
· Wikis
· E-rulemaking and regulation processes
· Face-to face data gathering exercises

Discussing and Connecting
· Text-enabled small-group dialogue
· Wired, welcoming hubs for participation

Disseminating Information
· Platforms for monitoring government spending and decisions
· Social media networks
· Tele-townhalls, robocalling, and e-blasts
· Civic health dashboards
· Serious games

future participation opportunities. In Chapter 8 and in the Participation Skills Module www.wiley.com/go/nabatchi, we discuss in detail how to do this well.

Tele-townhalls, robocalls, and e-blasts. These primarily one-way vehicles for communication are being used increasingly by legislators, and to some extent by state and federal agencies. They should be connected to other opportunities that give people a chance to be heard; otherwise, citizens may be frustrated by them or tune them out entirely.

Civic health dashboards. Groups like the National Conference on Citizenship, a congressionally chartered organization, have pioneered the use of dashboards and indices to help track the levels of voting, volunteerism, and other civic activities. This kind of information dissemination vehicle provides a picture of the overall state of civic infrastructure, a clearer articulation of why different organizations (including state and federal agencies) should be working together toward more holistic goals, and a way to measure their progress. This idea could be easily adapted to both legislative and administrative projects, programs, and activities.

Serious games. Online games are being used by legislators and agencies to educate citizens. One example, the Maryland Budget Game, challenges players to balance spending priorities and revenue-raising options in the Maryland state budget. In these experiences, citizens gain information and grapple with policy tradeoffs in a way that is interactive and fun.

Gathering Input and Data

Vehicles that allow citizens to provide information to state and federal governments have also proliferated. To maximize their potential as elements of participation infrastructure, state and federal governments ought to explore ways of linking these vehicles with one another. Officials should also work on better connecting public input processes to official decision making and explaining to the public how their ideas will be used. Finally, officials should think about how to use these input and data collection tools and processes with participation opportunities focused on discussion, decision making, and public work.

E-petition platforms. The use of e-petition platforms is expanding and increasingly enabling citizens to raise issues that transcend legislative and administrative boundaries. We the People is perhaps the most well-known e-petition platform. There are several ways to improve this and other e-petition platforms; one particularly useful idea is to incorporate a variety of responses or actions (e.g., forwarding a petition to a relevant agency official or requiring agency action) that are triggered at different signature thresholds.

Crowdsourcing exercises and competitions. Crowdsourcing exercises enlist a large number of people to share information or provide input on a particular task or project. Sometimes participants are paid, and sometimes they are awarded a prize if their work is selected. These tools allow government to "harness the problem-solving prowess of our fellow citizens" on a wide variety of issues and with a wide variety of government organizations (Dorgelo & Forde, 2014). In 2013, federal agencies ran more than eighty-five competitions that resulted in creative solutions to a wide variety of issues, from improved astronaut space suit gloves, to innovative tools for job seekers, to new ways to block illegal robocalls (Dorgelo & Forde, 2014).

Wikis. Wikis, websites where content can be created, edited, discussed, and changed by users working in collaboration, are increasingly prominent in government. Citizens are invited to submit their own ideas, comment on submissions, and help formulate final policy documents. (For more information on the use of wikis, see Mergel, 2011.)

E-rulemaking and regulation processes. E-rulemaking, or electronic rulemaking, occurs when government agencies use digital technologies in their rule, regulation, and other decision-making processes. Federal agencies have made particular use of e-rulemaking through regulations.gov, a website created under the Open Government Initiative that allows people to search, review, and comment on proposed regulations and related documents published by the U.S. federal government, as well as on comments submitted by others. However, while a fact sheet posted on regulations.gov claims that public participation matters in the rule-making process, it is unclear how much these public comments affect the formulation of final rules (see www.regulations.gov/docs/FactSheet_Public_Comments_Make_a_ Difference.pdf). Examining, determining, and reporting the degree to which public comments are used should be a focus of government officials.

Face-to-face data-gathering exercises. Listening sessions, charrettes, focus groups, and other in-person events (of various scales and sizes) can also be used to solicit ideas and feedback from citizens. These processes can supplement online and survey-based forms of data-gathering.

Discussing and Connecting

Encouraging social connections among citizens seems far afield from the things we expect state and federal governments to do. And yet how often have we heard a president or another prominent public official call for a "national dialogue" or "national conversation" on race, immigration, mental health, or some other critical public issue? These appeals are usually treated as empty rhetoric rather than serious policy proposals (Lozada, 2013). One recent op-ed piece was entitled: "Please, President Obama. Not Another 'National Conversation'" (Lozada, 2013). This need not be the case; state and federal governments have concrete ways—old and new—to promote civic discussion and connection.

Many of the tools and processes we identified above and elsewhere, such as games, wikis, online platforms, and face-to-face exercises, can also be used to enable citizens to discuss issues and connect with one another and with government. In addition to expanding the purpose and role of these tools, government should look to other opportunities to better enable discussion and connection.

Text- or online-enabled small-group dialogue. The "Text, Talk, and Act" process developed for President Obama's National Dialogue on Mental Health (see Box 7.3) is one illustration of how texting and other online connections can be used to encourage, organize, and connect face-to-face discussions that are happening across a state or nation. This kind of activity is a logical extension of the work in the first two building blocks: it can help citizens process information they have received and talk through input they might want to give, while at the same time strengthening their most immediate relationships. Because polling questions (and real-time reporting on poll responses) can be built into these platforms, and because they work well with Twitter and other social media

---

Box 7.3. "Text, Talk and Act"

"Text, Talk, and Act" is an example of how thick and thin forms of participation can be combined. It was launched in 2013 by a coalition of nonprofit organizations and a federal agency, the Substance Abuse and Mental Health Services Administration (SAMHSA), as part of the National Dialogue on Mental Health. The process, which has now been repeated several times, is a text-enabled, small-group dialogue that happens nationwide on a single day. Participants are recruited, primarily through social media, and asked to form in-person groups of three to four people. They text "start" to a pre-assigned code, and then receive a series of text messages, including discussion questions for the group; process suggestions; polling questions that can be answered from phones; and requests to respond with action ideas and commitments they will make to strengthen mental health in their school or community. Throughout the process, participants receive links by text that allow them to see how people in other parts of the country have responded to the polling and action questions. Participants can post pictures of their groups on Twitter using the hashtag #texttalkact. The experience is designed to last roughly one hour, although groups can move as quickly or slowly as they want. As of 2014, more than 8,500 Americans, many of them young people, had taken part in Text, Talk, and Act.

Link

www.creatingcommunitysolutions.org/texttalkact

---

networks, it is now possible to create an experience that is both personal and national.

Wired, welcoming hubs for participation. Long before any buildings were "wired" for the Internet, the New Deal and other spending programs created a physical infrastructure of public buildings that we still use today (see Chapter 3). Today, state and federal funds are still being used to help construct schools, hospitals, libraries, municipal buildings, community centers, train stations, and other structures and facilities. State and federal governments can bolster communities by maximizing the suitability of these spaces for various forms of participation. These meeting spaces can encourage face-to-face connections, and their computer centers and free wireless networks can facilitate online engagement.

Enabling Community Decision Making

While state and federal policies typically receive more headlines, the roles that legislators and agency officials play in local decisions—from how to allocate stimulus funding to how to clean up a toxic waste site—are more likely to bring them into direct contact with citizens. How these decisions are made is important, not only because they affect policies, but also because they influence how people feel about state and federal government. Legislators and agencies can instigate and support more productive forms of participation in these site-specific situations in several ways.

Participatory public meetings. The most obvious and straightforward change that legislators and agencies can make is to replace conventional opportunities with more productive forms of participation. Public hearings, tele-town halls, and other kinds of interactions set up by federal and state officials could be supplanted or at least augmented by meetings that employ better participation practices. Box 6.5 in Chapter 6 offers several ideas for revamping and improving public meetings.

Proactive engagement efforts on key issues and decisions. In situations where federal or state decisions seem likely to have a significant or controversial local impact, thicker, more deliberative participation processes are needed (see Chapter 2 for a more detailed exploration of these kinds of thick participation processes). Participant recruitment (an issue discussed further in Chapter 8) is critical to the success of these efforts. When recruitment is managed well, deliberative processes allow a critical mass of people to more deeply understand the issue and provide meaningful input on potential problems, opportunities, and actions.

Clear procedures for reacting to citizen concerns and ideas. In addition to legally required meetings and temporary outreach efforts, many state and federal employees need a clearer sense of how to conduct participation in the day-to-day work of the agency. "The big engagement initiatives are fine, but it is the regular ongoing processes that need to change," says Ben Gerhardstein of the Agency for Toxic Substances and Disease Registry (ATSDR) (Dudley, Leighninger, & Gniady, 2014). "We need ways to do this as part of the everyday work of agency. If we can, that will then create more of an expectation and general level of input—it would improve public perception and understanding of our work and a more collaborative working relationship." The most common way this happens is through public comment periods for new rules and regulations—a process that is largely dominated by lobbyists and special interest groups. The CDC's Julie Fishman asserts that "we really need to understand people's underlying philosophical goals and interests, rather than specific comments—understanding the tradeoffs, getting people's thoughts and having more of an ongoing dialogue" (Dudley, Leighninger, & Gniady, 2014).

Revised participation guidelines must be easy for citizens and other stakeholders to find and understand, and they must be clear about how and when obtaining a diverse, representative sample of the public matters. What kinds of efforts will state and federal agencies conduct to ensure that the comments or complaints they receive are truly representative of the community? What steps should community groups, businesses, or advocacy organizations take to show that their ideas or concerns are broadly supported by other citizens? In what situations does it become necessary to bring together divided groups of citizens and stakeholders to find common ground? Establishing clear procedures for these decisions will help the relationship between communities and agencies and help both decide when and how to launch more proactive participation efforts.

Enabling State and Federal Decision Making

As state legislatures and Congress find it harder to make decisions because of partisan gridlock, involving citizens productively holds the possibility of making state and federal government more decisive and efficient. There are several ways to facilitate this kind of participation.

Advisory bodies that help lead participation efforts. Advisory boards, committees, and commissions could adopt more explicitly democratic roles, helping to engage citizens through social media, random-sample exercises, public deliberation processes, and other tools and techniques. These bodies could make greater use of another element in the existing federal infrastructure: the We the People e-petition website. For example, advisory committees could create new petitions as a way to test public support for their proposals or to invite citizens to submit new ideas for the committee to consider in its work.

Proactive thin and thick engagement efforts on key issues and decisions. Combining thick and thin participation opportunities in large-scale processes is another way to better enable state and federal decision making. Large- and small-scale face-to-face deliberative forums, coupled with online opportunities such as crowdsourcing, social media, wikis, and text-enabled dialogues, would be extremely useful. The Public Engagement Project on Pandemic Influenza, the National Conversation on Chemical Exposures, and the National Dialogue on Mental Health, which featured "Text, Talk, and Act" (see Box 7.3) are all examples to consider.

Random-sample deliberative processes. On some issues and decisions, agencies and legislators can aid decision making by convening a deliberative, random-sample process like a citizen jury or citizen assembly (see Chapter 8). In these processes, participants are randomly selected from the population, and the role of experts is to enrich and inform their discussions. When the results of these deliberative processes are publicized, legitimized by public officials and organizations outside government, and connected to other sorts of participation opportunities, they may achieve the political weight necessary to influence policy decisions.

Policy conferences. Policy conferences are delegate-based systems in which people at the local level choose representatives to carry forward their interests and priorities to higher levels of government. In Brazil, policy conferences have been used for many years to connect citizen voices with state and federal decision making and have been successful at mobilizing large numbers of citizens (Pogrebinschi & Samuels, 2014). One of the strengths of the Brazilian system is that the conferences have been organized repeatedly and have become a well-known aspect of the political routine. Such approaches could be adapted and used in the United States.

Ballot initiatives and referenda. Many states allow initiatives and referenda in which voters approve or reject particular pieces of legislation. One of the drawbacks of this practice is that citizens are often unaware of the costs and benefits of the legislation and therefore cast uninformed votes. Innovations such as the Oregon Citizens' Initiative Review, discussed earlier in this chapter, could be employed by states to provide objective information to the public.

Encouraging Public Work

Our federal and many of our state governments have already made significant investments in encouraging volunteerism, from the "Points of Light" campaign of President George H.W. Bush in the early 1990s to the Edward M. Kennedy Serve America Act of 2009.

Collaborative approaches to maintenance of public resources. A number of federal and state agencies have long histories of working with community groups to inspire and support public work. For example, the EPA has galvanized volunteerism on watershed preservation through trainings, workshops, and joint activities, resulting in successes like the cleanup of Chesapeake Bay (Sirianni & Friedland, 2001). A range of new, inexpensive, portable technologies give citizens new ways to contribute, for example, by measuring water and air quality. When these opportunities are combined with chances to give input on agency work, citizens exhibit higher levels of responsibility for public resources (Sirianni & Friedland, 2001).

Service opportunities that are connected to problem solving for public issues. Federal and state agencies can also create service opportunities to engage the public in problem solving. For example, challenge.gov administered by the U.S. General Services Administration in partnership with government agencies and OSTP, lists the challenge and prize competitions run by more than sixty-five agencies across federal government. The challenges include technical, scientific, ideation, and creative competitions where federal agencies seek innovative solutions to problems from the public. Similarly, the National Aeronautics and Space Administration (NASA) runs NASA Solve to involve the public in solving tough mission-related problems (www.nasa.gov/solve/).

STRENGTHENING THE INFRASTRUCTURE: SYSTEMIC SUPPORTS FOR PARTICIPATION IN STATE AND FEDERAL GOVERNMENT

Building a strong participation infrastructure at the state and federal levels requires not only the building blocks, but also systemic supports. We describe a number of possible supports in this section, culminating in the Open Government Initiative and how it could be used to improve state and federal participation infrastructures.

Training and Skill Development

Legislators and agency officials who see the merits of participation often lack the knowledge, skills, and abilities to launch effective and meaningful programs. Therefore, training and skill development are critical to upgrading our participation infrastructure. To help build their capacity, agencies and legislators could take several steps, including identifying a participation point of contact; supporting opportunities for training and continuing education; creating and sharing participation materials; creating platforms that collect and report examples and innovations in participation; and supporting communities of practice. These approaches can help government officials engage in peer-to-peer learning, share ideas and best practices, generate innovations, and sustain momentum (PARCC, 2013).

These training and skill development opportunities require support from senior leadership, which is often lacking. Deborah Dalton, who has led public engagement efforts at the EPA for many years, says that one of their challenges is being able to "Convince senior leadership of other ways of operating [and] that town halls and hearings don't produce what [they] are looking for" (Dudley, Leighninger, & Gniady, 2014). Putting more emphasis on training and skill development would help empower agency staffers, but will not have a dramatic impact unless governments embrace and champion public participation. "The leadership matters, not just the language," says Dr. Marva King of EPA.

Professional Incentives for State and Federal Officials

It is not enough to give people training and skills in participation; they also need incentives. Government officials should be encouraged to conduct good public participation and be rewarded when they are successful. This is particularly important at the state and federal levels given that so many officials have had negative experiences with public participation. In addition to incorporating participation indicators into performance appraisals, simple motivational tools such as awards, prizes, and bonuses could go a long way toward incentivizing participation. Again, of course, developing and implementing professional incentives requires support from senior leadership.

Funding and Budgeting

Government officials are likely to fret about the costs of upgrading our participation infrastructure. In an era of cutbacks and sequestrations, supporting additional funding for participation is unlikely to be popular either among government officials or citizens. However, the lack of funding support is likely traceable to the negative experiences people have had with conventional participation. To the extent that new and better methods of public participation are devised and used, support for funding is likely to grow. Moreover, it is useful to point out that governments already expend significant resources, including money, time, and human capital, on conventional participation. These same resources could be channeled into improving specific participation opportunities and the overall participation infrastructure.

Policies and Procedures

Although public administrators are subject to a range of legal requirements for public participation, many of the laws, policies, projects, and initiatives that claim to promote participation do not support one another. Instead, they often put forth very different sets of goals, based on very different assumptions about citizens and their potential roles in democracy. The federal Open Government Directive and state-level open government initiatives hold promise for improving policies and procedures. In particular, they could help government agencies understand the kinds of strategic planning and outreach they must do to conduct effective public participation. To maximize the potential of such efforts to strengthen participation infrastructure, state and federal open government policies could:

1. *Define public participation, describe its basic principles, and provide examples of how to do it well.* This is the approach being taken at the local level by the Working Group on Legal Frameworks for Participation, an alliance of local government and legal associations that created a model ordinance on public participation. The ordinance (and a companion state act, developed by the same group) defines participation and describes its basic principles. (In the early days of the Open Government Directive, similar lists of principles were proposed to the White House by organizations and alliances such as the International Association for Public Participation (IAP2), the National Coalition for Dialogue and Deliberation (NCDD), and Strengthening Our Nation's Democracy (SOND), but none were incorporated by the administration.) During discussions of the Working Group on Legal Frameworks for Participation, Lisa Amsler commented that clarifying the definition of public participation would have a positive effect; because "public participation"

appears in so many laws and policies, defining the term would give those laws and policies greater meaning and purpose.

2. *Clarify how public participation laws should be interpreted.* Laws like FACA and PRA seem to be more of an impediment than an aid to public participation. Better definitions of participation would help, but there is also work to be done (partly through discussions among agency legal personnel) to ensure that the laws are interpreted and enforced fairly and consistently. The people conducting participation in federal agencies are often unsure of where they stand legally, say the CDC's Julie Fishman and Jennifer Van Skiver (Dudley, Leighninger, & Gniady, 2014).

3. *Help agencies think through how to embed participation in more routine ways, not just in special projects.* While federal agency staffers can point to some successful temporary participation projects, they have a harder time envisioning how to conduct participation in the day-to-day work of the agency. Open government initiatives could be used to help government officials recognize that participation is more than just a one-off obligation; it can be used over the lifecycle of an issue, with a wide range of different tools, tactics, and techniques and for a wide variety of purposes (PARCC, 2013). In particular, open government initiatives could be used to help agencies raise the bar for participation formats and use a wider variety of participation methods, including in-person, online, mobile app, and hybrid arrangements. They could also be used to encourage cooperation among government, civil society, and academia.

4. *Empower agencies to better evaluate their participation work.* "What gets counted—that's what happens," says the EPA's Deborah Dalton (Dudley, Leighninger, & Gniady, 2014). If federal and state governments followed through on the Open Government commitment to establish participation metrics, then agencies, advisory bodies, and interest groups would have greater incentives to become participation leaders and more clarity on how participation would matter to decision-makers. However, several laws, rules, and regulations limit agencies' ability to collect and use data for evaluations of participatory processes. Without such information, agencies are severely restricted in their ability to evaluate, learn from, and improve their methods of participation. At the federal level, the Administration could direct the development of a generic, OMB-approved

(and PRA-acceptable) tool that all agencies can use to collect common data about individual participants for routine uses (PARCC, 2013). Similar approaches could be used at the state level. In addition, governments could encourage cooperation with civil society organizations and academic institutions to assess and evaluate participation opportunities.

SUMMARY

Public participation in state and federal government has both great challenges and tremendous potential. On the legislative side, officials are increasingly wary of conventional participation and its inability to deal with citizen anger. Projects initiated by civil society organizations have been more successful at overcoming polarization, but the policy impacts of such processes are not always clear. On the administrative side, government agencies typically find themselves constrained by an outdated legal framework, which pushes them into using conventional participation processes. While the Open Government Directive was intended to provide some clarity, most open government measures have focused on data sharing and transparency rather than participation.

We provided a number of suggestions about how to strengthen the participation infrastructure of state and federal governments. Specifically, we asserted that participation can be improved if:

1. *Leaders and networks for participation are activated and empowered.* State and federal governments should tap into a range of networks that can play an active role in participation, including civil society organizations, foundations, universities and colleges, private sector organizations, and media institutions. Doing so could go a long way toward shoring up the infrastructure for participation in state and federal government.

2. *The six building blocks of participation activities are put into place.* State and federal governments already use a number of activities to disseminate information, gather input and data, discuss and connect, enable community decision making, enable state and federal decision making, and encourage public work. The participation infrastructure of state and federal government can be strengthened if legislators and agency officials think more broadly about participation and incorporate a wider variety of thin and thick participation tools or vehicles into these activities.

3. *Systemic supports are used to make participation sustainable, strong, and resilient.* To help people to take on new roles, connect the different building blocks to one another, and institutionalize participation in the regular functioning of state and federal governments, several systemic supports are needed, including training and skill development, professional incentives, policies and procedures, and funding and budgeting. Open government plans and initiatives hold promise for helping to improve policies and procedures.

To achieve the benefits of participation, state and federal governments need to take stock of the current picture of engagement, consider the kinds of participation activities they want to foster and support, and make changes that will enable government to operate in more democratic ways.

DISCUSSION QUESTIONS

1. What are the challenges of using participation in the legislative branch of state and federal government? Do you think it is appropriate to use public participation in the legislative branch? Why or why not?

2. What are the challenges of using participation in administrative agencies at the state and federal levels of government? Do you think public participation at these levels is appropriate? Why or why not?

3. What is the Open Government Directive? How does it promote public participation? What are potential challenges in implementing this directive? Do you think it effectively encourages public participation?

4. What is the link between access to information and participation? Do you think that access to data through Open Government initiatives will increase public participation in policymaking? Why or why not?

5. Micah Sifry claims that the White House's "We the People" e-petition platform is "becoming a genuine digital public square capable of gathering the collective attention of millions of Americans." Do you agree? Why or why not?

6. The authors presented three different views of who and what constitutes the public: those who are potentially concerned, the best brains available, and the best brains online. What assumptions underlie each of these views? Do you agree with any of these views? Why or why not?

7. Review the official settings for participation in state and federal government shown in Figure 7.1. Have you ever engaged in government through one of those avenues? What were your experiences?

8. Numerous actors and networks could be convened to address state or federal policy issues. Pick a state or federal policy issue and map the potential participation leaders and networks that could be involved.

9. Review the six building blocks for a stronger participation infrastructure in state and federal government (Figure 7.3). Which building blocks are present in your state? Are the activities offered by your state conventional, thin, or thick? Which opportunities would you like to see more of and why?

10. What kinds of skills, training, and incentives do you think would work best to support participation at the state and federal levels of government? Why?

References

Alexander, Lamar. (1995). *We know what to do: A political maverick talks with America.* New York, NY: William Morrow.

Berry, Jeffrey M., Portney, Kent E., & Thomson, Ken. (1993). *The rebirth of urban democracy.* Washington, DC: Brookings Institution Press.

Bingham, Lisa. (2007). Give the masses more ways to enter political conversation. *Indianapolis Star.* Available at http://archive.indystar.com/article/20071026/OPINION01/710260393/Give-masses-more-ways-enter-political-conversation.

Bingham, Lisa Blomgren. (2010). The next generation of administrative law: Building the legal infrastructure for collaborative governance. *Wisconsin Law Review, 10*: 297–356.

Breitman, Kendall. (2014). Poll: Congress approval hits new low. *Politico.* Available at www.politico.com/story/2014/08/poll-congress-approval-rating-low-109721.html#ixzz39zwljgzE.

Bull, Reeve T. (2011). *The Federal Advisory Committee Act: Issues and proposed reforms.* Washington, DC: Administrative Conference of the United States. Available at www.acus.gov/sites/default/files/documents/COCG-Reeve-Bull-Draft-FACA-Report-9-12-11.pdf .

Dorgelo, Cristin, & Brian Forde. (2014). By the people, for the people: Crowdsourcing to improve government. *Wired*. Available at www.wired.com/2014/04/people-people-crowdsourcing-improve-government/.

Dudley, Larkin, Matt Leighninger, & Noel Gniady. (2014). *Federal agencies and public participation*. Dayton, OH: Kettering Foundation.

Esterling, Kevin, Archon Fung, & Taeku Lee. (2010). *The difference that deliberation makes: Evaluating the "Our Budget, Our Economy" public deliberation*. Chicago, IL: John D. and Catherine T. MacArthur Foundation.

Exley, Zack. (2008). The new organizers: What's really behind Obama's ground game. *Huffington Post*. Available at www.huffingtonpost.com/zack-exley/the-new-organizers-part-1_b_132782.html.

Feynman, Richard P. (1959). *There's plenty of room at the bottom: An invitation to enter a new field of physics*. American Physical Society Meeting, Caltech, Pasadena, CA.

Freitag, Christian. (2010). *An institutional analysis of the National Environmental Policy Act in the United States Forest Service*. Bloomington, IN: Indiana University.

Friedman, Will. (2006). Deliberative democracy and the problem of scope. *Journal of Public Deliberation*, 2(1): Article 1.

Fung, Archon, & Taeku Lee. (2008). *The difference deliberation makes: A report on CaliforniaSpeaks statewide conversation on health care reform*. Washington, DC: AmericaSpeaks.

Fung, Archon, Taeku Lee, & Peter Harbage. (2008). *Public impacts: Evaluating the outcomes of the CaliforniaSpeaks statewide conversation on health care reform*. Washington, DC: AmericaSpeaks.

Gastil, John. (2007). Government by the people. *Seattle Times*. Available at http://seattletimes.com/html/opinion/2003960790_johngastil19.html.

Gastil, John, & Katie Knobloch. (2011). *Evaluation report to the Oregon state legislature on the 2010 Oregon Citizens' Initiative Review*. Seattle, WA: University of Washington. Available at www.la1.psu.edu/cas/jgastil/CIR/OregonLegislativeReportCIR.pdf.

Hamlett, Patrick, Michael D. Cobb, & David H. Guston. (2008). *National citizens' technology forum: Nanotechnologies and human enhancement*. Phoenix, AZ: Arizona State University Center for Nanotechnology in Society.

Jones, Jeffrey M. (2014). Illinois residents least trusting of their state government. *Gallup Politics*. Available at www.gallup.com/poll/168251/illinois-residents-least-trusting-state-government.aspx.

Kamensky, John. (2012). *Engaging citizens vs. streamlining bureaucracy*. Washington, DC: IBM Center for the Business of Government. Available at www.businessofgovernment.org/blog/business-government/engaging-citizens-vs-streamlining-bureaucracy.

Katz, James E., Michael Barris, & Anshul Jain. (2013). *The social media president: Barack Obama and the politics of digital engagement*. New York, NY: Palgrave Macmillan.

Kraushaar, Josh, & Lisa Lerer. (2009). Health care town hall anger rages on. *Politico*. Available at www.politico.com/news/stories/0809/26049.html.

Kroll, Andy. (2011). Congress has an answer for public wrath: Eliminate town halls. *Mother Jones*. Available at www.motherjones.com/mojo/2011/08/paul-ryan-congress-town-hall.

Leighninger, Matt. (2006). *The next form of democracy: How expert rule is giving way to shared governance—and why politics will never be the same*. Nashville, TN: Vanderbilt University Press.

Leighninger, Matt. (2012). Mapping deliberative civic engagement: Pictures from a (r) evolution. In T.Nabatchi, J.Gastil, M.Weiksner, & M.Leighninger (Eds.), *Democracy in motion: Evaluating the practice and impact of deliberative civic engagement*, 19–39. New York, NY: Oxford University Press.

Levine, Peter. (2010). *The path not taken (so far): Civic engagement for reform*. Available at www.peterlevine.ws/mt/archives/2010/01/the-path-not-ta.html.

Levine, Peter. (2013). *We are the ones we have been waiting for: The promise of civic renewal in American*. New York, NY: Oxford University Press.

Lozada, Carlos. (2013). Please, President Obama. Not another "national conversation." *Washington Post*, February 1.

Lukensmeyer, Carolyn J. (2013). *Bringing citizen voices to the table: A guide for public managers*. San Francisco, CA: Jossey-Bass.

Lukensmeyer, Carolyn J., Joseph P. Goldman, & David Stern. (2011). *Assessing public participation in an open government era: A review of federal agency plans*. Washington, DC: IBM Center for the Business of Government.

Marks, Joseph. (2013). When We the People talks, it's not always pretty. *Nextgov*. Available at www.nextgov.com/emerging-tech/2013/01/when-we-people-talk-its-not-always-pretty/60664/.

McCain, John. (2001). Putting the "national" in national service. *Washington Monthly*. Available at www.washingtonmonthly.com/features/2001/0110.mccain.html.

Mergel, Ines. (2011). *Using wikis in government: A guide for public managers*. Washington, DC: IBM Center for the Business of Government.

Mergel, Ines. (2012). *Social media in the public sector: Participation, collaboration, and transparency in a networked world*. San Francisco, CA: Jossey-Bass.

Nabatchi, Tina. (2014). *Open government? Check. Public participation? Not yet*. Available at http://conflictandcollaboration.wordpress.com/2013/12/20/open-government-check-public-participation-not-yet/.

Nabatchi, Tina, & Lisa Blomgren Amsler. (2014). Direct public engagement in local government. *American Review of Public Administration*, 44(4suppl): 63s–88s.

Nabatchi, Tina, & Cynthia Farrar. (2011). *Bridging the gap between public officials and the public*. Washington, DC: Deliberative Democracy Consortium.

NCoC. (2008). *Americans favor policy change to institutionalize civic engagement*. Washington, DC National Conference on Citizenship. Available at http://ncoc.net/213.

Noveck, Beth Simone. (2010). *Wiki government: How technology can make government better, democracy stronger, and citizens more powerful*. Washington, DC: Brookings Institution Press.

Noveck, Beth Simone. (2011). What's in a name? Open gov and good gov. *Huffington Post*. Available at www.huffingtonpost.com/beth-simone-noveck/whats-in-a-name-open-gov-_b_845735.html.

Noveck, Beth Simone. (2012). Open data: The democratic imperative. *Crooked Timber*. Available at http://crookedtimber.org/2012/07/05/open-data-the-democratic-imperative/.

NPR. (2013). White House's "We the People" petitions find mixed success. National Public Radio. Available at www.npr.org/2013/01/03/168564135/white-houses-we-the-people-petitions-find-mixed-success.

Obama, Barack. (2007). Illinois Sen. Barack Obama's announcement speech. Available at www.washingtonpost.com/wp-dyn/content/article/2007/02/10/ar2007021000879 .html.

O'Reilly, James T. (2011). *Federal Advisory Committee Act: Inhibiting effects on the utilization of new media in collaborative governance and agency policy formation*. Washington, DC: Administrative Conference of the United States. Available at www.acus.gov/sites/default/files/documents/OReilly-FACA-Report-4-15-2011-FINAL.pdf.

PARCC. (2013). *Priorities for public participation and open government: Recommendations to President Obama*. Syracuse, NY: Program for the Advancement of Research on Conflict and Collaboration.

Peters, Jeremy W. (2013). A former engine of the G.O.P., the town hall meeting, cools down. *The New York Times*. Available at www.nytimes.com/2013/08/13/us/politics/a-former-engine-of-the-gop-the-town-hall-meeting-cools-down.html?ref=politics&_r=1&.

Piotrowski, Suzanne J., & Erin Borry. (2010). An analytic framework for open meetings and transparency. *Public Administration and Management*, 15(1): 138–176.

Pogrebinschi, Thamy, & David Samuels. (2014). The impact of participatory democracy: Evidence from Brazil's national public policy conferences. *Comparative Politics*, 46(3): 313–332.

Public Agenda with the New Jersey Coalition for the Public Good. (2003). *A citizens' assembly on New Jersey's tax system*. New York, NY: Public Agenda. Available at www .publicagenda.org/files/nj_tax_reform.pdf.

Rupp, Keith Lee. (2011). R.I.P. town hall meeting. *U.S. News and World Report*. Online. Available at www.usnews.com/opinion/blogs/keith-rupp/2013/08/26/why-congress-town-hall-meetings-may-become-history.

Sifry, Micah L. (2013). How the White House petition site is becoming a digital public square. *TechPresident*. Available at http://techpresident.com/news/23402/how-white-house-petition-site-becoming-digital-public-square.

Sirianni, Carmen, Lisa B. Bingham, Kirk Emerson, Archon Fung, B. Israel, S. R. Smith, et al. (2010). *Partnering with communities: federal models of community-based programs*. National Workshop on Federal Community-Based Programs. Washington, DC: Brookings Institution.

Sirianni, Carmen, & Lewis Friedland. (2001). *Civic innovation in America: Community empowerment, public policy, and the movement for civic renewal*. Berkeley, CA: University of California Press.

Steinhauser, Paul. (2014). CNN poll: Trust in government at all-time low. *CNN Politics*. Available at http://politicalticker.blogs.cnn.com/2014/08/08/cnn-poll-trust-in-government-at-all-time-low-2/.

White House. (2011). *The Open Government Partnership national action plan for the United States of America*. Washington, DC: The White House.

White House. (2013). *The Open Government Partnership second open government national action plan for the United States of America*. Washington, DC: The White House.

Zeleny, Jeff. (2010). Democrats skip town halls to avoid voter rage. *The New York Times*. Available at www.nytimes.com/2010/06/07/us/politics/07townhall.html?_r=0.

PART THREE

Participation for Democracy, Present and Future

Participation Scenarios and Tactics

I n Part Two of this book, we explored what stronger participation infrastructures might look like in education, health, land use, and state and federal government. But while long-term, overarching visions for public participation may be compelling, they are less useful for those who have pressing participation goals and needs. Building a better infrastructure takes time, and some challenges must be dealt with now, not later. The purpose of this chapter is to describe a wide range of participation tactics and to help participation leaders decide how to use those tactics to meet the short-term needs and scenarios they face.

Whether participation leaders are planning for the short or the long term, they must always consider the relationships being built with citizens. Even if the tactic being used is designed to end next week, or next year, the participation experience itself is likely to have long-term effects (good or bad) on how people perceive their community, their government, and each other. To be successful in the short or the long term, public participation must work for both the "engagers" and the "engaged."

This chapter takes stock of those relationships by first taking a closer look at how people typically interact in conventional public meetings. Understanding the assumptions made by public officials, public employees, and citizens in conventional processes can help change the relationship between the engagers and the engaged. We then describe the main strategic questions that must be answered when choosing or designing a participation process. Finally, we examine common participation scenarios, provide a set of participation tactics and suggest strategies to address specific real-world situations.

TRAPPED IN THE FOXHOLE: CONVENTIONAL PARTICIPATION

As we have noted throughout this book, conventional opportunities—including public notice and comment periods, advisory boards, and traditional public meetings—are the most common forms of participation. They also exert a huge influence on the relationship between citizens and institutions, as well as how people perceive the word "participation." This is not just an intellectual point, but an emotional one: people who have been part of conventional processes (whether they are officials, staff, or citizens) often have scars from their experiences, and those past encounters affect their willingness to consider new forms of participation.

Most people in conventional participation feel as if they are trapped in a foxhole. Public officials struggle because the role they have been given is not necessarily the one they envisioned (or wanted). Whether they are elected or appointed, officials come into office with a rush of confidence, trust, and respect—only to find that when the first controversy or key policy decision emerges, the meeting room is full of angry faces. (And if the controversy is being discussed online, the exchange is likely to be even less civil.) Over time, this dynamic becomes entrenched in the thinking of public leaders, and conventional public participation—which, in the minds of most officials, means any kind of public participation—quickly becomes something they dread.

In another part of the meeting room sit the public employees, staffers who have many of the same hurt feelings about the lack of citizen trust and respect. The frustrations of both citizens and officials are often taken out on the relatively defenseless staff. Because they are afraid of these reprisals, and because they feel they are "in this for the long haul," the public employees are usually the silent, stoic characters in the room. They are often just keeping their heads down, trying to ride out the emotional turmoil of the meeting so that everyone will just allow them to go back to work.

This attitude of government staff reflects and reinforces their own blindered set of assumptions about their role: they think of themselves as public problem-solvers. They view the "politics" of public meetings as a side show to their main job, which is to ensure that the streets are cleaned, potholes are filled, buses run on time, criminals are apprehended, and children are educated. All other aspects of public life, especially the ways in which citizens connect with one another, are secondary to the central function of public employees and public institutions. In this way of thinking, citizens are not problem-solvers—and because they have no connection with problem solving, most people are unaware of the dedication and commitment of public employees.

The citizens who attend the meeting are, at least visibly, the most frustrated of all. The opportunity they are given—which in most cases consists of two to three minutes at an open microphone to express themselves to the entire room—reaffirms their role as protesters of public policy, testifying to their complaints about decisions that were made without their knowledge or input. In some public meetings, the officials and staff are barred from responding to anything said by citizens at the microphone (typically this is because open meetings laws prevent discussion by officials of any topic that was not placed on the agenda seventy-two hours before the meeting).

Even the physical setup of the room reinforces the disparity in power and authority: citizens sit in rows, without nametags, with their single microphone in the middle, while the officials loom above them on a raised dais with engraved name plaques and comfortable chairs. The conventional format favors the most confident, educated, and infuriated speakers—and since they seldom feel heard by the officials, it usually leaves them even more frustrated, angry, and distrustful than before.

In almost every case, the vast majority of the people simply stay home. Not showing up to public meetings could be labeled as apathy or ignorance, but in fact, it is a reflection of quite rational thinking on their part: since "getting involved" in this way does not provide them with what they want—problem solving, civility, or community—why should they participate? This same basic parent-child dynamic is prevalent in public meetings at every level of government. But the meetings are only symptomatic of the larger malaise: after they end, everyone goes home and continues working under those same small-minded assumptions about their roles in public life.

How can we get out of these foxholes? Public officials, staff, and citizens have to examine their assumptions about one another and about public participation itself (see Table 2.2 in Chapter 2). From one scenario to the next, they need to think through their participation goals and consider the goals that others bring to the table—this is fundamental to building an adult-adult relationship. Many people, whether they work inside government or not, have the potential to be participation leaders. In the following section, we address four key questions that people should take into account when planning for participation.

PLANNING FOR PARTICIPATION: KEY QUESTIONS TO ANSWER

Throughout this book, we have provided numerous examples of participation tools, techniques, and processes. Here, we want to take a closer look at how these approaches differ. Although participation opportunities vary in a number of ways (see Box 8.1), we focus on four that are important for both immediate participation needs and building stronger participation infrastructure. These differences are easily understood as strategic questions:

- Who should participate and how will participants be recruited?
- How will participants interact with each other and with decision-makers?
- What information do participants need?
- How will participation impact policy decisions, problem-solving efforts, or other kinds of public action?

Before examining these questions, it is useful to make three points about the overarching context for public participation. First, how participation leaders answer these questions will depend on other factors, such as the goals for participation (why participation is needed and the hoped for accomplishments); timing (how quickly a decision needs to be made or an action taken); mandates, laws, rules, and/or regulations; and system context and organizational conditions (budget, human and other resources, available technologies, and logistical constraints), among other issues (Nabatchi, 2012c).

Second, participation leaders should understand the distinction between positions and interests. *Positions* are what a person or group wants; they represent the demand being made. In contrast, *interests* are the reasons—the needs, values, or concerns—underlying a position; they represent why a person or group wants something. For any given issue, people generally have only one position but many interests, with some interests being more important than others. Moreover, people with conflicting positions often have interests in common. (For more information about positions and interests, see the Participation Skills Module, available at www.wiley.com/go/nabatchi.) When participation focuses on positions, discussions are more likely to become adversarial, with people taking up conflicting one-sided arguments. (If I want a mall to be built and you do not, we do not have much room to do anything but argue.) However, when participation focuses on interests, discussions can become more cooperative, constructive, and productive. (If you and I agree that both green space and economic development are important, then we can have a conversation about how to satisfy both of those interests.) If participation is position-based, people are more likely to stay in the foxhole; but if participation is interest-based, they stand a better chance of getting out (see Nabatchi, 2012c).

Box 8.1. Some Variations in Direct Public Participation

General Purpose and Objectives. Direct participation has many general purposes, for example, gathering or disseminating information, resolving disagreements, fostering collaborative action, making decisions, developing plans.

Size. The number of participants involved can range from a few to hundreds or thousands.

Participant Recruitment. Recruitment strategies may include broadcasting announcements through the media, recruiting proactively through networks, and selecting by random sample.

Participation Tactic. Participation can involve in-person, remote, and/or online tactics. In-person tactics may use a large-group or small-table format and may or may not be facilitated. Remote and online tactics differ in terms of how participants interact with the technology; whether, where, and how participants interact with each other; and whether the interaction is moderated. Some tactics have official names and may even be trademarked, whereas others are not.

Interaction Mode. Direct public participation may involve one-way, two-way, and/or deliberative communication.

Communication Plan. Participation approaches may (or may not) include a strategy to assist with the dissemination of information to the attendees and the broader community about the process, its results, and how and why public input is (or is not) being used in official decision making.

Participant Preparation. Informational and other materials may or may not be used to prepare participants.

Locus of Action. Participation may have intended actions or outcomes at the individual, family, organizational, network, neighborhood, community, municipal, state, national, or even international level.

Specificity of Recommendations. Participation may produce a variety of outcomes, ranging from fairly generic recommendations to highly specific proposals or judgments.

Recurrence and Iteration. Participation may involve a one-time event, a series of single events over the course of time, or a longer-term, ongoing endeavor.

Connection to Policy and Decision Making. Participation may have weak or strong connections to policy and decision-makers, or it may be intended to invoke individual or group action or change.

For more discussion about these and other variations in direct participation, see Nabatchi & Amsler (2014); see also Bingham, Nabatchi, & O'Leary (2005); Bryson, Quick, Slotterback, & Crosby (2013); Fung (2003, 2006); Hoppe (2011); and Nabatchi (2012a, 2012b, 2012c).

Third, it is important to consider the level of concern or controversy surrounding the issues being addressed. Some issues have low stakes, where most people are relatively unconcerned and do not have fixed positions; others have high stakes, where many people are very concerned and hold strong positions;

and still others are of low stakes to some people, and high stakes to others. In general, a high-stakes issue requires more attention to interests than a low-stakes issue does (Fung, 2003; Nabatchi, 2012c; Nabatchi & Amsler, 2014). These points about positions, interests, and stakes become clearer in light of the four strategic questions.

Who Should Participate and How Will Participants Be Recruited?

Who should participate is a central issue in public participation (cf. Bryson, Quick, Slotterback, & Crosby, 2013; Fung, 2003, 2006; Nabatchi, 2012c; Thomas, 1995, 2012). Most agree that getting the "right" people to the table is important, but decisions about who the "right" people are depend not only on what participation leaders are trying to do, but also on how people perceive and are affected by the issue.

A first step in determining who should participate is to examine who is affected by the issue. Some issues may affect the "public" (the broad and general populace) or "citizens" (eligible voters), while others may affect "community members" (those who live in a particular city or town) or "residents" (inhabitants of a particular locale such as a neighborhood, housing subdivision, or building), and still others may affect only a sub-set of people within any of these categories (Nabatchi & Amsler, 2014: 65). A second step is to examine the stakes involved for those who are affected. In general, if an issue deeply affects people, and/or if it is controversial, then it is important to devote significant amounts of time and energy to recruitment.

After deciding who should be involved, participation leaders must determine a recruitment strategy. Here, we identify three primary recruitment strategies, which may be used alone or in combination with one or more of the others: (1) broadcasting announcements through the media; (2) recruiting proactively through networks; and (3) selecting by random sample (Fung, 2003, 2006; Leighninger, 2012; Nabatchi, 2012c; Nabatchi & Amsler, 2014; Ryfe & Stalsburg, 2012). For all of these approaches, it is important for organizers to put themselves in the shoes of potential participants and think about the incentives that might compel them to engage (Will it make an impact on an issue I care about? Will it give me information I need? Will it be fun?) and the barriers that may stand in their way (Will there be child care? Will people speak my language? Will it be easy to get there?). Recruitment skills are described more extensively in the Participation Skills Module.

The most common recruitment strategy, and the default approach for conventional participation, is *broadcasting announcements through the media*. This approach is used most often for public meetings and online opportunities that are open to anyone. It relies on simple advertising—placing notices in newspapers, on the radio, and on websites, and perhaps distributing flyers. This approach is sometimes referred to as "voluntary self-selection" because people who see or hear the advertisements voluntarily decide whether to attend. The benefit of this recruitment strategy is that it is relatively easy and inexpensive. However, this strategy has drawbacks. If the issue has low stakes, then very few people turn out, and those who do tend to be wealthy, older, and white, since this population generally has the resources and time to participate; if the issue is of high stakes, then those who turn out tend to be people who have strong opinions and positions on the issue (Fung, 2003; Nabatchi, 2012c). In either case, this recruitment strategy creates "participation bias," which means that those who attend are not representative of the community in terms of socio-demographic characteristics, political or ideological perspectives, or viewpoints on the issue (Fung, 2003; Nabatchi, 2012c).

Because the success of a participation project often depends on whether it attracts a diverse, critical mass of people, many participation leaders use *proactive, network-based recruitment* strategies. This is sometimes also referred to as "targeted demographic recruitment." The first step is to map community networks; these could be political or advocacy groups, but they could also be networks centered on neighborhoods, schools, faith communities, workplaces, or other shared interests. Participation leaders then capitalize on the relationships they have (or ones they can build) with influential people in those networks. If certain populations seem especially critical—either because they are more likely to be affected by the issue being addressed or because they have traditionally been marginalized and are less likely to participate—then organizers may focus extra attention on building relationships and recruiting proactively within those networks.

Although this recruitment approach still largely relies on voluntary self-selection, it also tends to reduce participation bias. It is also more time- and labor-intensive, mainly because it relies on relationships of trust, which take time and effort to build. The main reason people participate is because someone they already know and trust asks them to do so; the challenge of proactive recruitment is to tap into (or in some cases, to establish) a sufficiently large web of trusting relationships to generate a large and diverse turnout. The advent of the Internet and the presence of social media have made this challenge a little less daunting because communication is almost instantaneous, and because networks are easier to find. However, recruitment remains one of the most difficult tasks in public participation.

Another method used to overcome participation bias is *random selection*, which essentially means picking participants by lot to produce a microcosm of the larger population. This strategy is much more resource-intensive, since participation leaders must often rely on paid consultants or polling firms who use random-digit dialing or other approaches to select potential participants. More recently, for-profit firms have assembled large panels of people who have agreed up-front to serve as poll and survey respondents on particular issues.

Of course, representativeness is only achieved if those who are selected or recruited choose to participate. Participation leaders using random-sample approaches sometimes offer incentives such as per diem payments, gift cards, or other monetary awards to participants. Organizers using proactive, network-based recruitment are more likely to use nonmonetary incentives (like food or music) that make the participation experience more enjoyable. All recruitment approaches are more effective and equitable when transportation, child care, translation, or other services that help remove the immediate barriers to participation are provided.

How Will Participants Interact with Each Other and with Decision-Makers?

Participation leaders should also consider the interactions, or how people will communicate with each other, within a participation opportunity. In general, there are three interaction or communication modes: one-way, two-way, and deliberative (Nabatchi, 2012c). Each has strengths and weaknesses, and the mode selected should depend on the stakes and what participation leaders are trying to accomplish. We discuss various skills that are useful for fostering productive participant interactions, such as moderation, facilitation, and ground rules, in the Participation Skills Module.

One-way and *two-way communication* are relatively straightforward. One-way communication is the unidirectional flow of information between people, and two-way communication is the reciprocal flow of information. One-way communication is generally fast and easy, but it does not allow for feedback or for negotiation. It is also sometimes hard to know whether the message has reached the intended audience and whether people understand it. Two-way communication does enable feedback and some negotiation, but it rarely allows for in-depth consideration of perspectives. Perhaps more importantly, both one- and two-way communication encourage position-based, rather than interest-based statements. For these reasons, one- and two-way communication are best used for low-stakes issues.

Other kinds of participation produce multi-way communication, in which citizens, public officials, and public employees can all interact with one another. In the realm of participation, the most important kind of multi-way communication is *deliberative communication*, a specialized mode of discussion that is structured and oriented toward problem solving (Gastil, 2008). Specifically, deliberation requires that a group of participants take part in an open and accessible process in which they "reflect carefully on a matter, [weigh] the strengths and weaknesses of alternative solutions to a problem [and] aim to arrive at a decision or judgment based on not only facts and data but also values, emotions, and other less technical considerations" (Gastil, 2005: 164). Deliberation also requires that all participants have an adequate opportunity to speak, listen attentively and consider carefully the contributions of other participants, and treat each other with respect (Gastil, 2008: 9–10). Most deliberation occurs in face-to-face settings, although platforms for online deliberation have been developed (see Chapter 2 and the Participation Skills Module).

Deliberation has many benefits: it gives everyone an opportunity to be heard and enables people to focus on interests rather than positions. This can foster cooperation and lead to more productive conflict management. However, deliberation also has drawbacks: it is labor-intensive and time-consuming. Deliberation is useful, and sometimes essential, for high-stakes issues.

What Information Do Participants Need to Be Prepared?

This question goes to the issue of participant preparation (Nabatchi, 2012c). A traditional criticism of participation is that the public is ignorant and rash, and consequently unable to give useful input on important public decisions. But research shows that participant input improves when they are given high-quality information (Delli Carpini, 2000) that provides context and history, is neutral and objective, and includes all perspectives (Lukensmeyer & Brigham, 2002). Deliberative processes require agendas or guides that "frame" the issue by laying out the main views or policy options to be considered. (For more information about how to develop informational materials and frame issues, see the Participation Skills Module.)

Of course, not all participation opportunities require preparatory materials. Whether information is needed, as well as what types of materials are appropriate, depends on the complexity of the issue being examined and the stakes involved. Some simple, low-stakes issues may not require participant preparation. Others may require specific information provided through websites, infographics, newspaper articles, short presentations, or expert or panel discussions. Complex and/ or high-stakes issues almost always require informational materials, such as issue guides, online resources, or experts who can answer technical questions.

How Will Participation Impact Policy Decisions, Problem-Solving Efforts, or Other Kinds of Public Action?

This is usually the most difficult question to answer, in part because impacts are dependent on the recommendations, ideas, and commitment of the participants. Some projects designed to affect policy changes lead instead to a wave of volunteer-driven problem-solving efforts; others that are intended to increase volunteerism instead change policy (Leighninger, 2006). Regardless, participation leaders can determine what kinds of questions and choices will best elicit citizen input for policymaking and can support participants in taking action.

When it comes to policymaking, an essential aspect of this question is how much decision-making authority is being given to participants. The International Association for Public Participation (IAP2) Spectrum of Public Participation (IAP2, 2007) provides a useful graphic for thinking about how public input will be used. Figure 8.1 presents an adapted version of the spectrum, including information about the communication modes, goals, and promise made to the public at each point along the continuum (for more about the adapted version of the spectrum, see Nabatchi, 2012b, 2012c).

At the first level of the spectrum are tactics that *inform* the public or "provide the public with balanced and objective information to assist them in understanding the problem, alternatives, opportunities, and/or solutions." Informational tactics typically use one-way communication and have no shared decision authority.

At the second level are tactics that *consult* with the public or "obtain public feedback on analysis, alternatives, and/or decisions." The promise in consultation is to "listen to and acknowledge concerns and aspirations, and provide feedback on how public input influenced the decision." They may use one-way or two-way communication, but provide minimal, if any, shared decision authority.

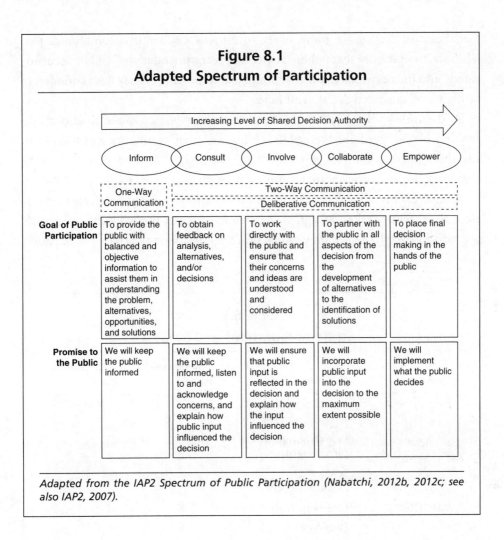

Figure 8.1
Adapted Spectrum of Participation

Increasing Level of Shared Decision Authority

	Inform	Consult	Involve	Collaborate	Empower
	One-Way Communication	Two-Way Communication / Deliberative Communication			
Goal of Public Participation	To provide the public with balanced and objective information to assist them in understanding the problem, alternatives, opportunities, and solutions	To obtain feedback on analysis, alternatives, and/or decisions	To work directly with the public and ensure that their concerns and ideas are understood and considered	To partner with the public in all aspects of the decision from the development of alternatives to the identification of solutions	To place final decision making in the hands of the public
Promise to the Public	We will keep the public informed	We will keep the public informed, listen to and acknowledge concerns, and explain how public input influenced the decision	We will ensure that public input is reflected in the decision and explain how the input influenced the decision	We will incorporate public input into the decision to the maximum extent possible	We will implement what the public decides

Adapted from the IAP2 Spectrum of Public Participation (Nabatchi, 2012b, 2012c; see also IAP2, 2007).

At the third level are tactics that *involve* the public, or "work directly with the public throughout the process to ensure that public concerns and aspirations are consistently understood and considered." Involvement tactics typically use two-way communication, although a few may use deliberative communication. These participation opportunities promise that public "concerns and aspirations are directly reflected in the alternatives developed." They have a low to moderate level of shared decision authority.

At the fourth level are tactics that encourage leaders to *collaborate* with the public, or "partner with the public in each aspect of the decision, including the development of alternatives and the identification of the preferred solution."

Collaborative tactics are more likely to employ deliberative communication. These tactics promise that public "advice and recommendations" will be incorporated "into the decisions to the maximum extent possible." They have a moderate to high level of shared decision authority.

At the fifth level are tactics that *empower* the public or "place final decision making in the hands of the public." Empowerment tactics are most likely to use deliberative communication and have the highest level of shared decision authority, because officials are promising to implement what the public decides.

Table 8.1 summarizes how the options for answering these four strategic questions fit with low-stakes or high-stakes public issues. Although these judgments are broad generalizations, they are helpful for considering various participation

Table 8.1
Strategic Questions and Stakes

Question	Options	Low-Stakes Issue	High-Stakes Issue
Recruitment	Broadcasting announcements	X	
	Proactive network recruitment		X
	Selecting by random sample		X
Interaction	One-way	X	
	Two-way	X	X
	Deliberative		X
Participant Preparation	No	X	
	Yes		X
Impact	Supporting ways for citizens to take part in problem solving	X	X
	Showing how input will influence resulting policy decisions		X

scenarios and tactics—some of which have their own built-in assumptions about recruitment, interaction, preparation, and impacts.

PARTICIPATION SCENARIOS: MATCHING THE GOALS OF "ENGAGERS" AND "ENGAGED"

How participation leaders answer the four strategic questions will depend on many factors, not the least of which are the participation scenario they face and the goals they have for engaging the public. In this section, we describe several of the most common scenarios, along with the typical goals that the engagers—and the engaged—bring to those situations.

The need to think through both the goals of participation leaders *and* the goals of the potential participants is perhaps the most complicated aspect of public engagement (see Box 8.2). Like many other aspects of this work, the dual nature of participation goals points up the importance of relationships—both specific personal relationships and broader relationships between individuals and institutions—since it is through these connections that goals are best articulated and negotiated.

The scenarios we describe in this chapter look similar to the six building blocks for participation infrastructure described in Chapters 4 through 7. This makes sense: many of the things we describe in Figures 4.3, 5.3, 6.3, and 7.3 are simply short-term participation activities that can be repeated, supported, and made easier. For example, crowdsourcing exercises and participatory budgeting processes can be organized as one-off projects—or they can be made part of the regular routine on a given issue. However, since meeting immediate participation needs is the focus of this chapter, two of the building blocks are not covered here. The first, discussing and connecting, does not typically come up as a short-term participation priority. (It is, however, still important; even short-term participation efforts rely on relationships, and they are hard to build in the midst of a controversy or a crisis.) The second, enabling student and family decisions (Chapter 4) or patient and family decisions (Chapter 5), does not come up here because these efforts are more likely to be tackled as long-term, highly context-specific priorities.

All four strategic questions are likely to be at least somewhat important in each of the scenarios; however, the discussion below highlights the most critical questions for each scenario. We also provide some general examples of participation tools and techniques in each scenario.

Scenario 1: Participation Leaders Want to Inform the Public

This is the most basic and common participation scenario. In fact, informing citizens in some way could be considered part of all these scenarios. Governments, civic organizations, universities, and civil society groups have a great deal of information they want—and need—to share. For example, participation leaders could be trying to inform citizens about the main expenditures in the city budget (Marois & Amsler, 2008), the threat of a flu pandemic (Liburd, Giles, & Jack, 2014), the way in which planning and zoning decisions are made (Amsler, 2008), how policing strategies are changing (Leighninger, 2006), or what to do in the event of a natural disaster (Lukensmeyer, 2013). Sometimes the information is basic and straightforward; other times the information might focus on a new issue or emerging problems, alternatives, opportunities, or solutions.

Participation leaders facing this scenario should ask themselves a basic question: Why do they want people to have this information? There are many possible reasons. Participation leaders may want to:

- Encourage people to change their behavior;
- Help people understand an issue, as well as the tradeoffs and options decision-makers face; and/or
- Help people understand how they can participate in decision making or problem solving on the issue.

Participants have their own goals in these situations, possibly including all of the goals listed above. In addition, participants may want to:

- Share information themselves or suggest new ways for information to be shared;
- Learn how to work with other people and organizations to do something about the issue; and/or
- Participate in decision making (including, in some cases, revoking a decision that has already been made).

The two most important strategic questions leaders should address in this scenario are recruitment and interaction. Recruitment speaks to the issue of who receives the information. In some cases, informational tactics need to reach a broad population (e.g., for flu prevention), whereas in others, they need to reach a specific population (e.g., parents of school-aged children).

Interaction concerns how information is communicated. One-way communication may be appropriate when the information is straightforward and the request being made of citizens does not require significant changes on their part ("to help prevent a flu pandemic, be sure to wash your hands frequently"). If the information is more complex and the request is more significant—or if the information will prompt citizens to become more involved in decision making and problem solving—then tactics that feature two-way or deliberative modes of interaction may be needed. Another way to say this is that simpler information sharing can be done effectively using thin participation tactics, whereas the more complicated situations require thick tactics. In part, this is because most people are visual and experiential learners—they learn better in interactive environments where they can envision how the information will affect their lives and where they can test the strengths and weaknesses of different ideas.

In some situations, the reaction of citizens may suggest a shift in scenarios: what participation leaders thought of as a need to share information is viewed by citizens as something that deserves greater deliberation, collaboration, or shared decision making. For a variety of reasons, participation leaders may not be able to accommodate these desires—for example, they are local officials bound to the constraints of a state or federal law, or a decision has been made that cannot be revoked. But even in these cases, it is important to be aware that the engagers and the potentially engaged have different perspectives on the nature of the scenario they are facing. Participation leaders should be clear about their expectations and constraints and open-minded about ways to adjust their participation plans.

Scenario 2: Participation Leaders Want to Gather Public Input, Feedback, and Preferences

Participation leaders are often faced with issues for which they want or need to know what citizens think. All kinds of activities, from campaign polls to opinion research, could fall under this very broad category of work. We focus here on efforts to gather feedback on what governments and other institutions are doing, how (and how well) they are doing it, and what they might do next. For example, participation leaders might want to know how parents feel about issues of race and difference at their child's school (Orland, 2007), how residents rank different public transit alternatives (Lazo, 2014), or how to allocate limited flu vaccines in the case of a pandemic (Leighninger, 2006).

Again, it is worth thinking through the potential goals of participation leaders, who may want to:

- Gauge public perceptions of a program or service;
- Hear reactions to different options for improving a service or implementing a plan; and/or
- Get a sense of citizen preferences, priorities, or rankings in the course of decision making.

Citizens, meanwhile, may want to contribute to these goals, and also:

- Suggest new ideas for improving a service or implementing a plan (including options that were discarded by decision-makers or that have not been considered so far);
- Devote some of their own time and energy to implementing those ideas; and/or
- Become more involved with participation leaders and other citizens in making a decision or developing a plan.

An important consideration in this scenario is how to reach and recruit the right group or mix of people. Participation leaders should determine whether they want a demographically representative sample of public opinion, the input of a specific set of people who use a particular service or are more likely to be affected by a certain issue, or just a general sense of what the most active and interested citizens think. Once again, being aware of the match or mismatch between the goals of engagers and engaged is important when thinking through how to describe a participation effort—and whether it needs to be adjusted.

Gathering input, feedback, and preferences lends itself easily to thin forms of participation, including surveys and polls conducted by telephone or online, canvassing door-to-door or at events, reaching out through online networks, using serious games, or aggregating the terms and opinions found in online discussions. If citizens require more information or participation leaders want them to delve more deeply into different options or tradeoffs, then thicker forms of participation may be more appropriate.

Scenario 3: Participation Leaders Want Citizens to Generate New Ideas or New Data

In addition to responding to questions from participation leaders, citizens can provide many other kinds of information, from big, creative ideas to small, but significant details. Many participation efforts tap this reservoir of knowledge, for example, to find "out of the box" thinking about how to improve community schools (Colorado Association of School Boards, 2003) or to uncover data about everyday problems (like potholes, graffiti, school absenteeism, or crime) that public institutions are trying to fix (Ganapati 2010). In some of these situations, citizens are encouraged to spend a great deal of their own time and effort developing their ideas, exploring the feasibility of their proposals, or refining or ranking the ideas contributed by others. In others, citizens are asked for specific pieces of data that help identify, tag, measure, or prioritize public problems.

Through these efforts, participation leaders may be trying to:

- Identify priority problems or issues;
- Gather data that helps employees address situations or meet public needs more effectively;
- Find creative ideas that their institutions can implement; and/or
- Find creative ideas that citizens will work to help implement.

Citizens who take part in these efforts may embrace these goals, and may also want:

- Public institutions to address priority problems, or implement the ideas that have been generated;
- Greater access to public data that will help them develop and refine their ideas; and/or
- Contact with public employees and other problem-solvers so that they can work on the feasibility and implementation of ideas, or find out why certain problems have not been addressed.

Here leaders should consider the strategic questions dealing with recruitment, preparation, and impact. Participation leaders should consider the degree to which representativeness, inclusion, and diversity are important and necessary for the issue and select recruitment strategies accordingly. They should think through what kinds of information, access to expertise, and other resources citizens may need to effectively contribute ideas and data. Finally, they should be sufficiently open-minded about the variety of suggestions they receive and sufficiently flexible to use or respond to them. Clear expectations are critical, particularly about the level of government or organizational resources that are available.

Scenario 4: Participation Leaders Want to Support Volunteerism and Citizen-Driven Problem Solving

In some situations, participation leaders realize that the problem or issue they are trying to address requires individual actions, behavioral changes, small-group efforts, or changes by organizations—or all of the above, on a large scale. Included among many examples are race and diversity issues (Walsh, 2007), crime and policing (Fung & Wright, 2003), childhood obesity (McCarron, Richartz, Brigham, White, Klein, & Kessel, 2010), and the preservation of watersheds and other environmental resources (Sirianni & Friedland, 2000).

Through these projects, participation leaders may be trying to:

- Increase the capacity of the community or society to solve the problem, and/or
- Raise awareness of the work being done by public institutions, civil society organizations, and other groups to solve the problem.

Citizens who participate in these efforts almost always share the first goal, and often the second. In addition, they may want to:

- Find more information about the issue, and

- Influence plans and policy decisions relevant to the issue.

It is relatively easy for citizens to recommend solutions for others to implement, but deciding to take action, even in minor ways, requires a higher degree of commitment. Building public ownership of public problems usually requires connecting people in information-rich environments in which they can decide not only what they want to do, but also how to do it. Accordingly, participation leaders should pay attention to strategic questions of recruitment, preparation, and impact. Recruitment is important in this scenario because higher numbers of volunteers usually means a higher capacity for problem solving. Preparation matters in the sense that citizens who know more about the issue and are better able to coordinate their efforts will be more effective. The question of impact is less tied to policy change and more tied to how citizens will be supported, recognized for their efforts, and asked to report back on accomplishments. This may require continuing opportunities for participation; if future events will feature their efforts, people are more likely to continue working together.

Scenario 5: Participation Leaders Want to Make a Policy Decision

Leaders sometimes use participation to address an immediate political peril, seize the opportunity of a policy window, or manage concerns or frustrations with the policymaking process (Nabatchi & Amsler, 2014). For example, public officials may use participation to generate the public will to help break a legislative deadlock or make a difficult decision on a controversial issue, such as school redistricting and closings (Leighninger, 2006), landfills (McComas, 2001, 2003), zoning for new developments (Gordon, Schirra, & Hollander, 2011), or statewide corrections reform (Leighninger, 2006). Even neighborhood-level concerns like bike lanes, dog parks, and community policing are critical topics for participation in public decision making.

Participation leaders dealing with this scenario typically want to:

- Ensure that citizens understand the basic facts on the issue, especially the tradeoffs among different options;

- Reduce the level of tension surrounding the decision; and/or

- Contain the political fallout from the decision—in other words, make it less likely that decision-makers will be fired or defeated for re-election based on the option they chose.

Citizens may also want to:

- Find more information about the issue;
- Feel that their opinions are valued and that they have a meaningful say in the decision; and/or
- Work in other ways to make an impact on the problem that the decision is trying to address—for example, they may want to help improve the quality of the school system and the education of students, no matter what happens with a school closing decision.

It is very difficult to overcome polarization among different segments of the population without bringing those people together in some kind of structured environment. Even the most carefully constructed compromises may not suffice without substantive public participation: citizens rarely accept compromises if they feel they had no say when the agreements were being negotiated. When people hear firsthand why others hold different opinions, and when people with divergent opinions have a chance to analyze the same information and consider different arguments or policy options, they usually are able to find some common ground.

All four of the key strategic questions—recruitment, interaction, preparation, and impact—are critical in this scenario. In high-profile, high-conflict situations, people pay attention to who is (and is not) in the room. Likewise, one-way and two-way communication are likely to foster a position-based discussion, which creates an adversarial, win-lose situation. Therefore, deliberative communication, where everyone has the opportunity to be heard, will be more effective (Nabatchi, 2012c). Because policy disagreements are often based on (mis)information and varying interpretations about information, participant preparation is critical; people need balanced, neutral, and objective data around which to center their discussions. Finally, participants want to know that their input had an impact on decision-makers. Even if they do not agree with the final decision or outcomes, people often value the participation opportunity when they feel that their contributions were carefully considered.

Scenario 6: Participation Leaders Want to Develop a Plan or a Budget

Developing a plan or a budget is perhaps the broadest participation scenario—in some cases, a planning process incorporates all five of the other scenarios. Because it may encompass all of the other scenarios, participation in planning and budgeting is the most likely to employ a wide range of engagement activities, tools, and processes. Participation has been used to develop plans relating to land use (Wates, 2000), health (Norris, 2014), school redistricting (Frey, 2014), disaster preparedness and recovery (Lukensmeyer, 2013), and many other issues. As we discuss in the next section, participatory budgeting and other engagement tactics centered on budgets have been used to inform or shape the financial decisions of local governments, school systems, housing authorities, and other organizations (Schugurensky, 2014).

In this scenario, participation leaders often have many goals, such as:

- Ensuring that people have a baseline of information about the issue or the community;
- Understanding public values and priorities;
- Encouraging citizens to contribute creative new ideas that could become part of the plan or budget;
- Encouraging citizens to contribute some of their own time and energy to implementing those ideas or other aspects of the plan;
- Establishing a general direction that is broadly supported by the population, so that in the future, people will understand the more specific decisions and actions taken by decision-makers; and/or
- Preparing for or making controversial decisions by framing them in the broader context of public values and what people want for their community.

This list of goals probably applies equally to citizens. The critical thing to discover is whether both the engagers and the engaged are interested in the same goals. This kind of clarification and negotiation is essential to successful planning or budgeting.

Implementation is also critical. Too many participatory processes have produced plans that failed to shape future actions and decisions. There are many reasons for this, but perhaps the most fundamental is that the participation opportunities ended when the plan was released: the engagers and engaged did not build in future meetings, online exchanges, dashboards, or other ways of benchmarking progress and holding one another accountable to commitments.

As with Scenario 5, and for the same basic reasons, all four key strategic questions will be important to answer in Scenario 6. Decisions about recruitment, interaction, preparation, and impact will have a critical impact on the success (or failure) of participatory planning or budgeting.

Table 8.2
Common Participation Scenarios and Strategic Questions

Scenario	Recruitment	Interaction	Participant Preparation	Impact
		Design Question		
Inform the public	X	X		
Gather input, feedback, and preferences	X			
Generate new ideas and information	X		X	X
Support volunteerism and problem solving	X		X	X
Make a policy decision	X	X	X	X
Develop a plan or budget	X	X	X	X

Although other participation scenarios certainly exist, these six arise most frequently. While participation leaders should always consider recruitment, interaction, preparation, and impact, some of these questions are more salient in some scenarios than in others. Table 8.2 summarizes the strategic questions that matter most in each scenario.

PARTICIPATION TACTICS: MATCHING APPROACHES TO SCENARIOS

Faced with these scenarios, and frustrated by the inability of conventional meetings and processes to address them, participation leaders have pioneered a wide range of participatory tactics. Table 8.3 specifies twelve common tactics—roughly organized from thinnest to thickest—and indicates which are most valuable in each scenario. Thinner tactics require simpler, quicker actions, usually by individuals acting alone, whereas thicker tactics require a greater commitment of time and energy from participants, mainly in small-group settings. Some tactics use digital tools, while others rely on face-to-face interactions, but most can be pursued either online or off (or through a combination of both).

Table 8.3

Participation Tactics and Scenarios

Tactic	Scenario 1 Inform the public	Scenario 2 Gather input, feedback, and preferences	Scenario 3 Generate new ideas and info	Scenario 4 Support volunteerism and problem solving	Scenario 5 Make a public decision	Scenario 6 Create a plan or budget
Social Media Aggregation		YES			YES—with other tactics	YES—with other tactics
Surveys and Polls		YES			YES—with other tactics	YES—with other tactics
Focus Groups		YES			YES—with other tactics	YES—with other tactics
Online Problem-Reporting Platforms			YES	YES—with other tactics		YES—with other tactics
Crowdsourcing and Contests			YES	YES		YES—with other tactics
Crowdfunding and Mini-Grants			YES	YES		YES—with other tactics
Serious Games	YES	YES	YES	YES	YES—with other tactics	YES—with other tactics
Wiki-Based Mapping and Writing Platforms	YES		YES	YES	YES—with other tactics	YES—with other tactics
Online Networks	YES	YES	YES—with other tactics	YES	YES—with other tactics	YES—with other tactics
Collaborative Planning Processes			YES	YES		YES
Participatory Budgeting	YES		YES	YES	YES—with other tactics	YES
Public Deliberation	YES	YES	YES	YES	YES	YES

Each tactic has strengths and limitations and, generally speaking, each will be most effective when conducted as part of a comprehensive strategy. In some scenarios—particularly Scenarios 1 and 2—some tactics used alone may be sufficient, whereas in other scenarios, tactics work best when used in combination. While many tactics are promoted as stand-alone models or tools, most experienced participation practitioners and researchers now agree that a multiple-tactic or "multi-channel" approach (Lukensmeyer, 2013; Peixoto & Weber, 2012) works best in most participation scenarios and is probably essential for Scenarios 5 and 6. Many of these tactics rely on skills described in the Participation Skills Module.

It is important to understand that this is not an exhaustive list: for decades, people have applied their creative energies to developing new formats for participation, and the result is a dizzying array of tactics. New innovations, especially tactics that capitalize on social media and other online tools, are emerging faster than ever. We also do not cover the most basic kinds of communication tools, like flyers, mailers, infographics, press releases, and static websites, even though these are common elements of participation projects. Additional resources for finding and understanding participation tactics include:

- Participedia (www.participedia.net)
- *IAP2 Public Participation Toolbox*, International Association for Public Participation (2007)
- *Organizing Community-Wide Dialogue for Action and Change*, Study Circles Resource Center (2001) (now Everyday Democracy)
- *Community Heart and Soul Field Guide*, Orton Family Foundation (2014)
- *Engagement Streams Framework*, National Coalition for Dialogue and Deliberation (2008)
- *Public Pathways: A Guide to Online Engagement Tools for Local Governments*, New America Foundation (2014)
- *Beyond the Ballot: 57 Democratic Innovations from Around the World*, The Power Inquiry (Smith, 2005)
- *Public Engagement: A Primer*, Public Agenda (2008)
- *Organizing for Participatory Budgeting*, Participatory Budgeting Project (www.participatorybudgeting.org/toolkit/)
- *A Refined Typology of Public Engagement Tools and Implements*, PE2020 Project (Mačiukaitė-Žvinienė, Tauginienė, Rask, Meijlgaard, Ravn, & d'Andrea, 2014)

The Participation Skills Module also contains a list of organizations that provide public participation resources.

Some of the tactics listed below were described or at least mentioned in Chapters 4 through 7. Many elements of the participation infrastructures described in those chapters may also apply to this one: structures like neighborhood associations, parent groups, advisory committees, and official public meetings might be useful elements of short-term participation projects. (In any case, the need for a comprehensive, multi-channel approach in most scenarios reinforces the importance of a stronger participation infrastructure that can support those kinds of strategies.)

Tactic 1: Social Media Aggregation

Aggregation tools, a relatively new technology, sift through social media networks to find common words and strings of words. They allow participation leaders to "listen in" on existing online discussions of public issues, rather than having to bring citizens to a meeting or a different online space. In fact, social media aggregation is not really a proactive participation tactic, but an approach that capitalizes on the fact that citizens have already participated in their online networks. CitizenScape, Measured Voice, and Cityzen are representative social media aggregation platforms. Another tool, Google Alert, notifies the user when a particular search term is used in social media.

Social media aggregation is useful for gaining a sense of citizen preferences (Scenario 2) and could also be part of a larger strategy for making decisions or developing plans (Scenarios 5 and 6). Participation leaders who aggregate comments on social media sometimes also introduce topics and questions within those setting, a practice that blends Tactic 1 with Tactic 9.

Aggregation is championed by some civic technologists, who characterize it as attending to participation from the "bottom-up," rather than trying to orchestrate it from the "top-down." One civic technologist claimed that "Listening to and participating in online conversations is quickly replacing polling as a way to understand what communities of interest are actually interested *in*" (Drapeau, 2009). "Above all, governments must expect to 'go where people are' when seeking to engage with them, rather than expecting people to come to government," wrote Joanne Caddy (OECD, 2009: 14), who has directed online engagement efforts for the Organization for Economic Co-operation and Development.

The more significant challenge with aggregation, however, is figuring out how participation leaders should interpret what they hear. Participant recruitment—or, in this case, selecting and filtering participant comments—is the only one of the strategic questions relevant to aggregation. At this point in their development, it is difficult for these tools to come close to the accuracy of a random-sample poll. Citizens participating in online discussions about policy are not necessarily more representative of the general public (and may in fact be less representative) than the organized lobbying groups—or even the "usual suspects" who show up at conventional public hearings. Furthermore, when political conversations are unstructured and isolated from the policymaking process, there is less incentive for the participants to deliberate, compromise, or even seek to understand each other better.

Tactic 2: Surveys and Polls

Surveys and polls are among the most basic participation tactics. They have traditionally been conducted by phone, by mail, and in person, but in the last ten years, online tools have made it easier to design and disseminate surveys and polls through email, texting, websites, and social media. Another method for surveying citizens is keypad polling, which is usually done in face-to-face meetings. In this method, participants vote on the same question at the same time, using handheld keypads (for tips on using keypad polling, see the Participation Skills Module). This method can be linked to online polls or to live keypad polling being conducted simultaneously in multiple places.

Like social media aggregation, surveys and polls are mainly useful for gathering citizen input, feedback, and preferences (Scenario 2), although they could be part of a larger strategy for one of the other scenarios, especially Scenarios 5 and 6. Many nonprofit and for-profit organizations specialize in polling and surveys. Online survey and polling platforms include SurveyMonkey, SurveyConsole, SurveyGizmo, Codigital, and Poll Everywhere, among others.

Many participation leaders have developed creative ways of gathering input and feedback, often using mobile technology, that push the boundaries of polls and surveys. For example, as part of an effort to create a regional plan for sustainable development in the Buffalo/Niagara Region, the organization Textizen posted questions about regional transit at bus stops, light rail stops, and on buses. People texted their answers, which were tabulated on the Textizen platform and made public as part of the planning process (Jacobs, 2014).

Participation leaders should pay attention to issues about participant selection and recruitment when using surveys and polls. In general, people who respond to surveys and polls tend to be more educated and more active citizens; this means that there can be biased responses. It can be useful to include questions that collect demographic data to provide a better idea of who is responding and how well they represent the broader community. Random sampling can also be used to generate more scientific surveys and polls that are more representative of the broader population; however, random sampling can be costly.

Box 8.3. Deliberative Polling

Deliberative polls have been used in numerous countries around the world. Their purpose is to gauge what citizens will support and why, and thus provide decision-makers with guidelines from which to act.

To conduct a deliberative poll, 200 to 500 people are randomly sampled from the population. Once identified, each participant is polled on a set of questions to establish a baseline about participants' opinions and knowledge. Participants are then paid to attend a summit that typically lasts one to two days. In advance of the summit, participants review information about the issue or decision being addressed. At the summit, participants work in small-group discussions with trained facilitators, punctuated with periodic presentations and briefings by experts. Following the deliberations, participants are polled again. The post-deliberation results are compared to the baseline data to determine any degree of refinement participants have made on their understanding of the issue.

Like other random-sample forms of participation, deliberative polls are seldom sufficient for planning or policymaking, since they do not produce the critical mass of participants or the political will necessary for action (see Chapter 2). However, they can be valuable—but costly—components of a broader strategy.

For more information, see http://cdd.stanford.edu/polls/; see also Fishkin and Farrar, 2005.

Another issue with surveys and polls concerns participant preparation. While survey and poll respondents tend to be more educated, this does not mean that they are more informed about the issue or issues being addressed. The framing, wording, and order of questions affect how people respond. Moreover, the kinds of questions used to gather reactions impacts the quality of the data. Multiple choice and other closed questions generate relatively limited data, whereas open-ended questions generate deeper data, for example, the interests that underlie positions or the terms people use to describe an issue.

Surveys and polls could perhaps be considered conventional forms of participation; they have certainly been a core feature of our political system for decades. Because the Internet has made surveys faster and easier, more versatile and at least potentially viral, surveys are being used more frequently as a form of "thin" participation. But they should treated as the thinnest of the thin, and usually need to be combined with other tactics. To overcome some of the limitations of traditional surveys and polls, some participation leaders have turned to deliberative polling, citizen's juries, and other methods that survey participants before and after they have had an opportunity to deliberate on an issue (see Box 8.3 and Tactic 12).

Tactic 3: Focus Groups

The use of focus groups is another longstanding participation tactic, with many organizations and consultants specializing in this approach. Focus groups typically involve between six and twelve people, although they may sometimes be larger. During a focus group, a facilitator guides the participants in discussion, usually around a preset list of questions. Sometimes, focus groups are used to better understand and delve more deeply into people's views and perspectives, as well as the values, needs, and concerns that lie behind people's beliefs. (In this way, focus groups can be a useful complement to surveys and polls.) Other times, focus groups are used to test how people's opinions change when presented with different options or pieces of information. Focus groups are essentially a more in-depth approach for Scenario 2, although they may also be incorporated into strategies addressing the other scenarios. (For more information about focus groups, see ctb.ku.edu/en/table-of-contents/assessment/assessing-community-needs-and-resources/conduct-focus-groups/main; www.griffith.edu.au/learning-teaching/quality/evaluation/focus-groups/focus-groups-examples; see also Simon, 1999).

Like the first two tactics, leaders of focus groups need to address participant selection and recruitment. The more that representativeness matters, the more important it is to use random sampling to select participants. For example, if participation leaders want to know what the patients think about options to improve a health clinic, they could recruit focus group participants from the people in the waiting room. If they want to get a sense of the options people might want to wrestle with in a large-scale deliberative process on a prominent issue, a more scientific sample may be essential.

Tactic 4: Online Platforms for Reporting Problems and Gathering Data

This tactic essentially automates the process of gathering data about particular problems and conditions. Whenever and wherever they want, citizens can make a record of what they see (and in some cases measure it) in a way that instantly uploads that information into a database that others can use. Most of these systems capitalize on the geographic information system (GIS) technologies that are now ubiquitous in smartphones, laptops, and other electronic devices. These systems sometimes include a process for users to rank or comment on the problems or data they are reporting and a feedback loop that explains whether and when government can fix the problem. This tactic is closer to the thin end of the participation scale, although it can encourage thicker forms of involvement by people who are particularly active users.

These platforms can be applied in many areas, such as crime and safety, land use and public works, education, and health. In these and other issue areas, online platforms make the most sense for generating new ideas and information (Scenario 3), although they may also be useful for supporting volunteerism and problem solving (Scenario 4) or for planning (Scenario 6). Representative tools include Open 311, SeeClickFix, Street Bump, FixMyStreet, Shareabouts, and PublicStuff.

Since these tools thrive when large numbers of people use them, especially those most affected by a particular set of public problems, recruitment is the most important issue to consider for this tactic. Is the tool sufficiently accessible and easy to use? How do people find out about it? Do they believe that if they participate, the data they report will lead to the problem being solved? This last question is important for recruitment, but it also gets to another consideration: whether and how the participation will make an impact. Tangible outcomes are more likely when platforms allow people to rank and comment on the data they have gathered, help people strategize about how to solve problems, and connect to other participation opportunities.

Tactic 5: Crowdsourcing and Contests

Crowdsourcing, or ideation, relies on some of the same thinking and technology that animates Tactic 4, but channels it in more creative, open-ended ways. Participation leaders issue a broad challenge to the public and encourage people to submit their best ideas. Some of these platforms, like the one used for the Knight News Challenge, allow people to vote for, rank, comment on, or propose collaborations with other participants. Others are framed as contests, with the most popular or useful entries winning prizes, badges, vouchers, or (in the case of Manor, Texas) the chance to be mayor for a day (Chafkin, 2010). There are many crowdsourcing platforms, including those operated by the organizations IdeaScale, Granicus, MindMixer, Crowd-Brite, SpigitEngage, Peak Democracy, TownHall Social, and MetroQuest. (For a list of crowdsourcing sites, see www.crowdsourcing.org/directory.)

Crowdsourcing is a logical vehicle for gathering new ideas (Scenario 3) and supporting volunteerism and problem solving (Scenario 4) and could be incorporated into a larger planning strategy (Scenario 6). For the people developing ideas, it can be a very thick, involved form of participation; for others who are simply commenting or ranking, the engagement is thinner.

The strategic questions most relevant to crowdsourcing are similar to the ones for Tactic 4. The main challenge is reaching a sufficient number of citizens, including people who have skills applicable to the challenge. While participants may be motivated by prizes and recognition, they are also more likely to contribute if they think their ideas will make an impact. Participation leaders can build this confidence by committing to implement ideas and/or by helping people find the resources they need to move forward.

Tactic 6: Crowdfunding and Mini-Grants

This tactic is quite compatible with the last one and capitalizes on the same citizen interests. Rather than asking people to identify problems or contribute creative ideas, crowdfunding platforms encourage them to donate money—and in some cases, information, connections, and constructive criticism—to projects and ideas proposed by others. Similarly, mini-grant programs run by local governments, community foundations, and other organizations make small investments that leverage commitments of ingenuity and sweat equity by citizens (Diers, 2008). Whether the participants give the money or receive it, the success of this tactic depends as much on their attachment to the process as on the funding itself. Examples of crowdfunding include platforms and processes organized by Ioby, Indiegogo, Kickstarter, CitizInvestor, neighbor.ly, and Crowdrise, among others (for a list of the top ten crowdfunding sites, see Barnett, 2013).

Some local governments and other institutions have organized crowdfunding exercises to improve public parks and other civic assets. Spark, a foundation based in San Francisco, goes beyond crowdfunding by asking its donors to vote on the projects it should fund. Then, at large face-to-face meetings, the members analyze project proposals and develop resource plans that may include in-kind assistance and expertise for each project.

Crowdfunding and mini-grants can be helpful for gathering new ideas (Scenario 3) and supporting volunteerism and problem solving (Scenario 4). They could also be incorporated into a larger planning strategy (Scenario 6). As with crowdsourcing, the thickness of the participation depends on the level and nature of citizen involvement. Once again, strategic questions relating to recruitment and impact are the most important to answer.

Tactic 7: Serious Games

Fun has become more than just a frill in public participation: games give citizens a chance to test their knowledge, strengthen their relationships, and come up with their own solutions to public problems. Representing one of the broadest categories of tactics, serious games have been developed in many different situations to achieve many different goals. Serious games can be used in Scenarios 1, 2, 3, and 4, and as part of a broader strategy in responding to Scenarios 5 and 6.

Games for participation come in a variety of forms. In *Making Democracy Fun*, Josh Lerner (2014) identifies five kinds of participation games: animation, team-building, capacity-building, analysis, and decision-making. There are online and face-to-face games in each category. "Theatre of the Oppressed," a face-to-face game first developed in the 1970s, helps people act out and analyze power relationships (Lerner, 2014). "Participatory Chinatown," a role-playing game developed for residents of Boston's Chinatown neighborhood, mixes online and face-to-face activities: the game is played online by residents in the same room, who then talk about the game and the outcomes in small groups (Shuman, 2010).

Some games are among the thinnest forms of participation, while others are thicker because they are more difficult, and potentially more rewarding, to play. Online games have the potential to spread virally if they are cleverly designed and disseminated, while some face-to-face games are so simple, versatile, and easy to set up that they can be used in a wide variety of situations. As a tactic, there is some overlap between games and other kinds of participation. As Lerner (2014: 7) argues, many public processes might be more effective (as well as more enjoyable) if they are designed with the gratification of participants in mind—in other words, if they are designed more like games. "Democracy has become the political version of spinach. Almost everyone says it is good, but few people actually want to eat it."

Depending on these variables, all four of the strategic questions can be relevant to serious games. If the success of the game depends on high numbers of users, recruitment is an important consideration. Deciding how you want people to play involves questions about participant interaction and preparation. The extent to which the game generates policy input or ideas for action raises questions of impact.

Tactic 8: Wiki-Based Platforms for Collaborative Mapping or Writing

Working together on a shared resource or statement is a more complicated endeavor than working separately on ideas that may or may not become part of a larger plan. Wiki-based technologies help surmount this challenge by incorporating individual contributions into a central map, database, or document and by including processes that help people to interact and negotiate in areas where their contributions differ (Mergel, 2011; Noveck, 2010; Scearce, Kasper, & Grant, 2010).

The earliest wikis were designed for shared writing and editing. GoogleDrive and Hackpad are document-focused wiki-based technologies commonly used today. These and other wiki platforms have become widely used in participation efforts; the nation of Iceland even tried using a wiki to allow citizens to help redraft the country's constitution (Landemore, 2014).

More recently, organizations have developed mapping wikis that capitalize on citizens' sense of place. These platforms allow users to map organizations and institutions, such as nonprofits, schools, or congregations, in relationship to needs in the community; overlay community indicators, such as unemployment rates, housing costs, health insurance, income, and poverty; assemble a centralized directory of services and volunteer opportunities; map specific problems like potholes or playgrounds that require maintenance; view publicly available financial information on community organizations; map schools and youth programs; and track quantifiable program outcome indicators, such as graduation rates or the number of families served; and connect with a national clearinghouse of resources. The Community Platform developed by the Urban Institute is one such example; it uses data assembled by the National Center for Charitable Statistics. Local Community Platform sites are now running in Connecticut, Florida, and the District of Columbia (Urban Institute, 2012). LocalWiki is another such resource, with the OaklandWiki in Oakland, California, perhaps the most advanced use of the technology (see Chapter 6). Wikiplanning (wikiplanning.org) helps communities use wikis for urban planning and other projects.

Wiki-based platforms are suitable for Scenarios 1, 3, and 4 and could be part of a larger strategy centered on Scenarios 5 and 6. Recruitment is once again the primary strategic consideration, although preparation and impact also matter. When participants invest significant amounts of time and effort on wiki platforms, it is certainly a thick participation experience; for casual users of the products of these processes, it is a thinner opportunity.

Tactic 9: Using Online Networks to Connect with Others

Because they encourage communication and collaboration within groups, and because participants often invest a great deal of time and energy in them, online networks could be considered thicker forms of participation. Although participation leaders sometimes create thin, temporary online networks—Facebook groups, email lists, blogs, and Twitter accounts that people are encouraged to follow and contribute to—there are also many thicker examples of networks that are set up for the long haul. Some of these networks were conceived in the midst of calamities: in places like Joplin, Missouri, and the Breezy Point neighborhood in Queens, online networks emerged from the efforts of residents to respond during and after natural disasters (Clift, 2014). Perhaps more than any other tactic on the list, online networks bridge short-term participation projects and long-term participation needs.

Because of this versatility, online networks can work well in all six scenarios. They are particularly useful avenues for informing citizens (Scenario 1), gathering input, feedback, and preferences (Scenario 2), and supporting volunteerism and problem solving (Scenario 4). They can also serve as vital recruitment tools for Scenarios 3 and 5, and as arenas where people bring ideas and concerns related to planning, budgeting, and decision making (Scenario 6).

One of the most important considerations participation leaders must make when using online networks is one that also applies offline: recruitment. Steve Clift of e-democracy.org recommends that anyone trying to start an online forum should gather 100 email addresses before launching the network. With that kind of critical mass, a forum can become self-sustaining without a great deal of effort from the moderator. The initial phase of recruiting those 100 participants and ensuring that they have a positive experience is critical. (For more discussion about the skills needed for building and moderating online networks, see the Participation Skills Module.)

Issues relating to interaction are also critical to these networks, because online forums can sometimes encourage more rash and disrespectful communication. This is directly related to the level of anonymity of the participants: some participation leaders insist that users register using their real names. This guideline is particularly effective in hyperlocal online networks, where participants are more likely to know one another in other settings. (For tips on moderating online networks, see the Participation Skills Module.)

Tactic 10: Collaborative Planning

Some collaborative planning processes bring people together to make determinations about relatively narrow issues, for example, the architecture, design, or layout of buildings or playgrounds, whereas others focus on relatively broader public issues, for example, economic development or transportation systems. Some processes are held in meeting rooms, others take place at the site or building being addressed, and still others are organized exclusively online.

There are dozens, if not hundreds, of methods for collaborative planning (Wates, 2000). Platforms like coUrbanize, EngagingPlans, and PlaceSpeak have been developed to facilitate collaborative planning online or to supplement face-to-face processes. Several of the most common types of face-to-face collaborative planning include:

- Charrettes, which are intensive workshops that involve architects, residents, developers, and other stakeholders (Freedman, 2014; Lennertz & Lutzenhiser, 2006). They typically focus on a building or distinct geographic area, enabling people to get critical design questions or concerns on the table early in the development process.

- Placemaking workshops, which focus primarily on public spaces like parks and plazas; they are intended to influence design, but also to help people plan for how they will use those places and how those places will evolve over time (Project for Public Spaces, 2014).

- Future search conferences, which sometimes focus on geographic places, but also have been used to develop plans that encompass a range of issues and priorities. They bring together sixty to eighty participants in one room, or many more working in parallel (Weisbord & Janoff, 2010).

Collaborative planning tactics, particularly when they occur in face-to-face settings, tend to be thick participation experiences for citizens. They can be quite similar to public deliberation (Tactic 12) in the sense that participants weigh different options or viewpoints about what should be done. The primary difference is that, in at least some collaborative planning processes, there is less emphasis on personal experience and the larger assumptions and conditions that underlie the different options.

Scenario 6 is the obvious use of collaborative planning, although it can also be helpful for generating ideas (Scenario 3) and supporting volunteerism (Scenario 4). Recruitment is a relevant strategic consideration, since the value of and support for the plan will depend in part on how many people helped to develop it and on whether the participants reflected the needs and goals of the population. Participant interaction and preparation are dictated in large part by the format or method chosen. The question of impact—specifically, whether and how plans will be implemented—is also critical.

Tactic 11: Participatory Budgeting

One of the most widespread and fastest-growing forms of participation, participatory budgeting (PB) engages large, diverse numbers of people in deliberative, informed discussions about how to spend public money. Most of these processes begin their annual cycle with neighborhood assemblies during which people talk about and vote on budget priorities. In most American examples of PB (and in other cases around the world), participants are invited to develop specific proposals for how to spend a specific, preset pool of funding. They usually form teams, research their proposals, and work with public employees and other stakeholders to refine their ideas. Many of the proposals promise to leverage citizens' sweat equity and other in-kind resources. At a subsequent large event, project teams advocate for their ideas and answer questions from other residents. The cycle concludes with an election in which residents of the city or ward vote on which of the project ideas should receive funding (for more information, see www.participatorybudgeting.org/).

Some PB processes also feature a set of "thematic" assemblies, at which participants focus on city-wide priorities like education, transportation, or health. In these meetings, citizens elect delegates to represent them at city-wide or regional forums that consider the investment priorities emerging from the assemblies. These delegates then decide how to allocate funding across the city and monitor the implementation of the chosen projects and policies (Baiocchi, Heller, & Silva, 2011; Smith, 2005; Wampler, 2007).

PB has been applied to more than just municipal budgets—it has been used to make budget decisions for schools, universities, housing authorities, workplaces, and nonprofit organizations (Schugurensky, 2014). The Participatory Budgeting

Project, a New York–based nonprofit that supports PB in the United States, even invites its supporters to allocate part of its organizational budget using a PB process. For the people who work on project ideas or serve as budget delegates, PB is one of the thickest participation processes. For residents whose participation is limited to voting on how to allocate the funding, it may not be as involved an experience. Naturally, PB is used most often for Scenario 6, developing a plan or budget, but because it is informative, generates new ideas, and supports volunteerism, it also fits into Scenarios 1, 3, and 4.

Recruitment is a key strategic consideration for PB, since it thrives on a high, diverse turnout. In South American cities where PB has been conducted as an annual process for years or even decades, tens of thousands of people have been involved. Since PB can encompass many kinds of interaction, including online communication as well as face-to-face meetings and assemblies, participation leaders have a number of options when implementing it. Participant preparation is essentially baked into the process, although here, too, there may be a number of ways to give citizens the information they need to participate in a meaningful way. When a separate fund has been set aside for allocation to ideas emerging from a PB process, a certain level of impact (and broad awareness of those impacts) is guaranteed.

Tactic 12: Public Deliberation

In this form of participation, citizens, public officials, public employees, and other stakeholders interact in small-group sessions where they share experiences, consider a range of policy options, and decide together what should be done. This most often occurs in projects that engage hundreds or even thousands of participants meeting simultaneously, but there are some models of deliberation that involve small, randomly selected groups of people. Because of the number of people involved, the amount of time they spend, and the intensity of the experience, public deliberation is probably the thickest form of participation practiced today. It can be used to address all six scenarios, although it is mainly used for Scenarios 5 and 6. Public deliberation is also labor-intensive (although not necessarily expensive), largely because of the time and effort required for recruitment.

Public deliberation can be a confusing category because it goes by many different names and takes several different forms (for some examples, see Box 8.4; for additional examples, see Gastil & Levine, 2005). Some processes and methodologies were named by the people and organizations that support them—such as

National Issues Forums, Dialogue-to-Change programs, and 21st Century Town Meetings. Others have more generic names, such as "community conversations," "study circle programs," "roundtables," or titles that refer to the places or issues on which they focus (e.g., Speak Up Austin and the National Dialogue on Chemical Exposures). Still others use the main principles of public deliberation, but remain nameless (Leighninger, 2012).

Some named public deliberation methods are exclusively small, random-sample processes. Daniel Yankelovich (1991) was one of the first to suggest the combination of random-sample selection and public deliberation in his book, *Coming to Public Judgment*. These methods include citizens juries (Crosby & Nethercut, 2005; see also Chapter 7), citizen assemblies (Warren & Pearce, 2008), consensus conferences (see Box 8.4), and deliberative polls (see Box 8.3). Participants in these processes spend at least a day, and in some cases up to eight days, learning about the issue, hearing from experts and advocates for particular solutions and weighing all the options before issuing their recommendations. Random-sample processes are better suited for narrow or technical issues for which larger-scale recruitment would be difficult. However, the impacts are dependent largely on whether voters (in the case of ballot initiatives) or public officials (in the case of policy decisions) agree with participant recommendations. Therefore, small-scale public deliberation processes are usually best when combined with other participation tactics—particularly those that amplify the findings and recommendations of the deliberation to a much larger number of people.

Some of the primary organizations supporting large-scale public deliberation projects are Everyday Democracy, the Kettering Foundation, Public Agenda, the National Institute for Civil Discourse, and the America*Speaks* Associates Network (see Leighninger, 2012). A number of local centers, some based at universities, have become regional hubs that provide technical assistance to participation leaders convening deliberative processes (Carcasson, 2014). While deliberative processes have relied mainly on face-to-face meetings, there are now a number of online platforms, such as Zilino, Common Ground for Action, E-Deliberation, Ethelo, Engagement HQ, and Loomio (Horose, 2014).

Public deliberation presupposes an intensive, structured form of participant interaction; virtually all of these methods include ways of informing and preparing citizens for the process. However, there are many options for recruitment and impact that leaders ought to consider. As with most participation tactics, the two questions are linked: impacts are more likely to occur when large, diverse numbers of people have been successfully recruited to take part in the effort.

Box 8.4. Some Methods for Public Deliberation

World Cafés. World cafés are used for generating and building consensus around ideas. Tables of four to eight people are set up, and participants rotate every twenty to thirty minutes for a total of at least three conversations. This allows participants to build shared understanding of a problem and develop shared ideas for action around that understanding. A World Café organizer typically sets up the room to mock an intimate café feel, sometimes using butcher paper on the tables, with markers to promote creativity (see www.theworldcafe.com/impact.html)

The Right Question Process. This approach to small scale deliberation, developed by Dan Rothstein and Luz Santana of the Right Question Project, is designed to build understanding, creativity, and accountability. Participants are usually convened around a broad and general topic. Participants first review the guidelines for the method and then brainstorm as many questions as they can about the topic. Then, they categorize each question on their list as open-ended or closed-ended, and think through the strengths and weaknesses of each question. They choose three priority questions and discuss why they chose them. Finally, they talk about how to use their questions in other settings and reflect on what they have learned (see www.rightquestion.org).

Appreciative Inquiry. Appreciative Inquiry was developed in the late 1970s at Case Western Reserve University and the Cleveland Clinic Foundation. Instead of asking people to identify problems, Appreciative Inquiry focuses on what is working and how to build on those assets. Appreciative Inquiry processes can be held as individual events over four or five hours, but many last for several days (see www.gervasebushe.ca/Foundations_AI.pdf; http://appreciativeinquiry.case.edu/; http://ncdd.org/rc/item/4856).

Consensus Conferences. Consensus conferences recruit a pool of volunteers from which participants are representatively sampled. Participants spend eight days learning about the issue, hearing from experts, considering opposing views, and developing their recommendations. Consensus conferences have been used extensively by the Danish Board of Technology Foundation, which has played a key role in Denmark's science and technology policymaking process for the last forty years (see www.tekno.dk/subpage.php3?page=forside.php3&language=uk/).

SUMMARY

We opened this chapter by asserting that participation leaders need to consider the relationships they are trying to build with citizens because short-term, mid-range, and long-lasting participation efforts all affect how people perceive and relate to their community, their government, and each other. Specifically, we asserted that participation leaders need to (1) understand the potential goals that participants may bring to the process; (2) think through how participants' input

278 Participation Scenarios and Tactics

and ideas will affect decisions, policies, and actions; and (3) offer meaningful ways for participants to remain connected to public institutions and to each other.

To illustrate these points, we examined how people typically interact in conventional public meetings. In these proceedings, public officials, staffers, and citizens often feel trapped, in large part because these processes foster a parent-child dynamic and small-minded assumptions about public life. To organize better forms of participation, leaders should consider the potential goals and answer four key strategic questions:

1. Who should participate and how will participants be recruited?
2. How will participants interact with each other and with decision-makers?
3. What information do participants need?
4. How will participation impact policy decisions, problem-solving efforts, or other kinds of public action?

How participation leaders answer these questions depends on the participation scenario they face. To illustrate our points, we discussed six of the most common scenarios:

1. Participation leaders want to inform the public.
2. Participation leaders want to gather public input, feedback, and preferences.
3. Participation leaders want citizens to generate new ideas or new data.
4. Participation leaders want to support volunteerism and citizen-driven problem solving.
5. Participation leaders want to make a policy decision.
6. Participation leaders want to develop a plan or a budget.

For each of these scenarios, we examined the typical goals that the engagers and engaged bring to those situations, as well as the key strategic questions that are likely to be the most critical in each.

Finally, we explored twelve participation tactics—both thin and thick—that participation leaders can use, including social media aggregation; surveys and polls; online problem-reporting platforms; crowdsourcing and contests; crowdfunding and mini-grants; serious games; wiki-based mapping and writing platforms; online networks; collaborative planning processes; participatory budgeting; and public deliberation. We described some of the most common tools and methods for each tactic and explained which tactics work well under which conditions and for which scenarios.

DISCUSSION QUESTIONS

1. Why do you think the authors put such a strong emphasis on relationships at the beginning of the chapter? What do participation goals have to do with relationships?

2. The authors assert that most people in conventional participation feel as if they are trapped in a foxhole. Why do they make this analogy? How do you feel about this analogy? What have been your experiences with conventional participation opportunities?

3. The authors identify four strategic questions that participation planners must address. Why are these singled out as being critical? Are there any other variations in direct public participation (see Box 8.1) that you believe are also critical? Why or why not?

4. Select a participation activity that you know about or have participated in. Analyze that activity based on the variations in direct public participation (see Box 8.1), as well as on the four key strategic questions about recruitment, interaction, participant preparation, and impact.

5. Most participation activities center on some issue or set of issues that have either low or high stakes. How does the difference in stakes affect the four strategic questions about recruitment, interaction, participant preparation, and impact? Use Table 8.1 to help explain your answers.

6. Participant recruitment is raised as a crucial issue throughout this book. Why is recruitment so important? Explain each of the recruitment strategies discussed in this chapter. What are the benefits and drawbacks of each?

7. Why do the authors discuss participation in terms of scenarios rather than goals? Do you agree with this approach? Why or why not?

8. How do the twelve tactics addressed in this chapter correspond to the adapted IAP2 Spectrum presented in Figure 8.1?

9. Select a method of public deliberation discussed in Tactic 12 or in Box 8.4. Analyze that tactic according to the four strategic questions and the other variations presented in Box 8.1.

10. Select a public issue—at the local, state, or federal level—that is important to you. If you were a participation leader, under which scenario or scenarios might this fall? Which of the twelve tactics would you use for participation and why?

References

Amsler, Terry. (2007). *Planning public forums: Questions to guide local officials.* Sacramento, CA: Institute for Local Government.

Amsler, Terry. (2008). Involving the public in city planning. *Western City.* Available at www.westerncity.com/pdfs/Civic_Partnership_Standalone_Final.pdf.

Baiocchi, Gianpaolo, Patrick Heller, & Marcelo K. Silva. (2011). *Bootstrapping democracy: Transforming local governance and civil society in Brazil.* Stanford, CA: Stanford University Press.

Barnett, Chance. (2013). Top 10 crowdfunding sites for fundraising. *Forbes.com.* Available at www.forbes.com/sites/chancebarnett/2013/05/08/top-10-crowdfunding-sites-for-fundraising/.

Bingham, Lisa Blomgren. (2010). The next generation of administrative law: Building the legal infrastructure for collaborative governance. *Wisconsin Law Review, 10*: 297–356.

Bingham, Lisa Blomgren, Tina Nabatchi, & Rosemary O'Leary. (2005). The new governance: Practices and processes for stakeholder and citizen participation in the work of government. *Public Administration Review, 65*(5): 528–539.

Bryson, John M., Kathryn S. Quick, Carissa Shively Slotterback, & Barbara C. Crosby. (2013). Designing public participation processes. *Public Administration Review, 73*(1): 23–34.

Carcasson, Martín. (2009). *Beginning with the end in mind.* New York, NY: Center for Advances in Public Engagement, Public Agenda.

Carcasson, Martín. (2014). The critical role of local centers and institutes in advancing deliberative democracy. *Journal of Public Deliberation.*

Chafkin, Max. (2010). Why the high-tech industry loves Manor, Texas. *Inc.* Available at www.inc.com/magazine/20100901/why-the-high-tech-industry-loves-manor-texas.html.

Clift, Steven. (2014). *Top tips for using social media for local community disaster recovery.* Available at http://bitly.com/localrecovery.

Colorado Association of School Boards. (2003). *Public engagement in five Colorado school communities: Report to the Kettering Foundation.* Denver, CO: Colorado Association of School Boards.

Crosby, Ned, & Doug Nethercut. (2005). Citizen juries: Creating a trustworthy voice of the people. In J. Gastil & P. Levine (Eds.), *The deliberative democracy handbook: Strategies for effective civic engagement in the 21st century*, 111–120. San Francisco, CA: Jossey-Bass.

Delli Carpini, Michael X. (2000). In search of the informed citizen: What Americans know about politics and why it matters. *The Communication Review, 4*(1): 129–164.

Diers, Jim. (2008). *From the ground up: The community's role in addressing street-level social issues.* Calgary, Canada: Canada West Foundation.

Drapeau, Mark. (2009). Government 2.0: From the Goverati adhocracy to government with the people. In J. Gotze & C. B. Pederson (Eds.), *State of the eunion: Government 2.0 and onwards.* Bloomington, IN: AuthorHouse.

Fishkin, James, & Cynthia Farrar. (2005). Deliberative polling: From experiment to community resource. In J. Gastil & P. Levine (Eds.), *The deliberative democracy handbook: Strategies for effective civic engagement in the twenty-first century*, 68–79. San Francisco, CA: Jossey-Bass.

Freedman, Robert. (2014). Engage; Don't rage: Use a design charrette to negotiate your next development proposal. Available at www.planetizen.com/node/68464.

Frey, Susan. (2014). Nonprofit and for-profit partners help Cincinnati transform its failing schools. *EdSource.* Available at http://edsource.org/2014/nonprofit-and-for-profit-partners-help-cincinnati-transform-its-failing-schools/63548#.VDF-F4Ra9bRc.

Fung, Archon. (2003). Recipes for public spheres: Eight institutional design choices and their consequences. *Journal of Political Philosophy, 11*: 338–367.

Fung, Archon. (2006). Varieties of participation in democratic governance. *Public Administration Review, 66*(s1): 66–75.

Fung, Archon, & Erik OlinWright (Eds.). (2003). *Deepening democracy: Institutional innovations in empowered participatory governance.* London, UK: Verso.

Ganapati, Sukumar. (2010). *Using geographic information systems to increase citizen engagement.* Washington, DC: IBM Center for the Business of Government.

Gastil, John. (2005). Deliberation. In G. J. Shepherd, J. St. John, & T. Striphas (Eds.), *Communication as . . . Perspectives on theory*, 164–173. Thousand Oaks, CA: Sage.

Gastil, John. (2008). *Political communication and deliberation.* Thousand Oaks, CA: Sage.

Gastil, John, & Peter Levine (Eds.). (2005). *The deliberative democracy handbook: Strategies for effective civic engagement in the 21st century.* San Francisco, CA: Jossey-Bass.

Gordon, Eric, Steven Schirra, & Justin Hollander. (2011). Immersive planning: A conceptual model for designing public participation with new technologies. *Environment and Planning B: Planning and Design, 38*(3): 505–519.

Hoppe, Robert. (2011). Institutional constraints and practical problems in deliberative and participatory policy making. *Policy & Politics, 39*(2): 163–186.

Horose, Caitlyn. (2014). Let's get digital! 50 tools for online public engagement. *Community Matters.* Available at www.communitymatters.org/blog/let%E2%80%99s-get-digital-50-tools-online-public-engagement.

IAP2. (2007). *IAP2 spectrum of public participation.* Thornton, CO: International Association for Public Participation. Available at http://iap2.affiniscape.com/associations/4748/files/IAP2%20Spectrum_vertical.pdf.

Jacobs, Garrett. (2014). *Beyond public hearings: Engaging in the 21st century.* San Francisco, CA: Code for America. Available at www.codeforamerica.org/blog/2014/06/25/beyond-public-hearings-engaging-in-the-21st-century/.

Landemore, Helene. (2014). Inclusive constitution-making: The Icelandic experiment. *Journal of Political Philosophy.* DOI: 10.1111/jopp.12032

Lazo, Luz. (2014). In the District, a transportation plan that boosts transit and discourages driving. *Washington Post.* Available at www.washingtonpost.com/local/trafficandcommuting/in-the-district-a-transportation-planthat-boosts-transit-and-discourages-driving/2014/06/03/c7721ac8-eb17-11e3-b98c-72cef4a00499_story.html.

Leighninger, Matt. (2006). *The next form of democracy: How expert rule is giving way to shared governance—and why politics will never be the same.* Nashville, TN: Vanderbilt University Press.

Leighninger, Matt. (2012). Mapping deliberative civic engagement: Pictures from a (r)evolution. In T. Nabatchi, J. Gastil, M. Weiksner, & M. Leighninger (Eds.), *Democracy in motion: Evaluating the practice and impact of deliberative civic engagement,* 19–39. New York, NY: Oxford University Press.

Lennertz, Bill, & Aarin Lutzenhiser. (2006). *The charrette handbook: The essential guide for accelerated, collaborative community planning.* Chicago, IL: American Planning Association.

Lerner, Josh. (2014). *Making democracy fun: How game design can empower citizens and transform politics.* Cambridge, MA: MIT Press.

Liburd, Leandris C., Wayne Giles, & Leonard Jack. (2013). Health equity. *National Civic Review,* 102(4): 52–54.

Lukensmeyer, Carolyn J. (2013). *Bringing citizen voices to the table: A guide for public managers.* San Francisco, CA: Jossey-Bass.

Lukensmeyer, Carolyn J., & Steve Brigham. (2002). Taking democracy to scale: Creating a town hall meeting for the twenty-first century. *National Civic Review,* 91(4): 351–366.

Mačiukaitė-Žvinienė, Saulė, Loreta Tauginienė, Mikko Rask, Niels Mejlgaard, Tine Ravn, & Luciano d'Andrea. (2014). *Public engagement innovations for Horizon 2020: A refined typology of PE tools and instruments D2.1.* Available at http://pe2020.eu/wp-content/uploads/sites/15/2014/02/D2-1-_PE2020_submission-1.pdf.

Marois, Deb, & Terry Amsler. (2008). Public involvement in budgeting: Options for local officials. *Western City.* Available at www.westerncity.com/Western-City/November-2008/Public-Involvement-in-Budgeting-Options-for-Local-Officials/.

McCarron, David A., Ninon Richartz, Steve Brigham, Molly K. White, Stephen P. Klein, & Samuel S. Kessel. (2010). Community-based priorities for improving nutrition and physical activity in childhood. *Pediatrics,* 126(suppl. 2): S73–S89.

McComas, Katherine A. (2001). Public meetings about local waste management problems: Comparing participants to nonparticipants. *Environmental Management,* 27(1): 135–147.

McComas, Katherine A. (2003). Citizen satisfaction with public meetings used for risk communication. *Journal of Applied Communication Research, 31*(2): 164–184.

Mergel, Ines. (2011). *Using wikis in government: A guide for public managers.* Washington, DC: IBM Center for the Business of Government.

Nabatchi, Tina. (2012a). An introduction to deliberative civic engagement. In T.Nabatchi, J. Gastil, M. Weiksner, & M. Leighninger (Eds.), *Democracy in motion: Evaluating the practice and impact of deliberative civic engagement,* 3–17. New York, NY: Oxford University Press.

Nabatchi, Tina. (2012b). *A manager's guide to evaluating citizen participation.* Washington, DC: IBM Center for the Business of Government.

Nabatchi, Tina. (2012c). Putting the "public" back in public values research: Designing public participation to identify and respond to public values. *Public Administration Review, 72*(5): 699–708.

Nabatchi, Tina, & Lisa Blomgren Amsler. (2014). Direct public engagement in local government. *American Review of Public Administration, 44*(4suppl): 63s–88s.

National Coalition for Dialogue and Deliberation (NCDD). (2008). *Engagement streams framework.* Boiling Springs, PA: National Coalition for Dialogue and Deliberation. Available at www.thataway.org/?page_id=1487.

New America Foundation. (2014). *Public-pathways: A guide to online engagement tools for local governments.* Washington, DC: New America Foundation.

Norris, Tyler. (2014). Healthy communities at twenty-five: Participatory democracy and the prospect for American renewal. *National Civic Review, 102*(4): 4–9.

Noveck, Beth Simone. (2010). *Wiki government: How technology can make government better, democracy stronger, and citizens more powerful.* Washington, DC: Brookings Institution Press.

OECD. (2009). *Focus on citizens: Public engagement for better policy and services.* Paris, France: OECD Publishing.

Orland, Catherine Brenner. (2007). *Teachers, study circles and the racial achievement gap: How one dialogue and action program helped teachers integrate the competencies of an effective multicultural educator.* Brattleboro, VT: School for International Training.

Orton Family Foundation. (2014). *Community heart and soul field guide.* Shelburne, VT: Orton Family Foundation.

Peixoto, Tiago, & Boris Weber. (2012). Technology drives citizen participation and feedback in Rio Grande do Sul, Brazil. *People Spaces, Deliberation.* Available at http://blogs.worldbank.org/publicsphere/technology-drives-citizen-participation-and-feedback-rio-grande-do-sul-brazil.

Project for Public Spaces. (2014). Eleven principles for creating great community places. Available at www.pps.org/reference/11steps/.

Public Agenda. (2008). *Public engagement: A primer from Public Agenda.* New York, NY: Public Agenda.

Ryfe, David M., & Brittany Stalsburg. (2012). The participation and recruitment challenge. In T. Nabatchi, J. Gastil, M. Weiksner, & M. Leighninger (Eds.), *Democracy in motion: Evaluating the practice and impact of deliberative civic engagement*, 43–58. New York, NY: Oxford University Press.

Scearce, Diana, Gabriel Kasper, & Heather McLeod Grant. (2010). Working wikily. *Stanford Social Innovation Review*. Available at www.ssireview.org/articles/entry/working_wikily.

Schugurensky, Daniel. (2014). *Evaluating participatory budgeting: Five dimensions*. Paper presented at the Third International Conference on Participatory Budgeting in North America. Oakland, California, September 25–27, 2014.

Shuman, Amanda. (2010). Interview: Eric Gordon on Participatory Chinatown. *Hashtac*. Available at www.hastac.org/blogs/amandaucsc/interview-eric-gordon-participatory-chinatown.

Simon, Judith Sharken. (1999). *How to conduct a focus group*. Los Angeles, CA: The Grantsmanship Center and Fieldstone Alliance.

Sirianni, Carmen, & Lewis Friedland. (2001). *Civic innovation in America: Community empowerment, public policy, and the movement for civic renewal*. Berkeley, CA: University of California Press.

Smith, Graham. (2005). *Beyond the ballot: 57 democratic innovations from around the world*. London, UK: The Power Inquiry.

Study Circles Resource Center. (2001). *Organizing community-wide dialogue for action and change: A step-by-step guide*. East Hartford, CT: Everyday Democracy.

Thomas, John Clayton. (1995). *Public participation in public decisions: New skills and strategies for public managers*. San Francisco, CA: Jossey-Bass.

Thomas, John Clayton. (2012). *Citizen, customer, partner: Engaging the public in public management*. Armonk, NY: M.E. Sharpe.

Urban Institute. (2012). *The community platform: Engagement, analysis, and leadership tools*. Washington, DC: The Urban Institute.

Walsh, Katherine Cramer. (2007). *Talking about race: Community dialogues and the politics of disagreement*. Chicago, IL: University of Chicago Press.

Wampler, Brian. (2007). *Participatory budgeting in Brazil: Contestation, cooperation, and accountability*. University Park, PA: Penn State Press.

Warren, Mark, & Hilary Pearse. (2008). *Designing deliberative democracy: The British Columbia Citizen's Assembly*. New York, NY: Cambridge University Press.

Wates, Nick. (2000). *The community planning handbook: How people can shape their cities, towns and villages in any part of the world*. London, UK: Earthscan.

Weisbord, Marvin, & Sandra Janoff. (2010). *Future search: Getting the whole system in the room for vision, commitment, and action* (3rd ed.). San Francisco, CA: Berrett-Koehler.

Yankelovich, Daniel. (1991). *Coming to public judgment: Making democracy work in a complex world*. Syracuse, NY: Syracuse University Press.

Assembling Participation Infrastructure

I n the previous chapter, we examined the scenarios participation leaders commonly face, and described tactics they could use to grapple with those scenarios. For the most part, however, these more productive forms of participation have not been incorporated into the official arenas for participation in education, health, land use, or any other issue. Planners conduct charrettes and then go back to contentious public hearings; healthy communities coalitions advocate healthier lifestyles, even as advisory committees flounder; school districts engage parents on bond issues while PTAs languish.

It is possible to develop a more sustained and productive system for participation on any one of these issues, without thinking of the others—but it would not be wise. Education, health, and land use are inextricably intertwined, and all three issues overlap with and are affected by a host of other issues, such as poverty, environmental protection, public safety, public finance, and economic development, to name but a few.

Citizens care about their children, their health, and their homes—and they care about many other problems and priorities as well. Instead of continuing to view the world through the professionalized, issue-delineated lenses that we first put on in the early 20th Century, we should embrace the holistic, democratic, citizen-centered view that has emerged in the early 21st Century. We can make progress on all these seemingly intractable public issues if we construct, renovate, or knit together a stronger legal, governmental, civic, electoral, and educational infrastructure for participation. This participation infrastructure should sustain and support regular opportunities, activities, and arenas for people to connect with each other, solve problems, make decisions, and celebrate community.

At the very least, we should not attempt to improve participation on one issue without developing some understanding of how these improvements could complement the settings and opportunities available for other issues. Although we may not often be able to create a new "big picture" for participation all at once, we can develop it in such a way that, like starting with the corners and then the edges of the puzzle, they fit together well with other current and future components.

In this chapter, we explore how the pieces of a stronger infrastructure can fit together. Specifically, we describe additional structures and supports that can connect and sustain participation in any issue, suggest some ways of helping people envision a stronger participation infrastructure, and lay out some guiding principles for infrastructure planning.

CONNECTING THE BUILDING BLOCKS FOR PARTICIPATION

The sections on "Strengthening the Infrastructure" in Chapters 4 through 7, and the corresponding figures within the sections, describe six main building blocks for participation infrastructure: disseminating information, gathering input and data, discussing and connecting, enabling smaller-scale decision making, enabling larger-scale decision making, and encouraging public work.

Some of the settings and processes that can support these building blocks already exist in many communities. For example, we explored and suggested ways to improve participation in parent-teacher conferences, school boards, and PTAs and other parent groups (Chapter 4); patient-caregiver interactions, advisory boards and commissions, and healthy community coalitions (Chapter 5); public meetings, planning commissions, and neighborhood and homeowner associations (Chapter 6); and in legislative and agency actions and decisions at the state and federal levels of government (Chapter 7). We also described a number of more cutting-edge vehicles and tactics for participation in education, health, and land use, as well as in state and federal government. These examples of democratic innovation are inspiring, but tantalizingly isolated from one another. Taking stock of the civic assets within a community and deciding which work well, which exist but need to be upgraded, and where there are gaps, is a practical way to approach infrastructure planning. There are also some obvious "universal pieces" that can support and connect participation infrastructures in many different issue areas. We described three of them extensively in other chapters:

- *Hyperlocal and local online networks.* This category of infrastructure is already rapidly growing, and holds great potential for connecting participation in many different issue areas.
- *Buildings that are physical hubs for participation.* The political philosopher Hannah Arendt is said to have remarked that "Democracy needs a place to sit down." Communities need accessible, welcoming, wired public spaces for participation on a range of issues.
- *Youth councils.* Perhaps the most undervalued of our civic assets, youth leadership should be cultivated and supported in settings specifically for young people.

One final universal piece that can support and connect participation in different arenas and issue areas is the use of participation commissions.

Participation Commissions

A local participation commission (or advisory board) can advise a community on the design, implementation, and evaluation of public participation tactics, and more broadly on building and embedding a sustainable participation infrastructure. Such a commission could be an official body constituted by local government, or a stand-alone entity recognized and supported by a range of community institutions, such as foundations, governments, school systems, Chambers of Commerce, and interfaith councils and faith institutions. At the state and federal levels, participation commissions could assist local efforts, support state and federal participation, and connect the work of people and groups inside and outside government.

A commission or board could have one or more of the following responsibilities:

1. Develop and propose a multi-year plan to guide public participation activities, programs, and policies;
2. Develop guidelines and recommendations for inclusive, effective public participation;
3. Provide advice and recommendations regarding the implementation of public participation guidelines and practices;
4. Establish participation measures, publicize and review the results, and help people use the results to improve participation policies and practices; and/or
5. Provide an annual report regarding the status of public participation activities.

A public participation commission or board ought to be constituted in a way that ensures geographically, demographically, and ideologically representative membership. It should adopt its own rules and bylaws, mirroring successful participation practices and including ways for larger numbers of citizens to contribute to the work of the commission (Working Group on Legal Frameworks for Public Participation, 2013).

One way for participation commissions to connect people working in different neighborhoods, communities, and issue areas—and to raise the profile of participation itself—would be to hold a large-scale deliberative process every year. This expectation could be codified in a local participation ordinance, or it could simply be part of a long-term participation plan upheld by a range of local institutions (for more information on public deliberation, see Chapter 8).

SYSTEMIC SUPPORTS FOR PARTICIPATION

In previous chapters, we discussed a number of systemic supports that can be incorporated into participation infrastructures. Here, we identify three additional supports that can buttress participation by helping people develop their skills for organizing, facilitating, clarifying, and measuring it.

Local Participation Ordinances

As we noted in previous chapters, most of the laws governing public participation are at least thirty years old; one of the most notorious, California's Brown Act, just turned sixty. Because these laws predate not only many of the innovations in face-to-face engagement, but also the Internet itself, it is unclear how they apply to:

- Social media platforms used by public officials and public employees;
- Participation by public officials and public employees in neighborhood online forums, email listservs, and other online arenas;
- Participation by public officials and public employees in small-group dialogue and deliberation as part of larger public engagement efforts;
- Use of online tools to announce and proactively recruit for public meetings (rather than the old formula still found in many laws, which require governments simply to post a notice about a meeting in a city bulletin); and
- Collaboration between public institutions and private, nonprofit, charitable, and faith-based institutions in organizing and supporting public participation.

In all of these scenarios, our laws ought to uphold the values of participation, transparency, privacy, inclusion, fairness, and freedom of speech. But in many cases, it is now difficult to decipher the letter or intent of the law.

One reason why there is more sustained participation in some countries in the Global South may be that they have newer constitutions and a more open-minded approach to the legal framework for participation. Participatory budgeting in Brazil and the Gram Sabha reforms in India have made productive participation a legally accepted and supported part of politics (Mansuri & Rao, 2013).

In the United States, a working group that includes representatives from the International Municipal Lawyers' Association, International City/County Management Association, American Bar Association, National League of Cities, National Civic League, Policy Consensus Initiative, National Coalition for Dialogue and Deliberation, and Deliberative Democracy Consortium has worked to produce new legal tools, including a model local ordinance for public participation (Working Group on Legal Frameworks for Public Participation, 2013). The model ordinance is intended to allow innovation, not require it. "We took as our inspiration the laws on alternative dispute resolution (ADR) enacted during the 1980s and 90s," says Lisa Blomgren Bingham (Working Group on Legal Frameworks, 2013: 6) of Indiana University, a public administration scholar who took the lead drafting role for the working group. "Simply by authorizing public agencies to use mediation, facilitation, and other ADR processes, those laws resulted in a dramatic proliferation of these practices at every level of the legal system."

Citizens' Academies and Other Participation Training Programs

To be successful, most of the building blocks described in this book require that the people developing and staffing participation activities have certain skills, many of which are described in the Participation Skills Module (see www.wiley.com/go/nabatchi). In many cities, the participation "skill base" is not deep enough to meet this challenge. In other places, the skills are there but so diffused throughout the community that it is not easy to find the people who could be helpful. Within city hall, these capacities are sometimes limited to a small cadre of public employees working out of departments for neighborhood services or human relations.

Many communities have "citizens' academies" or other training programs that are designed to boost public participation. However, these programs are often limited to informing participants about "how government works"—for example, how to apply for a zoning variance or how the police department deploys officers

(Morse, 2012). These may be important facts for citizens to know, but they are insufficient for supporting robust public participation.

Nevertheless, citizens' academies and other training programs have huge potential for supplying the kinds of skills and supports needed for a sustainable participation infrastructure. Specifically, they could be used to inform citizens about why participation is important, issue areas where participation could be useful, and skills that are necessary for improving participation in practice. Moreover, these training programs will work best when:

- They are provided as part of an ongoing program that can train large numbers of people over time.
- Participants are recruited proactively, with a special emphasis on reaching segments of the community that historically have been marginalized or under-represented.
- The curricula and content are publicly available online and in the different languages spoken in the community.
- They help prepare and recruit citizens for membership on public commissions and advisory boards.
- Citizens, public officials, and public employees take part in the trainings together (sometimes as trainers, sometimes as trainees) so that they learn the same skills and build relationships with the other participants.

Online Participation Dashboards

In Part Two of this book, we discussed the use of online dashboards for sparking participation on numerous issues; however, online dashboards can also be used more broadly as supports for participation infrastructure. Specifically, they can be used to track data like turnout, demographics, and participant satisfaction and to make that information publicly available online. In doing so, dashboards can help organizers and participants measure the quality of participation efforts and decide how to improve them.

Some state and local governments are already using performance dashboards to help people visualize spending and program performance by agencies and departments. These online platforms show "how we can much better evaluate and communicate government programs," writes Pete Peterson (2013). There also dashboards for civic indicators, such as state and local versions that use the Civic Health

Index methodology created by the National Conference on Citizenship (2010). These indices take some of the "meta-data" about citizen engagement, such as rates of voting and volunteerism, and track them over time. Although these kinds of dashboards are valuable and revealing, they would be even more helpful if they allowed communities to track finer-grained data about particular participation efforts.

One of the biggest challenges to evaluating public participation efforts is gathering the data, even on simple measures like turnout. But by following the approach and using some of the technological tools inherent in online platforms, communities can tap the capacity of citizens to contribute. "An online platform to evaluate public participation can provide benefits to all the involved parties by lowering the costs of data collection and data sharing," write Mariana Becerril-Chavez, Katharyn Lindemann, Jack Mayernik, and Joe Ralbovsky (2012: 23).

ENVISIONING STRONGER PARTICIPATION INFRASTRUCTURE

Grand plans are made of small elements. Like arraying puzzle pieces on a table, identifying potential building blocks and systemic supports makes it possible to envision how participation infrastructure might actually look and work.

Many different and complementary visions are possible at all levels of government. For example, in *Bringing Citizen Voices to the Table*, Carolyn Lukensmeyer (2013) suggests several infrastructure components that support national democracy, including: (1) a legislative mandate for participation, (2) safe, accessible physical spaces, (3) broader access to technology, (4) a facilitation infrastructure, (5) an organizational infrastructure, (6) a trustworthy, fact-based media, and (7) robust civic education. Similarly, many things can be done to support the creative process of envisioning a stronger local participation infrastructure. Here we suggest five: making it clear that participation is a cross-sector priority; using plainer, more compelling language; encouraging both progressive and conservative visions of and prescriptions for participation; providing visual aids, like charts and maps; and encouraging artistic expressions of future forms of democracy.

Making It Clear That Participation Is a Cross-Sector Priority

In Chapters 4 through 6, we described the official, governmental settings for public participation in education, health, and land use, and suggested ways to improve them. We also pointed out that many organizations and networks have a current or potential role in public participation. On almost every issue, from public safety to public finance, one could assemble similar lists of extra-institutional allies with a stake in participation.

It should be clear from these descriptions that public participation is more than a governmental responsibility. A strong, healthy local democracy is something that benefits every community member, every organization, and every local leader. City hall can play a key role in improving and sustaining local democracy, but it should not dictate the plan and it cannot bear the whole burden of implementing it. The Institute for Local Government (n.d.: 3–4) urges public officials to develop "mutual partnerships" by engaging with "neighborhood and community organizations to involve their members, or through these groups to involve the wider community, in appropriate public engagement activities over time. In some cases this may include structured relationships/agreements between neighborhood associations or community groups with . . . local government departments."

It may be that community foundations, along with other nonprofit groups that have a long-term stake in the community and are above the political fray, are best positioned to convene infrastructure planning efforts (Gibson & Leighninger, 2013). In any case, planning for stronger participation infrastructure should be a cross-sector, collaborative endeavor.

Using Plainer, More Compelling Language

"Participation infrastructure" is a dry and abstract-sounding term. Furthermore, the term "public participation" is often used interchangeably with many other civic synonyms, such as public engagement, democratic governance, citizen participation, participatory democracy, civic engagement, public involvement, citizen-centered work, public work, and public deliberation (Lee & Polletta, 2010; Nabatchi, 2014; Nabatchi & Amsler, 2014; Thomas & Leighninger, 2010). None of these terms is likely to grab the attention of the average person, let alone serve as a rallying cry for change. Participation leaders can use plainer, more compelling language to describe the potential features and benefits of a more participatory community. The "Civic Utopia" example in Box 9.1, which was developed by the Community Matters Partnership convened by the Orton Family Foundation, is one example of how to do this.

Encouraging Both Progressive and Conservative Visions

Participation is often stereotyped as a "liberal" project, despite the fact that some of the most interesting innovations, such as the British Columbia Citizens' Assembly, came from the imaginations of right-of-center public officials—and despite the fact

Box 9.1. Civic Utopia Combining Democratic Innovations to Create the Community We Want

A Vision Statement from the Community Matters Partnership

What is the future of civic engagement and local democracy? Two years ago, a set of organizations convened by the Orton Family Foundation began meeting around this question. All of the groups were involved in helping communities engage citizens or build community, but in very different ways—from online engagement to face-to-face dialogue, from public deliberation to community development, from grantmaking to placemaking.

Through these conversations, the organizations realized that our different perspectives and areas of expertise could be combined into a common, compelling vision about the kinds of communities people want. We formed the Community Matters Partnership to help communities work on their own visions:

- Imagine living in a neighborhood that had inviting public spaces, indoors and outdoors, attracting all kinds of people.

- Imagine going to a city council, school board, or zoning meeting and spending most of the time in a small-group discussion where you were able to learn, listen, talk—and feel like your views would contribute to policy decisions.

- Imagine living in a community with a steady supply of small grants available for teams of everyday people to work on local problems.

- Imagine living in a city where your ideas and projects were considered when shaping the city budget.

- Imagine being part of an online neighborhood network you could tap into quickly and easily to ask questions like: "Who can recommend a good plumber?" "Who has a canoe I can borrow?," "What is in the school system's redistricting plan?"

- Imagine being able to report public problems—from potholes and graffiti to low test scores at the grade school—in a way that captured the attention of public decision-makers and that gave you opportunities to help solve the problem.

- Imagine having an easily accessible map of your neighborhood that showed what new buildings were being proposed, what zoning issues were on the horizon, and how you could take part in those decisions.

- Imagine a school in which you and other parents met regularly with the teacher to discuss how things were going in the classroom.

- Imagine living in a community with a system of youth councils that gave students the chance not only to learn leadership skills for the future, but to exercise leadership in the present.

For more information, see www.communitymatters.org/

that evidence about the aggregate impact of thick participation on public opinion does *not* suggest a left-leaning bias (Weiksner, Gastil, Nabatchi, & Leighninger, 2012). Nevertheless, the language used to advance participation is commonly associated with "liberal" or "left-leaning" terms and goals, such as equality (of voice and opportunity), concern for the disenfranchised, and appeals to consensus and community. Participation can also be articulated in "conservative" or "right-leaning" terms and goals, such as non-governmental action, local authority, and the power of citizens to control public decisions and spending. Prime Minister David Cameron's vision of the "Big Society" in the United Kingdom could be considered a conservative picture of civic infrastructure (Peterson, 2010).

Both as an inspiring vision and as a practical plan, the need for stronger participation infrastructure should be couched in both progressive and conservative ways. We should describe the challenge in ways that invite responses and prescriptions from all political parties and across the ideological spectrum (Nabatchi, 2014).

Using Visual Aids, Like Charts and Maps

Using charts that describe the kinds of activities that are (or will be) happening in a more participatory community can help supplement and clarify the language of participation. The "Participation Infrastructure" figures in Chapters 4 through 7 could serve as visual aids that elucidate participation activities in different issue areas. Other charts such as the "Spectrum of Public Engagement Activities" produced by the Democratic Governance Panel of the National League of Cities (Leighninger & Mann, 2011) could be adapted to show the range of participatory activities happening in a community.

A second way of providing visual aids is to map the activities taking place in a community. In Chapter 8, we explored mapping as a specific participatory tactic; here, we suggest that mapping can be done more broadly. Interactive maps that encompass a wide range of local information, including opportunities for participation, can be extremely useful for helping people to take stock of the settings, vehicles, and hubs of participation—to see what is available, what is coming, and where there are gaps.

Encouraging Artistic Expressions of Democracy

Finally, envisioning a stronger participation infrastructure can be facilitated by tapping into citizens' creative impulses and encouraging more artistic expressions of how participation infrastructure might look. A fairly common practice in land use planning and visioning is to invite participants to take photographs or draw pictures of places in their community that they value or that need upgrading. This same approach can be used to more broadly imagine the possibilities for participation infrastructure in communities.

Inspired by the work of artist Leandro Erlich (shown in the bottom right corner), Figure 9.1 uses physical architecture as a scaffold for participation opportunities. Figure 9.2 offers a map of online communities around the world. Both figures provide creative examples of what a civic infrastructure might look like. Another artistic expression, suggested by John Stephens (forthcoming), is to use the human body as a metaphor for the body politic. Using these kinds of analogies, along with their own artistic impulses, people may be able to envision participation infrastructure in ways that are more compelling, understandable, and fun.

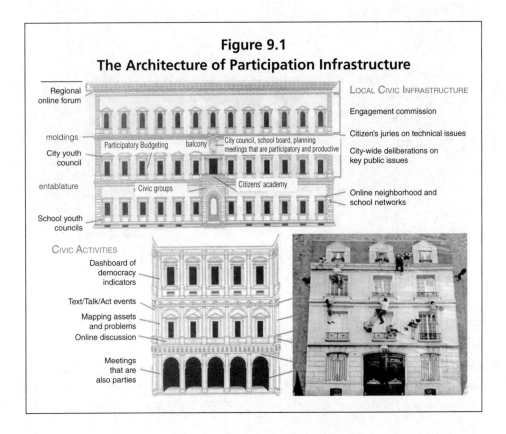

Figure 9.1
The Architecture of Participation Infrastructure

Regional online forum

moldings

City youth council

entablature

School youth councils

Civic Activities

Dashboard of democracy indicators

Text/Talk/Act events

Mapping assets and problems

Online discussion

Meetings that are also parties

Participatory Budgeting   balcony

Civic groups

City council, school board, planning meetings that are participatory and productive

Citizens' academy

Local Civic Infrastructure

Engagement commission

Citizen's juries on technical issues

City-wide deliberations on key public issues

Online neighborhood and school networks

Figure 9.2
A Map of Online Communities

SMALL "d" DEMOCRATIC PLANNING FOR SMALL "d" DEMOCRATIC INFRASTRUCTURE

Creating grand visions of how participation infrastructure might look, and surveying the potential components of such an infrastructure, can be inspiring but also daunting. Communities ought to embrace this challenge, at regular intervals, in the same way that land use comprehensive plans are devised and revised every few years. But if this is not possible, all is not lost. The fact is that most of the time, most of us do not have realistic chances to re-imagine how our communities should work—or, at least, we do not have realistic chances to implement those visions. It is much more likely that we can change how participation works in the context of a single neighborhood, a single school, or a single issue area (although we still need to contemplate and understand potential effects on other settings and issues).

Although that kind of piecemeal approach may not be as inspiring, it is also not as daunting. It reflects the fact that most infrastructures, whether they are physical, technological, or conceptual, are not built all at once. They are assembled over time, with different people and organizations taking a hand in different places. One might even argue that the idea of grand plans revisited periodically is itself a relic of early 20th Century Progressive thinking. The 21st Century mode of planning (and replanning), exemplified by shared resources like Wikipedia, is piecemeal, collective, collaborative, crowdsourced, and constant. Instead of a grand plan, we need a series of smaller plans that are united through their common principles and practices—what Abhi Nemani (2014), one of the founders of Code for America, calls a system of "small (city) pieces, loosely joined." If this book describes more participatory forms of governance—democracy with a small "d"—then perhaps these systems are best constructed in small "d" democratic ways.

What, then, are those common principles of small "d" democratic planning for small "d" democratic infrastructure? No matter what issue or geographic jurisdiction they are working on, planners of participation infrastructure ought to:

- Cross silos within government and between different sets of experts;
- Understand and articulate the broader context and reasons why people might want to participate, going beyond the specific policy decision to the bigger picture;
- Find out where citizens are already assembled, face-to-face and online, and how to tap into those settings;
- Assemble people in new settings and in ways that make further assembly and reassembly more likely;
- Map everything, and make those maps transparent and responsive;
- Build databases and other repositories of information on the community and people who live there;

- Facilitate accountability as much as possible—by giving participants decisions to make and/or by giving decision-makers many chances to respond; and

- Measure participation in ways that match with other measurement efforts and allow citizens to be part of the measuring.

With these principles in mind, it is also important to remember that participation infrastructure can be built in many different ways. In some places, there may already be so many civic assets and opportunities for citizens that little actual building is necessary; rather, efforts would be focused on improving the settings and opportunities and connecting them with one another as part of an overarching community plan. In other communities, there may be more gaps in the civic picture, and new building blocks must be added to fill them. Some places may be able to create a comprehensive plan for participation infrastructure all at once, whereas other communities may make slower, more incremental progress. Every place is likely to have its own unique culture of participation.

But however it is built, however slowly or quickly it develops, and whatever it looks like in the long run, the participation infrastructure has to work—both for the individuals it serves and the institutions it encompasses. Builders of participation infrastructure must periodically ask several questions:

- Why will people care about this?
- How will it serve our needs as citizens?
- Why will people participate?
- How will this make the work of public officials, public employees, and other stakeholders easier, more effective, and more gratifying?

To the extent possible, they must develop ways of measuring and benchmarking their answers to these questions.

Above all, the local infrastructure for participation must reflect the needs and goals of ordinary people. Generating broader public understanding and ownership of participation infrastructure may be important—and may even be absolutely necessary—for building and sustaining that infrastructure. As John Stephens and Matt Leighninger (forthcoming) write:

> The democratic principles that animate this work suggest that citizens should, as a matter of right, have a say in how their communities function. If they do not, the design of civic infrastructure could

be yet another aspect of public life that is controlled and concealed by a small elite. In other words, the public should have the opportunity to participate in designing, supporting, and improving public participation.

SUMMARY

In this chapter, we made the case for holistic models of participation infrastructure. While it is possible to strengthen the infrastructure for one issue, we argued that communities are better off taking a more multi-faceted, citizen-centered view of participation. Efforts to renovate official settings and create new opportunities for participation should be connected to other pieces, so that the whole is greater than the sum of its parts.

There are no "cookie-cutter" recipes for this work: every community should develop ideas and plans that fit local needs, assets, and goals. To help assemble the participation infrastructure for a community, we identified several "universal pieces" that would help people address many different issues and challenges, including hyperlocal and local online networks, buildings that are physical hubs for participation, and youth councils. The most helpful piece may be participation commissions, which can advise communities and agencies on the design, implementation, and evaluation of public participation tactics, as well as on building and embedding a sustainable participation infrastructure. Next, we turned to some of the systemic supports that are needed for participation infrastructure and specifically examined local participation ordinances, citizens' academies and other training programs, and online participation dashboards.

With these pieces and supports in mind, it becomes easier to envision how a stronger participation infrastructure might actually look and work. We suggested five ways to support the creative process of envisioning a stronger participation infrastructure in communities: making it clear that participation is a cross-sector priority; using plainer, more compelling language; encouraging both progressive and conservative prescriptions for participation; providing visual aids; and encouraging artistic expressions. Finally, we suggested that more participatory forms of governance are best constructed in participatory ways. To that end, we identified several common principles of small "d" democratic planning for small "d" democratic infrastructure.

DISCUSSION QUESTIONS

1. In the opening of this chapter, the authors assert that more productive forms of participation are not often incorporated into the official settings for participation in education, health, land use, or any other issue. Why do you think this is the case?

2. Develop a plan for creating a participation commission in your community or for an issue. Where would it be housed? Who would be on it? What would be its responsibilities?

3. Do you believe it is important to develop a local participation ordinance? Why or why not?

4. Does your community have a citizens' academy or other training programs? If so, what is the current curriculum for that program? Does it include participation? How might participation be incorporated into that program?

5. The authors assert that the language of participation is not clear or compelling, and that it fails to capture both progressive and conservative visions. Do you agree with these claims? Why or why not? What are your suggestions for talking about participation in a way that is exciting and understandable to people, regardless of their political views?

6. How would you go about mapping the participation activities taking place in your community? What information, opportunities, and other ideas are available? Where are there gaps?

7. Channel your inner creative genius and develop an artistic expression of a participation infrastructure. Why did you make the choices you made?

8. Some have suggested using analogies to explain the idea of a participation infrastructure, for example, likening it to a human body or to physical architecture. What analogy or analogies would you use to explain participation infrastructure?

9. What do the authors mean by small "d" democratic planning and small "d" democratic infrastructure? Do you agree with the common principles of democratic planning for democratic infrastructure? Why or why not? What would you add or eliminate?

10. What are the tradeoffs between grand visions and piecemeal approaches to developing a local participation infrastructure? Which approach do you think is better and why? How would you go about engaging others in discussions about developing stronger participation infrastructure in your community?

References

Becerril-Chavez, Mariana, Katharyn Lindemann, Jack Mayernik, & Joe Ralbovsky. (2012). *A SeeClickFix for public participation? Assessing the feasibility of an online platform for evaluating public participation activities.* Syracuse, NY: Maxwell School of Citizenship and Public Affairs, Syracuse University.

Gibson, Cynthia, & Matt Leighninger. (2013). *Deepening community engagement: What community foundations can do.* Phoenix, AZ: Alliance for Innovation.

Hoene, Christopher, Christopher Kingsley, & Matthew Leighninger. (2013). *Bright spots in community engagement: Case studies of U.S. communities creating greater civic participation from the bottom up.* Washington, DC: National League of Cities.

Institute for Local Government. (n.d.). *Three orientations of local government to public engagement: Passive—active—sustaining.* Sacramento, CA: Institute for Local Government.

Lee, Caroline, & Francesca Polletta. (2009). *The 2009 dialogue and deliberation practitioners survey: What is the state of the field?* Easton, PA: Lafayette College. Available at http://sites.lafayette.edu/ddps/.

Leighninger, Matt, & Bonnie Mann. (2011). *Planning for stronger local democracy: A field guide for local officials.* Washington, DC: National League of Cities.

Lukensmeyer, Carolyn J. (2013). *Bringing citizen voices to the table: A guide for public managers.* San Francisco, CA: Jossey-Bass.

Mansuri, Ghazala, & Vijayendra Rao. (2014). The challenge of promoting civic participation in poor countries. In P. Levine & K. Soltan (Eds.), *Civic studies,* 59–72. Washington, DC: Bringing Theory to Practice.

Morse, Ricardo. (2012). Citizens academies: local governments building capacity for citizen engagement. *Public Performance & Management Review, 36*(1): 79–101.

Nabatchi, Tina. (2014). Deliberative civic engagement in public administration and policy. *Journal of Public Deliberation, 10*(1): Article 21.

Nabatchi, Tina, & Lisa Blomgren Amsler. (2014). Direct public engagement in local government. *American Review of Public Administration, 44*(4suppl): 63s–88s.

National Conference on Citizenship. (2010). *A civic nation: Executive summary of America's first civic health assessment.* Washington, DC: The National Conference on Citizenship.

Nemani, Abhi. (2014). Small (city) pieces, loosely joined. Available at https://medium.com/@abhinemani/small-city-pieces-loosely-joined-5202fb5a93e3.

Peterson, Pete. (2010). Cameron's "big society" and its discontents. Front Porch Republic. Available at www.frontporchrepublic.com/2010/04/camerons-big-society-and-its-discontents/.

Stephens, John, and Matt Leighninger. (Forthcoming). Charting participation. On file with authors.

Thomas, Nancy L., & Matt Leighninger. (2010). *No better time: A 2010 report on opportunities and challenges for deliberative democracy.* Washington, DC: Deliberative Democracy Consortium.

Weiksner, Michael, John Gastil, Tina Nabatchi, & Matt Leighninger. (2012). Advancing the theory and practice of deliberative civic engagement: A secular hymnal. In T. Nabatchi, J. Gastil, M. Weiksner, & M. Leighninger (Eds.), *Democracy in motion: Evaluating the practice and impact of deliberative civic engagement*, 261–273. New York, NY: Oxford University Press.

Working Group on Legal Frameworks for Public Participation (Ed.). (2013). *Making public participation legal.* Denver, CO: National Civic League.

Building Democracy

Throughout this book, we have suggested that public participation is more than a set of processes, tactics, and skills. Philosophically and practically, it is the essence of a new political system—of new, more democratic forms of democracy. In this latest phase of a long history, democratic development is being driven by a fundamental shift in citizen capacities and attitudes and the need for public institutions to respond to these changes or perish.

We acknowledged that many readers would be surprised by this argument and used the analogy that they might feel like aspiring mechanics confronted by the need for a new kind of car. But while we empathize with the reader, we make no apologies. History marches on into the future, shaped by forces that are partly— but not completely—beyond our control.

Throughout this book, we have described ways to take control of our democratic future, to seize on the opportunities and minimize the difficulties in new forms of democracy. In Part One, we explained why conventional participation is problematic for public officials, staffers, and citizens and how thin and thick forms of participation could better serve everyone. We provided a brief history of democratic development and the ways in which democratic participation has led repeatedly to republican reforms. In Part Two of the book, we explored the potential of public participation to improve education, health, and land use, as well as governance more broadly at the state and federal levels. Within each of those chapters, we examined three steps to building better participation infrastructures: empowering and activating participation leaders and networks; using the six building blocks of participation activities; and incorporating systemic supports for participation. In the first two chapters of Part Three, we explored participation tactics and discussed how to assemble the pieces of a participation infrastructure.

In this concluding chapter, we locate these ideas and prescriptions in the broader context of political and societal change. We ask where democracy is headed and describe three significant trends affecting its course: the shift in how people consume and interact with information and the media; the role of citizens in decisions on how to spend public resources; and the relationship between citizens across the lines of race, ethnicity, religion, and other differences. Finally, returning to the themes we introduced in Part One, we explain why it is essential for us to adopt a broader, clearer message about public participation, and we make the case for why talking about democracy can make the struggle of public participation easier and clearer.

WHERE IS DEMOCRACY HEADED?

The future course of democratic development will undoubtedly be influenced by many forces, some of which we cannot anticipate. There are, however, three significant trends that are already affecting participation today and that seem likely to remain critical. In fact, it is hard to imagine a future in which these three trends are no longer important: the ways in which people receive information, their appetite for an authoritative role in public spending, and how they relate to one another in our increasingly diverse society.

Trend 1: People and Information

As Leighninger (2014a: 6) reports in *Infogagement: Citizenship and Democracy in the Age of Connection*, many journalists, public officials, and technologists feel that:

> information overload is bringing a kind of mutual, creative destruction to their fields, and that the consequences will be dramatic. People who work in these three fields all seem to feel that, somehow, their worlds are colliding, either with a sudden, thunderous boom or in wrenching super slo-mo. The fusion of these forces could be called "infogagement."

Traditional thinking about the relationship between information and participation puts information first: people need to become informed before they can become politically involved. In this view, the presence of an independent, impartial news media is essential (cf. Lukensmeyer, 2013). It is increasingly clear, however, that people do not just receive information anymore. Instead of a linear progression from education to participation, public life seems to seethe and spark with connections and reactions that are often unexpected and always hard to map. We now live in a hyper-informed, over-stimulated era, bombarded by facts, data, and stories in all their blurring and bewildering forms. The first line of the Pew Research Center's (Anderson & Rainie, 2012) *Future of Big Data* report reads: "We swim in a sea of data . . . and the sea level is rising rapidly." Similarly, Eric Newton of the Knight Foundation says that "Media is becoming increasingly personal, portable, and participatory" (Leighninger, 2014a: 18).

In this explosion of information and information sources, journalists have lost some of their status as trusted correspondents. Just as we have become more skeptical of experts, scientists, elected leaders, and other figures once treated as "truth-tellers," we also have become more skeptical of journalists. Given the competition in information provision and the erosion of their truth-telling status, it is no accident that the institutions of journalism are going through a painful transition period. Over one-fifth of the jobs in the newspaper industry were lost between 2000 and 2010, and the trend seems to have accelerated since then: newspaper revenues have gone down 40 percent in the last three years, according to Michael Maness of the Knight Foundation (Leighninger, 2014a: 13).

However, new collaborative practices, "hyper-local" innovations, and participation activities (including the use of participation as a revenue source) may be signaling the rebirth of journalism. A new category of nonprofit organizations dedicated to investigative reporting has emerged. These groups, which include ProPublica, the Center for Investigative Reporting (CIR), Zócalo Public Square, and the Investigative Reporting Workshop, are pioneering a hybrid business model that combines sales of content or advertising, memberships, and grant funding. Some of these new outfits are "hyperlocal" media organizations—the "mom-and-pop" shops of the journalism industry. Most of these hyperlocals focus on a neighborhood, a suburb or town, a school system, or a particular issue within a metro region (for example, Urban Milwaukee covers planning issues in Milwaukee, and PlanPhilly does the same in Philadelphia). New communication "labs" have also been established in universities such as the Massachusetts Institute of Technology, University of California-Berkeley, and Emerson College, using the resources of higher education to support innovation in journalism.

Participation is a key part of this transformation of journalism. Media organizations are trying several kinds of engagement that test new possibilities for the way they interact with the truth—and with their audiences. CIR demonstrates one type by engaging citizens to find out what issues or topics they would like the organization's journalists to cover. CIR "goes into the community before they do the journalism," says John Esterle of the Whitman Institute, a CIR funder. "They want to find out, 'What are the stories that need to be covered?'" (Leighninger, 2014a: 19). A national version of this idea, the Public Insight Network, was created by American Public Media. People sign up for free to offer insights and tips and to answer targeted questions; journalists then use the information to identify and research stories.

Josh Stearns of the media advocacy group Free Press wonders whether newspapers should take this one step further and experiment with converting their editorial boards (which, in many cases, no longer take decisive stands on issues like endorsing political candidates) into engagement boards. "What if editorial boards opened up the meetings in which they debate who they will endorse and turned them into something akin to a town hall? I think we can create a better endorsement, one that more concretely serves the local community and builds engagement and trust amongst readers" (Leighninger, 2014a: 20; for more on the relationship between elections and public deliberation, see Charles, Sokoloff, & Satullo, 2005).

Other media organizations employ a different type of participation: using news stories and opinion pieces to frame an issue, inform participants, and present a range of views. This practice, which is at the heart of what has been called "public journalism" or "civic journalism," was pioneered in the 1990s by newspapers such as the *Wichita Eagle, Charlotte Observer*, and *Portland Press Herald* (Rosen, 1999). The support of the *Portsmouth Herald* has been a key element of the award-winning public engagement work of Portsmouth Listens over the last twelve years (Ames, 2012). If the CIR work exemplifies engagement "at the front end" of the journalistic process, as John Esterle puts it, this second practice is engagement "at the back end."

Joe Mathews of Zócalo Public Square argues that this second type of engagement provides a way out of the "objectivity trap." In his view, when journalists help convene events, frame and inform the discussions, and then report on what people said to one another and how leaders responded, they strengthen the reputation of journalists as skillful, trusted arbiters of the truth. "If your game is to piss people off, like Fox or MSNBC, you can't be impartial because you need to get attention," says Mathews. "But if you're a convener, you can live in impartiality. After all, the media you want is a media that forces people to talk to each other, both online and face to face" (Leighninger, 2014a: 20).

But perhaps the most intriguing development is the growing awareness that convening public participation can be profitable. A rising number of traditional media companies and enterprising new startups convene public meetings and hold real-time online discussions as a way to sell advertising dollars, in addition to fulfilling other aspects of their missions. These include the *Texas Tribune*, Zócalo Public Square, and ideastream, a collaboration of public broadcasters in Northeast Ohio. John Esterle predicts that "As journalism reinvents itself, engagement won't just be a good thing to do, it will be an economic necessity" (Leighninger, 2014a: 13).

The shifts in journalism, and in the interactions between information and participation, have provoked a great deal of soul-searching among journalists—but also an opportunity for them to clarify what they want to do. Paula Ellis, a former newspaper editor who served as an executive at Knight-Ridder and the Knight Foundation, reports that "Old-line journalists would always say to me, 'We're in service to democracy'—and then never ever say what that means" (Leighninger 2014a: 21). The shifts in public participation would seem to provide journalists, and everyone else, new opportunities to get in on this conversation. The free exchange of factual information would seem to be the lifeblood of almost any vision of a supportive participation infrastructure.

Trend 2: People and Public Money

Another trend with significant implications for participation is the advance of participatory budgeting (PB) and other formats that give citizens a role in allocating public resources (for more information on PB as a participation tactic, see Chapter Eight). Perhaps the fastest-growing form of public engagement in the world, PB was first developed in thirteen Brazilian cities in the late 1980s, of which Porto Alegre became the most famous example. It has since spread to over 1,500 cities on six continents (Peixoto, 2014). Many of the cities are shown on the map in Figure 10.1.

From the beginning, the PB experiment was an attempt to rectify the relationship between the individual and the institution. It was implemented soon after the end of Brazil's military dictatorship; democratic governance had become possible, but most Brazilians had neither faith in government nor any experience with democracy in practice. The members of the Workers' Party who prevailed in Porto Alegre's 1989 municipal election wanted a tangible way to show citizens that the changes were real—that the new local regime would not just be responsive to their interests, but would also give them a meaningful measure of power and authority (Abers, 1998; Altschuler, 2013; Wampler, 2012).

Figure 10.1
Map of Participatory Budgeting Projects

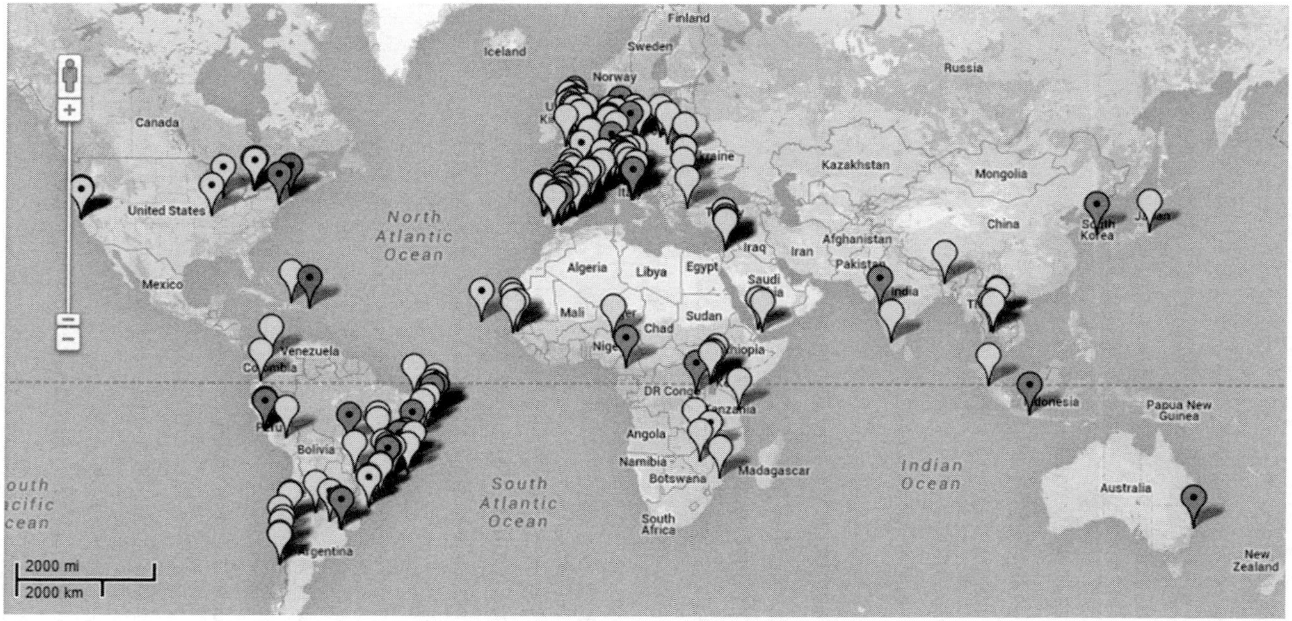

From GoogleMaps.

The current wave of PB in the United States began in 2009 with Alderman Joe Moore in Chicago's 49th Ward (Schugurensky, 2012). Pioneered and assisted by the Participatory Budgeting Project, this single-councilmember model of PB takes advantage of the unusual budgeting configuration—and political calculus—of large cities like Chicago and New York. In those cities, councilmembers have their own separate city funds to direct. In the United States, PB has spread to five districts in Chicago, twenty-three in New York City (representing over half the city), a city-wide process in Vallejo, California, projects with online elements in Detroit and St. Louis, and a youth-focused process in Boston.

While PB began as a purely face-to-face process, and still usually relies on in-person meetings, many cities have added technology-based elements. One of the first was the Brazilian city of Belo Horizonte, which launched an online budgeting platform in 2006 that allowed participants to discuss and vote on how to spend the equivalent of $11 million (U.S.) in public works funding. Almost 10 percent of the city's population took part (Peixoto, 2008). In a number of cities, citizens can vote by texting with their cellphones. The best PB efforts accommodate a wide range of technologies. PB advocates now champion the use of "multi-channel" approaches that encompass a variety of online and offline opportunities (Peixoto & Weber, 2012).

Although PB can be implemented as a one-time-only project, it is often embedded as a regular, annual feature of local democracy. This allows a PB experience to grow over time. In Porto Alegre, for example, participation estimates range from 17,000 to 35,000 people per year, and a World Bank (2008) survey found that almost 20 percent of the population had participated. This scale and staying power may account for some of the more eye-opening characteristics and impacts of PB (Peixoto, 2012):

- Unlike almost every other example of public participation, PB in Brazilian cities has attracted low-income, less-educated people at rates that are equal to, and sometimes even higher than, those of wealthier, better-educated people (Pateman, 2012).
- In cities using PB, public resources are more likely to be spent in low-income neighborhoods with fewer public amenities—and perhaps as a result, PB is "strongly associated with a reduction in extreme poverty and increased access to basic services" (Baiocchi, Heller, Chaudhuri, & Silva, 2006).

- Cities that have used PB for at least eight years have spent more on education and sanitation than other cities and have collectively reduced infant mortality rates by over 20 percent (Touchton & Wampler, 2014).

- When identified through a PB process, government-funded projects are more likely to be completed and efficient, and less likely to run over budget (Schneider & Goldfrank, 2002).

- PB cities have fewer instances of corruption (Touchton & Wampler, 2014; Zamboni, 2007).

- Residents of PB cities are less likely to evade taxes, consequently local tax revenues are higher (Baquero, Schneider, Linhares, Alves, & Pereira, 2005; Cabannes, 2004; Zamboni, 2007).

- Elected officials who support or initiate PB processes are 10 percent more likely to be reelected than local officials who do not (Spada, 2010, 2012).

Despite these benefits, PB does have critics. One of the charges is that citizens are usually not making decisions on the entire city budget—they have a say over only 5 to 20 percent of the municipal budget, even when the process determines 100 percent of all new capital spending. Thus, critics assert that PB is some sort of shell game, where citizens are distracted by one small slice of the public pie while public officials and special interests divvy up the rest. However, there is no reason why PB has to be limited to capital spending. In a number of cases, including the earliest American PB projects conducted in the 1990s in Eugene, Oregon, and Sacramento, California, citizens deliberated on the entire municipal budget (Weeks, 2000). Furthermore, because participating in PB seems to raise citizens' knowledge of government and attentiveness to local politics (which may explain why it tends to reduce corruption), PB seems likely to increase accountability for the entire budget.

Beyond these critiques, there are also examples of poorly implemented PB projects, along with projects that are labeled "participatory budgeting" but that seem to be nothing more than attempts to manipulate citizens. As political theorist Carole Pateman (2012: 10) warns, the PB concept has proliferated and diversified so much that there is a danger we will "drain the term 'participatory budgeting' of meaning." This is a predictable problem in the rapid dissemination of an idea and a challenge for many other participatory tactics as well.

PB is not the only successful process for engaging citizens in budget decisions. Approaches like Priority-Based Budgeting (Kavanagh, Johnson, & Fabian,

2011), online platforms like www.bipart.it in Italy, serious games like the "San Jose Budget Game," and high-profile examples like "Listening to Toronto" have all provided meaningful opportunities for people to have a say in public finance.

The differences between these approaches, and even among the many other processes calling themselves PB, seem to pivot around whether they:

- Give citizens a chance to vote on priorities and projects, or simply to give comments;
- Allow citizens to elect and serve as delegates to play more intensive roles in the process;
- Focus on capital spending, or on a fund set aside for the process, or on the budget as a whole;
- Feature structured meetings and/or online experiences where people deliberate on budget decisions; and
- Use proactive, network-based recruitment to involve large, diverse numbers of people.

Participatory budgeting is more than just a successful participation tactic; its true potential may be as a new feature in the infrastructure for participation. PB came about because of a desire to repair the relationship between individuals and institutions—not only in the shadow of Brazil's military dictatorship, but as a consequence of other governmental transitions, such as the City of Vallejo, California, declaring bankruptcy in 2008 (Altschuler, 2013). Alderman Joe Moore started using PB after he was almost defeated for re-election in 2007; in the following election, he won in a landslide. In 2012, Moore said:

> I take the result of the last election as a sign of popular support for participatory budgeting and any similar initiatives that nurture citizen engagement and promote participatory governance. I take it as a sign that people in the 49th ward want to be active participants in governing rather than being passive observers of government. I also take it as a sign that people are hungry for more open and transparent ways of making decisions that affect them. (Schugurensky, 2013: 170)

As they try to weather the difficult financial conditions affecting state and local governments, officials like Moore are realizing that giving citizens a say in budgeting may be key to restoring the fiscal stability of government. The most striking example of this may be in Vallejo, California, where four members of the PB steering committee have since been elected to the city council.

The growth of PB, Carole Pateman (2012: 10) argues, "shows how central components of participatory democracy can be institutionalized successfully in what is conventionally seen as an expert, technical area." This institutionalization of PB is not simply a matter of continuing the process year after year. Rather, as Pateman asserts, it is important that "Citizen participation in decisions about the municipal budget is established as a *right* of citizens—a step necessary for democratization." In his research on PB in Italian cities, Stefano Stortone (2010) finds that the processes were more likely to be sustained in places where citizens viewed them as a right rather than a government service.

The institutionalization of PB may also be a consequence of the social appeal of the process. Particularly in the Latin American examples, PB has become a part of the social and cultural fabric of communities. In *Making Democracy Fun*, Josh Lerner (2014) describes how annual PB processes have been peppered with games, festivals, contests, and other celebrations of community.

In a world where people have become accustomed to choice—about where to live, what to buy, how they receive their news—it makes sense that they are compelled by the opportunity to make choices about how public institutions spend tax revenucs. This "demand for democracy," as Elena Fagotto and Archon Fung call it (2009: 4), may well get louder, and any attempt to create a stronger participation infrastructure would do well to accommodate it.

Trend 3: People and Cultural Difference

We increasingly live in multi-racial, multi-ethnic, multi-religious societies where at least some of the residents are people who have recently arrived from other regions or other countries. Although this rich diversity can pose a challenge to participation leaders who are trying to engage a broad cross-section of the population, it can also be a tremendous asset both to participation efforts and to the community as a whole. To sustain successful participation, communities need regular, routine ways for people to address their cultural differences, celebrate their cultures without being isolated from one another, and gauge the impact of participation on social and economic inequities. Simply put, sharing the responsibilities of governance means sharing our differences (Leighninger, 2006).

As we described Chapter 3, the need to address cultural differences has been a key driver of innovation in public participation. The projects that emerged in the 1990s after the Rodney King and O.J. Simpson controversies helped set the template for engagement on all kinds of issues. They confirmed the importance of giving people a chance to share their stories and experiences, reinforced the value of impartial facilitators, demonstrated how network-based recruitment could bring in people from populations that were previously considered "hard to reach," and established that many citizens wanted to plan for action in addition to taking part in dialogue. And while many of these projects were prompted by obvious cases of racism and bias, participants showed an appetite for delving into more complex theories of institutional and structural racism (Leighninger, 2006, 2010; Walsh 2007).

In the 2000s, an increasing number of local leaders recognized the need to strengthen civic engagement among recent immigrant communities. This led to many different kinds of efforts, including some immigration-focused participation projects that used similar tactics as the processes focused on race. Most of these were one-time efforts, but a few, like the Jane Addams School of Democracy in St. Paul, Minnesota (Leighninger, 2006), have become sustained elements of civic infrastructure. This work is sometimes described as immigrant "integration." But advocates of integration often seem to make two dubious assumptions: first, that there is already a robust, participatory, empowering civic culture into which we simply need to integrate "those new people," and second, that the new people bring nothing to the table, other than perhaps some interesting new kinds of food, music, and art.

The political and cultural traditions that newcomers bring with them, or that already exist in marginalized populations, are sometimes more vibrant, participatory, and democratic than the ones we currently have in place. Attempts to strengthen participation infrastructure ought to identify and honor these assets, and above all, people should not feel that they have to give up or turn their backs on their own culture to be counted as members of the larger society (Mann & Leighninger, 2010). The Knight Foundation's *Soul of the Community* research (2010) suggests that the level of "openness" people feel toward their cultural backgrounds has a significant effect on whether they feel attached to that community—which in turn drives economic growth.

One way of assessing our levels of openness and cultural interaction is by mapping how people connect online (Leighninger, 2014a). Of course, this is only one analytical tool, and it leaves out the face-to-face connections among people who are not Internet users. It can, however, help identify the people and groups that are node connectors (many of whom may serve this role offline as well as online), helping to inform and empower people who traditionally have not been included in public life.

Any understanding of cultural difference ought to include the important, ongoing conversation about the relationship between participation and equity. Many advocates of public participation argue that equitable and just processes will lead to equitable and just outcomes. They feel that participation is an important tool for achieving social justice and racial equity, even if those goals are seldom listed explicitly by the initiators of a project. In fact, many argue that naming equity and justice as explicit goals is counterproductive because it deters the participation of people who are not already committed to those causes. Often, practitioners with a more explicit focus on justice and equity use the term "democracy" to imply equitable outcomes, not just equitable processes. "Democracy is about more than just ensuring that every voice is heard," says Danielle Atkinson, a community organizer in Michigan. "In fact, sometimes participation must be inequitable in order for outcomes to be equitable" (Leighninger, 2010: 11).

In practice, this kind of "inequitable participation" has been carried out in two main ways. First, some practitioners focus on numbers and representation during recruitment and try to ensure that the "marginalized" or "under-represented" members of a community constitute the majority of the voices at the table. The assumption here is that the voices of the powerful, and those who benefit from the status quo, are already well-represented in public life and decision making, and so any attempt at broader engagement should favor populations who have not benefited—typically the poor, people of color, and youth. John Gaventa of the Institute for Development Studies, who has worked extensively on civic engagement efforts in the Global South, argues that much of this work relies on "creating situations where a public official or some other leader is in a room with people who are poor and disadvantaged, and has to listen carefully to what they are saying" (Leighninger, 2010: 11).

Second, some practitioners facilitate the discussions or meetings differently. Facilitators can argue for viewpoints that are under-represented, present information that supports those claims, or lead exercises that prompt participants to think more critically about mainstream views. "Facilitators need to understand power dynamics and structural racism, and have the skills necessary to intervene—which includes questioning stereotypes," says Maggie Potapchuk (Leighninger, 2010: 11). "It also means asking questions about the impact of policy decisions on different groups, having historical knowledge of cumulative and systemic advantages for whites and disadvantages for people of color, and discussing common values to ensure equity for ALL, not some."

There are strong disagreements about these tactics among participation practitioners and facilitators. Some uphold the need to bring a higher percentage of "under-represented" voices to the table and reject the idea of non-neutral facilitation. For example, Atkinson suggests, "If you have the right mix of people in the room, passive facilitation is better" (Leighninger, 2010: 11). However, others support the latter and reject the former. For example, William Burton says, "I hate the idea of just bringing the 'marginalized' together. There has to be a point in time where we can all interact and talk about common aspirations. In fact, the idea that we can't create level playing fields may itself be discriminatory" (Leighninger, 2010: 11).

Fundamentally, these differences relate to how people view their relationship with government. Some community organizers and policy advocates think of their work as taking place outside "the system"—they are mobilizing people to have an impact on the leaders who retain decision-making power. To them, trying to create impartial processes and arenas seems like a distraction at best; at worst, bringing in other viewpoints may weaken the independent voice and power of the base they have built in the community. Other organizers and participation practitioners are not trying to affect the system, but rather are trying to reconstitute the system along more participatory lines. They are not building an independent power base to challenge or negotiate with decision-makers—they are trying to change where and how the decision is made.

People on both sides of this debate agree that adopting better ways of measuring equity—in both process and outcome—is important for understanding how public participation and cultural difference intersect. The Philanthropic Initiative for Racial Equity argues that participation leaders should use a "racial equity lens" when they are planning, implementing, and evaluating their efforts to engage citizens (GrantCraft, 2007). They describe this lens as having four facets:

1. Analyzing data and information about race and ethnicity;
2. Understanding disparities and learning why they exist;

3. Looking at problems and their root causes from a structural standpoint; and

4. Naming race explicitly when talking about problems and solutions. (GrantCraft, 2007; Potapchuk, 2008)

This multi-faceted lens could be used by participation commissions (see Chapter 9) and other leaders who are trying to understand whether and how their work is affecting issues of equity and cultural difference.

All of these efforts, from candid discussions of difference to ways of measuring equity, could reinforce what seems to be a natural link between public participation and cultural diversity. To bring a diverse array of people to the table, one has to acknowledge the differences between people, affirm that all cultures and groups are valued, and give people a sense that their past experiences with discrimination and bias will be rectified—or at least not repeated. In turn, it is difficult to make progress on issues of discrimination and bias without bringing a diverse array of people to the table. The two enterprises, improving participation infrastructure and increasing intercultural understanding, complement and may even require one another.

WHAT WE ARE TALKING ABOUT WHEN WE TALK ABOUT PARTICIPATION

"Participation infrastructure" may be helpful as a technical term, but as a banner for advocacy—a declaration of what citizens want—it will never do. People are more likely to care about these improvements in (and to) their communities and be better able to articulate why they matter, if they have better words to use.

Furthermore, "participation" and its civic synonyms, like engagement and involvement, are misleading words because they describe activities: it is often unclear what they are for and who should be participating (Nabatchi, 2014; Nabatchi & Amsler, 2014). This point of confusion is more than just a language problem or a marketing challenge. The real issue, as Leighninger (2014b) argues, is that, although participation leaders may all agree that their work relates somehow to democracy, they have not established—or, at least, have not articulated—a common vision of what that really means.

In fact, when first confronted with the term, most people assume that participation means engaging citizens within the confines of a primarily representative system, in which almost all of the decisions continue to be made by elected officials. But the successes and limitations of public participation point us toward democratic reforms, not republican ones. Successful participation efforts demonstrate that all kinds of people are ready for meaningful opportunities to make public decisions and solve public problems (Hoene, Kingsley, & Leighinger, 2013; Leighninger, 2006). They show us the definition of democracy (see Box 10.1) is a practical one: a political system where the "supreme power is vested in the people," where citizens have both formal and actual equality, where power can be "exercised directly" by "common people." Participation also demonstrates that primarily republican systems of government are largely inadequate for responding to and capitalizing on that new citizen energy.

Box 10.1. de·moc·ra·cy [dih-mok-ruh-see]

noun, plural de·moc·ra·cies.

1. government by the people; a form of government in which the supreme power is vested in the people and exercised directly by them or by their elected agents under a free electoral system.

2. a state having such a form of government.

3. a state of society characterized by formal equality of rights and privileges.

4. political or social equality; democratic spirit.

5. the common people of a community as distinguished from any privileged class; the common people with respect to their political power

(www.dictionary.com)

The lack of a clear vision about the relationship between participation and the political system has dire consequences. It has produced rifts and misunderstandings between academics and practitioners, community organizers and deliberative democrats, civic technologists and dialogue practitioners, policy advocates and consensus-builders (Nabatchi, 2014). It divides people on the left from those on the right, and the supposedly "advanced" countries of the Global North from the more democratically innovative nations of the Global South. It helps perpetuate official processes that claim to uphold democratic governance but in fact hamper and discourage it. Worst of all, the lack of clarity about democracy provides no help to people who are trying to create sustainable, participatory political systems in Egypt, Thailand, Ukraine, and many other countries (Benhabib, Cameron, Dolidze, Halmai, Hellmann, Pishchikova, & Youngs, 2013; Gaventa & Barrett, 2010).

The confusion about participation is due partly to the fact that participation leaders have so many different starting points. As we have described in this book, people in a wide range of fields and professions have developed successful tactics for helping citizens make decisions, solve problems, and build community.

The result of this mismatch between tactics and system, compounded by our inability to articulate the full meaning of this work, is that public participation is misunderstood even by people who should be allies:

- The "civic technologists" who have pioneered most of the new online forms of thin participation have repeated some of the same mistakes made by the inventors of face-to-face deliberative processes, producing innovative apps and tools that often falter because they are not anchored in a larger plan or infrastructure for participation.

- Some scholars continue to believe that "public deliberation" can happen only in exorbitantly expensive, highly facilitated processes in which a small, scientifically assembled microcosm of the public spends many days deliberating on a policy issue before issuing recommendations to public officials.

- Many people who describe themselves as community organizers see participation as simply an alternative form of advocacy—one that emphasizes friendly, urbane conversations and suppresses questions of power. Ironically, interviews of community organizers often reveal the same frustrations about the limitations of their work, and the same zeal to transform systems, as participation practitioners do (Leighninger, 2010).

- Participation advocates and practitioners in the Global South, who pioneered participatory budgeting and many other forms of participation, do not sense a similarly democratic energy in the North—and many of us in the North do not realize how much we can learn from civic innovations in the South.

- People on the right often see participation processes as stalking horses for a Progressive "big government" agenda; they do not recognize how participation can uphold the problem-solving capacity of citizens. People on the left do not recognize—or are not comfortable with—the fact that participation challenges the expert orientation to governance that took over during the Progressive Era a century ago.

The conversations between these potential allies tend to focus on tactics. They should instead be focusing on strategies and systems—not because we are likely to agree on every aspect of the democracy we want, but because the dialogue is more likely to be clear, constructive, and consequential.

Meanwhile, the most conventional, outdated forms of public participation still predominate at every level of government. For most people, most of the time, the only ways to take part in public decision making are public hearings and public comment periods. Practitioners and public officials often think of conventional participation as a necessary hindrance, and they sometimes organize better meetings and processes as a way to augment or work around the official ones. But as we argued in Chapter 2, conventional participation is far more damaging and costly than we realize. Because it requires time and resources to organize, conventional participation diverts public officials and employees from more productive pursuits. Because it erodes trust and communication, it makes public problem solving more difficult. And because it damages the relationship between citizens and government, it may also have an impact on tax revenues and the financial and political sustainability of public institutions.

Furthermore, because conventional processes are far more common than productive forms of engagement and deliberation, and because in many cases they are required by law or at least entrenched in the way governments function, they dominate people's perceptions of public participation. So as we struggle as a field to describe our work, the continuation of conventional participation makes citizens less receptive to any interaction with public institutions and erodes their faith in democracy—because, ironically, the "democracy" they have experienced is not actually democracy at all (Anderson, 1998; Peixoto, 2014). Similarly, the "democracy" we attempt to export to other countries follows this same, weak, primarily republican formula of elections, hearings, and committees. It does not sustain the participation, enthusiasm, or power of Egyptians, Thais, or Ukrainians any more than it appeals to Americans.

Authoritarian regimes have repeatedly been toppled by the commitment, ingenuity, and self-sacrifice of people who use democratic tactics—both thick and thin—to mobilize their neighbors and fellow citizens. But these democratic movements seldom produce more democratic systems. In most of these new regimes, the main opportunity for participation is at the ballot box. People who had a range of options for deliberation, negotiation, and public work while they were trying to overthrow the government are confined to the conventional formats once their revolution succeeds. Our romantic view of democratic movements like the Arab Spring is that protesters become citizens; in fact, what happens is that citizens become protesters.

WHAT KIND OF DEMOCRACY DO WE WANT?

In a sense, we have already done the hard part: we have established that large, diverse numbers of people have the capacity and appetite for genuinely democratic experiences. We have a wide variety of successful tactics and a good sense of the essential skills in public participation. From both academic research and anecdotal experience, we know why people will, and will not, participate in public life (Neblo, Esterling, Kennedy, Lazer, & Sokhey, 2010). Returning to Oscar Wilde's formulation, we can clearly differentiate "charming" participation opportunities from those that are "tedious."

Throughout this book we have described potential elements of participation infrastructure. But none of these tactics and assets will be put to their best use if we do not admit, to ourselves and to the world, their true significance. These are not just props for conventional processes, but building blocks for new political systems. We should not just be asking how to help citizens participate in democracy; we should be asking citizens what kind of democracy they want.

We should also be fully prepared for their answers. Once people have had a taste of meaningful, powerful public participation, they sometimes begin to think and talk about it as not just an interesting exercise or a valued opportunity, but as a right. This way of talking can have an impact: several studies of embedded participatory processes argue that those structures are more likely to be sustained when people make these rights-based claims (Fagotto & Fung, 2009; Stortone, 2010). As former Brazilian president Luiz Inácio Lula (2013) declared in a *New York Times* op-ed:

> People do not simply wish to vote every four years. They want daily interaction with governments both local and national, and to take part in defining public policies, offering opinions on the decisions that affect them each day. In short, they want to be heard. This creates a tremendous challenge for political leaders.

We agree that it is a tremendous challenge, but we also see it as a tremendous opportunity. However we talk about participation, as a right or as a privilege, as a democratic revolution or as an institutional reform, we should embrace the positive possibilities as well as the necessity for difficult change. As Lula himself demonstrated, it is possible to lead and effectively wield power by empowering citizens. It is possible to achieve reasoned, data-driven policies by trusting citizens to learn and deliberate. It is possible to overcome deep tensions and divisions by asking citizens to communicate, negotiate, and empathize. It is possible to build institutions that are both republican and democratic.

We face daunting problems, and we have remarkable capacities. Democracy, our greatest invention and still-unfinished project, is the key to both.

SUMMARY

In this concluding chapter of the book, we asserted that public participation forms the basis of new, more democratic forms of democracy. This wave of innovation is being driven by a fundamental shift in the capacities and attitudes of citizens and by the need for public institutions to respond to those changes. We also asserted that the future of our democracy is being shaped by three significant participatory trends: shifts in how people receive (and process) information, citizens' growing appetite for a meaningful role in public spending, and changes in how people relate to each other across cultural differences in our increasingly diverse society. These three trends seem likely to become even more influential over the coming years.

We then explored the potential (or lack thereof) of terms such as "participation" and "participation infrastructure" for capturing and clarifying what citizens want. These terms may work for practitioners and researchers, but they are not suitable for helping citizens articulate their growing demands for problem solving, civility, and community. This issue with language is more than a simple academic problem; it blurs the relationship between participation and our political system, creates divides among people, perpetuates conventional processes (and their shortcomings), and offers little help to those who are trying to create sustainable, participatory political systems around the world.

The good news is that we know people want democratic experiences, and we know how to use participatory tactics and skills to give them what they want. This knowledge is incredibly powerful: it provides us—empowers all of us—with the tremendous opportunity to harness our growing capacities as citizens, improve problem solving, civility, and community, and advance public participation for 21st Century democracy.

DISCUSSION QUESTIONS

1. Do you agree that public participation is more than a set of processes, tactics, and skills? Do you believe that it is the "essence of a new political system" driven by a shift in citizen capacities and attitudes and the need for public institutions to respond to those changes? Why or why not?

2. What is infogagement, and how does it connect to public participation? Why is the connection between people and information so important for public participation and democracy?

3. What is participatory budgeting (PB)? What role do you think average citizens can (and should) play in determining how taxpayer dollars are spent in their communities?

4. Why is it important to think about the role of cultural difference in public participation? What are the potential challenges and benefits of doing so?

5. The authors write that "'Participation infrastructure' may be helpful as a technical term, but as a banner for advocacy—a declaration of what citizens want—it will never do." Why do they make this claim? How would you describe the meaning and importance of "participation infrastructure"?

6. What do the authors mean by participation systems that are small "r" republican and small "d" democratic?

7. Review Box 10.1. Which of the definitions of democracy resonate with you? How would you define democracy, and what is the role of participation within it?

8. Why is there so much confusion about participation? What steps would you recommend to address and ameliorate this confusion?

9. How would you describe participation and democratic innovation to people who are not versed in this field? What terms would you use? What kinds of stories would you tell? Are there other ways you would communicate these ideas?

10. What kind of democracy do you want?

References

Abers, Rebecca. (1998). Learning democratic practice: Distributing government resources through popular participation in Porto Alegre, Brazil. In M. Douglass and J. Friedmann (Eds.), *Cities for citizens: Planning and the rise of civil society in a Global Age*, 39–66. Chichester, UK: John Wiley & Sons.

Altschuler, Daniel. (2013). Participatory budgeting in the United States: What is its role? *Nonprofit Quarterly*, *20*(1). Available at https://nonprofitquarterly.org/policysocial-context/22157-participatory-budgeting-in-the-united-states-what-is-its-role.html.

Ames, Steven. (2012). *Stewarding the future of our communities*. Shelburne, VT: Orton Family Foundation.

Anderson, Gary L. (1998). Toward authentic participation: Deconstructing the discourses of participatory reforms in education. *American Educational Research Journal*, *35*(4): 571–603.

Anderson, Janna, & Lee Rainie. (2012). *The future of big data*. Washington, DC: Pew Research Center, Internet & American Life Project.

Baiocchi, Gianpaolo, Patrick Heller, Shubham Chaudhuri, & Marcelo Kunrath Silva. (2006). Evaluating empowerment: Participatory budgeting in Brazilian municipalities. In R. Alsop, M. Frost Bertelsen, & J. Holland (Eds.), *Empowerment in practice: From analysis to implementation*, 94–124. Washington, DC: World Bank.

Baquero, Marcello, Aaron Schneider, Bianca Linhares, Douglas Santos Alves, and Thiago Ingrassia Pereira. (2005). Bases for a new social contract? Taxes and the participatory budget in Porto Alegre. *Opiniao Publica*, *11*(1): 94–127.

Benhabib, Seyla, David Cameron, Anna Dolidze, Gabor Halmai, Gunther Hellmann, Kateryna Pishchikova, & Richard Youngs. (2013). *The democratic disconnect: Citizenship and accountability in the transatlantic community*. Washington, DC: Transatlantic Academy.

Cabannes, Yves. (2004). Participatory budgeting: A significant contribution to participatory democracy. *Environment & Urbanization*, *16*(1): 27–46.

Charles, Michelle, Harris Sokoloff, & Chris Satullo. (2005). Electoral deliberation and public journalism. In J. Gastil & P. Levine (Eds.), *The deliberative democracy handbook: Strategies for effective civic engagement in the 21st century*, 59–67. San Francisco, CA: Jossey-Bass.

Fagotto, Elena, & Archon Fung. (2009). *Sustaining public engagement: Embedded deliberation in local communities*. East Hartford, CT: Everyday Democracy and Kettering Foundation.

Gaventa, John, & Gregory Barrett. (2010). *So what difference does it make? Mapping the outcomes of citizen engagement*. Brighton, UK: Institute of Development Studies.

GrantCraft. (2007). *Grant making with a racial equity lens*. New York, NY: Foundation Center.

Hoene, Christopher, Christopher Kingsley, & Matt Leighninger. (2013). *Bright spots in community engagement: Case studies of U.S. communities creating greater civic participation from the ground up*. Washington, DC: National League of Cities.

Kavanagh, Shane C., Jon Johnson, & Chris Fabian. (2011). *Anatomy of a priority-driven budget process*. Chicago: IL: Government Finance Officers Association.

Knight Foundation. (2010). *Soul of the community 2010. Why people love where they live and why it matters: A national perspective*. Miami, FL: Knight Foundation.

Leighninger, Matt. (2006). *The next form of democracy: How expert rule is giving way to shared governance—and why politics will never be the same*. Nashville, TN: Vanderbilt University Press.

Leighninger, Matt. (2010). *Creating spaces for change: Working toward a "Story of Now" in civic engagement*. Battle Creek, MI: W.K. Kellogg Foundation.

Leighninger, Matt. (2014a). *Infogagement: Citizenship and democracy in the age of connection*. Washington, DC: Philanthropy for Active Civic Engagement.

Leighninger, Matt. (2014b). What we are talking about when we talk about the "civic field." *Journal of Public Deliberation, 10*(1): Article 8.

Lerner, Josh. (2014). *Making democracy fun: How game design can empower citizens and transform politics*. Cambridge, MA: MIT Press.

Lukensmeyer, Carolyn J. (2013). *Bringing citizen voices to the table: A guide for public managers*. San Francisco, CA: Jossey-Bass.

Lula, Luiz Inácio. (2013). The message of Brazil's youth. *New York Times*. Available at www.nytimes.com/2013/07/17/opinion/global/lula-da-silva-the-message-of-brazils-youth.html?_r=0.

Mann, Bonnie C., & Matt Leighninger. (2010). *Civic engagement and recent immigrant communities*. Washington, DC: National League of Cities.

Nabatchi, Tina. (2010). Addressing the citizenship and democratic deficits: Exploring the potential of deliberative democracy for public administration. *American Review of Public Administration, 40*(4): 376–399.

Nabatchi, Tina. (2014). Deliberative civic engagement in public administration and policy. *Journal of Public Deliberation, 10*(1): Article 21.

Nabatchi, Tina, & Lisa Blomgren Amsler. (2014). Direct public engagement in local government. *American Review of Public Administration, 44*(4suppl): 63s–88s.

Nabatchi, Tina, & Cynthia Farrar. (2011). *Bridging the gap between the public and public officials: What do public officials want and need to know about public deliberation?* Washington, DC: Deliberative Democracy Consortium.

Neblo, Michael, Kevin Esterling, Ryan Kennedy, David Lazer, & Anand Sokhey. (2010). Who wants to deliberate—and why? *American Political Science Review, 104*(3): 566–583.

Pateman, Carole. (2012). Participatory democracy revisited. *Perspectives on Politics, 10*(1): 7–19.

Peixoto, Tiago. (2008). *E-participatory budgeting*. Aauru, Switzerland: E-Democracy Centre.

Peixoto, Tiago. (2012). The benefits of citizen engagement: A (brief) review of the evidence. *Democracy Spot*. Available at http://democracyspot.net/2012/11/24/the-benefits-of-citizen-engagement-a-brief-review-of-the-evidence/.

Peixoto, Tiago. (2014). Social accountability: What does the evidence really say? *Democracy Spot*. Available at http://democracyspot.net/2014/05/13/social-accountability-what-does-the-evidence-really-say/.

Peixoto, Tiago, & Boris Weber. (2012). Technology drives citizen participation and feedback in Rio Grande do Sul, Brazil. *People Spaces, Deliberation*. Available at http://blogs.worldbank.org/publicsphere/technology-drives-citizen-participation-and-feedback-rio-grande-do-sul-brazil.

Peterson, Pete. (2013). Did democracy bankrupt our cities? *Zócalo Public Square*. Available at www.zocalopublicsquare.org/2013/09/11/did-democracy-bankrupt-our-cities/ideas/nexus/.

Potapchuk, Maggie. (2008). Building capacity and cultivating interdependence for racial justice. Available at www.opensourceleadership.com/documents/WKKF%20Interdependence.pdf

Rosen, Jay. (1999). *What are journalists for?* New Haven, CT: Yale University Press.

Schneider, Aaron, & Benjamin Goldfrank. (2002). *Budgets and ballots in Brazil: Participatory budgeting from the city to the state*. Brighton, UK: Institute of Development Studies.

Schugurensky, Daniel. (2012). Working together in the city that works. *Sharable.net*. Available at www.shareable.net/blog/the-city-that-works-works-together-participatory-budgeting-in-chicago.

Schugurensky, Daniel. (2013). Volunteers for democracy: Informal learning through participatory budgeting. In F. Duguid, K. Mündel, & D. Schugurensky (Eds.), *Volunteer work, informal learning and social action*, pp. 159–176. Rotterdam, The Netherlands: Sense Publishers.

Schugurensky, Daniel. (2014). Evaluating participatory budgeting: Five dimensions. Paper presented at the Third International Conference on Participatory Budgeting in North America. Oakland, California, September 25–27, 2014.

Spada, Paolo. (2010). The effects of participatory democracy: Evidence from Brazilian participatory budgeting. Paper presented at the American Political Science Association. Washington, D.C., September 2–5.

Spada, Paolo. (2012). Political competition in deliberative and participatory institutions. Dissertation Manuscript. New Haven, CT: Yale University.

Stortone, Stefano. (2010). Participatory budgeting: Heading towards a "civil" democracy? In M. Freise, M. Pyykkönen, & E. Vaidelytė (Eds.), *A panacea for all seasons? Civil society and governance in Europe*, 99–119. Baden-Baden, Germany: Nomos.

Touchton, Michael, & Brian Wampler. (2014). Improving social well-being through new democratic institutions. *Comparative Political Studies*, 47(10): 1442–1469.

Walsh, Kathy Cramer. (2007). *Talking about race: Community dialogues and the politics of disagreement*. Chicago, IL: University of Chicago Press.

Wampler, Brian. (2012). Participatory budgeting: Core principles and key impacts. *Journal of Public Deliberation*, 8(2): Article 12.

Weeks, Edward C. (2000). The practice of deliberative democracy: Results from four large-scale trials. *Public Administration Review, 60*(4): 360–372.

World Bank. (2008). *Brazil: Toward a more inclusive and effective participatory budget in Porto Alegre.* Washington, DC: World Bank.

Zamboni, Yves. (2007). *Participatory budgeting and local governance: An evidence-based evaluation of participatory budgeting experiences in Brazil.* Washington, DC: World Bank. Available at http://siteresources.worldbank.org/INTRANETSOCIALDEVELOPMENT/Resources/Zamboni.pdf.

NAME INDEX

Page references followed by *b* indicate a box.

A

Abelson, Julia, 33
Abers, Rebecca, 60, 309
Abt, Clark C., 17
Adamec, Shaun, 93
Adams, Brian, 25
Adams, John, 50*b*
Addams, Jane, 52
Aleshire, Robert A., 54
Alexander, Lamar, 196
Altschuler, Daniel, 309, 313
Alves, Douglas Santos, 312
Ames, Steven C., 98, 160, 308
Amini, Fari, 140
Amsler, Lisa Blomgren, 6, 14, 24, 30, 53, 166, 185, 204, 218, 230, 246, 254*b*, 259, 294, 318
Anderson, Gray L., 321
Anderson, Sarah, 24
Andersson, Edward, 32
Arendt, Hannah, 46
Arnstein, Sherry R., 57, 58, 161
Arras, John, 144
Atkinson, Danielle, 316, 317

B

Baiocchi, Gianpaolo, 27, 275, 311
Baldwin-Philippi, Jessica, 27, 63, 64
Balestra, Martina, 27, 63, 64
Baquero, Marcello, 312
Barnes, William, 184
Barnett, Chance, 270
Barrett, Gregory, 320
Barris, Michael, 196

Barron, David J., 53
Bartman, Dan, 182
Beaulieu, Bo, 36
Becerril-Chavez, Mariana, 293
Becker, Jack, 8, 23, 82
Benhabib, Seyla, 320
Berman, Sheldon H., 89
Bernier, Roger, 124
Berry, Harry C., 85
Berry, Jeffrey M., 55, 56, 169, 218
Bessette, Joseph M., 14
Best, Nina J., 31, 36
Bhatia, Rajiv, 138
Bieber, Justin, 212*b*
Bingham, Lisa Blomgren, 53, 196, 204, 245*b*, 254*b*, 291
Birnback, Lara, 32
Bishop, Bill, 157
Black, Alissa, 163
Black, Laura, 30
Bockmeyer, Janice, 58
Bohman, James, 15
Bonner-Thompkins, Elaine, 82
Boone, Richard W., 55
Borry, Erin, 204
Boyte, Harry, 105
Brand, Ronald, 58
Brandeis, Louis, 210
Breitman, Kendall, 196
Bridgeland, John M., 79
Brigham, Steve, 249, 258
Brown, Alison, 158
Bryan, Frank M., 50

Morgan, Piers, 212*b*
Morison, Karen Burke, 79
Morone, James, 46
Morse, Ricardo, 292
Moses, Robert, 158
Mossberger, Karen, 176
Moynihan, Daniel Patrick, 55, 56
Muhleberger, Peter, 33, 48
Muhlestein, David, 130

N

Nabatchi, Tina, 6, 8, 14, 23, 24, 30, 36, 37, 53, 63, 198, 199, 202, 203, 204, 210, 213, 218, 244, 245*b*, 245*t*, 246, 247, 248, 249, 250, 251, 254*b*, 259, 260, 294, 318, 319
Neblo, Michael, 322
Nedland, Marcia, 182
Nemani, Abhi, 19, 163, 164, 177, 299
Nethercut, Doug, 277
Newman, Kathe, 58
Newman, Oscar, 161
Newton, Fred, 307
Neyestani, Bita, 163
Nicolato, Courteny, 126, 135, 141
Norris, Tyler, 132, 135, 261
Noveck, Beth Simone, 210, 272

O

Obama, Barack, 62, 124, 196, 210, 223
Oldenburg, Jan, 125, 135
O'Leary, Rosemary, 245*b*
Olien, Jessica, 6, 31
Olson, Linda, 120
O'Reilly, James T., 207
Orland, Catherine Brenner, 82, 256
Ostrom, Elinor, 173
Oza, Priyanka R., 136

P

Palmer, Patsy, 160
Paredes, Maria, 101*b*
Park, Todd, 211
Patel, Mayur, 18
Pateman, Carole, 23, 311, 312, 314
Pearce, Hilary, 277
Pearce, Kimberly A., 5, 25
Pearce, W. Barnett, 5, 25
Peixoto, Tiago, 31–32, 264, 309, 311, 321
Pereira, Tiago, 312
Perry, Marlo A., 79
Peters, Jeremy W., 199
Petersen, Matthew, 130

Peterson, Pete, 63, 295
Pfeifer, Laura, 182, 183
Piotrowski, Suzanne J., 204
Pishchikova, Kateryna, 320
Pittman, Mary, 119
Pogrebinschi, Thamy, 32, 226
Polletta, Francesca, 66, 109, 294
Popper, Ben, 172
Portney, Kent E., 55, 56, 169, 218
Postel, Charles, 52
Potapchuk, Maggie, 60, 317
Potoski, Matthew, 24
Potter, Gwen, 166
Prugh, Tom, 34–35
Putnam, Robert, 178

Q

Quick, Kathryn S., 245*b*, 246

R

Rainie, Lee, 64
Ralbovsky, Joe, 293
Rao, Vijayendra, 46, 291
Rask, Mikko, 264
Raudenbush, Stephen W., 31
Rauzon, Suzanne, 121
Ravn, Tine, 264
Reedy, Justin, 24
Reich, Jay, 167
Renner, Michael, 34–35
Richartz, Ninon, 258
Ridini, Steve, 132, 135
Riis, Jacob, 118
Roberts, Nancy C., 6, 50, 51, 53
Robinson, Elizabeth L., 119, 140
Robinson, Eric W., 47, 48
Roggio, Armando, 97
Rosen, Jay, 308
Rosenberg, Heidi, 79, 80, 85, 101*b*
Ross, Robert K., 119, 212
Rothstein, Dan, 218, 278*b*
Roudman, Sam, 138
Roulier, Monte, 119, 123, 130, 147, 148
Rubio-Cortés, Gloria, 117, 120
Rupp, Keith Lee, 25, 199
Rush, Benjamin, 50
Ryfe, David M., 27, 30, 246
Rylands, C. J., 179*b*

S

Safran, Charles, 124
Sampson, Robert J., 31

Willems, Patricia P., 78, 79, 80, 100, 107
Williams, Alex T., 97
Wohlstetter, Priscilla, 85
Woudstra, Ronald, 182
Wright, Erik Olin, 258
Wu, Yonghong, 176

Y
Yankelovich, Daniel, 59, 277
Young, Tamara V., 93

Youngs, Richard, 320
Youniss, James, 8

Z
Zamboni, Yves, 312
Zeleny, Jeff, 199
Zuckerman, Ethan, 14
Zyda, Michael, 17

SUBJECT INDEX

Page references followed by *fig* indicate an illustrated figure; followed by *t* indicate a table, followed by *b* indicate a box.

A

Accountability: how participation increases elected officials,' 34; public deliberation designed to build, 278*b*; small "d" democratic principle on, 300

Accountable Care Organizations (ACOs), 128, 130–131, 141, 144

Action strategy, 16–17

Administrative participation: the "best brains available" argument driving, 206–207, 210–213; development of, 203–213; legal framework for, 204–205; National Action Plans for Open Government for, 209–210; Open Government Directive (OGD) driving, 63, 203–204, 207–210, 222, 229; Open Government requirements for participation federal agency, 209*b*, 222; outside pressure and the potentially concerned public impact on, 205–206

Administrative Procedure Act (APA) [1946], 53

Adult-adult participation relationships: engaged in participation response to common health issues, 118–127*t*; forms of participation and attributes of an, 28, 29*t*; how "good" participation creates a, 25–29*t*; planning and land use participation, 158–166. *See also* Public participation

Advisory boards (participation commissions), 289–290, 318

Affiliation opportunity, 19

Affordable Care Act (ACO), 125, 128, 141, 148

Agency for Toxic Substances and Disease Registry (ATSDR), 225

Alternative dispute resolution (ADR), 291

American Academy of Pediatrics, 130

American Bar Association, 291

American Institute of Architects, 158, 160

America*Speaks,* 201

Appreciative Inquiry, 18*b*, 278*b*

Apps: CDC's "Solve the Outbreak," 137; disseminating planning and land use information on, 176; health participation, 128, 145; planning and land use, 186; public work in education, 106; reporting problems with school physical infrastructures, 98

The Architecture of Participation Infrastructure, 297*fig*

Arnstein's Ladder of Participation, 57*fig*–58

Asthmapolis project (2012), 138*b*

Athenian *Ecclesia* (citizen participation), 48

B

Balancing Justice in Oklahoma (1996), 201

Ballot initiatives and referenda, 227

BANANA (Build Absolutely Nothing Anywhere Near Anything), 159, 190

Bang the Table, 177

Baron, Mark, 79

Belo Horizonte (Brazil) Participatory Budgeting project, 311

"Best brains available" participation argument, 206–207, 210–213

Beyond Random Act report (2010), 79

Beyond the Ballot: 57 Democratic Innovations from Around the World (The Power Inquiry), 264

"Big Dig" (Boston), 158

"Big Society" (UK's David Cameron's vision), 63, 295

Booths (fairs and festivals) thin participation, 20b

Boston Globe, 87b

Boston Open Data Innovation Summit, 172

Boston's "Big Dig," 158

Boule (Council of 500) [ancient Athens], 48

Bowling Alone (Putnam), 178

Brazilian Participatory Budgeting (PB) projects, 60, 291, 311

Bridging the Gap between Public Officials and the Public (Nabatchi and Farrar), 198

Bringing Citizen Voices to the Table (Lukensmeyer), 293

British Columbia Citizens' Assembly, 294–295

Brown Act (California), 290

Buckhannon Meet and Eat lunches, 179b

Budgeting. *See* Funding and budgeting; Participatory Budgeting (PB)

Built environment, 155. *See also* Planning and land use

Bush's Points of Light campaign, 227

C

California Endowment, 119

California Healthy Cities and Communities program, 121–122

California Speaks project (2007), 123

California's Brown Act, 290

California's Convergence Initiative, 132–133

CaliforniaSpeaks project, 201

"Campfire" democracies, 47

Case Western Reserve University, 278b

CAVE (Citizens Against Virtually Everything), 159, 190

Center for Advancing Health (CAH), 117, 124, 125, 126, 128

Center for Investigative Reporting (CIR), 307, 308

Center for Urban Pedagogy, 176

Centers for Disease Control and Prevention (CDC): flu vaccine policy of, 32; health volunteer coordination recommendations by, 144; impact of the Congressional dynamic on budget allocation and, 203; projects that engage citizens in health policymaking, 123–124; *Public Health Preparedness Capabilities: National Standards for State and Local Planning* by the, 144; "Solve the Outbreak" app and "Zombie Pandemic" comic book series, 137; Twitter followers of, 135–136

ChangeByUs, 106, 162, 186

Change.org, 20b

Chapel Hill 2020, 18b

Charlotte Observer, 308

Charrettes, 274

Chicago Public Schools, 88–89

Chicago's 49th Ward Participatory Budgeting Project, 311

Cincinnati Public Schools, 81

Citizen advisory boards, 145b

Citizen assemblies, 18b

Citizen capacity: failure of public participation to tap into, 4; the reality of rising, 3

Citizen Congresses, 196

Citizen juries, 18b

Citizens: allowing them to tell their stories, 26–27; assumptions and realities about public participation and, 36t; BANANA (Build Absolutely Nothing Anywhere Near Anything) attitudes of, 159, 190; CAVE (Citizens Against Virtually Everything) types of, 159, 190; changing relationship between health experts and, 117–118; citizen's academies to provide participation training to, 291–292; encouraging social connections and national dialogue among, 222–224; engaging them in health policymaking, 123–124; "good" participation by creating an adult relationship with, 25–29t; government "induced participation" versus "organic participation" by, 46; government that provides "customer service" to, 58–59; NIMBY (Not in My Back Yard) accusations against, 59–60, 159, 190; and patient level of health participation, 131; polls showing dissatisfaction with political processes and institutions by, 196–197; "right to the city" of, 158; scenario on gathering public input from, 256–257, 262t, 263t; scenario on participation for problem solving driven by, 258–259, 262t, 263t; skepticism about public officials by, 3, 4–5; social media connections versus sense of social isolation of, 5–6; tensions between government and (1990s), 60–61; urban renewal (1940s) and participation limited to "blue-ribbon," 54. *See also* Networks; Public meetings

Citizen's Academies, 291–292

Citizens' Statement (CIR), 202

CitizenScape, 265

Citizenship: "active," 196; how online technologies have impacted, 63–65

Citizinvestor, 20b, 106, 270

City Creator, 20b

Cityzen, 265

Civic health dashboards, 221

Civic Health Index, 292–293

D

Dana-Farber Cancer Center, 144

Danish Board of Technology Foundation, 278*b*

Dashboards: civic health, 221; community and neighborhood, 176; online participation, 292–293

Data: dashboards and apps for community and neighborhood, 176–177; gathering health input and, 138*b*–139; information overload and having just too much, 306; providing citizens with factual information and, 26; providing discrete pieces of, 19; scenario of leaders wanting citizens to generate new ideas or, 257–258, 262*t*, 263*t*. *See also* Disseminating information; Information

Data collection: crowdsourcing (crowdfunding) for, 222; of health data, 138*b*–139; online platforms and tools for public, 20*b*; participation tactic of reporting problems and, 263*t*, 269; for planning and land use participation, 177–178; scenario on public input, 256–257, 262*t*, 263*t*; for schools from the local community, 96*fig*, 98–99

Data.gov, 209

"Datapaloozas" events, 211

The Death and Life of Great American Cities (Jacobs), 158

Decatur Next, 18*b*

Decision makers: how participants should interact with, 248–249, 252*t*, 262*t*, 263*t*; identifying and recruiting participants, 246–248, 252*t*, 262*t*, 263*t*. *See also* Participation leaders; Public officials

Decision making: avenues for participation in state and federal agency, 213*fig*, 215–216; enabling a community's education, 103–105; enabling community health, 143–145*b*; enabling community planning and land use, 183–184*b*; enabling family and student, 96*fig*, 100–103; enabling government participation and, 224–227; enabling neighborhood, 180–183; enabling patient and family, 141–143; monitoring government spending and, 219–220*fig*; planning and land use zoning, 158–159, 165*t*. *See also* Problem solving

Deliberative communication, 249

Deliberative Democracy Consortium, 291

Deliberative Polling, 18*b*

Deliberative polling tactic, 267*b*

Democracy: barriers to successfully exporting to other countries, 321–322; creating a civic utopia by using innovative, 295*b*; deciding what kind we really want, 322–323; deciding what kind we want, 322–323; dictionary definitions of, 319*b*; encouraging artistic expressions of, 297*fig*–298*fig*; equitable outcomes vs. equitable processes and, 316–318; etymology of, 48*b*; Founders' views of popular, 50*b*–51; founding of the United States role of republicanism and, 49–51; hunter-gatherer societies' "tribal" or "campfire," 47; journalism role in free exchange of information supporting, 307–309; "nanodemocracy" or "microdemocracy" forms of, 218; pre-Columbian, 49; role of education in public participation and, 77–110; roots of participation in the ancient world, 47–48; small "d" democratic planning for small "d" democratic infrastructure, 298–302

Democratic trends: regarding participatory budgeting (PB), 309–314; regarding people and cultural differences, 314–318; regarding people and information, 306–309

Demonstration Cities and Metropolitan Development Act (1966), 56

Detroit 24/7 game case study, 176*b*

Detroit City Futbol League, 180

Dialogue-App, 18*b*

Dialogue-to-change programs, 277

DiscoverBPS (Boston), 87*b*, 88, 103

Disseminating information: government sector, 219–221; health sector, 135–137; to participants for public participation, 249–250, 252*t*, 262*t*, 263*t*; planning and land use sector, 174–177. *See also* Data; Information; Journalism

E

E-blasts, 221

E-Deliberation, 277

E-domocracy.org, 64, 178

e-Petition, 20*b*

E-petition tools, 20*b*, 212*b*, 221

E-rulemaking (or electronic rulemaking), 222

Economic Opportunity Act (EOA) [1964], 55

Education: building blocks for participation in, 95–106; development of participation in, 78–85; disseminating information about schools and, 96*fig*–98; fundamental role in participation and democracy by, 77–78; official settings for participation in, 85–91; as public participation infrastructure component, 8; recommendations for improving participation in, 110; role of leaders and networks in strengthening participation infrastructure role of, 91–93*b*; systemic supports for participation in, 106–109. *See also* School systems; Student learning

Education participation building blocks: discussing and connecting, 96*fig*, 99–100; disseminating information about schools and education, 96*fig*–98; enabling community decision making on education issues, 96*fig*, 103–105; enabling family and student decision making, 96*fig*, 100–103; encouraging public work, 96*fig*, 105–106; gathering input and data, 96*fig*, 98–99; strengthening the, 95–96

Educators: participation training and skill development of, 107; professional participation incentives for, 107–108

Edward M. Kennedy Serve America Act (2009), 227

Elected officials. *See* Public officials

Electoral participation: description of, 8; Obama's presidential campaign (2008) application of, 61–63, 196

Emerson College, 307

Engagement Game Lab, 177

Engagement HQ, 18*b*, 277

Engagement Streams Framework (NCDD), 264

EngagingPlans, 274

Environmental Protection Agency (EPA), 203, 215–216, 228

Equitable outcomes vs. processes, 316–318

Ethelo, 277

Ethical Guidance for Public Health Emergency Preparedness and Response, 144

Ethnic differences. *See* Racial and ethnic differences

Eugene Decisions (Eugene city council), 34

Everyday Democracy, 16, 264, 277

F

Face-to-face processes: for thick participation, 18*b*; for thin participation, 20*b*

Facebook: used for indicating public preferences, 20*b*; school district presence on, 88, 89. *See also* Social media

Families: academic parent-teacher teams, 101, 101*b*; enabling decision making by students and, 96*fig*, 100–103; enabling health decision making by patients and, 141–143; engagement in students' participation education by, 79–80, 84*t*; how connections and relationships for improving health of, 139–141; parent-teacher conferences involvement by, 101; Patient-Family Advisors to, 126, 131, 143. *See also* Parent organizations

Farmer's Alliance (19th century), 51–52

Federal Advisory Committee Act (FACA), 204, 207, 230

Federal agencies. *See* Government agencies

Federal Register (online edition), 210

Feedback: online platforms and tools for public, 20*b*; public participation scenario on gathering public input, preferences, and, 256–257, 262*t*, 263*t*

First 5 LA initiative (Los Angeles), 99, 100, 106–107, 140

FixMyStreet, 20*b*, 162, 269

Focus groups: gathered by community on schools, 98–99; as public participation tactic, 263*t*, 268

"Food deserts" areas, 123, 137

foreignassistance.gov, 219

Fox News, 308

Free Press, 308

Fremont Street Troll (Seattle), 32, 33*e*

Front Porch Forum, 64

Funding and budgeting participation: government participation, 229; health participation, 148; planning and land use participation, 188; school participation, 109. *See also* Participatory Budgeting (PB)

Future of Big Data report (Pew Research Center), 307

Future search conferences, 274

G

Games: Detroit 24/7 case study on participation through, 176*b*; online platforms and tools for, 20*b*; as thin participation strategy, 19. *See also* Serious games

Ganas (equal), 47

Geomedicine technologies, 139

GIS (geographic information system): online platforms for reporting problems and gathering data, 269; participatory, 162–164*b*, 178

Global North: comparing Global South public participation to, 319–322; state of public participation in the, 23. *See also* United States

Global South: barriers to public participation in, 319–322; barriers to successfully exporting democracy to the, 321–322; Brazilian Participatory Budgeting (PB) projects in the, 60, 291, 311; efforts to increase public participation in the, 31

"Good" public participation: defined as treating citizens like adults, 25–28; how it helps to solve problems, 29–36; Lakewood public meeting (Colorado, 2004) as example of, 26

Google Alert, 265

GoogleDrive, 272

Governance: how conventional participation can harm, 25; how technology facilitates bigger, 63–65; "voice of the whole people," 46

IAP2 Spectrum of Public Participation, 108, 145*b*, 161, 230, 250, 251*fig*
IBM Center for the Business of Government, 207
ICivics, 177
IdeaScale, 20*b*, 270
Ideastream, 309
Ideation: how participation helps generate, 35; online platforms and tools for, 20*b*; scenario of leaders wanting citizens to generate new data or, 257–258, 262*t*, 263*t*
Incentives. *See* Professional incentives
Incivility trend, 5
Indian self-governing republics, 47–48
Indiana University, 291
"Induced participation," 46
Industrial Workers of the World, 52
Infogagement: Citizenship and Democracy in the Age of Connection (Leighninger), 306
Information: journalism role in free exchange of, 307–309; to prepare participants for public participation, 249–250, 252*t*, 262*t*, 263*t*; providing citizens with factual, 26; traditional thinking about the relationship between participation and, 306–307. *See also* Data; Disseminating information
Information overload, 306
Institute for Family-Centered Care (IFCC), 144
Institute for Local Government, 294
Interactive maps. *See* Mapping
International Association for Public Participation (IAP2) Spectrum of Public Participation, 108, 145*b*, 161, 230, 250, 251*fig*
International City/Management Association, 291
International Municipal Lawyers' Association, 291
Interviews (community), 98–99
Investigative Reporting Workshop, 307
Ioby, 270
Issue framing, 16

J

Jane Addams School of Democracy (St. Paul), 100, 315
Johnstown Flood, 52
Journalism: changing trust status in, 307; collaborative practices signaling rebirth of, 307; participation as key to transformation of, 307–308; practice of participation in public or civic, 308–309. *See also* Disseminating information; Social media

K

Kettering Foundation, 277
Kickstarter, 20*b*, 270

Kirkwood city council shooting (2008), 24
Knight Foundation: *Soul of the Community* research by, 5, 31, 162, 315; on state of journalism, 307, 309
Knight News Challenge, 269
Knight-Ridder, 309
Kony controversy (2012), 35

L

"A Ladder of Participation" (Arnstein), 57*fig*–58
Lakewood public meeting (Colorado, 2004), 26
Land use. *See* Planning and land use
Leaders. *See* Participation leaders
Legislation: Administrative Procedure Act (APA) [1946], 53; Affordable Care Act (Obamacare), 125, 128, 141, 148; Civil Rights Act (1964), 54; Demonstration Cities and Metropolitan Development Act (1966), 56; Economic Opportunity Act (EOA) [1964], 55; Edward M. Kennedy Serve America Act (2009), 227; Federal Advisory Committee Act (FACA), 204, 207, 230; local participation ordinances, 290–291; Medicare, 125, 130, 148; National Environmental Policy Act, 204; No Child Left Behind Act, 81; Paperwork Reduction Act (PRA), 204–205; Section 508 (Rehabilitation Act), 205; Voting Rights Act (1965), 54; Workforce Investment Act (1998), 205. *See also* Public participation infrastructure; United States
Legislative branch participation: challenge of scale and policy connection in, 202–203; development of, 197–203; how the "mad and angry folks" contributed to, 198–199; influence of other non-governmental organizations on, 200–202
Legitimacy (political), 27
Lerner Center for Public Health Promotion (Syracuse University), 142*b*
LinkedIn, 20*b*
Listening to Toronto (serious game), 313
Local Education Funds (LEFs), 91–92
Local Health Information Networks (Ontario), 128
Local participation ordinances, 290–291
localocracy, 64
LocalWiki, 20*b*, 176, 272
LogoLink, 158
Loomio, 277

M

Making Democracy Fun (Lerner), 28, 271, 314
Mapit, 20*b*

Mapping: disseminating planning and land use through interactive maps, 176; "food deserts" interactive maps, 123, 137; health inequities of communities, 122–123, 127t; A Map of Online Communities, 298fig; online platforms and tools for, 20b; participatory budgeting projects, 310fig; wiki-based platforms for collaborative writing or, 263t, 272–273

Mapumental, 20b

Maryland Budget Game, 221

Massachusetts Institute of Technology (MIT), 307

Measured Voice, 265

Medicare, 125, 130, 148

MetroQuest, 16, 18b, 270

"Microdemocracy," 218

MindMixer, 20b, 270

Mini-grant programs: online platforms for, 270; as participation tactic, 263t, 270–271; planning and land use, 186; school-based crowdfunding and, 106

Montgomery County schools, 82

MSNBC, 308

N

National Coalition for Dialogue and Deliberation (NCDD), 230

"Nanodemocracy," 218

NASA (National Aeronautics and Space Administration), 227

National Action Plans for Open Government, 209–210

National Center for Charitable Statistics, 272

National Civic League (NCL), 90, 119, 159–160, 291

National Coalition for Dialogue and Deliberation (NCDD), 254b, 264, 291

National Commission on Fiscal Responsibility and Reform, 200

National Conference on Citizenship (NCoC), 195, 221, 293

National Dialogue on Chemical Exposures, 277

National Dialogue on Mental Health (2013), 124, 223b

National Environmental Policy Act, 204

National Institute for Civil Discourse, 277

National issues forums, 18b

National Issues Forums Institute, 16, 277

National League of Cities, 184, 291

National Physicians Alliance, 147

National Policy Forum for Family, School, and Community Engagement, 79

National School Public Relations Association (NSPRA), 83, 109

Neighborhood associations, 169–170, 180–183

Neighborhood councils, 169–170

Neighborhood dashboards, 176

Neighborhood online forums, 178–179

Neighborhoods: enabling decision making by, 180–183; planning and land use participation in, 166fig, 168–170; public officials developing "mutual partnerships" with, 294; revitalizing groups that serve, 181b

neighbor.ly, 20b, 270

Nellie Mae Education Foundation (NMEF), 90, 93

Network-based recruitment, 16

Networks: education participation, 91–93b; government participation, 216–217fig; health participation, 132–134; Hospital Engagement Networks (HENs), 129; participation tactic of using online, 263t, 273–274; patient online forums and, 140; planning and land use participation, 170–172b; public participation infrastructure empowering civic, 66. See also Citizens

New America Foundation, 264

New Deal, 53

New England Town Meetings, 50

New Jersey Coalition for the Public Good, 201

New Jersey Peoples' Tax Assembly (2003), 201

New Jersey Tax Assembly and Citizens' Technology Forum, 202

New York Times, 322

NextDoor, 64, 171, 172

NIMBY (Not in My Back Yard), 59–60, 159, 190

No Child Left Behind Act, 81

NoiseTube, 20b

Nojaim Brothers Supermarket (Syracuse), 142b

O

OaklandWiki, 163, 272

Obama administration: National Commission on Fiscal Responsibility and Reform of the, 200; Open Government Directive (OGD) of the, 63, 203–204, 207–210, 222, 230–231

Obamacare (Affordable Care Act), 125, 128, 141, 148

Obama's presidential campaign (2008): participatory breakthrough during the, 61–62; participatory principles used during the, 62–63, 196; "Stories of Self, Us, and Now" during, 62

O.J. Simpson verdict, 60, 315

One-way communication, 248–249

Online forums: neighborhood, 178–179; participation tactic of creating online networks through, 263*t*, 273–274; for patients, 140; school-based, 100

Online National Dialogue on Reforming Government Websites, 211

Online platform tools: "best brains" online driving government participation using, 210–213; bigger governance through, 63–65; data gathering and feedback, 20*b*; e-petitions, 20*b*, 212*b*, 221; games, 19, 20*b*, 176*b*; indicating preferences on social media, 20*b*; mapping, 20*b*, 122–123, 127*t*, 137, 176, 263*t*, 272–273, 298*fig*, 310*fig*; for mini-grant programs, 270; monitoring government spending and decisions, 219; for Open Government transparency, 209; participation dashboards, 292–293; participation tactic of reporting problems and gathering data, 263*t*, 269; for patients and families, 141, 145; planning and land use participation, 164*b*, 186; polls, 20*b*, 98–99, 196–197, 263*t*, 266–268; public deliberation, 277, 278*b*; for public work in education, 106; reporting problems and prioritizing improvements using "participatory GIS," 162–164*b*, 178; school-based crowdfunding and mini-grant programs, 106; serious games, 17, 18*b*, 19, 177, 221, 263*t*, 271–272, 313; surveys, 20*b*, 98–99, 263*t*, 266; for tracking student learning progress, 102; wiki, 20*b*, 163, 176, 222, 263*t*, 272–273. *See also* Crowdsourcing (crowdfunding); Technology

Open Government Directive (Obama administration), 63, 203–204, 207–210, 222, 229, 230–231

Open houses, 20*b*

Open Space, 18*b*

OpenDataPhilly, 172

OpenStreetMap, 20*b*, 176

OpentheGovernment.org, 210

OpenTownHall, 20*b*

Oregon Citizens' Initiative Review (CIR), 201–202

"Organic participation," 46

Organizing Community-Wide Dialogue for Action and Change (Study Circles Resource Center), 264

Organizing for Participatory Budgeting (Participatory Budgeting Project), 264

Orton Family Foundation, 264, 295*b*

Our Budget, Our Economy (OBOE), 200

P

Paperwork Reduction Act (PRA), 204–205

Parent cafés (Jane Addams School of Democracy), 100

Parent organizations: encouraging public work, 105–106; facilitating participation in school board meetings, 92*fig*, 103; Parent-Teacher Association (PTA), 88–89, 104*b*; participatory budgeting (PB) role by, 103–104; school council role of, 104–105. *See also* Families

Parent-Teacher Association (PTA), 88–89, 104*b*

Parent-teacher conferences, 101

Park Forest Elementary School (Pennsylvania), 89–90

Participants: adapted spectrum of participation by, 251*fig*; deciding how they interact with decision-making and other, 248–249, 252*t*, 262*t*, 263*t*; deciding on information required to prepare, 249–250, 252*t*, 262*t*, 263*t*; how they will impact policymaking, 250–251–253, 252*t*, 262*t*, 263*t*; knowing how they will impact policymaking, 250–253, 252*t*, 262*t*, 263*t*; recruitment of, 245*b*, 246–248, 252*t*, 262*t*, 263*t*; strategic questions and stakes for, 252*t*. *See also* Cultural differences

Participation commissions (or advisory boards): description and participation function of, 289; "racial equity lens" recommended for, 318; responsibilities of, 289–290

Participation leaders: government participation, 216–217*fig*; messaging healthy behavior, 118–119; mismatch between systems and participation tactics used by, 320; planning and land use participation infrastructure role of, 170–172*b*; professional incentives for health participation by, 147–148; public participation infrastructure empowering, 66; scenario on developing a plan or budget, 260–262*t*, 263*t*; scenario on participation and policymaking, 259–260, 262*t*, 263*t*; scenario on supporting volunteerism and citizen-driven problem solving, 258–259, 262*t*, 263*t*; scenario on wanting citizens to generate new ideas or data, 257–258, 262*t*, 263*t*; scenario on wanting to inform the public, 254–256, 262*t*, 263*t*; scenario on wanted to gather public input, 256–257, 262*t*, 263*t*; training and skill development for health participation by, 146–147. *See also* Decision makers

Participatory Budgeting (PB): Brazilian projects for, 60, 291, 311; Chicago's 49th Ward project for, 311; community decision making on school district, 103–104; Eugene Decisions (Eugene city council) experience with, 34; as form of thick participation, 18*b*; global map of projects for, 310*fig*; as "good" participation, 27; Gram Sabha reforms in India on, 291; increasing participation trend of, 309–314; local ordinances supporting,

291; as participation tactic, 263*t*, 275–276; Priority-Based Budgeting approach to, 312–313; scenario on, 260–262*t*, 263*t*. *See also* Funding and budgeting participation; Public participation tactics

Participatory Budgeting Project, 264

Participatory Chinatown (3-D game), 17

Participatory Chinatown (serious game), 177, 271

"Participatory Democracy Revisited" (Pateman), 23

"Participatory GIS" platforms, 162–164*b*, 178

Participatory populism (19th century), 51–52

Participedia, 264

"Partnering with Communities" (Sirianni and others), 206

Patient-caregiver interactions, 141

Patient-centered care, 124–126, 127*t*

Patient Engagement Committees, 128

Patient-Family Advisors, 126, 131, 143

Patients: enabling decision making by family and, 141–143; encouraging civic engagement by health practitioners with, 147; health participation level, 129*fig*, 131; how connections and relationships for improving health of, 139–141; online forums and networks for, 140, 145; providing care rating systems to, 139. *See also* Health practitioners

PatientsLikeMe online community, 140

PE2020 Project, 264

Peak Democracy, 20*b*, 270

Peer to Patent initiative, 211

Peterson, Pete, 292

Petitions: e-Petition, 20*b*, 221; online platforms and tools for, 20*b*; thin participation through, 20*b*; "We the People" online petition platform, 212*b*

Pew Research Center: *Future of Big Data* report of, 307; *Neighbors Online* report by, 172

Pew Research Center for the People & the Press, 5

The Philanthropic Initiative for Racial Equity, 317

Pittsfield Middle-High School (New Hampshire), 90

Placemaking workshops, 274

PlaceSpeak, 274

Planning and land use: BANANA (Build Absolutely Nothing Anywhere Near Anything) attitude toward, 159, 190; CAVE (Citizens Against Virtually Everything) attitude toward, 159, 190; contentious struggle for control over, 156; major zoning decisions for, 158–159, 165*t*; NIMBY (Not in My Back Yard) attitude toward, 59–60, 159, 190; official settings for participating in, 166*fig*–170. *See also* Built environment

Planning and land use participation: barriers to, 155; community and neighborhood visioning, 159–161, 165*t*; community development, 161–162, 165*t*; Create Buckhannon case study on, 179*b*; Detroit 24/7 case study on, 176*b*; Detroit City Futbol League, 180; development of, 156–166; examples of online platforms for assistance, 164*b*; funding and budgeting, 188; major zoning decisions, 158–159, 165*t*; official settings for, 166*fig*–170; policies and procedures for, 188; professional incentives for planners and leaders in, 187–188; recommendations to improve, 189; reporting problems and prioritizing improvements, 162–166, 165*t*; strengthening the infrastructure for, 170–188; tactical urbanism form of, 182–183

Planning and land use participation infrastructure: assessing state of planning and land use, 172*bb*; building blocks for, 173–186; leaders and networks, 170–172; systemic supports for, 186–188

Planning and land use participation settings: community level, 166*fig*–168; neighborhood level, 166*fig*, 168–170

Planning charrettes, 18*b*

"Please, President Obama. Not Another `National Conversation'" (Lozada), 223

Points of Light campaign (George H. W. Bush), 227

Policies and procedures participation: government participation, 229–231; health participation, 148; planning and land use participation, 188; school participation, 108. *See also* Public policies

Policy conferences, 226–227

Policy Consensus Initiative, 291

Political legitimacy, 27

Polk County health plan (Iowa), 120–121

Poll Everywhere, 266

Polls: deliberative, 267*b*; gathered by community on schools, 98–99; online platforms for, 266; as public participation tactics, 263*t*, 266–268; showing American dissatisfaction with political processes and institutions, 196–197; thin participation through, 20*b*

The Populist Moment (Goodwyn), 52

Portland Press Herald, 308

Porto Alegre (Brazil) Participatory Budgeting (PB), 60, 91

Portsmouth Herald, 308

Portsmouth Listens, 18*b*, 308

Poway Unified School District (California), 98

The Power Inquiry, 264

Pre-Columbian democracy, 49

Presidential campaigns: George H. W. Bush's Points of Light, 227; Obama's 2008, 61–63, 196

Priorities for Public Participation and Open Government: Recommendations to President Obama report (PARCC), 204, 228, 230

Priority-Based Budgeting, 312–313

Problem solving: how good participation helps in, 29–36; ranking ideas for, 19; scenario on participation for citizen-driven, 258–259, 262*t*, 263*t*. *See also* Decision making

Problems: apps for reporting school infrastructure, 98; caused by conventional participation, 23–25; how good participation helps to solve community, 29–36; participation tactic of gathering data and reporting, 263*t*, 269; participation used to solve U.S. policymaking and public, 32; reporting planning and land use, 162–166, 165*t*

Professional incentives: education participation, 107–108; government participation, 228–229; health participation, 147–148; planning and land use participation, 187–188

Progressives movement, 52–54, 299

Project for Public Spaces, 274

Project Open Data, 209

ProPublica, 307

The public. *See* Citizens

Public Agenda: on classroom level participation, 91; on improving education accountability, 80; issue framing by, 16; New Jersey Coalition for the Public Good work with, 201; public deliberation projects of, 277; *Public Engagement: A Primer* by, 264; revamping the planning and land use, 184*b*; on school-based participation training, 107

Public deliberation: as participation tactic, 263*t*, 276–277; some methods for, 278*b*

Public Engagement: A Primer (Public Agenda), 264

Public Engagement Pilot Project on Pandemic Influenza (PEPPPI), 123–124

Public Health Preparedness Capabilities: National Standards for State and Local Planning (CDC), 144

Public Insight Network, 308

"Public journalism," 308–309

Public meetings: cultural differences that may impact, 316–317; dealing with hostile and uninformed citizens in, 24–25; government participation during, 224; limits of the "three-minutes-at-the-microphone," 214; procedures required for, 21–22*e*; school board, 103; tele-townhalls, 221; traditional New England Town Meetings, 50; 21st Century Town Hall

Meetings, 18*b*, 123, 198–199, 221, 277; typically low attendance on CDBG grants, 24. *See also* Citizens

Public officials: citizen skepticism about, 3, 4–5; developing "mutual partnerships" with neighborhoods and communities, 294; government participation incentives for, 228–229; government participation through interactions with, 213*fig*–214; government participation training provided to, 228; how participation increases accountability of elected, 34. *See also* Decision makers; Government agencies

Public participation: adapted spectrum of, 251*fig*; assumptions and realities about citizens and, 36*t*; challenge of defining, 14; deciding what kind of democracy we want, 322–323; as the democracy in our political system, 4; democratic roots in the ancient world, 47–48; distinguishing "good" from "bad," 13; examining the future of, 8–9; health sector, 117–150; ineffective for overcoming divide of citizens and government, 3–4; information required to prepare participants for, 249–250, 252*t*, 262*t*, 263*t*; misunderstandings regarding the meaning of, 318–322; participatory populism in nineteenth century America, 51–52; in planning and land use, 155–190; traditional thinking about relationship between information and, 306–307; urban renewal (1940s) and increased need for, 54. *See also* Adult-adult participation relationships

Public participation forms: conventional, 15*fig*, 21–25, 38, 242–243, 321; "good," 25–36; illustrated diagram of the different, 15*fig*; "organic" versus "induced," 46; thick, 14–18*b*, 28, 29*t*, 38; thin, 15*fig*, 18–21, 29*t*, 38; why "bad" participation happens to good people, 36–37

Public participation goals: description and variation in, 254*b*; matching tactic approaches to scenarios on, 262–277; six scenarios on matching engagers and engaged, 253–262*t*, 263*t*

Public participation infrastructure: ancient world democratic roots of, 47–48*b*; artistic expressions of democracy and, 297*fig*–298*fig*; assembling participation building blocks through, 66–67; citizen's academies, 291–292; civic, 7–8; Community Action Agencies (CAAs), 55–56; connecting the building blocks for participation, 288–290; educational, 8, 77–111; electoral and government, 8, 61–63, 195–233; empowering and activating leaders and networks, 66; encouraging both progressive and conservative visions, 294–295; envisioning stronger, 293–298fig; failure of the, 6–8; founding of the U.S. democracy and republicanism, 49–51; governmental, 7; health sector, 132–148; how technology has impacted, 63–65; local participation ordinances, 290–291; participation commission role in assembling, 289–290, 318; participatory populism in 19th century America, 51–52; using plainer and more compelling language as part of, 294; pre-Columbian democratic, 49; Progressive movement influence on, 52–54, 299; providing systemic supports, 67; small "d" democratic planning for small "d" democratic, 298–302; UK's David Cameron's "Big Society" vision of, 63, 295; using visual aids to demonstrate and visualize, 296; War on Poverty and expansion of, 54–58. See also Legislation

Public participation scenarios: creating a plan or a budget, 260–262t, 263t; gathering public input, feedback, and preferences, 256–257, 262t, 263t; generating new ideas or data, 257–258, 262t, 263t; inform the public, 254–256, 262t, 263t; making a policy decision, 259–260, 262t, 263t; for matching goals of engagers and engaged, 253–262; matching tactics and, 262–277; supporting volunteerism and citizen-driven problem solving, 258–259, 262t, 263t

Public participation tactics: additional resources on, 264; being trapped in the same old conventional, 242–243; collaborative planning processes, 263t, 274–275; for conventional participation, 242–243; deciding who should be recruited to participate, 246–248; e-petitions, 20b, 212b, 221; focus groups, 263t, 268; information needed to prepare participants, 249–250; knowing how participation will impact policymaking, 250–253; matching scenarios and, 262–277; mismatch between system and, 320; online networks, 263t, 273–274; online platforms for reporting problems and gathering data, 263t, 269; planning for participation, 243–246; public deliberation, 263t, 276–278b; serious games, 17, 18b, 19, 177, 221, 263t, 271–272, 313; social media aggregation, 263t, 265–266; some variations in direct, 245b; surveys, 20b, 98–99, 263t, 266; wiki-based platforms for collaborative mapping or writing, 263t, 272–273. See also additional information under specific tactic; Crowdsourcing (crowdfunding); Participatory Budgeting (PB)

Public Pathways: A Guide to Online Engagement Tools for Local Governments (New America Foundation), 264

Public policies: how conventional participation can harm, 25; providing citizens with choices in, 27. See also Policies and procedures participation

Public policymaking: challenge of connecting legislative branch participation to, 202–203; engaging citizens in health-related, 123–124; knowing how participation will impact, 250–253, 252t, 262t, 263t; participation for facilitating problem solving and, 32–36; scenario on making decisions for, 259–260, 262t, 263t

Public work: encouraging government participation and, 227; encouraging planning and land use, 185–186; encouraging school participation, 105–106

PublicStuff, 20b, 26, 106, 162, 186, 269

Q

Quad Cities, 122–123, 137

"Quantified self" technologies, 142

R

Racial and ethnic differences: resolving injustice related to, 316–318; in student achievement gaps, 82. See also Cultural differences

Racial Equity, 317–318; equitable outcomes vs. processes for, 316–318; "racial equity lens," 317–318

Rank ideas, 19

recovery.gov, 219

Referenda and ballot initiatives, 227

A Refined Typology of Public Engagement Tools and Implements (PE2020 Project), 264

regulations.gov, 222

Republicanism, 49–51

Right Question Institute, 218

Right question process, 278b

Right Question Project, 278b

Robert's Rules of Order, 89, 181

Robocalls, 221

Rodney King verdict (1992), 60, 315

S

San Jose Budget Game (serious game), 313

Sanghas (assembly), 47

Scenarios. See Public participation scenarios

School board meetings, 103, 104fig

School districts: establishing participation policies and procedures, 108; participatory Budgeting (PB) for, 103–104; school board meetings, 103

School fairs, 102–103

School participation: classroom level, 86fig, 90–91; district level, 86fig–88; encouraging public work,

105–106; First 5 LA initiative (Los Angeles) reports on, 99, 100, 106–107, 140; funding and budgeting for, 109; parent organizations' roles in, 88–89, 92*fig*, 103–105; recommendations for improving, 110; school level, 86*fig*, 88–90; school task forces and advisory committees, 105; student government and youth councils, 105; training and skill development to facilitate, 107

School systems: assessing the state of participation in a, 93*b*; Boston's DiscoverBPS program for placing students in, 87*b*, 88, 103; Common Core State Standards goals and testing impact on student learning, 81–82, 84*t*; Creighton Elementary School District parent-teacher teams, 101, 101*b*; disseminating information about education and, 96*fig*–98; how redistricting, school closures, and funding impact student learning, 80–81, 84*t*; official settings for participation found in, 85–93*b*; school-based online forums organized by, 100; social media presence by, 88, 89; student-centered learning teams organized by, 101; student learning and impact of standards and testing by, 81–82, 84*t*. *See also* Education

Section 508 (Rehabilitation Act), 205

SeeClickFix, 20*b*, 26, 162, 269

Serious games: description of, 17; as face-to-face process for thick participation, 18*b*, 19; focusing on planning issues, 177; Listening to Toronto, 313; Maryland Budget Game, 221; as participation tactic, 263*t*, 271–272; San Jose Budget Game (Italy), 313. *See also* Games

Shareabouts, 106, 186, 269

Small-group facilitation, 16

Social capital-public life relationship, 178

Social media: citizens' sense of social isolation versus constant connections of, 5–6; disseminating information about health through, 135–136; disseminating information about the government through, 220; disseminating planning and land use through, 175–176; online platforms and tools for indicating preferences on, 20*b*; school district presence on, 88, 89. *See also* Facebook; Journalism; Technology; Twitter

Social media aggregation tactic, 263*t*, 265–266

Social networking sites: Facebook, 20*b*, 88, 89; LinkedIn, 20*b*; percentage of adult participation on, 5–6; Twitter, 20*b*, 88, 135–136, 136, 175–176

"Solve the Outbreak" app (CDC), 137

Soul of the Community (Knight Foundation), 5, 31, 162, 315

Speak Up Austin, 277

Spectrum of Public Participation (IAP2), 108, 145*b*, 161, 230, 250, 251*fig*

SpigitEngage, 20*b*, 270

St. Joseph's Hospital Health Center, 142*b*

State agencies. *See* Government agencies

State and federal government. *See* Government

State of the World report (Worldwatch, 2014), 34

Stop Online Piracy Act/Protect Intellectual Property Act (SOPA/PIPA), 35

Stories/storytelling: allowing citizens to tell their, 26–27; how it helps citizens to relate to one another and build civility, 30; "Stories of Self, Us, and Now" (Obama's 2008 presidential campaign), 62

Street Bump, 269

Strengthening our Nation's Democracy (SOND), 230

Student learning: achievement gaps in, 82, 84*t*; Common Core State Standards goals and testing of, 81–82, 84*t*; family engagement in, 79–80, 84*t*; how redistricting, school closures, and funding impact, 80–81, 84*t*; online tools for tracking progress of, 102; school safety and bullying issues in, 83, 84*t*, 85; school settings for participation and, 85–91; student-centered learning teams organized to support, 101. *See also* Education

Study circles, 18*b*

Study Circles Resource Center (now Everyday Democracy), 264

Substance Abuse and Mental Health Services Agency (SAMHSA), 119, 124, 139

Sumerian primitive democracy, 47

Sunlight Foundation, 210

Super City, 20*b*

Superstorm Sandy, 163

SurveyConsole, 266

SurveyGizmo, 266

SurveyMonkey, 266

Surveys: gathered by community on schools, 98–99; online platforms for, 266; as public participation tactics, 263*t*, 266–268; thin participation through, 20*b*

Sustained dialogue, 18*b*

T

Tactical urbanism, 182–183

Tactics. *See* Public participation tactics

Teacher unions, 92–93

Teachers. *See* Educators

Technology: bigger governance through, 63–65; geomedicine, 139; GIS (geographic information system), 269; "quantified self," 142. *See also* Online platform tools; Social media

TechPresident, 21
Tele-townhalls, 221
Telephone hotlines, 20*b*
Telephone-related participation activities, 20*b*
Texas Tribune, 309
"Text, Talk, and Act" (CCS), 124, 223*b*
Thick participation: as activating individual
    participation of people, 18–19; compared to
    thin participation, 19, 21; description of, 14–15,
    38; face-to-face processes used for, 18*b*; forms
    of participation and attributes of an adult
    relationship in, 28, 29*t*; illustrated diagram of
    public participation role of, 15*fig*; inside and
    outside tactics used for, 16–17; online and
    digital applications for, 18*b*, 20*b*; "serous games"
    category of, 17
Thick participation tactics: an action strategy,
    16–17; a discussion sequence, 16; issue framing,
    16; proactive network-based recruitment, 16;
    small-group facilitation, 16
Thin participation: compared to thick
    participation, 19, 21; description of, 18, 38;
    face-to-face or telephone activities for, 20*b*;
    forms of participation and attributes of an adult
    relationship in, 29*t*; illustrated diagram of public
    participation role of, 15*fig*; online and digital
    applications for, 20*b*; types of activities included
    in, 19, 21
Tidepools project (Red Hook, Brooklyn), 163
Town All Meetings, 18*b*, 123
Town hall meetings: tele-townhalls, 221; traditional
    New England, 50; the 21st century version of,
    18*b*, 123, 198–199, 277
TownHall Social, 270
Training and skill development: citizen's academies
    for, 291–292; education participation, 107;
    government participation, 228; health
    participation, 146–147; planning and land use
    participation, 187
Trayvon Martin case, 35
Triangle Shirtwaist Fire, 52
"Tribal" democracies, 47
21st Century Town Hall Meetings, 18*b*, 123,
    198–199, 221, 277
Twitter: CDC's network on, 135–136; disseminating
    planning and land use through, 175–176;
    Healthcare Hashtag project on, 136; used for
    indicating public preferences, 20*b*; school district
    presence on, 88. *See also* Social media
Two-way communication, 248–249

U

Unified New Orleans Plan, 32
United States: democracy and republicanism in
    the founding of the, 49–50; Founders' views of
    popular democracy in the, 50*b*–51; participation
    to solve policymaking and public problems in
    the, 32; participatory populism (19th century),
    51–52; Progressives movement in the, 52–54,
    299; state of public participation in the, 23; War
    on Poverty (1960s) in the, 54–58. *See also* Global
    North; Legislation
University of Buffalo Center for Urban Studies, 93
University of California-Berkeley, 307
Urban Institute, 272
Urban Milwaukee, 307
Urban renewal (1940s), 54
U.S. Code of Federal Regulations, 204
U.S. Department of Health and Human Services
    (HHS): health literacy programs of the, 137;
    health volunteer coordination recommendations
    by, 144; Healthy Communities Access Program
    of the, 120
U.S. Department of Housing and Urban
    Development (HUD), 210
U.S. Forest service (USFS), 204
U.S. General Services Administration, 227
U.S. Public Health Services, 119
USASpending.gov, 219
Ushahidi, 26

V

Village Academy (Delray Beach, Florida), 32
Visioning neighborhood and community, 159–161,
    165*t*
Volunteerism: CDC recommendations on
    coordinating health, 144; scenario on supporting
    citizen-driven problem solving and, 258–259,
    262*t*, 263*t*
Voting Rights Act (1965), 54

W

Walkshops, 182
War on Poverty (1960s): Arnstein's Ladder of
    Participation in the, 57*fig*–58; Community
    Action Agencies (CAAs) created by the EOA
    during, 55–56; description of the, 54; increased
    participation structures created through, 54–58
Waze, 20*b*
"We the People" online petition platform, 212*b*

"What a Difference a Friend Makes" campaign (SAMHSA), 119, 139
White House Office for Science and Technology Policy (OSTP), 210
Whitman Institute, 308
Why We Engage (Gordon, Baldwin-Philippi, and Balestra), 63
Wichita Eagle, 308
Wikipedia, 299
Wikiplanning, 20*b*, 272
Wikis: gathering government input and data through, 222; interactive planning and land use maps on, 176; LocalWiki, 20*b*, 176, 272; OaklandWiki, 163; online platforms and tools for, 20*b*, 272–273; as participation tactic for collaborative mapping or writing, 263*t*, 272–273

Workforce Investment Act (1998), 205
Working Group on Legal Frameworks for Public Participation, 7, 229, 290, 291
Works Progress Administration, 53
World Café, 18*b*, 278*b*
Worldwatch Institute, 34

Z

Zilino, 18*b*, 277
Zócalo Public Square, 307, 308, 309
"Zombie Pandemic" comic book series (CDC), 137
Zoning decisions, 158–159, 165*t*